GACarter

PRINCIPLES
AND
PRACTICES
FOR
BAPTIST
CHURCHES

PRINCIPLES AND PRACTICES FOR BAPTIST CHURCHES

EDWARD T. HISCOX

KREGEL PUBLICATIONS
Grand Rapids, Michigan 49503

Principles and Practices for Baptist Churches, published in 1980 by Kregel Publications, a division of Kregel, Inc. Grand Rapids, Michigan 49501. This work was originally published as *The New Directory for Baptist Churches* by Judson Press in 1894 and Kregel Publications in 1970.

Library of Congress Catalog Card Number 71-125 114
ISBN 0-8254-2840-8

Printed in the United States of America

CONTENTS

3

APPENDIX

PUBLISHER'S FOREWORD

It is in response to an increasingly felt need that this reprinting of Hiscox's *Practices and Principals for Baptist Churches* (formerly *New Directory*) appears. Long recognized as the most authoritative and comprehensive work on Baptist polity ever written, its preservation and perpetuation have been deemed an absolute necessity by a host of Bible-believing Baptists. A decision on the part of the original publisher to produce a "revised" abridged edition and allow the original work to go out of print has brought forth a multitude of requests for a reprinting of that complete and unabridged work of Hiscox.

The "revised" edition referred to above (published as *The Hiscox Guide for Baptist Churches*) was produced ostensibly to make the book more modern in style and more reflective of the numerous changes which have taken place in Baptist polity and circles since Hiscox completed his work in 1893. In the view of many Baptists, however, the editors of the "revision" have actually weakened the original by deleting vast pertinent sections and altering much of what remained. Many who have sought to use that edition have found it inadequate to answer the questions and meet the demands of even the most basic polity decisions. It is the premise of the publishers that Hiscox still speaks clearly and pertinently today to those who seek to follow Biblical patterns of church government. Although a few references and statistics in the book are obviously dated, and changed conditions may have invalidated an even smaller number of citations, the vast majority of the contents are not only valid and pertinent, but vital and essential.

In a day of deteriorating church standards and confused church operation, it is our sincere hope that this reprint of the genuine classic might not only prove helpful to many but that it might also be used of the Lord to preserve the Biblical faith of Baptists in a Scriptural manner.

PREFACE

THIRTY-FOUR years ago (1859) the Baptist Church Directory was published as an ecclesiastical manual for use among Baptists. It met with immediate and hearty approval by both pastors and members of the churches, and was welcomed at once by a large circulation. That such a book is still needed is proven by the fact that after a constant and uninterrupted use for an entire generation, it is in as great demand as ever. This, for a book of the kind, is declared by the publishers to be a case " altogether phenomenal." Since its first issue, within its field of denominational literature, probably a dozen different books treating of some departments of Baptist Church polity have appeared, had a brief run, then disappeared. The Directory, by its general plan, method of treatment, and exposition of principles, has so commended itself to the denomination as to be declared as nearly a " standard" on the subjects of which it treats, as anything short of the New Testament can be. About *sixty thousand* copies have been circulated in this country, while it has

7

been translated more or less fully into at least *seven* different languages, by our missionaries in foreign lands, for use among the native churches. For such signal service rendered to Gospel truth and our distinctive faith, the author is devoutly thankful.

Since the first appearance of the Directory the author has published several other manuals, mostly smaller, designed to meet the needs of specific departments in our Church life, usage, and order. In all, there are now *nine* of these manuals, the combined circulation of which, in this country, so far as can be ascertained, is not less than *one hundred and sixty thousand copies.* The Standard Manual has been translated into Spanish, for use in our churches in Mexico, Cuba, and elsewhere, among Spanish-speaking peoples.

The present work, though constructed on the same general plan as the Directory, is an entirely new book, much more comprehensive, and contains more than double the amount of matter. It is entirely in harmony with previous manuals, as to Baptist polity, and neither abrogates nor antagonizes any of the fundamental principles announced or advocated in those previous issues. During the past quarter of a century the author has been written to repeatedly, asking his opinion and advice as to perplexing cases in Church order and discipline, such as will frequently arise, and which no prescriptive rules can possibly anticipate. This work is intended, so far as possible, to meet such cases, by more extended explanations of general principles. The arrangement of subjects and matter is lucid, the style is plain and simple, and the arguments are believed to be convincing. The book, it is confidently expected, will commend itself to the people as a careful and sound exposition of Baptist Church polity and practice.

When the Directory was issued in 1859, American Baptists numbered less than *one million* Church members. Now they have about *three and one-half millions*. Many thousands of young people, and persons from other denominations and from families without religious instruction, are yearly gathered into our churches. These recruits came among us with all the rights of franchise, but with little or no previous instruction as to their exercise. They need to be taught as to the nature, duties and privileges of membership in the Church of Christ, if their admission is to be made a blessing. Our Church members also, both young and old, need instruction as to our distinctive principles, and the reasons for them, if the integrity of our faith is to be preserved. If there be reasons for the maintenance of a distinct denominational existence, there is special urgency for the declaration and the defense of those reasons. The principles on which this Manual is constructed are drawn from the New Testament, and never in our history was there so much need of such an exposition and guide for members in our Church fellowship, as there is to-day. Let the necessity be recognized and met.

May the favor of our gracious Heavenly Father attend this, as it has sanctioned previous efforts in the same direction, and make it a means of furtherance to the unity, harmony, spiritual vitality and efficiency of the churches, resulting in the glory of our Lord Jesus Christ, through the salvation of souls and the edification of the saints, is the sincere and prayerful desire of the writer,   E. T. H.

CHAPTER 1

PROPOSITIONS AND STATEMENTS

PROP. I. The Bible is a Divine Revelation given of God to men, and is a complete and infallible guide and standard of authority in all matters of religion and morals; whatever it teaches is to be believed, and whatever it commands is to be obeyed; whatever it commends is to be accepted as both right and useful; whatever it condemns is to be avoided as both wrong and hurtful; but what it neither commands nor teaches is not to be imposed on the conscience as of religious obligation.

PROP. II. The New Testament is the constitution of Christianity, the charter of the Christian Church, the only authoritative code of ecclesiastical law, and the warrant and justification of all Christian institutions. In it alone is life and immortality brought to light, the way of escape from wrath revealed, and all things necessary to salvation made plain; while its messages are a gospel of peace on earth and of hope to a lost world.

PROP. III. Every man by nature possesses the

right of private judgment in the interpretation of the Scriptures, and in all religious concerns; it is his privilege to read and explain the Bible for himself, without dictation from, or dependence on, any one, being responsible to God alone for his use of the sacred truth.

PROP. IV. Every man has the right to hold such religious opinions as he believes the Bible teaches, without harm or hindrance from any one on that account, so long as he does not intrude upon, or interfere with, the rights of others by so doing.

PROP. V. All men have the right, not only to believe, but also to profess and openly declare, whatever religious opinions they may entertain, providing they be not contrary to common morality, and do no injustice to others.

PROP. VI. All men possess the common right to worship God according to the teachings of the Scriptures, as they understand them, without hindrance or molestation, so long as they do not injure or interfere with the rights of others by so doing.

PROP. VII. Civil governments, rulers and magistrates are to be respected, and in all temporal matters, not contrary to conscience and the word of God, to be obeyed; but they have no jurisdiction in spiritual concerns, and have no right of dictation to, of control over, or of interference with, matters of religion; but are bound to protect all good citizens in the peaceable enjoyment of their religious rights and privileges.

PROP. VIII. No organic union of Church and State

should be tolerated, but entire separation maintained: the Church should neither ask for, nor accept of, support from civil authority, since to do so would imply the right of civil dictation and control. The support of religion belongs to those who profess it.

PROP. IX. Christian men are to be good and law-abiding citizens, sustaining and defending the government under which they live, in all things not contrary to conscience and the word of God; while such government is bound to protect them in the full enjoyment of all their rights and privileges, both civil and religious.

PROP. X. Religion is to be free and voluntary, both as to faith, worship and service; neither conformity to, nor support of, religion in any form, should be compulsory. Christian faith and practice are matters of conscience and personal choice, and not subject to official dictation; and for either civil or ecclesiastical authority to enforce conformity, punish dissent, or compel the support of any form of worship, is a crime against the rights of man, an assumption of divine prerogatives, and treason against Christ, the only Lord of the conscience and sovereign of the soul.

PROP. XI. None but regenerated persons ought to be, or properly can be, members of a Christian Church, which is a spiritual body separate from the world and distinct from the state, and to be composed of spiritual members only.

PROP. XII. Pastors are not to be imposed on churches nor taken from them without their consent;

but are to be chosen by them, each for itself, at its own option, as by free men in Christ, who have a right to the choice and election of their religious teachers.

PROP. XIII. Christ is the only Head over, and Lawgiver to, His churches. Consequently the churches cannot make laws, but only execute those which He has given. Nor can any man, or body of men legislate for the churches. The New Testament alone is their statute book, by which, without change, the body of Christ is to govern itself.

DISTINCTIVE CHARACTERISTICS

In what respects do Baptists differ from other Christian denominations?

This is a question sometimes asked, and one which even Baptists themselves not unfrequently find it difficult to answer. If others misunderstand or misinterpret them, they should understand their own position, and be able to give a reason for it; they of all men, should be well instructed in the " kingdom of heaven," especially so far as relates to their peculiar faith and order. Every honest mind searching for truth will ask, " What does the Bible teach?" rather than, " What do men believe?" Yet the former is often better learned by well understanding the latter. The opinions of men and the creeds of the churches are important to be known, for information if not for authority.

The following points indicate the more important

respects in which Baptists differ from others, as to religious opinion and practice:

1. *As to a Christian Church*

They hold that a Church is a company of disciples, baptized on a profession of their faith in Christ, united in covenant to maintain the ordinances of the Gospel, and the public worship of God; to live godly lives, and to spread abroad the knowledge of Christ as the Saviour of men.

Consequently an ecclesiastical system consisting of many organic units, a confederation of religious societies under one general government or head, is not a Christian Church, though sometimes bearing that designation.

2. *As to Baptism*

They believe that *baptism* is the *immersion*, dipping, or burying a candidate in water, on a profession of his faith in Christ, and that such is the only form of baptism taught in the New Testament, or practised by the Apostles and first Christians. Consequently the form is essential to the ordinance, and nothing but immersion can be scriptural baptism.

Therefore sprinkling, pouring, and whatever other use of water may be resorted to, are not baptism at all, but substitutes for it. On the contrary, Pedobaptists hold that sprinkling and pouring are equally valid baptism with immersion, and because more convenient, are to be preferred.

3. *Proper Subjects for Baptism*

Baptists assert that the only proper *subjects* for baptism are regenerated persons; those who have exercised and professed a saving faith in Christ, and are living orderly Christian lives.

On the contrary, some hold and teach that unregenerate persons may be baptized as a means of grace; while all Pedobaptists claim that unconscious infants, unregenerate and incapable of faith, should receive baptism on the faith of parents, or sponsors. All of which Baptists declare to be plainly contrary to the word of God and the economy of grace.

4. *Proper Subjects for Communion*

As to who have the right and properly should come to the Communion of the Lord's Supper, Baptists claim that only regenerate persons, baptized on a profession of their faith, and living in a godly and Christian manner as members of a church, have a right to, or can properly partake of, the Supper. Of course, then, baptism is prerequisite to the Supper; of course, also, the Church is to judge the qualifications of those who enjoy its privileges.

On the contrary, some believe and teach that baptism is not prerequisite to the Communion, therefore unbaptized persons may rightfully come to the Lord's table; some also teach that conversion is not prerequisite to baptism and church-membership, while others assert that each one should judge of his own fitness, and the Church cannot properly deny the privilege to any one who desires it.

All Pedobaptists invite to the Supper persons only sprinkled, whom Baptists regard as unbaptized; the Roman Church gives to the laity the Communion in one kind only, withholding from them the cup, and the Greek Church gives the Eucharist, as they do baptism, to unconscious infants. All of which Baptists consider contrary to the Scriptures, and subversive of Gospel order in the churches.

5. *Subjects for Church Membership*

What class of persons should be admitted as members to the fellowship of Christian churches? Baptists say that godly persons, baptized on a profession of faith, are the only proper and suitable persons. That all others should be denied admission, and if already within the Church should be cast out.

Consequently, to receive unconverted persons, whether infants or adults, destroys the spiritual character of the body, and forms an unholy alliance with the world, instead of maintaining a broad and distinctive separation between them.

6. *The Form of Church Government*

Is there any form of government for the churches taught in the New Testament? And if so, what is it? Baptists assert that each particular local Church is self-governing, and independent of all other churches, and of all persons and bodies of men whatever, as to the administration of its own affairs; that it is of right, and should be, free from any other human authority, whether civil or ecclesiastical, and that this is the New Testament idea of church government.

Others, however, with great diversity of opinion, hold and teach that local congregations of Christians should not govern themselves, but be governed by popes, bishops or priests, assemblies, conferences, conventions, councils, consociations, synods or presbyteries. All of which Baptists consider as contradictory of the New Testament and the practice of the primitive churches.

7. As to Church Officers

What and how many are the Scriptural officers of a Christian Church? Baptists hold that they are *two; pastors* and *deacons:* besides these, there are no others. They assert that *bishop* and *elder* in the primitive churches were identical in office and authority, being *pastors* when holding the superintendence of churches, and *evangelists* when preaching from place to place; and that ruling and teaching elders were not, and properly should not be, distinct and separate offices in the churches. Consequently *bishops* are not a superior order of the clergy, nor ruling elders an order distinct from teaching elders.

On the contrary, other denominations claim more than two orders in the ministry and officers in the churches, running through a long list from pope to pastor, from cardinal to curate, from dean to deacon.

8. *As to Doctrinal Belief*

In doctrine, Baptists agree very nearly with other evangelical Christians. They are what is usually called Calvinistic, as opposed to Arminian views of free-will and the sovereignty of grace. They hold the unity of the Godhead, and the equal Divinity of the Father, Son and Spirit: a full and free salvation proclaimed to all in Christ; the atonement and redemption by the meritorious sacrifice of Christ; justification by faith, not by works; the absolute necessity of regeneration in order to salvation; the Holy Spirit the author and finisher of saving faith and sanctification; the personal election of believers; the perseverance of the saints by upholding grace; the resurrection of the body, and the life everlasting; also the endless duration of rewards and punishments, to be assigned by Christ, the judge of quick and dead, at His coming and glory.

There may be others, but the above named constitute those which chiefly mark the difference between Baptists and other Christians. These are the questions in respect to which misapprehensions most frequently arise, and on which information is most likely to be sought. And on all of them, while Baptists do not claim to be faultless, nor beyond the possibility of mistake and error, they appeal to the Bible, to history, to philology, in justification of their views, and in support of their position.

CHAPTER 2

A CHRISTIAN CHURCH

A CHRISTIAN CHURCH is a company of regenerate persons, baptized on a profession of faith in Christ; united in covenant for worship, instruction, the observance of Christian ordinances, and for such service as the gospel requires; recognizing and accepting Christ as their supreme Lord and Lawgiver, and taking His Word as their only and sufficient rule of faith and practice in all matters of conscience and religion.

I. MEANING OF THE WORD

The word *Church* is of uncertain derivation : English, *Church;* Scottish, *Kirk;* Anglo-Saxon, *Cyric;* German, *Kirche;* Danish, *Kyrke;* Swedish, *Kyrka;* Russian, *Zerkow*. It is used as the equivalent, if not derived from the Hebrew *Kahal;* Latin, *Curia*, and has usually been derived from the Greek *Kuriakon*—"belonging to the Lord." This is, however, disputed by good authority. But *Ekklesia* is the accepted equivalent Greek word used in the New Testament, and translated *Church*. This word is used to designate the visible " Kingdom of heaven " on earth, the company of God's elect people chosen in Christ Jesus; His spiritual Israel of the New Dispensation—what Alford calls "the congregation of the faithful."*

Ekklesia is composed of *ek*, from, or out of, and *kaleo*, to call—called out from. It denotes a company, or assembly of persons, called out, selected, chosen and separated from a larger company, a more general concourse of people. According to the usages of Greek civil life, the *Ekklesia* was, as the lexicons define it, "an assembly of citizens called together for deliberative purposes; a legislative assembly, called to discuss the affairs of state." It was an orderly and an organized assembly, consisting of those possessing the rights of citizenship, for the consideration of public affairs, and the enactment and enforcement of laws pertaining to the public welfare, as distinguished from the common populace at large, an incidental concourse, or a disorderly crowd of people.†

BISHOP TRENCH gives the following elucidation :

"We have *Ekklesia* in three distinct stages of meaning—the Heathen, the Jewish, the Christian. In respect of the first, *Ekklesia*, as all know, was the lawful assembly in a free Greek city of all persons possessed of the rights of citizenship for the transaction of public affairs. That they were *summoned*, is expressed in the latter part of the word; that they were summoned *out of* the whole population, a select portion of it, including neither the populace, nor yet the strangers, nor those who had forfeited their civic rights; this is expressed

---

* See Matt. 16: 18; 18: 17.

† See Grimms-Wilkes N. T. Lexicon, Liddell & Scott, Robinson, *et al.*

in the first part. Both the *calling*, and the calling *out*, are moments to be remembered when the word is assumed into a higher Christian sense, for in them the chief part of its peculiar adaptation to its auguster uses lies."—*Synonyms of the New Testament, pp. 17, 18; Ed. 1857.*

Still true to its original classical idea and scope of meaning, when the word was adopted into Christian literature and applied to higher and more sacred uses, it designated a company called out from the world, elected, chosen and separated—*Eklektoi*, the elected, the faithful, called to be saints. And thus a selected and separated company, to constitute "the Kingdom of Christ," "the Church of the living God," "a peculiar people" sanctified to Himself. Here, also, we have the further idea, fundamental to its primitive meaning, of an organized company, with laws, officers and ordinances for the orderly transaction of affairs, and the performance of service contemplated in their calling and institution.

II.   USES OF THE WORD

The word *Ekklesia* is found *one hundred and fifteen times* in the New Testament. In *one hundred and ten* of these instances it has reference to the institution known as the *Church*. In *three* instances it is used in what Trench calls the "heathen sense," being applied to the assembly gathered at Ephesus, on the occasion of the riot incited against Paul and his associates—Acts 19: 32, 39, 41. Notice, however, that the excited and riotous multitude was the *oklos*—a crowd, a confused and disorderly multitude, Acts 2: 35, and not the *Ekklesia*, which was the official and authoritative assembly, to which such cases of popular disturbance and disorder were appealed for suppression and settlement. In *two* cases this word is used in the "Jewish sense," being applied to ancient Israel as God's chosen and separated people. In the address of Stephen before his accusers, when referring to Mosaic history, he said: "This is he that was in the Church (*Ekklesia*) in the wilderness, with the angel which spoke to him."— Acts 7: 38; and in the Epistle to the Hebrews, a citation from the Twenty-second Psalm, according to the Seventy, "I will declare thy name unto my brethren; in the midst of the Church (*Ekklesia*) will I sing praise unto thee."—Heb. 2: 12; Ps. 22: 22. The Alexandrian translators of the Hebrew Scriptures into Greek used this word to designate the entire congregation of Israel, the whole Hebrew commonwealth, as an organic unity. Under the theocratic government of the Old Dispensation, the seed of Abraham constituted a distinct congregation, called out and separated from all other peoples and races, organized under a polity peculiarly their own, with laws, ordinances and services as distinct as their own calling and race life. Hence the propriety and force of this word as a designation of the Hebrew people.

In the "Christian sense" the word *Ekklesia* has a twofold signification in the New Testament. *First,* it is used, in its primary and literal sense, to desig-

nate a visible, local congregation of Christian disciples, meeting for worship, instruction and service.
Second, it is used in a secondary and figurative sense,
to designate the invisible, universal company, including all of God's true people on earth and in
heaven. There is, then, the visible, local Church,
and the invisible, universal Church. In the latter
case the word represents a conception of the mind,
having no real existence in time or place, and not a
historical fact, being only an ideal multitude without organization, without action, and without corporate being.

Of the *one hundred and ten* instances in which
Ekklesia is rendered *Church* in the New Testament,
more than *ninety* are applied to a visible, local congregation, or company of disciples, meeting in a
given place, for a given purpose. This is the primary and literal signification of the word. Thus it
is said, "Paul called the elders of the Church;"
"The Church of God at Corinth ;" "The Seven
churches of Asia;" "The Church of Ephesus;" "The
churches of Galatia." But when it is said, "Christ
also loved the Church, and gave Himself for it, that
He might present it to Himself a glorious Church,"
etc., Eph. 5 : 25, 27, it presumably refers to no particular congregation of believers, but to the entire
company of the saved — the universal, invisible
Church. In the same way is interpreted the much-
quoted declaration of Jesus : "On this rock will I
build my Church."—Matt. 16: 18. Also, "To the
intent that now . . . . might be known *by the*

Church the manifold wisdom of God."—Eph. 3 : 10, "He is the head of the body, the Church."—Col. 1 : 18. "The general assembly and Church of the first-born, which are written in heaven."—Heb. 12 : 23. These, with a few other passages, are supposed to refer not to any localized congregations of believers, but to the universal fellowship of the faithful. And yet it is likely that some of the passages usually thus interpreted might, by a more careful exegesis, be found to bear the primary and literal meaning of a particular congregation. Certain it is that this literal meaning of the word is its first and ruling signification, as is certified in a vast majority of cases. And if in certain cases another meaning attaches to it, such other meaning is purely tropical and secondary. And such secondary meaning grows directly out of, and bears a strict resemblance to, the primary.

The word *Church*, in common language, is used with a large latitude of meaning. It is applied to a congregation of Christian worshipers, to a religious establishment, to a given form of ecclesiastical order, to the aggregate of all the saints, and to a building used for religious purposes. This last-named use, though common, is hardly legitimate, and the passages of Scripture sometimes cited to justify it (Rom. 16: 5; 1 Cor. 11: 18; 14: 19, 28) will not warrant such application. And to call the aggregate of those who profess the Christian faith—of all names in all the world—"the Christian Church," is a misuse of the word not warranted by the Scriptures.

There is no such thing as a universal Church on earth embraced in one grand communion. Equally baseless and unsupported by Scripture is the claim that all the religious congregations of a nation, or of a given form of faith in a nation, constitute a national, or a denominational church. It contradicts the New Testament idea. It is common to speak of "the Church of England," or "the Church of Russia," or "the Church of Rome." We understand what is intended, but such terms are extra-evangelical, and untrue to the New Testament idea.

III.   MARKS OF A TRUE CHURCH

Are there any marks, or signs, by which a true Church can be known? If so, what are they? If our ideas as to what constitutes a true Church be erroneous or confused, we shall be likely to go astray as to all that follows, and misinterpret its polity, order, ordinances, its structure, government and purpose. All the various Christian communions, both ancient and modern, have, in their dogmàtic symbols, more or less fully, given their conception of a true Church. These definitions are found in their standard creeds and confessions of faith; and it is to be observed that they all assume to start with the New Testament idea. But as they proceed they do more and more diverge, and complicate the primitive simplicity with their ecclesiastical surroundings, their educational prepossessions, or with what trusted authority decides a Church ought to be, rather than what it is.

It may be noted that our Savior used the term *Ekklesia* but on two occasions, in both briefly, and without definitions or explanations, as reported in the Gospel narratives—Matt. 16: 18; 18: 17. His oft-repeated expression was, "the Kingdom," "the Kingdom of God," many times repeated; "the Kingdom of heaven;" "the Son of man coming in His Kingdom;" "my Kingdom;" "the children of the Kingdom." Now, it is manifest that the *Kingdom* and the *Church* are vitally related, but not identical. The Kingdom is a fact in the world, being a moral and spiritual reign of truth and righteousness in the hearts and lives of men, Christ Himself being King, His word law, and His Spirit the indwelling life. But there is no outward form, no organization, no corporate life. The Church is the outward, visible, organic expression and development of this spiritual, real, but invisible Kingdom of Christ; not a perfect counterpart, but an imperfect representation; since the Church may contain some not in the Kingdom, and the Kingdom may contain many not in the churches.

THE LATIN CHURCH gives this definition of a Church :

"The company of Christians knit together by the profession of the same faith, and the communion of the same sacraments, under the government of lawful pastors, and especially of the Roman bishop, as the only vicar of Christ on earth."—*Bellarmine De Eccl. Mil., III., 2.*

THE GREEK CHURCH gives this definition :

"The Church is a divinely instituted community of men,

united by the orthodox faith, the law of God, the Hierarchy, and the sacraments."— *Full Catec. of the Orthodox Est. Church.*

THE CHURCH OF ENGLAND defines after this manner :

" A congregation of faithful men, in which the pure Word of God is preached, and the sacraments duly administered according to Christ's ordinances, in all those things that of necessity are requisite to the same."—*Thirty-Nine Articles, Art. XIX.*

THE AUGSBURG CONFESSION has the following :

" A congregation of saints, in which the gospel is purely preached, and the sacraments are rightly administered." —*Aug. Conf., Art. VII.*

THE HELVETIC CONFESSION states it thus :

" The Church is a community of believers, or saints, gathered out of the world, whose distinction is to know and to worship, through the Word and by the Spirit, the true God in Christ the Savior."—*Helv. Conf., Art. XVII.*

THE BELGIC CONFESSION gives this definition :

" A true congregation or assembly of all faithful Christians, who look for their salvation only from Jesus Christ, as being washed by His blood and sanctified by His Spirit." —*Belg. Conf., Art. XXVII.*

THE SAXON CONFESSION defines in these words :

" A congregation of men embracing the gospel of Christ, and rightly using the sacraments."—*Saxon Conf., Art. XII.*

THE SCOTTISH CONFESSION puts it in these words:

" The Church is a society of the elect of all ages and

countries both Jews and Gentiles; this is the Catholic, or universal Church. This Church is invisible, and known only to God."— *Scot. Conf., Art. XVI.*

THE WESTMINSTER ASSEMBLY'S definition is this:

"Particular Churches in the primitive times were made up of visible saints, viz., of such as being of age, professing faith in Christ, according to the rules of faith and life taught by Christ and his Apostles, and of their children."*— *West. Assem. Directory ; Neal's Hist. Puritans, Vol. II., p. 469, Appendix.*

Baptists have attached less importance to creed statements than most other denominations Nevertheless they, too, have some historical symbols which they respect and use, but to which they are not bound.

A CONFESSION OF FAITH, issued by seven Baptist Churches in London, put forth A. D. 1643, as a vindication from the aspersions and calumnies of their opponents and enemies, defines a Church as follows :

"Jesus Christ hath here on the earth a spiritual kingdom which is His Church, whom He hath purchased and redeemed to Himself, as a peculiar inheritance : which Church is a company of visible saints, called and separated from the world by the Word and Spirit of God, to the visible profession of the faith of the gospel; being baptized into that faith, and joined to the Lord, and to each other, by mutual agreement, in the practical enjoyment of the ordinances by Christ their head and King."—*Bap. Conf., 1643, Art. XXXIII.*

---

*See Schaff's Creeds of Christendom; Smith's Bible Dict. ; Append. B., Art. Ch.; Cyclop. Bib. Eccl. and Theo. Lit. Art. Ch. *et al.*

A BAPTIST CONFESSION, put forth by the elders and brethren of many Baptist congregations in London, 1677, evidently based on that of 1643, and adopted by the " General Assembly" of ministers and delegates of more than one hundred "baptized Churches," in 1689, says:

"The Lord Jesus Christ collecteth out of the world to Himself, through the ministry of His Word by His Spirit, those that are given to Him by the Father, that they may walk before Him in all the ways of obedience, which He prescribeth to them in His Word. Those thus called He commandeth to walk together in particular societies or churches, for their mutual edification, and the due performance of the public worship which He requireth of them in the world. The members of these churches are saints by calling, visibly manifesting and evidencing their obedience unto the call of Christ; and do willingly consent to walk according to the appointment of Christ, giving up themselves to the Lord, and one to another, by the will of God, in professed subjection to the ordinances of the gospel." *—Art. XXVI., secs. 5, 6.

THE NEW HAMPSHIRE CONFESSION more briefly gives the following definition of a Church:

" A visible Church of Christ is a congregation of baptized believers, associated by covenant in the faith and fellowship of the Gospel; observing the ordinances of Christ, governed by his law, exercising the gifts, rights, and privileges invested in them by His Word."—N. H. Conf., Art. XVI.

* In 1742 the old Philadelphia Association adopted, with some additions and changes, this English Confession of 1689, since which it has been known in this country as " The Philadelphia Confession."

IV. SIGNS OF A TRUE CHURCH

By what signs, notes, or attributes may a true Church of Christ be known ?

To this question the Roman Catholic Catechism answers: "Unity, holiness, catholicity, apostolicity, and perpetuity." To these, Bellarmine and others, from the ultra papal standpoint, add various others. These attributes Protestants accept as signs, only with their own definitions. But, if accepted, they must be predicated, to a certain extent, of "the invisible, universal Church." More distinctively Protestant, however, are added these marks, oft-repeated in their definitions, "the preaching of the pure Word of God, and the right administration of the sacraments." But these have reference rather to the *action* of the Church's life, than to the *substance* of that life—to what is *done* in the Church, rather than to what *constitutes* the Church.

1. *Unity.* This is true from the New Testament point of view, which Baptists emphatically accept as thus taught: "Endeavoring to keep the unity of the Spirit, in the bond of peace. There is one body, and one Spirit, even as ye are called in one hope of your calling; one Lord, one faith, and one baptism; one God and Father of all, who is above all, and through all, and in you all."—Eph. 4 : 3–6. There is one head—Christ. There is one body—the Church. But the doctrine that the unity of the Church consists in the combination of many separate congregations of Christians into one general or universal assembly

of like faith and order, whether taught by Catholics or Protestants, is not taught in the Scriptures, and is repudiated by Baptists. There is, however, a spiritual unity in the " Communion of Saints," existing among all who are truly born of God, however various and dissimilar their ecclesiastical polity and relations may be.

2. *Holiness*. This marks a true Church, because only such as are born of the Spirit, and become " new creatures in Christ Jesus " are suitable persons to be, or can properly become, members of it. They are called " saints," sanctified ones. " Unto the Church of God, which is at Corinth, to them that are sanctified in Christ Jesus, called to be saints."—1 Cor. 1:2. "As the elect of God, holy and beloved."—Col. 3:12. " Ye also, as lively stones, are built up a spiritual house, a holy priesthood, to offer spiritual sacrifices."—1 Peter 2:5. This holiness may not be perfect and absolute as to any one member, much less as to the entire body; nevertheless it is what the gospel claims, and is the prevailing mark of those who are united to Christ, as the branch is to the vine. Being characteristic, therefore, of individual believers, it becomes characteristic of the congregation of believers. But the papal claim that holiness comes from a union with that, as the only true Church, is an absurd fiction, not to be credited, or seriously considered.

3. *Catholicity*. Various ecclesiastical establishments arrogate, each to itself, universality, and claim to be the only " Catholic Church." Such a

claim is made by the Latin, the Greek, the English, and other prelatical systems. Such claims, however, have no foundation whatever in the historical, or doctrinal teachings of the New Testament. But if catholicity may be interpreted to mean a recognition of the essential spiritual unity of the faith in all of Christ's redeemed people, and a willingness to accord sainthood to all of every name and nation who bear the image and have the spirit of their Lord, then every congregation of evangelical disciples is a Catholic Church. "Of a truth I perceive that God is no respecter of persons; but in every nation, he that feareth Him, and worketh righteousness, is accepted of Him."—Acts 10:34, 35. "For the same Lord over all, is rich unto all that call upon Him."—Rom. 10:12.

4. *Apostolicity*. It is the claim of the Roman, and of some other prelatical and High-Church communions, that they have an unbroken succession of ministerial gifts and ordinations direct from the Apostles—what is sometimes termed "the historical episcopate." And if a succession in the ministry, then a succession largely also in Church order, and sacramental efficacy. This claim is historically groundless, and doctrinally useless. But the true apostolicity consists not in *succession*, but in *possession;* for they who possess and exhibit the doctrines, the spirit and the life of the Apostles, have right to claim this mark of a true gospel Church. "For other foundation can no man lay, than that is laid, which is Jesus Christ."—1 Cor. 3:11. "Now there-

fore ye are no more strangers and foreigners, but fellow citizens with the saints, and of the household of God; and are built upon the foundation of the Apostles and prophets, Jesus Christ Himself being the chief corner-stone."—Eph. 2 : 19, 20.

5. *Perpetuity.* This has reference, not to a continuance of official administration, as in the previous note, but to visible and corporate Church life. And, strange to say, some Baptists have been courageous enough, and indiscreet enough to assert that an unbroken succession of visible, organized congregations of believers similar to their own, and therefore substantially like the primitive churches, can be proven to have existed from the Apostles until now. Such claims may well be left to papal audacity. For those who learn from that storehouse of sacred truth—the New Testament—what are the spirit, doctrine, ordinances, and polity of a Church of Christ, and practice the same, it matters nothing whether the chain of organic perpetuity may never have been broken, or broken a thousand times. They are the true disciples of Christ who have His spirit; the true successors of the Apostles who follow their teachings, and imitate their lives. " They continued steadfastly in the Apostles' doctrine, and fellowship, and in breaking of bread, and in prayers."— Acts 2 : 42. "And you being in time past alienated and enemies in your mind, by wicked works, yet now hath He reconciled, in the body of His flesh, through death, to present you holy and without blemish, and unreprovable before Him; if so be that

ye continue in the faith, grounded and steadfast, and be not moved away from the hope of the gospel."—Col. 1 : 21–23.

Strictly speaking, perpetuity is predicated of the invisible Church only. It is "the kingdom of heaven" on earth; "the Messiah's reign," which is perpetual. "In the days of these kings shall the God of heaven set up a kingdom which shall never be destroyed."—Dan. 2 : 44. "But the saints of the Most High shall take the kingdom, and possess the kingdom forever, even forever and ever."—Dan. 7 : 18. "Upon this rock will I build my Church, and the gates of Hades shall not prevail against it."—Matt. 16 : 18. "Lo, I am with you **alway, even** unto the end of the world."—Matt. 28 : 20.

But visible churches—local congregations—are largely subject to the mutations of human society. They rise and fall; they grow and decay; they flourish, decline and disappear. Many a "candlestick" has been removed out of its place, and many more will be. But the cause is imperishable, and the foundations shall never be removed.

V. NOT A CONFEDERATION

A Christian Church, therefore, is not a confederation of many local congregations, under some one general head, whether that be a person, as bishop, patriarch, or pope; or under some system of government, as presbytery, synod, conference, or assembly. It is not an ecclesiastical system, extending over a wide area of country, claiming the right of control over all of similar faith within such territory. Such, at least, is far from the New Testament idea of a Church. The expressions found in the Acts and the Epistles clearly define and fix the primitive notion of a Church.

We read : "Then had the *churches* rest," and " were established in the faith." Not "the *Church*," mark, as if all disciples were grouped in one comprehensive body. "The *churches* of Christ salute you." " The *churches* of Galatia;" not " *the* Church." "The *churches* of Asia salute you." "Messengers of the *churches*." "The churches throughout all Judea and Galilee and Samaria;" "the churches of Macedonia;" "the Church which was at Jerusalem;" "the Church of the Thessalonians;" "the Church of the Laodiceans." "As I teach in every Church." "Ordained elders in every Church." "The Church which is at Cenchrea." "Greet the Church that is in their house." "If therefore the whole Church be come together into one place." "With the Church in their house." No one can fail to understand the force of such expressions.

NOTE 1.—An organization of professing Christians may fail in some respects to meet the requirements of the Gospel, and still be a Church, providing it fulfills the fundamental conditions of a Scriptural faith and practice, holding the headship of Christ, maintaining the Ordinances and the ministry of the word in their purity.

NOTE 2.—But if it ceases to recognize and submit to Christ as its supreme ruler, and to receive His word as its supreme law, then it ceases to be a Church of Christ, though it may still preserve its religious character and retain many evangelical marks.

NOTE 3.—No Church, however sound its orthodoxy, or perfect its order, can fulfill the conditions of its existence without the indwelling life of Christ in its members, they walking in the Spirit, and not fulfilling the lusts of the flesh. Its importance and efficacy, therefore, depend not on mere mechanical conformity to any, even a divine model, so much as on the life and power of godliness in its constituent elements.

VI. ANALOGICAL DEFINITIONS

The Church is not unfrequently spoken of in the New Testament in figurative language, in which certain analogies are suggested, in the use of which the nature, purpose and relations of this institution are more clearly represented. The fact that these tropes were not intended as logical definitions, and do only incidentally define, makes them perhaps the more interesting. The similarities elucidate, and the comparisons, so far as they were intended to apply, are accurate and instructing.

" And gave Him to be head over all things to the Church, which is His body. "—Eph. 1: 22. Christ the *head*, and the Church His *body*. This is equally true of the Church universal and invisible, and of the Church local and visible. Head over all things, and in all respects. The head is the intelligent director, the authoritative lawgiver, to the body, and furnishes the will-force for active obedience. The Church as the body is to obey the directions, and to execute the authoritative mandates of Christ, the head. The figure indicates the intimate, sensitive, and sacred relation existing between Christ and His people. Also observe, there are not many heads, but one only—Christ. A many-headed body would be a monstrosity. In God's methods and operations there are the beauty and the symmetry of a sacred unity.

" Husbands, love your wives, even as Christ also loved the Church, and gave Himself for it." " So ought men to love their wives as their own bodies " " For no man ever yet hated his own flesh; but nourisheth it, even as the Lord the Church." " This is a great mystery; but I speak concerning Christ and the Church."—Eph. 5: 23–32. Here the relation subsisting between Christ and the Church, is illustrated by the relations of husband and wife. A relationship intimate, tender, affectionate, sacred; on the recognition of which relations, cherishing their proper spirit, and discharging their implied obligations, depends the success of the purpose for which they exist. If to the husband be accorded, in the divine economy, headship over the wife, it is not for her servile subjection, but for the common good ; and that his affection, protection, and support, may be made the more manifest, and the more abiding. If the Church is to be subject to, and directed by, its Head, it knows that " Christ loved the Church, and gave Himself for it."   And if He seems exacting in His requirements, for its service and its sanctity, it is, " that He might present it to Himself, a glorious Church, not having spot, or wrinkle. or any such thing."

"The house of God, which is the Church of the living God, the pillar and ground of the truth."— 1 Tim. 3 : 15. If "the pillar and ground of the truth" refer to the "Church of the living God," as is almost universally conceded, and indeed is almost necessary to suppose, and not to the "mystery of godliness," as some would make to appear, but which would seem forced and harsh, then we have a vivid conception of the importance of each individual congregation of the saints, as the organized unit of the "kingdom of heaven," in the world. The *pillar* supports the superincumbent portion of the building. The *ground*, literally *foundation*, is that on which the building rests, and upon which it is reared. Thus, while in an emphatic sense Christ is the only foundation for the faith of saints, the hope of souls, yet in a very important sense does the Church become the support of all Christian endeavor, whether for the edification or the sanctification of the saints, or the spread of the gospel and the evangelization of the world. As a historical fact the churches of Christ have acted this part, and served this purpose, and are now serving it—indeed, this is the very end for which they were instituted. Without them, all those Christian activities which are filling the world with light and blessing, would soon become inert and fail. It is from beneath the threshold of the sanctuary, the river of life flows forth to the nations. "Out of Zion, the perfection of beauty, God hath shined."—Ps. 50: 2. No human influence is so much a pillar and foundation to the truth as a spiritual, orderly, active Church, composed of godly members, well ordered and faithful to their Lord.

But may there not be a still further resemblance, intended or implied, in this use of the "pillar?" The *stylos* often had a memorial as well as an architectural value. The obelisk was reared to perpetuate the memory of great men, and of noble deeds. It preserved the records of historical events, and both instructed and inspired succeeding generations, by its inscribed memorials. It cultivated a becoming pride in national character, and sustained a worthy patriotism for national defence. The churches of Christ are monumental. Their preservation is miraculous ; their very existence is a wonder. They perpetuate the grandest events in human history : the Incarnation, the Crucifixion, the Resurrection, the Ascension, and the Mediation of Christ. They do not simply honor the name and the deeds of the greatest and best of men, but of Him who is Lord of lords, and King of kings. In all senses each true Church is a pillar for Him, who is the Truth, and aids to support and to proclaim the profound mystery of godliness.

"Ye are God's building." "Know ye not that ye are the temple of God, and that the Spirit of God dwelleth in you?"—1 Cor. 3: 9–17. This is true, in a very important sense, of each individual Christian. But here it was declared true of the Corinthian Church. The Apostle asserted that he had laid the foundation of the edifice, and others had built upon it. He declares the building to be holy, as the shrines of heathen gods even, were supposed to be; and cautions them not to defile this sanctuary. It is the abiding presence of the Spirit in a Church, that gives importance to its existence, and efficacy to its ministrations. As a mere human organization it would not rise above the level of other moral and benevolent institutions. But the divine element in it lifts it to a loftier position. An ornate and costly material structure, a magnificent and imposing ritual, numbers, wealth, fashion, social attractions, can never meet the demand, nor realize the sacred purpose of the churches' life, without the indwelling presence of the Spirit, as the presence of the Shekinah in the Tabernacle of old.

All this is suggestive to those who are active in planting, and laborious in building up the churches. No mistake should be made as to what manner of institutions they are to be. A salutary discipline is implied, as is elsewhere plainly enjoined, since "the temple of God is holy." While this spiritual house "groweth up," each one in his place, and according to his ability, is to aid in rearing the sacred edifice, and at the same time each member as a "living stone," is "builded together for a habitation of God through the Spirit."—Eph. 2 : 22. But Christ is the "Chief Corner-stone," and the abiding life, "in whom all the building, fitly framed together, groweth unto a holy temple in the Lord."—Eph. 2 : 21.

"As we have therefore opportunity, let us do good to all, especially unto them who are of the household of faith."—Gal. 4 : 10. Here the household, or family idea, represents the Church in the Apostle's mind, and gives direction to his counsel. The chapter begins with directions as to the proper spirit in which disciplinary culture is to be administered in the churches; for this epistle is dedicated, not to the saints at large, "but unto the churches of Galatia." By a natural and easy transition the writer conceives of each particular Church as a family, a household, where mutual affection should rule; the members careful for each other's good, bearing one another's burdens, and with fraternal solicitude, striving to restore to the truth such as are faulty and out of the way. A similar idea underlies the Apostle's address to the Ephesian Church. " Now, therefore, ye are no more strangers and sojourners, but ye are fellow-citizens with the saints, and of the household of God."—Eph. 2 : 19. Here is a double metaphor. The Church is likened to a state, a commonwealth, of which the saints have been made citizens, now no longer strangers, temporarily sojourning, but naturalized and permanently abiding, entitled to all the immunities of citizens native born.

And then, in a narrowed circle, but a more intimate and sacred relationship, they are represented as members of the holy family of God, the Father. And if it may be said that the *family* here bears a more general signification, a wider application than to the individual Church, yet it must be remembered that the whole address is to a particular Church, " the saints which are at Ephesus;" and out of this specific idea grows the more general notion of the larger fellowship of the saints, which the tropes supply, of citizenship in the state and membership in the family. Thus, again to the Ephesians, Paul says, "I bow my knees unto the Father of our Lord Jesus Christ, of whom the whole family in heaven and on earth is named."—Eph. 3:15. Or, as the New Version renders it, "from whom every family in heaven and on earth is named." The thought is distributive, and the conception is individualized. If the idea be that of the completed company of the saints, the Church universal both above and below, it manifestly aggregates it out of all the individual families of the faithful, the separate and distinct churches of Christ, called to be saints.

In the closing chapter of the Revelation we have the Church idea brought to view in a somewhat strange commingling of figures. But it is the Church triumphant; and the unusual mixing of the metaphors gives a strange and vivid picturesqueness and beauty to the conception. It represents the company of the saved, both as a *bride*, and as a *city*, and Christ as a *bridegroom*, and as a *lamb*. "And I John saw the holy city, New Jerusalem, coming down from God, out of heaven, prepared as a bride adorned for her husband. And there came unto me one of the seven angels . . . . saying, 'Come hither, and I will show thee the bride, the Lamb's wife.' And he carried me away in the spirit to a great and high mountain, and showed me that great city, the holy Jerusalem, descending out of heaven from God."—Rev. 21:2, 9, 10. The purity, beauty and glory of the redeemed saints are implied in the bridal relation, and the affection of the Lamb, who is the Bridegroom, and his joy at the final reception of his bride, so beautiful, for whom he had suffered so much, and waited so long, that he might present her to himself, "a glorious Church, not having spot or wrinkle, or any such thing." It realizes the prophet's declaration to Zion, " As the bridegroom rejoiceth over the bride, so shall thy God rejoice over thee."—Is. 62: 5. The added conception of a city to represent the company of glorified saints, may imply the transcendent glory of the final habitation of the righteous; and that the Church triumphant shall be orderly and active as well as blissful and glorious; governed by a polity as really as is the Church militant, law-abiding and obedient, under the joyous and loving reign of their Lord, the prince of life, "the King eternal, immortal, invisible."

Thus the teachings of Scripture as to the Church idea do show the peculiar place in human society which this sacred brotherhood, this divinely appointed institution holds, as well as explains the purpose which, in the economy of redemption, and in God's purposes of mercy to a lost world, the Church was designed to serve.

VII.   THE NATURE OF A CHURCH

The Christian Church is the only divinely organized society among men. It was instituted for a purpose by Christ, who gave to it laws, and an economy of methods and order by which to accomplish its sacred mission, and who still retains headship and kingship over it. A Church is the "Society of Jesus" in a truer and better sense than Loyola knew when founding the order of Jesuits. Each such organized company of saints constitutes a body politic in a spiritual realm; in the world, but not of it; being able to maintain its existence and discharge its functions in all conditions of social and civil life, under all forms of human government: while not untrue to any, yet is in subjection to none, but gives allegiance to a foreign potentate, "the Prince of the kings of the earth." Jesus said, "My kingdom is not of this world."—John 18 : 36. And of his disciples he said, "They are not of the world even as I am not of the world."—John 17 : 16.

Members of the Church have all the rights, privileges, and immunities of citizens in civil government, as others have, and owe allegiance to that under which they live, in all matters temporal, so long as such allegiance does not interfere with perfect obedience to the claims of Christ upon them. But if human laws, and the demands of human governments, contravene the divine claim, or in any way interfere with the rights of conscience or religious faith, and the freedom of belief and worship, then God is to be obeyed rather than man. His claims are supreme, and annihilate all rival claims. "Render unto Cæsar the things that are Cæsar's, and to God the things that are God's." Christian men should be good and law-abiding citizens, unless obedience to human law demands a violation of divine law. Their fealty to the higher law must be prompt and unquestioned. "Submit yourselves to every ordinance of man, for the Lord's sake; whether it be to the king as supreme, or unto governors, as unto them that are sent by him for the punishment of evil doers, and for the praise of them that do well. For so is the will of God, that with well-doing ye may put to silence the ignorance of foolish men."— 1 Peter 2:13–15. As to things spiritual, the state has no right of control over, or interference with, them. Matters of conscience, faith, and worship the civil power has no right to meddle with, so long as the government is not injured, nor the rights of others put in jeopardy by their exercise.

The nature of a Church is very different from that of other societies and associations. Its members may be connected with other organizations, whose objects contemplate the furtherance of commerce, literature, science or the arts; they may be moral, philanthropic, and even religious. But they do not reach the high ideal of the Church's vocation, nor fill the broad sphere of the Church's mission. That is no less than the glory of God and the salvation of souls. Fellowship in such other associations will be consistent and harmless—it may be even commendable—providing the objects they seek, and the methods by which they are sought, be consistent with Christian morals; and providing, also, their duties to these in no way interfere with their duties to, and usefulness in, the Church, whose claims are first and most imperative. In such other associations good may be accomplished by the wider diffusion of intelligence, the cultivation of social morals and of public virtue, the mitigation of human suffering, and the advancement of a true civilization.

All these aims are good, and all good men should encourage them. But all these aims are contemplated by a Christian Church, and can and will be better reached by a Church, if true to its calling and mission, than by any other society; while beyond and above all these remains the one special and unique object of the Church's life, which all other societies lack; a regenerated humanity, in order to constitute the ultimate " Church of the first-born, which are written in heaven."—Heb. 12:23. Did not He who founded the Church, who knew what was in man, and who understood the world He came to save, who gave Himself to restore the divine image in man, and the divine authority over man, know what sort of organized endeavor, what kind of a society would be best adapted to accomplish the simple but sublime object contemplated? Every effort at social virtue and moral reform should find its best example and its most efficient advocacy in the Church of God. It would be a shame for those who are expressly set forth to be the " light of the world,* and the " salt of the earth," to fall below the standard of goodness in worldly societies, or the conceptions of virtue in carnal minds. Then would they no longer be " holding forth the word of life."

VIII.   THE AUTHORITY OF CHURCHES

All associations of men are supposed to possess such and so much authority as may be needful to control their members within the limits of their associational relations, to guard their organizations against perversion and disaster, and to secure the objects for which they exist. This authority they have the consequent right to exercise, and power to enforce. It is derived either from voluntary compact, where each individual surrenders to the body a part of his personal freedom of action, or else is conferred by some external and superior authority. Thus with churches.

Its members, on uniting with a Church, do voluntarily surrender some personal prerogatives, that they may be invested in the body, the organic whole. But such personally surrendered prerogatives constitute but a small part of its authority. Its chief authority is given by Christ alone. The state cannot bestow it; nor can legislatures, or courts of civil jurisdiction, or princes, or parliaments, either bestow or annul the charter by right of which the churches of Christ exist and act. Quite as little can that authority emanate from any ecclesiastical source, since all ecclesiastical orders emanate from, and grow out of, the churches, and are created by them — do not create them. Popes, patriarchs, bishops, priests, synods, assemblies, conventions, conferences, supposing they were Scriptural, do not make churches, but are made by them; cannot in-

vest churches with authority, since they possess
no antecedent authority in the premises, but are invested by the churches, directly or indirectly, with
all the authority they claim to possess. All rightful authority, therefore, is conferred by Christ, the
king in Zion. He builds them: "On this rock will
I build my Church." He commissions them: "Go
ye, therefore, and teach all nations, baptizing them
in the name of the Father, and of the Son, and of
the Holy Ghost." He is personally ever with them,
superintending, and giving them success: "Lo, I am
with you **alway,** even unto the end of the world."—
Matt. 16:18; 28:19, 20. What He does not give is
not possessed. What He does not sanction is not
legitimate. What He does bestow is a sacred trust,
to be guarded and used for His purpose and praise.
This, then, is the source, and the only authoritative
source, of the Church's right of rule. It can assume
none and derive none from any other source.
This authority a Church can exercise on none but
its own members. They can bring the moral force
of their persuasion, of their consistent living, and of
their Christian character, to bear on all around them,
as indeed they should; but as to authoritative administration, they can claim no right of interference
with any except those with whom they hold covenant relations in the fellowship of the body. Said
the Apostle to the Corinthians, "For what have I
to do to judge them also that are without? Do
not ye judge them that are within?"—1 Cor. 5:12.
Nor can a Church exercise authority over its own

members in any respect except as to spiritual concerns. With their personal rights and duties as members of society, it cannot interfere. It cannot dictate what they shall eat or drink, or wherewithal they shall be clothed; what business they shall pursue, what associations they shall keep, what privileges they may enjoy; *except*, that in all these they shall do nothing which shall be inconsistent with their position and profession as Christians ; nothing that shall harm or hinder the gospel of Christ; nothing that shall destroy their influence for good, place a stumbling-block in the way of unconverted men, or cast a reproach on the Christian name. And of all these questions the Church has the right to judge. The sphere of a Church's authority is therefore distinctively and exclusively moral and spiritual. Those so-called churches, whether of the past or present, that have assumed dictatorship over their communicants in all matters both sacred and secular, have forfeited their claim to be recognized as true churches of Christ, and are to be held as religious societies only. They have transcended all proper bounds, violating personal rights by their assumptions.

Nor yet can a Church dominate the faith or conscience of its members. With such personal religious liberty no man, or combination of men, **has** a right to interfere. For such liberty and its lawful exercise each one is responsible to God alone. The Church's authority goes not so far. It can and should secure harmony in the faith and fellowship of the body. But to what extent it may require doctrinal conformity, and how it should treat dissent, whether it may or may not become a court of jurisdiction in matters of faith, or only of morals, and whether its acts may be punitive, will be considered more at length in the chapter on discipline.

IX. THE COMITY OF CHURCHES

Churches hold relations of comity and fraternal courtesy with each other, but sustain no legal governmental or organic connections. No Church can exercise discipline upon another, or for another, or interfere in any way with another's disciplinary acts. No member has a right to vote in the meeting of any Church but his own, or even to be present at such a meeting, or participate in the Communion except by invitation and as a matter of courtesy. No pastor has a right to exercise his ministry in any Church but his own except on invitation. Churches, however, are fraternal and exchange courtesies, dismiss members by letter to each other, and receive those dismissed, respect each other's disciplinary acts, but are not bound by them. Pastors exchange pulpits. Churches unite fraternally in associations for mutual benefit and for missionary work. They bear themselves toward each other with that respect and affection which become disciples of a Common Master, but to talk of an *interdependence* of organic and official Church life and action, as some have done, is most absurd. There is no such thing. These questions will be more fully considered in another place.

X. CHURCHES CONSTITUTED

Churches are constituted by voluntary covenant on the part of those who wish to become members. The *constitution* of a Church, strictly speaking, is to be found in the New Testament only, as regards both faith and practice. But it is customary to have these formulated, which thus become creed symbols, and to a certain extent serve as standards. And though no Church and no Church-member is asked to sign them, or is required to pledge allegiance to them, yet a general and substantial assent and conformity to them is expected, in order that harmony in the churches and among the churches may be secured. And this harmony is secured to a remarkable degree among Baptists. when we consider the great number of their churches, the wide extent of territory over which they are scattered, and the great diversity of social life, local customs, and educational bias which naturally influence them; and especially when we consider the tenacity with which they maintain the independence of the individual Church, and the right of private judgment in the individual member.

The process by which new churches are constituted is very simple. The necessity for, and the practicability of, organizing one, must be decided by those who are to constitute it, and who are to bear the expense and the responsibility of its support. These may be persons belonging to some other Church or churches, who find themselves living where there is none, but where one is believed to be needed, and where the increase of population shows a need for increased religious privileges. Or such persons may be converts from some recent revival in a neighborhood where there seems both room and a demand for another Church. After mature deliberation on the part of such persons, meeting together for consultation, canvassing all sides of the question, taking counsel of wise and discreet brethren, with much prayer for divine direction—since such a movement is one of grave concern—general agreement being secured, a meeting is finally called for the organization. A committee most likely has been previously appointed to secure some approved form of Church Covenant, and Articles of Faith,* to be considered and adopted by the body.

Before the organization actually takes place, however, such persons as propose to constitute the body, should procure letters from the churches of which they are members, given *for the purpose of forming a new Church*. Should there be among them persons who have been members of regular Baptist churches, but have for any reason lost their mem-

---

* Such a form of Covenant, prepared for this work, widely adopted, and many years in use, may be found in this volume, as also well-known and extensively used Articles of Faith. See Appendix.

bership without special fault of their own, who are living consistent Christian lives, and are acceptable to the others, they can, by consent of the company, be admitted as constituent members. So can others who have been baptized on profession of their faith in Christ, for the purpose of so uniting in the formation.

The "Constituting act" would properly and appropriately be the unanimously voting—perhaps by rising—a resolution like this :

"*Resolved*, That, guided as we believe by the Holy Spirit, and relying on the blessing of God, we do, here and now, by this act, constitute ourselves a Church of Jesus Christ to perform His service, and to be governed by His will, as revealed in the New Testament. And to this end we do hereby adopt and agree to the following Covenant and Articles of Faith." Here let the Covenant be read, to which agreement may be witnessed by each one raising the right hand. Prayer for strength, guidance, and blessing should follow. Such an act makes such a company of disciples, *ipso facto*, a Church of Christ with all the rights, powers, and privileges of any New Testament Church. Officers can afterward be chosen, as seems to them best, a pastor, deacons, trustees ; only that some one should at once be selected, temporarily or permanently — unless previously chosen—to act as clerk, to preserve a minute of these and of all subsequent proceedings, as well as the antecedent proceedings which have led to this organization.

Some churches, at their organization, adopt a very elaborate and complicated " constitution and by-laws " for their guidance, a course of very doubtful expediency. They are never necessary, and often more trouble than help. The well - understood teachings of the Scriptures are a sufficiently plain guide in all matters of morals and discipline, and such special cases as may arise can be dealt with on their merits at the time, or provided for by standing resolutions to be placed upon the records, as subsequent guides in all similar cases. For instance, if the body wishes to make any deliverance or establish any rule, as may be the case, on the subjects of Temperance, Missions, Sunday-schools, Sabbath-keeping, or Covetousness, they can embody their views in standing resolutions, place them on their minutes, and hold them as standards for subsequent action in similar cases.*

NOTE 1.—The multiplication of feeble churches should be guarded against; and the organization of new interests without the prospect of becoming independent and efficient, should not be encouraged, especially in a community already well supplied with religious privileges.

NOTE 2.—More particularly should the formation of new churches as the outgrowth and fruit of strife and dissension in older ones, be avoided and discountenanced, except in extreme cases. A large and careful observation proves that very few churches so constituted ever attain to any considerable degree of prosperity or usefulness.

NOTE 3.—The existence of officers is not essential to the

* See " Optional Resolutions " in Appendix.

existence of churches, possessing all ecclesiastical possibilities and powers. Officers are developed out of the membership by election and investiture by the Church. And in the absence of formally invested officers, the Church can select some of its members to officiate, temporarily, in all departments of its service; either to conduct its Worship, dispense the Word, or administer the Ordinances.

XI. CHURCHES RECOGNIZED

It is customary for a new Church to call a Council to *recognize* it. Occasionally this precautionary act takes place at the time of the constitution of the body. More frequently at a subsequent period. The object of the Council is to examine their doctrines, inquire into the circumstances, and the reasons for their organization, so as to be able to express approval of their course, and certify to the churches they represent, their fellowship for the new body as a regularly constituted Church of the same faith. The calling of a Council for this purpose is entirely optional with the Church. It is a prudential measure, very proper and well to be continued as a guard against irregularities in doctrine or practice, and is likely to secure the sympathy and approbation of sister churches; but it is in no sense essential. The body is no more a Church for having the approval of a Council, and no less one for being without it.

The object of the Council, after being organized, is to inquire into the facts of the case for which they were convened. They hear a statement made by some person selected to speak for the Church ; examine their Articles of Faith and Covenant, the letters by which those from other churches have united in the organization ; carefully consider whether there be apparent need of a Church in that particular field ; and when the whole subject is fully before them, vote approval of the steps taken, if they do approve, or advise to the contrary if they disapprove. It is customary to hold some public religious service appropriate to the occasion, calculated to give them encouragement in their enterprise, and assure them of the fellowship and sympathy of sister churches. Such services may take any form preferred by the body or advised by the Council ; usually there is a *discourse* preached, a *charge* given to the Church, and the *hand of fellowship* extended, with remarks, through some one chosen by the Council, to some one selected by the Church to receive this expression of fraternal goodwill.

NOTE 1.—If a Council should decline to recognize a newly constituted Church, deeming the organization unwise and uncalled for, still that Church would have the right to maintain its organization and to continue its work and its worship. The Council could not unmake it, and it would as really be a Church without, as with their sanction. It would seldom, however, be wise to proceed against the wisdom and advice of pastors and members of other churches assembled in a Council. Such adverse decision would lessen their influence in the community, and abate the sympathy and confidence of sister churches.

NOTE 2. — It not unfrequently happens that a Council

doubts the propriety of recognizing a new Church, and yet hesitates to refuse, lest a refusal might be a mistake, place difficulties in the way of a struggling interest, and hinder a good cause. In such cases the wise course is for the Council to adjourn for a specified time—three or six months—and wait developments. At the end of that time the case may be clearer, and admit of definite settlement.

NOTE 3.—To prevent mistakes in organizing churches, some hold that the Council should be called before constitution, to advise as to whether it is best to constitute, rather than afterward to recognize. This course would doubtless avoid some mistakes, though it is open to some objections, and is not usually followed—possibly because of the independency of those concerned in the formation of new churches.

XII. CHURCHES DISBANDED

It sometimes happens, under stress of circumstances, that it becomes needful, or at least seems wise, to abandon Church organizations and to transfer the efforts made for their support to new fields, or to a union with other churches. It is always a matter of serious concern thus to remove the candlestick out of its place, and should be determined on only after long consideration, much prayer, and consultation with wise and unbiased brethren. But duty may require that it shall be done. Cases have occurred, where complicated and inveterate troubles in the body have been so long continued as to discourage all hope of further comfort, edification or usefulness, promising only further contention and scandal to the Christian name. The only resort may be to disband, and the members go into other

churches, or, such as believe they can free themselves from the old troubles, and work harmoniously
together, unite in forming a new Church, leaving
out the old roots of bitterness and seeds of contention.

Of the wisdom and propriety of such a step the
body itself must be the judge, with all the light
it can obtain; and since this step will most likely
be opposed by some, the question must be finally
decided by a majority of the members, as in other
cases. There are some things, however, that ma-
jorities even cannot rightfully do, and they must proceed cautiously.

1. Each member has an indefeasible right to all the
immunities of Church membership, whether moral,
spiritual, social or otherwise; which rights cannot
be abrogated or alienated, and must be regarded as
sacred. If the Church be disbanded, therefore, letters must be given to all the members, which will
secure them admission to other churches, without
loss of position or privilege.

2. There are rights of property also to be considered, if the Church holds property, purchased or
given for religious uses. The deed by which such
property is held, or the charter by which the Church
has become a body corporate for the purpose of
holding and controlling temporalities, would have to
be well understood, so that such property might not
be lost, or diverted to other uses than those for
which it was given or purchased. The laws of the
state, and the decisions of courts would have to be

consulted, so that such property should still be used according to its original design.

3. If a Church be disbanded, and absolutely dissolved, and a new one constituted on the same ground, and of the same materials, the new one cannot hold the property, retain the officers, perpetuate the history, or claim the immunities of the old one, but must begin anew, unless, indeed, it may so far be allowed by legal process to hold the property, appropriating it to its legitimate use.

The process by which the organization is disbanded, or dissolved, is very simple. After all preliminary preparations are attended to—for no Church acts can be performed after the final act of dissolution has been passed—letters having been voted to its members, and the clerk authorized to give such letters to any person who may subsequently appear, and have right to them; then a simple vote, " that we do here and now, by this act, disband as a Church, and cease to exist as a corporate and covenant organization," will accomplish the purpose. What disposition shall be made of the records, of any furniture, or other effects belonging to them, would previously have been determined.

CHAPTER 3

CHURCH MEMBERSHIP

THE character of a building depends very much on the materials of which it is constructed. Christian disciples " are builded together for a habitation of God, through the Spirit." Any society or association is largely what its constructive elements are. Combination and intercourse may, to a certain extent, modify individual peculiarities, but the corporate character will be the result of the various personalities which compose the body. The estimation in which will be held its internal life and order, the efficiency with which it will work toward its purposed end, will all be determined by the character of its individual elements.

It is sometimes said that a Church is a *voluntary society*. This is true in a sense, and only with an explanation. It is true in that no external force or authority can compel the relation of membership to be formed, or dissolved. The Church can compel no one to unite with it, nor can the individual oblige the body to receive him. But it is not true that it is a matter merely optional and indifferent whether or not a believer identifies himself with the Household of Faith. He is under moral obligation to do that. It is for his own spiritual good to do it; it is one of the appointed means of grace; the Church needs his presence and influence, and the cause of Truth is furthered by a combination of Christian influence and effort. All are under law to Christ, and are bound by sacred obligations to obey and please Him. He has ordained that His followers should associate themselves together in these brotherhoods of faith and affection. A Church, therefore, is more than a voluntary society: it is a society under law to Christ.

Church membership, therefore, becomes a question of grave moment, and should be carefully studied and well understood.

Let it be observed:

NOTE 1.—The character of the persons who are to constitute the churches and hold membership therein, is fixed and prescribed by Christ Himself, and is to remain permanent and unchanged.

NOTE 2.—Consequently, the Church, by whose act persons are to be formally admitted to membership, has no right or authority to alter the terms or conditions of membership, but must conform strictly to those prescribed by the Lawgiver; much less can the wish or the will of the pastor be allowed to change these conditions, since he has no authority in the case; still less can the desire or judgment of the candidate himself modify the divinely prescribed conditions.

NOTE 3.—The benefits to be derived by Church association and fellowship, whether to the individual or to the body, can be certainly anticipated only by exact conformity to the prescribed qualifications of admission, and subsequent conformity to the principles of the Church's internal polity.

NOTE 4.—Decline, perversion and decay of spiritual life and evangelical doctrine, are more likely to result from the admission of unsanctified and unsuitable materials into its membership than from almost any other deviation from the divinely constituted order of building the spiritual temple.

NOTE 5.—The moral purity and spiritual vitality of the membership is the best conservation and the surest guaranty of the doctrinal soundness and spiritual vitality of the ministry itself. Where vital godliness rules in the body, the same will be demanded and supported in a teacher and leader, and there an unevangelical ministry will not long be tolerated. But a carnal membership will endure, and even demand a carnal ministry. " Like people, like priest."

I.   CONDITIONS OF MEMBERSHIP

The very great importance of the subject hereby becomes apparent, and the question of who may and who may not be admitted to membership is one of primary moment. What are the scriptural qualifications for citizenship in this spiritual kingdom, for brotherhood in the family of the faithful, for membership in the society of Jesus ? What are the conditions on which this privilege depends ?

These conditions are *four:*

1. A regenerate heart. 2. A confession of faith. 3. The reception of baptism. 4. A Christian life.

1. *A regenerate heart*

None but converted and godly persons have any right in the Church of Christ as members. To admit the ungodly and the profane to the fellowship of the holy, to share the privileges of the faithful, and partake of the sacred Communion of the Body and the Blood of Christ, would be a scandal and a shame, not to be perpetrated or endured by those who profess to be His disciples. Nor is it enough that one's moral character be without reproach, and his life orderly. He must give good evidence that he is " a new creature in Christ Jesus," that he " has passed from death unto life," and that " Christ is formed in him," or he has no place in His body, which is the Church. If our churches are to fulfill their mission, remain true to their traditions, and honor their apostolical pretensions, they must insist, with unabated vigor, on *a regenerated membership*. Nor must they insist on it in theory only, but take every precaution to maintain it in practice.

This position, however, is one with which many Christians, deemed evangelical, not a few Christian teachers, and some entire denominations do not agree; such persons claiming that nothing more than good moral character and a serious disposition to attend to religious instruction should be demanded in candidates for Church membership. Their theory is, that *within* the Church regeneration and salvation are to be found, rather than before entering it. By this practice the holy and the profane are brought into unseemly fellowship in the body of Christ, the broad distinction between the Church and the world is diminished or obliterated, the salt loses its savor, and the city set on a hill to that extent is hid, and ceases to be á monument of grace to men. This becomes more emphatically true, since churches which hold this theory hold also to infant baptism and Church membership without pretension of saving faith or spiritual birth. Such associations lose the foremost characteristic of Christian churches, and become religious societies, where carnal and spiritual mingle in inharmonious fellowship, only a part of which can pretend to be members of the body of Christ.

The teachings of the New Testament are clear and emphatic on this point. Both Jesus and His Apostles made it manifest that His kingdom was not of this world, and those who constituted it were such as are born of the Spirit. In the constitution of the first churches, both Jewish and Gentile, the persons who composed them were not indiscriminately gathered, but those *called out* from the masses of the people on a confession of faith in Christ, and a change which betokened a regenerate nature. This was the case at the Pentecost, and subsequently it was " the saved " who were added to the churches. So was it at Samaria, at Antioch, at Ephesus, at Corinth, at Philippi—everywhere.

The Church at Rome was addressed as " Beloved of God, called to be saints." — Rom. 1 : 7. And these same disciples Paul reminds of their former condition, " When ye were servants of sin," and contrasts it with their present condition: " But now, being made free from sin, and become servants to God, ye have your fruit unto holiness, and the end everlasting life."—Rom. 6 : 20, 22. The salutation to the Corinthians is, " Unto the Church of God, which is at Corinth, to them that are sanctified in

Christ Jesus, called to be saints."— 1 Cor. 1 : 2.
His second epistle he inscribes: " Unto the Church
of God, which is at Corinth, with all the saints which
are in Achaia."—2 Cor. 1 : 1. The Ephesians he
addresses as: " The saints which are at Ephesus,
and the faithful in Christ Jesus." He says they
" were sealed with the Holy Spirit of promise."
Also, they " were dead in trespasses and sins," but
God had " quickened them together with Christ."—
Eph. 1 : 1; 2 : 1, 6.

The broad distinction between what they once
were and what they had become, indicative of the
great change, is carried through all the epistles.
To the Philippians, it is, " To all the saints in
Christ Jesus, which are at Philippi."—Phil. 1 : 1.
Elsewhere it is the same : " To the saints and
faithful brethren which are at Colosse."—Col. 1 : 2; 3:3.
He says: " Ye are dead, and your life is hid with
Christ in God." Peter, addressing the saints, says:
" Ye also, as living stones, are built up a spiritual
house, to be a holy priesthood, to offer spiritual sacrifices, acceptable to God, through Jesus Christ."
And further, he declares: " But ye are a chosen
generation, a royal priesthood, a peculiar people;
that ye should show forth the praises of Him who
called you out of darkness into His marvellous
light."— 1 Peter 2 : 5, 9. The unvarying tone of
New Testament utterance is the same. Those gathered in fraternal fellowship to constitute the churches
of our Lord, are such as have been called out of
darkness into light, and from the powei of Satan

unto God. Once were they darkness, now are they light in the Lord.

Were it not for a too ready disposition in many quarters to admit to the churches almost any one who might desire to enter, or could be induced to come—not only gold, silver and precious stones, but wood, hay and stubble as well—it would appear puerile to insist on a spiritual nature, a regenerate heart, as the first requisite for membership in the Church of Christ.

2. *A professed faith*

Before the Church can consistently welcome one to its fellowship, the members must obtain the evidence that he, too, is of like precious faith with themselves; that he has also passed from death unto life, and become a new creature in Christ. The bond of fellowship among the saints is the love of Christ shed abroad in all hearts alike, binding all in a common experience, a common hope and a common sympathy to the Cross, the one common centre of their new life. In order to make this fellowship real and personal to each, the new-comer who seeks admission to their company must give them the evidence that he, too, has been born of the Spirit, and become an heir of God. How is he to give and they to obtain this evidence? By a confession to that effect, and by such change in character and conduct on his part as he is able to show. Without this, no evidence of fitness for membership with the disciples becomes apparent, and no fraternal fellowship is begotten.

This confession of faith is made verbally, by a declaration of the great change which has transpired. He who remains silent, and can bear no testimony to the loving kindness of the Lord, gives small reason to believe that he is a child of God. The declaration of those who experience this spiritual transformation in all ages, climes and conditions, is substantially the same: "Come and hear, all ye that fear God, and I will declare what He hath done for my soul."—Ps. 66: 16. And thus is realized the declaration: "With the heart man believeth unto righteousness, and with the mouth confession is made unto salvation."— Rom. 10 : 10. Without a confession of saving faith in Christ, and a profession of pardon and peace through the blood of the Covenant, there can be no spiritual fellowship, and membership in the Church would be little more than a pretense. Those who accept Christ as their Lord and Saviour are expected to declare their new obligation. By this confession largely the Church gains the evidence that they have passed from death unto life. The old Baptist way, from times immemorial, is, to have persons wishing to unite with the Church, to come personally before it and "relate their experience," tell what the Lord had done for them and in them. However much such matters may be referred to pastor or deacons or committees, as preliminary, candidates must come personally before the Church and speak for themselves. And this custom should be heroically maintained. They need not plead timidity, and say they cannot speak in the presence of others. They deceive themselves. If they have experienced anything, they can say something about it. If their hearts have been changed, they can speak of it. If they know the love of God, they can say so.

3. *A Reception of Baptism*

Especially is a confession of faith to be made in baptism. A regenerate heart constitutes the spiritual qualification for Church membership. A professed faith and a consistent Christian life constitute the moral qualifications. And baptism constitutes the ritual or ceremonial qualification for that sacred fellowship. Except by baptism no person can be received as a member of the Church, without violating the prescribed conditions, and vitiating the divine method. One may become a member of "the kingdom of heaven" by being "born from above," but he cannot become a member of the visible Church except he confess that spiritual change in the waters of baptism. In that symbolic act he declares himself dead to the world and sin, buried, and raised up to newness of life through the death and resurrection of Jesus Christ from the dead. The spiritual change of the new birth begets *Christian* fellowship; but to secure *Church* fellowship, that change must be confessed in baptism. This is the New Testament order. At the first it was so; they repented, they believed, they were baptized, then added to the Church. Without confession in baptism there could be no Christian churches.

4. *A Christian deportment*

This condition must appear manifest. The first act of Christian obedience after conversion, is, naturally, baptism. In most cases, in primitive times, it followed immediately after an exercise of saving faith. " They believed and were baptized." There was, consequently, little or no opportunity to test the sincerity of their profession, or prove the genuineness of their conversion by a well-ordered life and godly conversation. With us it is usually somewhat different; for while no specified time is required for probation, or proof of sincerity, some time usually does, and prudently should, elapse after a profession of faith, before Church membership is consummated. Union with the Church usually follows baptism immediately, but baptism does not usually follow conversion immediately, as it might lawfully do.

But whatever time and opportunity there may be for observing the spirit and conduct of professed converts, that spirit and conduct should be found in harmony with the professed change of heart. If they still choose their old companions, find pleasure in their old pursuits of worldliness, are captivated with the vanities and frivolities of life, to say no more, who could believe that any vital and radical change by grace had passed upon the soul? If the old things have not passed away, and all things become new how can a Christian character be detected in them ? And if that be not apparent, how can they be fit members for the Church of God ?

An external Christian life must corroborate the profession of an internal Christian faith. This apostolic injunction must, to a good degree, be made manifest to all in every professed disciple. " If ye then be risen with Christ, seek those things which are above, where Christ sitteth on the right hand of God; set your affections on things above, and not on things on the earth. For ye are dead, and your life is hid with Christ in God."—Col. 3 : 1, 2. No amount of attestation can make the world believe that he is a Christian whose conduct does not correspond to his profession. And if there cannot be a good degree of conformity between the professed and the practical, persons had better remain out of the Church than to enter it. Positively so, if there be a manifest disparity and contradiction between the two.

NOTE 1.—Not every person can give an equally satisfactory relation of Christian experience before the Church, nor are those always the most certainly regenerate who can tell the most remarkable experience. But no person can consistently be admitted to its fellowship unless the Church in some way obtains satisfactory evidence of his conversion, and hears him personally declare his faith.

NOTE 2.—Persons on entering a Church may be ignorant of many things in Christian doctrine, and must be ignorant of many things in practical Christian life, which they will afterward learn. Nor should they be rejected simply on that account. Indeed, they enter the Church as a school of sacred learning, to be instructed. But no one should be admitted who holds and maintains matters, either of faith or morals, *contrary* to the Scriptures, as understood by the Church. Especially so, if such differences are likely to be proclaimed and advocated. For, even admitting that the candidate may be right and the Church wrong in the matters wherein they differ, such oppositions would produce discords and dissensions, interrupting the harmony of the body, and thus becoming obstructive, both to its peace and to its usefulness.

NOTE 3.—In all matters fundamental, both as to faith and practice, members of the same Church should hold and act alike, since harmony in the body is of the greatest importance. But it would be unreasonable to demand or expect that considerable numbers of persons, differing in education habits of thought, constitution of mind and independent opinions, could attain perfect uniformity of belief in all matters of Christian truth. This would be impracticable, and in minor matters large Christian liberty should be allowed.

NOTE 4.—The relation of Christian experience before the Church, while the practice should be maintained, cannot usually give full and satisfactory evidence of conversion. The excitement of the occasion and the timidity of the candidate may do injustice to the most devout and pious persons. The pastor, deacons and others should, by personal intercourse and private conversation, obtain the facts in the case, and lay them before the body as evidence.

NOTE 5.—In the relation of experience it is not so much the words spoken as the manner by which, and the spirit in which, they are spoken, that convince and satisfy those who hear. And it is more difficult to judge, and requires more caution in the case of strangers, with whose history, manner of life and habits of thought they are unfamiliar, than of those well known.

NOTE 6.—Those pastors make a grave mistake, and are grievously in fault, who hurry persons into the Church without giving the body a fair and full opportunity of gaining evidence of their regenerate state. They may ask a few leading questions themselves, which any one, saint or sinner, could answer, and virtually debar others the privilege of asking others, call a vote on their reception, to which a few will respond and many remain silent. No fellowship is accorded by the body, since no evidence is obtained. The Church may seem to be prosperous, because baptisms frequently occur; but the moral strength of the body is weakened, rather, and disorder introduced where order should prevail.

NOTE 7.—Neither age, sex, race, past character, nor condition in life should serve to keep one out of the Church, if the evidence be abundant and satisfactory that such an one be a subject of renewing and saving grace; and that the character and conduct since professed conversion be in accordance with the gospel of Christ.

II.   MODES OF ADMISSION

It is not proposed to admit persons to membership by an imposing ceremonial, the better to impress on them and others the importance of the act, as is done in some societies, and even in some churches. For, though the act be an important one, the simplicity of Christ does not call for parade to make it seem impressive. The form is simple, though the act be serious. While no gorgeous pageant marks initiation to the fellowship of the Christian mysteries, it may well be questioned if we do not hold too lightly and make too little of admission to membership in this sacred brotherhood.

There are *three* ways in common use, by either of which persons may be admitted to the Church, according to their religious standing and their relation to a profession of faith. But the difference in either case has reference to the form or mode, the substantial act in all these cases being the same, viz.: a *vote of the body* to receive the candidate. Each new member must be admitted by the free and voluntary consent and approval of those already members, which consent is usually expressed by a formal vote. By this method alone, and not by the personal action of the minister, nor yet by the decision of a board of official members, nor yet by some executive committee specially appointed for this purpose, are new members to be received, if the sympathy and confidence of the body are to be secured to each one added. An examination before the pastor and deacons, or before some official consistory or committee, might be preferred by many candidates, and even to others might seem more desirable, because more private. All this may be had, but if had, it is preliminary and precautionary. The final and efficient act is the vote of the Church in its corporate capacity, after having listened to the candidate's personal statement, and being satisfied as to his fitness.

The following are the *three modes* of admission :

1. *By Baptism* —A person may be admitted to the Church, on a profession of faith in Christ, by baptism. This is the more common method. Such an one makes known his Christian hope and desire for baptism and union with the Church, to the pastor or brethren. If they, after proper investigation of the case, become satisfied of his fitness for that

step, he is encouraged to come before the Church at such time as they are accustomed to receive candidates, relate his Christian experience and his desire to be received to their fellowship. After he has made this relation and retired, the Church considers the question of his reception, hears the testimony of those who have become familiar with the case, and then, if satisfied, it is moved and voted that he be received as a member, *on being baptized.*

2. *By Letter* —In the changes of social and domestic life, which are constantly transpiring, members often remove from the vicinity of the Church with which they have united. Then it becomes their duty, and should be their desire, to connect themselves with a Church of the same faith near their new home, where they can conveniently work and worship. By the comity of Christian fellowship, and by that courtesy which each Church owes to each other, the one of which he is a member gives him a *letter* of commendation and dismission, by which his membership may be transferred to the other. This letter certifies to his good Christian character and regular standing, and commends him to the confidence of, and membership in, the other Church. If satisfied, he is received by a vote of the Church, as in the former case—the letter serving as a certificate of character and standing, with permission to unite. Though not considered essential, yet it is desirable that the person should be present when his letter is read, and verbally express his desire to be received.

3. *By Experience* —It sometimes happens that persons who have been baptized, but by some means have lost their membership, desire to unite with a Church. They bring no letters, nor are they re-baptized; but give an account of their conversion and Christian life, which, being satisfactory, they are received by vote on their confession—or, as it is usually stated, " on experience."

NOTE 1.—In some churches the names of all candidates are announced at a meeting previous to that on which action is to be taken, in order that all may be acquainted with the fact, and make objection, if they know of any good reason for objection.

NOTE 2.—In some churches, also, there is a standing committee, before which all applicants for membership must first go, and if that committee regard the application unfavorably, it is not presented to the Church at all. Such action may at first appear somewhat arbitrary, perhaps, but in cities and other crowded communities great care is needed to guard against imposition by designing and unworthy persons, who may be influenced by sinister motives in such a step. Of course, a final appeal is to the Church, and not to a committee.

NOTE 3.—In some churches, particularly in large communities where individuals may not be so well known, the pastor requests some careful and competent member to act as committee to ascertain the facts in the case of each one applying for membership. Or there may be a standing committee, to which all such cases are referred. Or if there be a prudential committee, through which all applications must come, they act in the matter. In either case a report is made to the church, when action is taken. But, in addition, a careful pastor will personally investigate every case.

NOTE 4.—Persons cannot be received to membership on

the credit of letters from other denominations. Such letters are accepted as testimonials of previous Church standing and Christian character; but the applicants are to be received by *baptism*—if not already baptized—or otherwise on their Christian *experience*, related in person before the Church.

NOTE 5.—It is a rule generally acted on, that no person shall be taken into the Church to the grief of any one already a member. Hence, members should be received not simply by a majority, but by a unanimous vote. If objection be made, the case should be postponed, to ascertain the facts. If the objections be found to be factious and unreasonable, they should not be further regarded; and if persisted in, would subject the objectors to reproof and censure.

NOTE 6.—At times it may be found expedient to postpone the reception of a candidate for a better acquaintance, and for greater harmony in action respecting him. Moreover, it is always better to use great deliberation than to proceed with great haste in such a matter. But the Scriptures certainly do not authorize any system of *probation* by which all candidates are required to wait a specified time before being admitted to the full fellowship of the body.

NOTE 7.—To baptize persons who do not unite with any Church, is considered bad policy, as subversive of good order and destructive of Church organization. They should be approved and received by the body for full fellowship *when baptized*. Yet there are possible exceptions to this rule where no Church exists, or where they are baptized to constitute one, and in some other unusual circumstances.

NOTE 8.—Nor is it expedient, or promotive of good order, for ministers to baptize persons who wish to unite with churches of other denominations. Such persons should receive the ordinance from the pastors of the churches with which they are to unite. Nor is it consistent Christian walking for such persons to unite with churches which uphold and practice a form of so-called baptism which they themselves reject and condemn.

NOTE 9.— Persons who fulfil! all the Scriptural conditions and possess all the requisite qualifications for membership, *have a right* to be admitted to baptism and the privileges of the Church, if they request it; though no extraneous force or authority can compel their admission.

NOTE 10.—Uniting with a Church must be a free and voluntary act on the part of the individual; there is neither civil nor ecclesiastical authority among us to compel or require it. But there is a moral obligation resting on every professed lover of the Saviour to identify himself in fraternal union with the company of His disciples.

NOTE 11.—No civil or religious disability can, with us, be inflicted on those who are not communicants, as is the case in countries where there is a state Church, and where religion is supported as a civil establishment. The gospel idea of religious faith and service is, that all should be voluntary and free, and that civil authority has no right of control over, or interference with, matters of religion.

NOTE 12.—It is customary, when members are admitted to the Church, whether by baptism, letter or experience, for the pastor to give them *the right hand of fellowship*. This is usually done at the communion service immediately before the elements are distributed. The candidate rises, while the hand is extended with a few words of kindly welcome. The act is fraternal, but not essential; is designed simply as an expression of the Church's welcome. It does not make them members, and adds nothing to their standing, but recognizes them in the presence of the body as fellow-disciples. In some churches—particularly at the South—in addition to the pastor's hand of fellowship, the various members pass by in order, each extending the hand of welcome; a practice which, though somewhat less conventional, is more expressive.

NOTE 13.—The reception of persons by *restoration* is not essentially different from that by experience, Members who have been excluded from fellowship may be received back, when the causes which led to the withdrawal of fellowship are removed, and the individual requests restoration—the Church, being satisfied with his fitness, votes his reception. The "hand of fellowship" properly follows in this case, as in the others. Such cases are reported as additions by "restoration."

NOTE 14.—Persons received to membership have equal rights and immunities with any and all other members, without distinction of sex, age or condition, unless for cause under discipline and censure. Persons not members enjoy the privilege of worship with the Church, but can claim no corporate rights, including the ordinances.

III. MODES OF DISMISSION

Church membership is held to be of *perpetual obligation*. What has been elsewhere said as to its voluntary character will apply to the dissolving as well as to the forming of this relation. No human authority can hold one in the Church, who resolves to go out of it. The Church is more than a mere confederation of men and women; it is "the body of Christ," where each one, "is a member in particular." Each one who unites with it does so, presumably, not as a mere matter of convenience, or personal caprice, but from a sense of religious obligation. Voluntarily and of choice indeed, yet still doing it, "as unto the Lord." When he becomes a member therefore, it is for life, unless some providential interposition should break the bonds. Baptists hold that Christians should not live outside the fold of the Good Shepherd, but within the shelter of its fellowship; unless, indeed, they become unworthy the position, and have to be "put away."

Provision is, however, made for a transference of membership from one Church to another.

There are *three ways*, by either of which the relation of members to the body may be dissolved:

1. *By Letter* —A member may, on application, receive a *letter* of commendation and dismission from his Church, with which to unite with another of the same faith, and thus, not pass out of Church relations, but be transferred from one fellowship to another.

2. *By Exclusion* —When the Church, in the exercise of its lawful authority and discipline, withdraws fellowship from one proven to be an unworthy member, his connection with the body is dissolved and thenceforth ceases.

3. *By Death* —The death of members of course dissolves the relation, and transfers them from the Church on earth, to that above.

No other modes of dismission, or disconnection are recognized among our churches.

NOTE 1.—It is customary for the validity of letters to be *limited* to some specified time—usually *six months*—after the expiration of which time they are worthless; but may be renewed, if satisfactory reason be given the Church for their non-use.

NOTE 2.—The one receiving a letter is still a member and subject to the authority and discipline of the Church granting it, until he has used it by actually connecting himself with another Church.

NOTE 3.—Letters thus given can be *revoked*, for cause, by the Church at its discretion, any time previous to their being used.

NOTE 4.—Any member in good standing has the *right* at any time to ask for, and receive from the Church a *certificate* of his membership and standing; but subjects himself to discipline if he use it for any improper purpose.

NOTE 5.—Letters cannot properly be given to be used in uniting with a Church of another denomination. It would be manifestly inconsistent for a Church to commend and dismiss its members to unite with those with whom it did not hold Church fellowship.

NOTE 6.—When a member unites with a Church of another denomination, the hand of fellowship is withdrawn from him, though otherwise of good Christian character, and though he may have acted conscientiously in what he had done. This act implies no censure; but since his Church is not in fellowship with that to which he has gone, they cannot consistently continue fellowship with him in that Church.

NOTE 7.—No member can *withdraw* from the Church. He must be regularly dismissed by the action of the body. Nor can one have his name *dropped*, or be *excluded* at his own request. Such action, if taken at all, must be taken by due process of discipline on the part of the Church.

NOTE 8.—Nor can the Church *compel* a member to take a letter and withdraw, without his consent. This would be a virtual *exclusion* from its fellowship; in order to which, due course of discipline must be pursued, on charges made, and for sufficient reasons.

NOTE 9.—When members remove their residence so far as to render worship with their Church impracticable, they should take letters, and unite where they go. Their churches should require this of them, if at all practicable. The too common practice of holding membership in one Church, and worshiping in another deserves severe reproof.

Note 10.—In voting on the reception, dismissal, discipline or exclusion of members, several cases should not be included in the same vote, but each one be acted on separately, and decided on its own merits.

NOTE 11.—The *dropping* of members is merely placing on a separate list the names of those of whom the Church has lost all knowledge. They are neither dismissed, nor reported as members; and whenever found, their names are restored to the record. No one can be dropped as an act of *discipline*, nor when his residence is known, nor simply to get rid of a disturbing element.

NOTE 12.—Persons *excluded* from one Church should not be received to the fellowship of another, except after careful investigation, and when most manifest injustice has been done such members; and also when the excluding Church refuses to correct the wrong done. Yet cases may, and do occur, where it is the duty of one Church to bear this testimony against the wrong done by another, and receive the unjustly excluded member to its fellowship.

NOTE 13.—Sometimes a letter of simple commendation, or *occasional communion*, is given to a member who is to be temporarily absent from home, for the purpose of affording him Christian introduction where he may visit, or worship during his absence. This may be given by the pastor, or clerk, or by the action of the Church, and should be limited to the time of his probable absence.

NOTE 14.—The conception of a perfect Christian brotherhood is not to be realized on earth. Many defects and faults may be expected, both in the individual, and in the body. The member may think the Church little better than the world; and the Church may regard the member as a burden rather than a blessing, and wish to be rid of him. But those who are truly Christ's, " have crucified the flesh with its affections and lusts," and must " bear one another's burdens," and take no unlawful or unkindly means to break the bonds of their fellowship, and sever their connection.

CHAPTER 4

CHURCH OFFICERS

EVERY form of organized society, whether civil, social or religious, is supposed to have officers, duly constituted to execute the laws, administer the government, and secure the ends contemplated by the organization. The Church is a commonwealth, a society, a family, and has its officers as leaders and administrators of its affairs. Officers, however, are not essential to the existence of a State, nor are they to the existence of a Church. They are nevertheless important to their highest efficiency, and the best exercise of their legitimate functions. The State does not lapse and cease to be, because its executive dies, resigns, or is removed. Nor does the Church cease to be a Church though it may be without officers. It was a Church before it had officers, and supplied these administrative functionaries from among its own members. And should they all resign, or be removed, the Church would still survive, and supply the deficiency by the election of others to fill their places.

What are the officers of a Christian Church? How are they secured? What are their functions? And whence is their authority? These are questions of importance to be asked and answered; and to which various replies will be given, according to the ecclesiastical theory on which the reply proceeds.

But suppose we make the questions somewhat more specific, and ask, " What are the Scriptural officers of a Christian Church ? " We shall by this means simplify the inquiry, and be directed not to ecclesiastical standards, but to the New Testament for an answer—a source of authority which to all Christians ought to be more satisfactory than any other, in such matters; and to Baptists, certainly will be, if they be true to their convictions as Bible Christians.

They are of two grades

In the New Testament we find but *two orders* pertaining to the ministry; but *two* officers to a Church. These are *pastors* and *deacons*. And, yet, this is a question still to some extent in dispute. All prelatical churches insist there are, and of right should be, *three orders*, and the Romish Church has carried the number up to ten or twelve.

But if the Scriptures be appealed to, and primitive churches be accepted as examples, it would seem to be a question settled, that in apostolic times, and for many years after, pastors and deacons only were known as permanent Church officers. The introduction of other orders subsequently, was a part of that system of change and perversion, which eventually reared a gigantic and corrupt hierarchy on the ruins of the simplicity of the Gospel, and substituted an oppressive and tyrannical worldly establishment for the Church of Christ. All of which changes and corruptions come largely through the unwarranted assumptions of the clergy themselves.

I. PASTORS

In the New Testament the term *episcopos*, which is usually rendered *bishop*, and *presbuteros*, which is rendered *elder*, are used interchangeably, and often applied to the same person. The *episcopos* was an *overseer*, what the term properly denotes; it was the word used chiefly by the Greek Christians as applied to the *pastor*, who had the oversight of the flock, and performed the work of a shepherd in spiritual concerns. The term *presbuteros* or *elder*, was evidently derived from the synagogue, and used chiefly by Jewish Christians, to designate the same person, especially as in the synagogue elderly and dignified persons were selected as the official directors of religious affairs.

The term *pastor* signifies a shepherd, and well indicates the nature of the relation he sustains to the Church; that of leading, feeding, guiding and guarding the flock committed to his care. He is also called a *minister* (*diakonos*), one who serves and ministers to others; as the pastor is supposed to minister in holy things to the Church. Thus the prelatical distinction of Bishops, Priests and Deacons, constituting three orders in the clergy, corresponding to the three orders, High-priest, Priest and Levite, in the Jewish hierarchy, finds no warrant in the use of the terms, *episcopos*, *presbuteros* and *diakonos*, in apostolic writings. And to this many distinguished prelatists, historians and commentators agree.

NEANDER, the most distinguished of Church historians, gives the following explanation :

"The name of *presbyters*, which was appropriated to this body, was derived from the Jewish Synagogue. But in the Gentile churches, formed by the Apostle Paul, they took the name (*episcopoi*) *bishops*, a term more significant of their office, in the language generally spoken by the members of these churches. The name of *presbyters* denoted the dignity of their office : that of *bishops*, on the other hand, was expressive rather of the nature of their office, to take the oversight of the Church. Most certainly no other distinction originally existed between them." "They were not designed to exercise absolute authority, but to act as presiding officers and guides of an ecclesiastical republic; to conduct all things with the coöperation of the communities; as their ministers, and not as their masters." "I can discover no other difference between the *elders* and *bishops*, in the Apostolic age, than that the first denotes the *dignity*, the second the *duties* of the office, whether the reference is to one or more."—*Ch. Hist. Vol. I.*, *p. 184; Plant. and Train, p. 147; Intro. to Coleman's Prim. Ch., p. 20; Plant. and Train, p. 148.*

MOSHEIM says :

"The rulers of the churches were denominated sometimes *presbyters* or elders—a designation borrowed from the Jews, and indicative rather of the wisdom than the age of the persons; and sometimes also *bishops;* for it is most manifest that both terms are promiscuously used in the New Testament of one and the same class of persons." "In those primitive times each Christian Church was composed of the *people*, the *presiding officers*, and the *assistants* or deacons.

These must be the component parts of every society. The principal voice was that of the *people;* or of the whole body of Christians."—*Eccl. Hist. Cent. I. part 2, ch. II., secs. 5, 8.*

WADDINGTON says:

" It is also true that in the earliest government of the first Christian Society—that of Jerusalem, not the *elders* only, but the whole Church, were associated with the Apostles; and it is even certain that the terms *bishop* and *elder,* or *presbyter,* were in the first instance, and for a short period, sometimes used synonymously, and indiscriminately applied to the same order in the ministry."—*Hist. Ch., chap. II., sec. 2.*

GIESELER says:

" The new churches everywhere formed themselves on the model of the mother Church at Jerusalem. At the head of each were the *elders* (presbyter, bishop), all officially of equal rank, though in several instances a peculiar authority seems to have been conceded to some one individual, from personal considerations."—*Ch. Hist., Period I., div. I., chap. II., sec. 29.*

COLEMAN says:

" It is generally admitted by Episcopal writers on this subject that in the New Testament, and in the earliest ecclesiastical writers the terms *bishop* and *presbyter,* or *elder,* are synonymous, and denote one and the same office." " The office of presbyter was undeniably identical with that of bishop, as has been shown above." " Only two orders of officers are known in the Church until near the close of the second century. Those of the first are styled either *bishops* or *presbyters;* of the second, *deacons.*"—*Ancient Christianity Exemplified, chap. VIII., sec. 6; chap. VI., sec. 5.*

This author still further cites many of the early Christian Fathers, who took the same view of the subject, declaring that only two orders existed in the primitive ministry, and that all pastors were of equal rank among themselves. Of these writers are: Clement of Rome, Polycarp, Justin Martyr, Irenæus, Jerome, Chrysostom, Theodoret and others; authorities extending from A. D. 100 to A. D. 1000, and nearly all of them defenders of prelatical supremacy.

DR. JACOBS, an Anglican churchman, says:

"The only bishops mentioned in the New Testament were simple presbyters; the same persons being called bishop (*episcopos*), superintendent, overseer, from his taking an oversight of his congregation, as is distinctly shown by Acts 22:20 and other passages; and a presbyter (*presbuteros*) or elder, from the reverence due to age. It may, however, be observed that the term *elder* is of Hebrew origin, while that of *bishop* is Hellenic, and is applied in the New Testament only to the officers of Gentile churches, though it did not supersede the use of the word *presbyter* among them."—*Eccl. Polity of N. T., pp. 72-3.*

SCHAFF says:

"Bishops or presbyters. These two terms denote in the New Testament the same office: the first signifying its duties; the second, its dignity."—*Hist. Christ. Ch., First period, sec. 42, 1.*

KURTZ says:

"That originally the *presbuteroi* (elders) were the same as the *episcopoi* (bishops), we gather with absolute certainty from the statements of the New Testament, and of Clement of Rome, a disciple of the Apostles."—*Text-Book of Ch. Hist., Vol. I., p. 67.*

PROF. FISHER says:

" Until we approach the close of Elizabeth's reign there is no trace in the Anglican Church of the *jure divino* idea of episcopacy—the doctrine that bishops are necessary to the being of a Church, and that without episcopal ordination the functions of the ministry cannot be lawfully discharged."— *History Christ. Church, p. 373.*

PROF. PLUMPTRE, a Church of England clergyman, and a prominent biblical scholar, declares the identity of *episcopos* and *presbuteros* in New Testament usage, and adduces four reasons from the Acts and the Epistles for this opinion. To his statement and proofs he adds:

" Assuming, as proved, the identity of *bishops* and *elders* of the New Testament, we have to inquire into : 1. The relations which existed between the two titles. 2. The functions and mode of appointment of the men to whom both titles applied. 3. Their relations to the general government and discipline of the Church."—*Smith's Bible Dict., Art. Bishop.*

THE ENCY. BRITANNICA says:

" The identity of the office of *bishop* and *presbyter* being thus clearly established, it follows that the presbyterate is the highest permanent office in the Church, and that every faithful pastor of a flock is successor to the Apostles in everything in which they were to have any successors."—*Art. Presbyterian.*

THE PANTALOGIA says:

" There is no scriptural difference between *bishop* and *presbyter*." Furthermore, the same competent authority adds: " To this purpose the declaration made of the functions of bishops and priests, signed by more than thirty civilians and divines, among whom were thirteen bishops, Cranmer and others included, affirm that in the New Testament there is no mention of any degrees or distinctions in orders, but only of *deacons*, or ministers, and *priests* or bishops."—*Arts. Bishop and Presbyter.*

In Acts 20 : 17 it is stated that Paul called together the *elders* (presbyters) of the Ephesian Church. But in Acts 20 : 18, he calls these same persons *bishops* (overseers). In this case both terms were applied to the same office, and were used interchangeably to designate the same officer.

DEAN ALFORD says:

" The E. V. has hardly dealt fairly in this case with the sacred text in rendering *episcopous*, v. 28, *overseers*; whereas, it ought there, as in all other places, to have been bishops, that the fact of *elders and bishops having been originally and apostolically synonymous*, might be apparent to the English reader."—*Com. on Acts*, 20 : 17. " The *episcopoi* of the N. T. have nothing in common with our bishops." " The identity of the *episcopos* and *presbuteros* in apostolic times is evident, from Titus 1 : 5–7."—*Com. on 1 Tim. 3 : 1.*

PAUL and TIMOTHY, in their address to the Philippian Christians, specify three classes as composing the Church, and manifestly consider these as constituting the entire body. They say: " To all the *saints* in Christ Jesus, which are at Philippi, with the *bishops* and *deacons*."—Phil. 1 : 1. Saints, bishops and deacons, therefore, comprised the entire membership—the whole Church. Bishops and pastors were identical.

TIMOTHY is instructed by Paul as to the qualifications necessary for those who should be chosen as pastors and placed over the churches. These officers are called *bishops*. Particular directions are given as to the choice of *bishops* and *deacons*, but no mention is here made of elders or presbyters, clearly because they were the same as bishops.— I Tim. 3 : 1–10.

TITUS is in like manner directed by Paul to place pastors over the churches in Crete. These pastors he calls *elders* in the fifth verse and *bishops* in the seventh. Here both terms are applied to the same persons, and must indicate the same office.—Titus I : 5, 7.

But little discussion would be needed on a question so clear, at least when viewed from the position of the apostolical epistles, were it not for the pertinacity with which the somewhat arrogant, and not seldom offensive assumption is put forth by Episcopal denominations—both clergy and laity— that there are no genuine churches save those duly organized with three orders in their ministry, and no scripturally ordained ministers except such as have been ordained by the imposition of hands by Episcopal bishops, as a superior order of the clergy. How groundless and absurd such lofty pretensions are, let any careful reader of the New Testament judge. The " historic episcopate " finds no foundation and no warrant in the New Testament.

During their lifetime the Apostles would, of necessity, be regarded with peculiar veneration, as having been the companions of, and received their appointment directly from, Christ Himself; and, also, as having been specially inspired and qualified for their work. But in all of this, they had no successors. After their death, such pastors as had associated with them, or had been appointed to office by them, would, for that reason, receive special regard from the churches and the younger ministry, and this special regard might deepen into reverence so profound as to concede them a foremost official position—a kind of patriarchal attitude among the churches, with a larger dignity of office and a larger liberty of action than was allowed to others. This in time could easily lead to the recognition of a higher rank and a superior order in the ministry.

Moreover, in process of time, as the first planted churches in the more important cities grew older and stronger, they might readily claim, and have accorded to them, a preëminence over the newer and feebler — especially the suburban and rural churches. In like manner the pastors of the older city churches could, without difficulty, assume a preëminence over the pastors of the smaller churches about them. In this way grew up the rule of the metropolitan churches over the provincial churches, and the authority assumed by the pastors of the former over their brethren in humbler positions, resulting finally in a clerical caste, or higher order of the clergy.

GIESELER, in his history of the Church, declares that:

"After the death of the Apostles and their pupils, to whom the general direction of the churches had always been conceded, some one among the presbyters of each Church was suffered gradually to take the lead in its affairs. In the same irregular way the title of *bishop* was appropriated by this first presbyter."—*Ch. Hist., Period I., div. I., chap. III., sec. 32.*

To the same effect is the testimony of Neander and nearly all early Church historians, including many prelatists. Moreover, it appears that each Church usually contained several elders, and the one among them who presided in their meetings, and, whether for age or ability, was more prominent, would come to be recognized as peculiarly the *episcopos*, though all were of equal rank. Thus gradually matured, through a course of years, either because of assumption on the one hand, or of concession on the other, or of both, that vast, complicated and despotical system of ecclesiastical domination and hierarchical tyranny, which culminated in the oppressive rule of the Greek and Roman establishments, falsely called churches.

This broad departure from apostolic practice, and from the order and simplicity of the Gospel, was natural, though unfortunate, and no imitation of it, however remote, should be countenanced or continued now. Its course of evil progress is easily traced in history, and generally conceded by scholars and divines. Not the less to be deplored that it was begun soon after the Apostles and their immediate successors had ceased to watch over and guide, by their wisdom and piety, the churches they had planted.

THE PASTORATE AND THE MINISTRY

The *Pastorate* and the *Ministry* are related, but not identical. A pastor is a minister, but a minister is not necessarily a pastor. The minister is the *kerux*, the herald, who preaches the Gospel, who proclaims the glad tidings to men. The pastor is the *poimen*, who folds and feeds and leads the flock. The pastor has the care of a Church; the minister is a preacher, and may or may not have the care of a Church. James is understood to have been pastor of the Church in Jerusalem; but Paul and Barnabas, Apollos and Cephas preached the Gospel from place to place, as ambassadors of Christ and heralds of the great salvation, planting churches and setting in order affairs, but without a local and permanent cure of souls.

In our time—though we have evangelists, missionaries and other ministerial service without pastoral responsibility—yet, for the most part, ministerial service is identified with the pastorate. It may be, as some have supposed, that in primitive times, when in each Church the Spirit developed a plurality of ministers, some—according to their peculiar gifts and graces—devoted themselves especially to pastoral work, as each Church might desire or have need, and some to preaching only, or chiefly. Certainly, in all ages, some have been better adapted to the one department of the ministry, and some to the other. Thus could the churches have the largest amount and the best application of the ministerial service, and be most edified.

The present discussion will be confined to the pastorate, its functions and relations, leaving a more general consideration of the ministry to another chapter.

1. *Nature of the pastor's work*

The religious cultivation of his Church and congregation constitutes the peculiar work of the pastor. It is the *shepherding* of the flock. He is not to be indifferent to their temporal interests, but their spiritual welfare is his special charge. He is to be the ever ready, sympathizing and helpful friend to all; but his endeavors should aim at, and be made subservient to, the ultimate purpose of the Gospel— to win souls to Christ, and edify the saints. The details of his work will be manifold; and while he should not assume too many duties, or take responsibilities alien to his proper calling, he must not too hastily repulse those who repose confidence in him, and whom he may be able in many ways to benefit by a variety of service.

The *pulpit* will constitute the stronghold of his power on his congregation and the community. For though a pastor, he must still be a preacher, a Gospel herald to his flock. The minister is, perhaps, first of all, a *teacher*. Therefore he must not neglect his preparations for the pulpit. If he cannot hold the people by his preaching, he cannot in any other way. Many devices may be resorted to, to draw and hold an audience, some of which deserve no better name than tricks, which if they serve their purpose at all, are short-lived, and fail utterly to command the confidence of thoughtful people. For, while some men have not, and cannot have the same attractive power in the pulpit as others, yet sound Gospel sermons, ably prepared, and earnestly delivered, constitute the only kind of pulpit service which can long commend itself to the consciences of the people. He who neglects his pulpit preparations for any cause whatever, will find frequent pastoral changes to be imperative— and possibly, not always in the most pleasant way. The same will be true of him who relies on a facility for extemporaneous discourse, under the inspiration of a present audience, to the neglect of previous careful preparation.

Emphasis must also be laid on *pastoral visitation.* Here peculiarly he is the pastor. He may not visit so much as many would wish. Some are never satisfied. Nor should he visit to the detriment of his pulpit preparation. Since, according to the present constitution of religious society, the Christian minister is expected to fill the twofold office of preacher and pastor, he should labor to discharge the functions of both, with the greatest possible fidelity and success, giving to each conscientiously its appropriate share of his ability. He must know his people in their homes; must know their joys and sorrows as they themselves will relate them. They must know him, as they cannot know him in the pulpit simply. Both he and they miss boundless good, if this be not done. These visits should be brief and religious. They should not degenerate into social chit-chat, or even into religious gossip. They must not be morose nor melancholy, but genial, gentle and sympathetic. Young ministers may find it hard work, and dread it as a drudgery; but they will come to feel differently when for a few times they have been able to comfort the sorrowing, relieve the burdened, and know the luxury of doing good to those in trouble.

It would not be just nor true to say, that the pastor's sphere is exclusively the spiritual life of the Church, while the deacons are assigned to its temporalities. The pastor has the oversight and superintendence of all the interests of the Church, and of all departments of its work, both spiritual and temporal. And while he should not lord it over God's heritage, he should feel himself responsible for the guardianship and watch-care of all with which he is put in trust. Nor should he needlessly interfere with the deacons, or trustees, or Sunday-school workers, nor assume dictatorial authority over others in their service. Yet it is his privilege and his duty to hold a watchful supervision over all, that all may be done to the edifying of the body of Christ.

The pastor should have great care for the religious culture of children and the youth. But not to the neglect of others. Class distinctions are invidious, unhappy in their influence in a Church, and should never be encouraged, or countenanced. As this is not a treatise on pastoral duties, it need be pursued no further than to say, the pastorate should be assumed, not of constraint, nor for selfish ends, but out of love to Christ, and for the triumphs of His truth.

NOTE.—Ministers are not *priests* in any ecclesiastical sense to offer sacrifices on behalf of the people, or propitiate an offended Deity; nor yet do they mediate between God and men, as is taught by the Romish, and other sacramentarian communions. They cannot *consecrate* elements, and have no exclusive right to the ministration of sacraments— indeed, there are no *sacraments*, in the commonly understood sense of that term, as means which in themselves effectually convey grace. The minister is not a priest, save in that sense in which all true Christians constitute a " royal priesthood." Sainthood, therefore, without distinction of rank or office, constitutes a spiritual priesthood. Thus also said Peter to the elect believers, scattered abroad. " Ye also as living stones, are built up a spiritual house, to be a holy priesthood, to offer up spiritual sacrifices, acceptable to God, through Jesus Christ." " A chosen generation, a royal priesthood, a holy nation, a peculiar people."—1 Peter 2: 5, 9. Christ Jesus, the Great High-Priest of our profession, is the one only mediator between God and men.

2. *How pastors are obtained*

If it be asked how the churches are to secure pastors, the reply is, by election, as the free choice of the people, in each individual Church. It is an essential part of the independency of the churches, the right to choose their pastors and teachers; and that no individual, or combination of men, can appoint pastors over them, or compel a Church to accept as officers those whom they have not chosen by their free suffrages. This is the polity of the New Testament, and has ever been the usage of our people. A free people demand and maintain the right to choose their own rulers. They may ask, or accept advice; but no man is a pastor to any people until he has been chosen by a majority vote of that Church. Nor does it require the consent of any synod, presbytery or council for him to enter at once upon the duties of the office. Primarily and properly, though not necessarily, the pastor is chosen from among the members, after the Church has had evidence that the Spirit had called to, and fitted him for, the work of the ministry; and after having abundant evidence of his adaptation to the position. But if not a member of that particular Church, he should become such before entering upon his official duties as pastor of it.

The selection and election of a pastor is one of the most important acts—if not the most important —pertaining to the independency of the Church. The interest of the body, and the welfare of religion depend so largely on it, that it should be entered upon with the utmost care, deliberation and prayer —prayer for divine direction. That a wise and safe leader, an able and instructing teacher, a devout, spiritual and holy man may be secured for the sacred office, and that the choice be influenced by no carnal ambition, by no personal prejudices, and for no selfish ends. When the choice is made, and the pastor secured, then let him be received, loved, supported, honored and obeyed, as one sent of God for this sacred work.

And let it be further considered that no man can do of himself all that is desired and expected of a pastor. He must not only have divine help, but he must have the sympathy, coöperation, and prayers of the Church. Some miserable failures in the ministry are due to the faults of the ministers themselves; still more are due to the churches, which too often abuse what they professed was the gift of God, when they secured their pastors.

3. *The Pastor's Authority*

The pastor is to be loved, honored and obeyed, in the Lord. He is placed over the Church by both the Head of the body, and by the free and voluntary act of the body itself. Though he professes no magisterial authority, and has no power, either spiritual or temporal, to enforce mandates or inflict penalties, yet the very position he occupies as teacher and leader supposes authority vested in him. On the one hand, the minister is not to be regarded with ignorant and blind devotion, as if possessed of superhuman attributes, whose official acts must be venerated even though his private life be scandalous; nor yet, on the other hand, is he to be considered a mere puppet for the capricious mistreatment of such as wish to show their independence, and "use their liberty for a cloak of maliciousness."

As a rule, the pastor who maintains a dignified and consistent Christian and ministerial life, commending himself to the confidence of the people, will receive all the deference he desires, and will have accorded to him all that personal respect and official reverence which he needs to claim. His authority will be a moral force, to which those who love and honor him will yield. He need not worry and fret because he does not receive the respect which he thinks his due. Let him command it by his character and deportment. He may too much attempt to enforce his authority. As a preacher of the gospel his authority is of another and a higher kind, in that he is an ambassador from the king, and speaks with an authority more than human. True, his words, even in the pulpit, are not beyond question, since they are to be judged by the infallible standard of the word of God. But in the administration of Church affairs he should secure the coöperation of his members, and gain his object by reason and persuasion, rather than attempt to force compliance by authoritative dictation.

4. *Length of the Pastorate*

The spirit of Christian liberty, and the voluntary principle on which all Christian institutions should be supported, control the relations of pastor and people. There is no power that can compel a Church to accept a pastor, or a pastor to accept a Church. The relation is formed by mutual agreement between them. And when once formed, the relation can be

dissolved by no external authority, civil or ecclesiastical, but by the mutual consent of the parties
themselves. In some of the other denominations,
where ecclesiastical systems instead of Church independency prevail, the relations of the pastorate
are regulated by higher official authority, instead of
by the mutual agreement of the parties. Even
there, however, the free spirit of religious life mani-
fests itself, indirectly, if not directly, and the churches
do not quietly consent to receive pastors unwelcome to them, nor to retain them when the relation
becomes irksome, notwithstanding the action of
bishops, conferences, or presbyteries.

The ideal pastorate is, no doubt, life-long; but in
practical life this is seldom realized. In theory
there is something beautiful in the case of a minister
who spends his whole life among the same people,
loved, honored and venerated till his death; around
whom the new generation grows up as his supporters, when the fathers have passed away. Honored
by his compeers, loved by the young, venerated by
the children, he becomes the typical patriarch and
shepherd of the flock. Such things have been; but
seldom can they now be found —certainly not in our
denomination. And perhaps, on the whole, it may
be just as well. The restless spirit of a headlong
age and a busy life demands change—change in hope
of progress, but change at any rate. The romance
of a beautiful theory cannot control the activities
of society, not even in Christian circles, since there,
also, a carnal, utilitarian spirit is likely to rule.

It is unquestionably true that the long pastorates have their trials no less severe—sometimes more painful—than short ones. The pastor has more than once seen the time when, restless and uneasy, he would gladly have resigned, had any eligible field elsewhere opened for him. And the Church has more than once seen the time when it would have rejoiced at a change, but had too much regard for him, and too much respect for themselves, to force a change. Many a pastor, who has the faculty of "holding on," has outlived his usefulness on a given field, either because devoted to the theory of long pastorates, or because he saw no way to better his situation ; and that, too, very likely, when he knew the people would be quite willing for a change Quite willing for a change for the sake of the cause. though they loved and honored him.

Quite as unfortunate in its effects, and more frequently than long and fruitless pastorates, is the sudden and hasty change so often made by many, and sometimes on the most trivial occasion. There are in every Church, most likely, mischief-makers, whose influence is chiefly felt in opposing others and stirring up strife. Let a pastor possess his soul in patience, and not be made unhappy by every little cross-current in his affairs. But if any considerable number of his kind, prudent and judicious brethren think a change is desirable ; or if he himself, after long and prayerful consideration, believes it his duty to leave, let him act accordingly. But let a minister flee " Church quarrels " as he would a pestilence. He may not be responsible for them, but if he becomes involved in them, though the merits of the case may be on his side, yet he cannot remain to fight them out without suffering more in peace of mind and reputation than any victory be can win will be worth. Let him retire to more quiet fields, where he can live in peace and do good without conflict, and leave the fighting to those who have less at stake. The world is wide, and he can do good and be happy in many another field.

5. *Pastoral Support*

A pastor should be well and generously supported as to his salary, according to the ability of the Church he serves. Few things exhibit the essential meanness of human nature—Christian human nature even—more clearly than for a people to stint and crowd a pastor down to the smallest pittance, while they have an abundance, or live in affluence. The true minister of Christ will cheerfully share necessities with his people. But it is cruel and contemptible for them to lade him with heavy burdens which they are not willing to help him bear. He will not expect to live up to the standard of the wealthiest; he ought not to be expected to live down to the standard of the poorest. And if there be one thing more dishonorable than cramping him to the smallest amount of salary, it is that refinement of cruelty of not paying him the salary agreed upon, when it is due, compelling him to endure the shame and grief of living in debt, unable to pay for the necessaries of life, while they have an abundance.

When the Church extends a call they name the amount they are willing to pay. Of course it is optional with him whether to accept the call on such conditions. If he does, he cannot find fault that they give no more. Unless, indeed, as is not unfrequently the case, they delude him with the promise that they will increase the amount the next year; a promise often made, but very seldom kept. But let the stipulated sum be regularly and promptly paid, otherwise he will not be able promptly to pay his debts, and his reputation will be compromised, and his character imperiled. It is a fearfully bad and injurious thing for a clergyman to get the name of not paying his debts. In the payment of salary, never allow donations and personal presents to be counted. It is little less than an insult to ask a minister to discount his salary for a bushel of potatoes, a bag of meal, or a barrel of apples. These personal presents are of value in the family; can often be made without sacrifice, and will go far to eke out a scanty support. But let them be personal presents and the salary come by itself, in full tale, and promptly.

It may be added also, with propriety, that a minister devoted to Christian work should not engage in secular employments simply for the purpose of making money. But if the Church cannot, or will not, support him in comfort, he may, if opportunity offers, add by the labors of his hands what will relieve himself and family from want—as Paul sustained himself by tent-making that he might the better preach the Gospel.

6. The Pastor a Peacemaker

Troubles in Church life unfortunately do sometimes arise. And whether the pastor be the cause, or only the victim of them, he always more or less suffers from them. Very many of these troubles are no doubt to be charged upon pastors themselves. If they do not originate them, their indiscreet and unwise management and partisan conduct foment instead of allaying dissension. Some pastors, like some private members, are imprudent, irascible, impetuous and severe. It is not wise to give heed to everything said and done. Many exasperating things are cured or conquered by letting them alone. A minister of the Gospel, of all men, should be a peacemaker. He should soothe and heal. It is better for himself and better for all concerned. He must " endure *hardness* as a good soldier of Jesus Christ." Of course he has his rights, which are not to be lightly invaded; he is not required to be trifled with, or trampled on, for the sport of the envious or the vile. But he is to be an example to the flock in patient endurance.

On the other hand, the Church should carefully guard the reputation and the feelings of their pastor, and not allow the gossip-loving or the envious to assail him. His people are bound to protect him. If he be in fault, let them tell him so, and win him from his mistakes. A pastor ought not to be compelled to stand guard as a watchful sentinel over his own good name, to defend it against the idle but wicked calumnies of mischievous tongues. There ought to be advocates and defenders on every side. Ordinarily there will be. Both pastor and people should regard all dissension and strife with so much dread as to check it by any amount of effort and sacrifice at the very beginning. If, however, it defies all attempts at repression, and involves the peace and harmony of the Church, the pastor will find it wise to flee from the windy storm, and serve the cause he loves in some more quiet sphere.

Churches cannot be expected to prosper, or the Gospel to have free course, while rent by dissension and strife, especially if it be strife connected with, or on account of the pastor. The philosophy of spiritual and religious growth is the same now as at first, when this record was made: "Then had the churches rest throughout all Judea and Galilee and Samaria, and were edified; and walking in the fear of the Lord, and in the comfort of the Holy Ghost, were multiplied."—Acts 9:31.

NOTE 1.—Great care is needed in the selection of a pastor. Grave interests are committed to his charge, as the religious teacher, leader, and example for the flock. Very serious responsibility devolves on the deacons and leading members of the Church especially. An act so vitally connected with the welfare of the cause and the spread of the Gospel, should be preceded by, and accompanied with, earnest and protracted prayer for divine direction in the choice.

NOTE 2.—In calling a man to the pastorate, the Church should take deliberate care to know his *record;* what he has done elsewhere, and how he is esteemed and valued where he has previously lived and labored. It is a piece of reckless folly, of which churches are often guilty—and for which they justly suffer—that on the credit of a few flashy or fascinating sermons, wholly ignorant of his private character and of his ministerial history, they call and settle a pastor. A man of deep piety, thoroughly in love with the word of God, is much to be preferred to the brilliant platform declaimer.

NOTE 3.—If a young man without a record is called to be ordained and begin his pastorate, his reputation for piety, sound sense, and pulpit ability should be carefully considered and well understood. If he be of the right spirit and the right material, he will grow into larger usefulness through study, the endowment of the Spirit, and the prayers of the people.

NOTE 4.—In giving a *call*, the Church usually appoints a meeting for that express purpose, notice being publicly given two Sundays in succession, the purpose of the meeting being distinctly stated in the notice, and a *three-quarters vote* of all present at such a meeting should be deemed essential to a call. Certainly no prudent or self-respecting man would accept a call on anything less than that. Nor even on that if but a very small number are opposed to him. Such meeting should be managed with Christian sincerity, without caucusing or partisanship for the purpose of electing a favorte man. The candidate should be informed *exactly* how the vote stands, and what the feeling toward him is, concealing nothing. Let there be transparent honesty in so delicate and important a matter, and no deception practised.

NOTE 5.—The connection between pastor and people is sometimes made for a specified and limited time. But more generally—now almost universally—for an indefinite time, to be dissolved at the option of either party, by giving *three months'* notice or otherwise by mutual agreement. Permanency in this relation is greatly to be desired, as tending to the best good of all concerned, if it be the permanency of active concord. Trifling disadvantages are better endured than remedied at the expense of more serious evils, which frequent changes seldom fail to bring to both pastor and people.

NOTE 6.—The too common practice of hearing many *candidates* preach on trial cannot be approved, and usually works evil to the Church which indulges in it. A few sermons preached under such circumstances form no just criterion of a man's ministerial ability, pastoral qualifications, or personal worth. If the churches wish to avoid men unsuited to them, and especially if they wish to escape the plague of unworthy men in their pulpits, they must use more caution in the calling and settlement of pastors.

NOTE 7.—Is it right for one Church to call a pastor away from another Church? Merely to call a man would be neither wrong nor dishonorable—would violate no law of personal courtesy or of Christian comity as among the churches. Let the responsibility, then, rest with *him* of accepting or declining the call. But if one Church should use other means to unsettle him by arguments, persuasions, and the offer of special inducements, it would be both unchristian and dishonorable. It would surely not be doing as they would wish to be done by.

II. DEACONS

The term *deacon* (*diakonos*) in the New Testament means a minister; a servant; one who ministers to, or serves others. This, taken in a large sense, gives a very wide range of meaning to the word. It is applied to the Apostles and even to Christ himself. In ecclesiastical usage, however, it designates an officer in the Church. But precisely what relation the *diaconate* sustains to the Church and the *pastorate* is a matter of opinion or of interpretation, in respect to which men differ.

Those who favor prelatical forms of Church organization and government, claim, as has been heretofore stated, a threefold ministry, and demand an *episcopate*, a *pastorate*, and a *diaconate*. The deacon, then, is the first and lowest order of the ministry. But Presbyterian and Independent Churches reject the episcopate, holding that bishop and pastor are the same, and the deaconship does not constitute an order in the ministry, taking that word in its ordinary sense, though the deacon be in the primitive sense a minister, but a minister of temporalities, and a helper to the pastor in his ministry of the Word.

1. *Their Origin*

The diaconate is usually supposed to have originated in the election of the Seven, as helpers to the Apostles, recorded in Acts 6 : 1 - 6 ; though they were not called *deacons*. Some, however, have regarded the election of the Seven as a temporary expedient to meet that special emergency, and claim that they had no successors. But inasmuch as a similar service in Church work became permanent, similar help would be permanently needed. Also since the Apostle subsequently recognized the office in the Epistles to Timothy and Titus, giving specific directions as to the qualifications necessary for those who should fill it, we are in no great perplexity as to the fact or the nature of the diaconate as permanent in the churches.

Subsequent to the Pentecost, the large ingathering of converts had so multiplied the number, that the care of the needy among them and such temporal concerns as were a necessity, became a burden to the Apostles, so great as seriously to interfere with their spiritual duties in the ministry of the word. Hence, having called the multitude of the disciples together, they explained the matter and requested them to select " seven men of honest report, full of the Holy Ghost, and wisdom," to whom this service should be committed, that they themselves might "give themselves continually to prayer and to the ministry of the word." This request was complied with and seven men selected, whom the Apostles, set apart to the work for which they were chosen, by prayer and the laying on of hands.

2. *Their Duties*

They are to be chosen by a free vote of the Church—"the multitude of the disciples"—and are to be faithful, prudent, experienced, and devout men. They are to have charge of the sick and needy members, and whatever temporal affairs may require attention. They are also to act as counselors and assistants of the pastor in advancing the general interests of the body, both temporal and spiritual. Of the original seven, Philip and Stephen were most effective preachers of the Gospel, but it was not for this they were specially chosen. With many of our churches the deaconship has come to be a merely nominal affair, regarded as of small importance, and accomplishing a questionable service. This ought not so to be.

3. *Their Number*

The number of deacons in a Church is a matter discretionary with the body. Usually it is from *two* to *seven*, according to the conditions and necessities of the case ; the latter being the original scriptural number, many unwisely consider it needful to have seven, whether the Church be large or small. Deacons, however, should not be appointed merely to keep the ranks full, nor as official ornaments, but only for real and needed service to be rendered by them. And the men appointed should be fit men for that service.

4. *Their Time of Service*

The period of time for which they are chosen, as well as the number, is discretionary with the Church, since no scriptural precept or precedent directs. More commonly they have been chosen for an *indefinite period*, which was substantially for life, unless they resigned, died, or removed. But since it not unfrequently happens that persons in the office become inefficient and sometimes obstructive, the practice of electing them for a *limited period* has come to be quite prevalent ; generally for three years. In this way the office expires by limitation, and if better men are available they can be chosen without offense. Which is the better rule, each Church must judge for itself. Other things being equal, permanency in this as well as in the pastoral office, usually tends to secure a higher regard for the office itself and greater usefulness on the part of those who fill it.

5. *Their Ordination*

The Seven were set apart to the discharge of their duties by prayer and the laying on of hands by the Apostles, as indicating the sacred and important duties committed to them. In our older churches this practice was carefully adhered to, as it still is by some, particularly at the South. But in many parts, of late, it has fallen very much into disuse, and the diaconate is regarded as little more than a committee service. The office is coming to be far too little esteemed, and the scriptural qualifications of the men chosen, too little insisted on. Ordination, if generally practised, would invest both with more importance. Too much care cannot be taken to secure the right kind of men for the office, when we consider that the permanent influence of a deacon is scarcely surpassed by that of the pastor himself. A good deacon is a peculiar blessing both to the pastor and the Church.

NOTE 1.—Notice that the deaconship was not instituted by Christ, but by the Apostles, and grew out of the emergencies of the case. The fact that Paul subsequently recognized the office and specified the qualifications which the incumbents should possess, shows that it was to remain a part of the permanent constitution of the churches.

NOTE 2.—The Seven were elected by the *Church*, that is.

by " the multitude of the disciples ; " they were chosen from among their own number, but their setting apart or designation to their work was by the Apostles with prayer and the laying on of hands. This is called their *ordination*, and gave added importance and impressiveness to the office, and the work to which they were chosen.

NOTE 3.—It deserves notice that while no instance is found in the New Testament in which any preacher of the Gospel was inducted into his office by formal ordination or by any ceremony whatever—hands were laid on Paul and Barnabas when sent to the heathen, but they had then been in the ministry many years—*now* ceremonial ordination to the ministry is strenuously insisted on. And yet, while we have primitive precedent for formal ordination of deacons, *now* that ceremony is very generally disregarded.

NOTE 4.—The qualifications made requisite for the office sufficiently indicate its importance, and the care with which it should be filled. " Men of honest report, full of the Holy Ghost and of wisdom." Indeed, these qualifications differ but slightly from those required for bishops or pastors.

NOTE 5.—It is evident from the character of the Seven, and the personal history of some of them subsequently, that while their specific official duties were the temporalities of the Church, yet at the same time they were foremost as counselors and co-adjutors with the Apostles in the spiritual interests as well. Having been among the most devout, prudent, and faithful before their election, and as the reason for their election, they would not be less so afterward. Such are the men for the office.

NOTE 6.—Some people and some churches seem to think, that about the only duty of a deacon is to pass the elements at the celebration of the Supper. And so the office becomes almost a nullity. Any one on whom the pastor may call can pass the elements. The original " serving of tables " was quite a different work from this. The diaconate implies a substantial and an important service in the Church, of which tne serving at the Supper is a proper, but only an incidental adjunct. If their practical relations to the Church be reduced to this, they may well be considered as little more than an ornamental appendage to an organization.

NOTE 7.—The secular concerns of the Church, including its financial affairs, would seem legitimately to be embraced in the duties of the deaconship according to the original purpose, as belonging to its temporalities, but now these matters are usually committed to an entirely different class of men known as *trustees*, elected under the specific direction of State laws.

NOTE 8.—Deacons should be watchful guardians of the purity and good order of the churches, striving to maintain a healthful tone of piety and Christian activity in the body. But they do not constitute a coördinate branch for the administration of its government, and in the exercise of their functions must act only in conjunction with the pastor, not independent of him ; possibly, *except* in very rare and urgent cases. Hence, while it is desirable for the pastor to have meetings with his deacons often or statedly for consultation and advice, it is not proper for them to hold meetings as a " board of deacons," independent of and without the advice of the pastor, as sometimes is done.

NOTE 9.—In the absence of a pastor it becomes the duty of the deacons to conduct the devotional meetings, provide for the supply of the pulpit and administer the affairs of the body generally. In case there be no pastor it would be legitimate for them to bring before the Church, as by them directed, such persons as were deemed suitable candidates for the pastorate. But this is often, perhaps usually, performed by a " pulpit committee " appointed for that purpose.

NOTE 10.—The deacons' wives (*gunaikos*), mentioned in 1 Tim. 3: 2, were probably not the wives of deacons, as has usually been inferred, but deaconesses or female assistants, appointed by the churches to minister to the sick and perform other services to those of their own sex, which could with more propriety be done by them than by the deacons or other male members   A few churches retain the practice; and since female members in all the churches are the more numerous, and as a rule, the more efficient in charitable ministrations, it is difficult to see why such a class of helpers, more or less formally designated for Christian work, should not be continued in our churches.

III.   OTHER OFFICERS

The above-named officers constitute a twofold ministry for the churches, and all that are provided for by the New Testament economy, and all that are necessary to the best organization and highest efficiency of these bodies, since all the functions essential to a working Church may be efficiently discharged by these alone.   Yet it is usual to supplement these by several called " Church officers," merely as a matter of convenience or of expediency.

Thus a *clerk* is appointed to take minutes and preserve records of its business proceedings, with all other papers belonging to the body.   A *treasurer* is chosen to hold, disburse, and account for moneys for Church purposes.   In most of the States, if not all, *trustees* are elected, as required by law, according to specified procedure, in order legally to hold property and rightly to administer its financial affairs.   But the duties of these various offices could well be performed by the deacons and constitute a part of their appropriate work.   Yet it may be right and wise to distribute the labors of the Church among its members, all the more so if those better fitted for these peculiar services can be found.   Especially should the requirements of civil law be conceded, as in the case of trustees, in order to enjoy the legal rights of corporate bodies as property holders.

NOTE 1.—The laws for the incorporation of religious societies differ in the different States. In some the Church itself can become an incorporate body, and thus control and administer its temporal affairs as it does the spiritual, without interference by any persons not Church members. This is right, and, according to the independent theory of Baptist Church government, they ought everywhere to be able to do this. In other States the corporate body is a *society* composed of all attendants who are regular contributors, whether members of the Church or not. This admits persons not Christians to participation in the management of Church affairs. Though usually no harm arises, yet harm is always liable to arise and the theory is wrong. Still, the churches should conform to the legal requisitions of the States where they are located.

NOTE 2.—Trustees are really a standing committee, appointed for a specific purpose. And since the *Church* is the responsible and authoritative body, even though there be a *society*, the trustees should hold themselves bound by every consideration of morality and honor to carry out the wishes of the Church and to act under their instructions, whatever technical rights civil laws and the decisions of courts may give them in certain emergencies.

NOTE 3.—The trustees have a treasurer through whose hands pass the funds for current expenses, including pastor's salary and other items, provided for by pew rents, subscription, and gifts for these uses. It is customary also to have a Church treasurer, usually one of the deacons, who receives and disburses, as directed, funds for benevolent purposes, moneys for the needy, and other uses not included in current expenses, or for care of the property.

NOTE 4.—It is supposed that the Church clerk will do more than keep in record the bare items which may be transacted at business meetings. His journal should show a condensed history of the Church's current life, including all items of note, and whatever transpires in its affairs of interest to be mentioned and preserved.

NOTE 5.—The various offices and responsible services in the Church should be as widely distributed as possible among the members, so that the same persons need not fill several offices at the same time. A few individuals should not be overburdened with service, nor should any one be tempted, by too much office, to dictatorial authority and an assumptive personal control of affairs. And yet incompetent and unfit persons should not be appointed to important and responsible positions, even though two offices might be imposed on the same individual.

NOTE 6.—It is undoubtedly true that the different official positions require somewhat diverse personal qualifications for their incumbents. Trustees, as having to transact business matters, should be sound, careful, and accurate business men. Deacons, as being more concerned in spiritual affairs, should in a marked degree be spiritually minded and devout. A Church clerk should be a good penman, prompt, careful, and accurate in detail. An appropriate fitness should be sought in all these affairs.

CHAPTER 5

CHRISTIAN ORDINANCES

CHRISTIAN ordinances are defined to be "institutions of divine authority relating to the worship of God, under the Christian Dispensation." In this general sense there are various ordinances ; since preaching and hearing the word, prayer, singing, fasting, and thanksgiving may all be considered as institutions of divine authority.

But in a narrower and a more distinctive sense it has been common to call *Baptism* and the *Lord's Supper* by this name, and to say they are the only Christian ordinances committed to the churches, and are for perpetual observance. These rites are also by some called *sacraments,** the number of which the Catholic Church has increased to seven, including, with Baptism and the Eucharist, Confirmation, Penance, Extreme unction, Matrimony, and Orders. But in the sense in which the Roman and Greek Churches explain the meaning of sacrament, to which meaning other ritualistic churches do strongly incline, Baptism and the Supper are not sacraments at all. Sacraments, by them, are interpreted to mean not simply outward signs of inward grace and

* From the Latin "Sacramentum," a soldier's oath of fealty and consecration to the military service in which he enlists.

spiritual operations, but outward rites which work grace and produce spiritual operations. This view of sacramental efficacy Protestant confessions reject, and against it Baptists do strongly protest.

These two, therefore, Baptism and the Supper, are the two sacred rites, and the only ones, enjoined by Christ for perpetual observance in His churches. They are not only visible signs which appeal to the senses, but they are teaching institutions which appeal to the understanding and the heart. They are the two symbols of the new covenant ; the two visible pillars of the spiritual temple ; the two monuments of the new dispensation. Christ has appointed no others. They are *positive* institutions, as distinguished from those of a purely moral character, their claim to honor and obedience arising exclusively from the fact that Christ has appointed and made them obligatory. Their claim to respect and observance rests not on their peculiar fitness, though that is manifest, but on the simple fact that Christ has established them and commanded their observance.

These ordinances, so simple in form, so expressive in action, and so intelligible in meaning, have been the occasions of heated, sometimes of bitter controversy through all the ages of Christian history. Their forms have been changed, their purpose perverted, the manner of their administration encumbered by numerous and puerile ceremonials, and their entire effect and efficacy misinterpreted and misstated. Baptists claim to hold and use them in their original simplicity and purity. But a fuller discussion of the subject must be reserved to another place.

I. BAPTISM

Baptism is sometimes called "the initiatory rite," because persons are not received to membership in the churches until they are baptized. But baptism of itself does not admit to the fellowship of the churches ; it, however, stands at the door, and admission is only on its reception. It has by some been called "the seal of the new covenant," as circumcision was the seal of the old. It is, however, a witness and a testimony to the covenant, since it is naturally and properly the first Christian act of the believer after an exercise of saving faith. It certifies therefore to the acceptance of Christ, and the union and fellowship of the renewed soul with its Saviour. It becomes a badge of discipleship, and is, in that sense, a seal of the covenant of grace.

1. *Its Institution*

Christian baptism was instituted by Christ, when He submitted to John's baptism, adopting its form, with some change of meaning. John's baptism was unto repentance and faith in Him who was to come. Jesus baptized (or His disciples did) into Himself, as the Messiah who had come, and as the sign that His kingdom had already been established in the hearts of those who received it.

This baptism did not come in the place of circumcision or any other sign or seal of the old covenant, but was ordained for the new. Thus, " John did baptize in the wilderness, and preached the baptism of repentance for the remission of sins."—Mark 1 : 4. " John answered, saying unto them all, I indeed baptize you with water, but one mightier than I cometh, the latchet of whose shoes I am not worthy to unloose ; He shall baptize you with the Holy Ghost and with fire."—Luke 1 : 16. " Then cometh Jesus from Galilee to Jordan, unto John, to be baptized of him. And Jesus, when He was baptized, went up straightway out of the water ; and lo, the heavens were opened unto Him, and He saw the spirit of God descending like a dove and lighting upon Him : and, lo, a voice from heaven saying, This is my beloved Son, in whom I am well pleased." —Matt. 3 : 13, 16, 17. "And He said to His disciples, Go ye therefore and teach all nations, baptizing them in the name of the Father, and of the Son, and of the Holy Ghost, teaching them to observe all things, whatsoever I have commanded you : and, lo, I am with you alway, even unto the end of the world."—Matt. 28 : 19, 20.

The circumstances in which this characteristic Christian rite was inaugurated, as well as the personal glory of Him who appointed, and who commanded it as a badge of discipleship for all who confess His name, make it impressive and august in its simple form, and sacred in its influence on both those who receive and those who witness it.

2. *Its Administration*

Christian baptism is defined to be the immersion of a person in water, on a profession of his faith in Christ, in, or into, the name of the Father, Son, and Holy Spirit. Baptism, therefore, is an *immersion* or dipping in water, with this meaning, and for this sacred purpose; and without this dipping there is no Scriptural baptism. The immersion is essential to the rite, and pouring or sprinkling water upon a person is not, and cannot be, baptism, as will hereafter be shown.

And this sign of the Christian dispensation is distinguished from all the ablutions, washings, and sprinklings of the Mosaic dispensation, for none of which was it a substitute. "And were baptized of Him in Jordan, confessing their sins."—Matt. 3:6. "And they went down both into the water, both Philip and the eunuch, and he baptized him."—Acts 8:38. "Therefore we are buried with Him by baptism into death."—Rom. 6:4. "Buried with Him in baptism."—Col. 2:12. This impressive form and manner of administration was practised by Christ and His Apostles, and continued unchanged in the churches for generations; but finally, at the dictate of prelates, or for the convenience of priests, it underwent changes which destroyed its beauty and robbed it of its significancy, and a human device was substituted for a divine ordinance.

3. *Its Subjects*

Baptism is to be administered to those, and to

those only, who have exercised and professed a saving faith in Christ; that is, to *believers*. This saving faith supposes an exercise of godly repentance for sin, and a turning to the Lord with full purpose of heart.

Pedobaptists say baptism is to be given to believers and their *children*. But that is a fiction of human ingenuity. The New Testament knows nothing of the baptism of unconscious infants, nor of unbelieving persons, either young or old. Neither does it teach or admit the inference that children can be partakers of the benefits of grace simply because of the faith of their parents. Each one must believe for himself in order to be saved. " He that believeth and is baptized shall be saved ; but he that believeth not shall be condemned."—Mark 16 : 16. But "when they believed they were baptized, both men and women."—Acts 8 : 13. " Then they that gladly received His Word were baptized." —Acts 2 : 41. " If thou believest with all thy heart, thou mayest."—Acts 8 : 36. None but believers were baptized.

If baptism be " an outward sign of an inward grace," showing forth the washing of regeneration and the renewing of the Holy Ghost, then it can have no significancy to those who have not received the inward cleansing of the Spirit.

4. *Its Obligation*

All men are under obligation to repent of sin, and believe on Christ as the only means of salvation. And all believers in Christ are bound by the most sacred considerations to obey their Lord's command, and confess Him before men in baptism. No one who trusts Him for salvation can lightly esteem His authority, or willingly disregard His command, nor yet neglect to profess a faith which to him is precious, by submitting to this ordinance.

It is not a question as to whether he can be saved without baptism; but whether he can be a true disciple, and refuse or neglect thus to obey and confess his Saviour. "Repent and be baptized, every one of you, in the name of Jesus Christ."—Acts 2:38. "Arise and be baptized, and wash away thy sins." — Acts 22:16. Baptism may not be essential to salvation, but it is essential to obedience. The wish to live unrecognized as a Christian, unwilling to share the responsibilities, or discharge the duties of discipleship, and yet hoping for all its blessings and rewards, is both selfish and mercenary, and indicates that the new birth has not yet transpired.

5. *Its Efficacy*

It may well be asked, What is the efficacy of baptism? What does it do for him who receives it? Is it an efficacious means of grace? In what respect is the disciple different, after his baptism, from what he was before? In reply it may be most positively stated that baptism does not produce faith and a new heart. It possesses no magical power to convert the soul. Baptismal regeneration, as taught by some, is altogether a false and pernicious doctrine. Regeneration is by the Holy Spirit alone, and should precede baptism. Out of this mistaken view of its efficacy grew the unscriptural dogma of infant baptism, in the early ages, since it was feared that dying infants could not be saved without it.

But as an act of obedience to Christ, the reception of this ordinance usually brings peculiar light, joy, and comfort to the soul. This is especially true as a witness usually borne soon after conversion, when every act of obedience is a service of love, and the soul's sensibilities are alive and tender. Moreover, the disciple feels that in baptism he has effectually and openly come out from the world, and committed himself to Christ and His service. This gives to the spirit a moral triumph, and fills it with boundless peace. Baptism, therefore, is an act of obedience, and as such brings the candidate into a more intimate and exclusive fellowship with his Lord; but it possesses no power in itself to remit sin, to change the heart, or sanctify the spirit.

6. *It is Commemorative*

Baptism has its retrospect. It points back to Christ in His humiliation, death, burial and resurrection; and keeps constantly in the minds of both candidates and spectators Him " who died for our sins and rose again for our justification." It testifies that He suffered, died, was buried, and rose from the dead, to perfect the work of redemption.

What Christ did and suffered gives to this ordinance its significance and its force. " So many of us as were baptized into Christ were baptized into

His death."—Rom. 6:8.   "Buried with Him in baptism, wherein also ye are risen with Him."—Col. 11:
12.   The past is brought to view.   There is "one
Lord, one faith, one baptism"—Eph. 4:5—thus forever connecting the disciple in this act with his
Lord.   "We are buried with Him by baptism, into
death."—Rom. 6:4.   If the past could be forgotten,
this sacred ordinance would lose its moral power

7. *It is Predictive*

That is, in the sense of looking forward and antici-
pating things to come, it foreshadows.   Most im-
pressively does it prefigure the resurrection of the
body from the grave, when one rises from the baptismal waters "like as Christ was raised up from the
dead by the glory of the Father."—Rom. 6:4.   "If
the dead rise not at all, why are they then baptized
for the dead?"—1 Cor. 15:29.   Though this passage
is of doubtful interpretation, yet in some sense it
clearly connects baptism with the resurrection from
the dead ;   thus uniting the hopes of the future
with the memories of the past, binding both in the
realities of the present by baptism.

8. *It is Emblematic*

Baptism is a creed; a confession of faith.   The
symbolism of that sacred rite teaches the great cardinal doctrines of the gospel.   It represents Christ's
death and burial for our sins, and His resurrection
from the dead for our justification.   "But I have a
baptism to be baptized with;   and how am I strait-

ened till it be accomplished ? "—Luke 12 : 50. It rep-resents the candidate's death to sin, and his rising to a new spiritual life in Christ, and, therefore, his fellowship with his Lord, both in dying and living. "For as many as have been baptized into Christ have put on Christ."—Gal. 3 : 27.

It teaches the resurrection of the saints, of which the resurrection of Christ is the prophecy and the pledge. "For if we have been planted together in the likeness of His death, we shall be also in the likeness of his resurrection."—Rom. 6 : 5. The life everlasting follows in sacred proximity the death to sin; for "if we be dead with Christ, we believe that we shall also live with Him."—Rom. 6 : 8. It represents in an outward sign the inward work of renewal and cleansing. "According to His mercy, He saved us by the washing of regeneration, and the renewing of the Holy Ghost."—Titus 3 : 5. This inward cleansing by the precious blood of Christ, through the operation of the Spirit, is symbolized in the submersion and ablution of baptism. "The like figure whereunto even baptism doth now save us (not the putting away of the filth of the flesh, but the answer of a good conscience toward God), by the resurrection of Jesus Christ."—I Peter 3 : 21.

It also shows the unity of the faith, and the fel-lowship of the true people of God, who, in the one baptism, profess their trust in the one Lord, and their acceptance of the one faith. "For by one spirit we are all baptized into one body."—I Cor. 12 : 13. Is not this impressive ordinance, therefore, a proclamation of the great cardinal doctrines of the gospel?

NOTE 1.—The beauty, impressiveness, and general effect of the sacred rite of baptism are not a little affected by the manner of its administration. It should be so carefully arranged, and performed with such propriety that no mistakes could occur, on the part either of the candidate or the administrator, to excite any other emotions, on the part of spectators, than those of reverence and devotion. Great haste and all excitement should be avoided, and all infelicities carefully guarded against. If the administrator be calm, self-possessed, acting under a sense of the importance and solemnity of the occasion, the candidate will usually be calm and free from agitation. The moral force of the ordinance, somewhat to the candidate, and largely to observers, depends on the dignity and propriety of its administration.

NOTE 2.—Baptism is usually administered by ordained *ministers*. And this is proper, regular, and orderly. But should occasion require, and the Church so direct, it would be equally valid if administered by a deacon or any private member selected for that service. The validity depends on the character and profession of the candidate, and not on that of the administrator. As to the qualifications of administrators the New Testament is silent, except that they were disciples. Nor need the churches deprive themselves of the ordinances because an ordained minister is not obtainable, as they, unwisely, often do.

NOTE 3.—The question has often arisen, in receiving to membership in our churches persons who have been *immersed* by ministers not themselves immersed, Is such baptism valid? or, should they be rebaptized in order to admission? In the South and Southwest our churches quite generally insist on rebaptism in such cases ; at the North, East, and West they do not. It has been almost universally conceded that the *validity* of baptism depends on the character of the candidate, and not on that of the administrator. If the candidate has received the ordinance properly administered in good conscience, in obedience to Christ, and on a profession of faith in Him, giving evidence of genuine conversion at the time, such baptism cannot be invalidated, whoever may have performed the ceremony.

NOTE 4.—Both ordinances are usually administered on Sunday, and commonly each month, particularly the Supper. But both the time when and the place where they shall be observed, are in the discretion of the Church, as circumstances may require.

NOTE 5.—Baptism, strictly speaking, is not to be *repeated*. But cases may occur in which it had been administered in form to candidates, who, at the time, as subsequently appeared, had not exercised a saving faith in Christ, and had not made an intelligent confession of such faith. In such cases baptism may be repeated, when the candidate becomes duly qualified. This would be rebaptizing in form, but not in fact, since, in the former case, a lack of faith made the act invalid. Such cases seldom occur, and, when they do, can be mutually adjusted by the candidate and the Church.

II. THE LORD'S SUPPER

The Eucharist, or Lord's Supper, is the other ordinance established by Christ, and ordained to be observed in His churches till the end of the time. It has equal simplicity and impressiveness with baptism, but holds a very different relation to the economy of grace, and the order of the Church; and as a teaching ordinance represents a different phase of vital doctrine. This, too, perhaps still more than baptism, has been the occasion of heated and often of bitter controversy among the professed followers of Christ, through the ages of Christian history.

1. *Its Institution*

The Supper was instituted by our Lord during, or at the close of, the last paschal supper which he observed with His disciples, on the evening before He suffered. It is thus described: " As they were eating, Jesus took bread and gave thanks, and brake, and gave it to the disciples, and said, Take, eat; this is my body, which is broken for you; this do in remembrance of me. And He took the cup, and gave thanks, and gave it to them, saying, Drink ye all of it; for this is my blood of the New Covenant, which is shed for many for the remission of sins. This do ye, as oft as ye drink it, in remembrance of me. For as oft as ye eat this bread, and drink this cup, ye proclaim the Lord's death till He come."— Matt. 26 : 26–28; Mark 14 : 22–26; Luke 22 : 14–20; I Cor. 11 : 23–26.

It will be noticed that in the various accounts of the institution there is a substantial agreement, with slight verbal differences. But each of the added sentences gives additional interest and impressiveness to the scene. It was at the close of, or immediately following, the passover supper, which was the seal of the Old Dispensation, now passed away, and sanctified by the sacrifice of the paschal lamb, that Jesus inaugurated His own memorial, which should be a seal of the New Dispensation, and a memorial of the sacrifice of the Lamb of God, who taketh away the sins of the world. The sad, tender, and sacred associations of the time and the place have all passed into history, and are reproduced in the hearts of all true and loving disciples, as they surround the table of their Lord.

2. *Its Administration*

The Supper is a provision of bread and wine—the *loaf*, and the *cup*—as symbols of Christ's body and blood, partaken of by the members of the Church assembled, to commemorate His sufferings and death for them, and to show their faith and participation in the merits of His sacrifice. The loaf is to be *broken*, and the wine to be *poured*.

Usually this is observed either at the close of a preaching service, or as a special service on Sunday afternoon, when more time and more prominence is given to it, though fewer usually attend at that time. Occasionally it is observed in the evening, being, as some think, a more appropriate time for a supper, but less favorable for the attendance of the members. If held as a distinct service, it is preceded with singing, prayer, reading the Scriptures, and brief remarks. If as a supplementary service, the introduction would be much abridged.

The pastor breaks the bread, and fills the cups in order, preceding each with a brief prayer of thanksgiving, as did the Lord, and passes the plates and cups in order to the deacons, who distribute to the members. It is customary for the deacons and pastor to partake after all the others are served.

Some ministers seem to lose sight of the real purpose of the service, or else lack the spirit of the occasion, and talk during the exercises. After very brief remarks to introduce the ordinance, and the equally brief prayer of thanksgiving, complete silence should prevail; a silence which the attendants, in passing the elements, should be careful not to break. It is presumption and folly for the pastor to draw the thoughts of the worshipers to himself, when they should remember only Him whose symbolic body is broken, and whose symbolic blood is shed. "This do, in remembrance of me."

It is an almost universal custom among our churches to take a collection at the close; "the offering for the sick and needy," of which the deacons are the custodians and almoners. It is also a well-nigh unvarying custom to close with singing, in imitation of Jesus and the Apostles; "and when they had sung a hymn, they went out into the Mount of Olives."

3. *Its Obligation*

It is a sacred privilege for every disciple to remember his Lord in the observance of the Supper, and it is his solemn duty as well. Few signs more effectually tell of a spiritual decline in the individual soul or in the Church than a neglect of the sacred Communion. It is the duty of every believer to be baptized, and the duty of every baptized believer to commemorate the dying love of his Lord at the Supper. "Take, eat; drink ye all of it." "Divide it among yourselves." "Do this in remembrance of me." Such were the words of

Jesus Himself. Let no disciple who loves his Lord lightly esteem or neglect this sacred rite.

Sometimes negligent Christians attempt to excuse their failures by saying there are unworthy members present, or that some member has done something wrong. That is no excuse. If Judas himself were present, it should keep no one else away. "This do in remembrance of *me*," not in remembrance of some one else deemed unworthy of the place. The communion is not with each other, save incidentally, but each one with his Saviour, who has promised to be present. Few Christians ever plead such excuses until their own hearts, and perhaps their lives likewise, are far out of the way. A neglect or misuse of the Supper not only reveals but produces spiritual derangement and decay. It was for this reason the Apostle reproved the Corinthians, when he wrote, " For this cause many are weak and sickly among you, and many sleep."—I Cor. 11 : 30.

4. *Its Subjects*

Who ought, and who have a lawful right to come to the Lord's Table will be seen by a careful study of the Scripture narratives. From these it is manifest that baptized believers, walking orderly in the faith of the Gospel, and in the fellowship of the Church, constitute the proper subjects for this privilege. And no others. Some have insisted on its having a wider scope; some even going so far as to hold that no limitations or restrictions whatever should be imposed on the privilege. This question is argued at length in another place.

Observe that our Saviour at the institution "sat down, and His Apostles with Him."—Luke 22 : 14. Here was a very restricted, and, so to say, close Communion. Neither His own mother, nor His brethren, nor the many relatives and friends who had followed Him, were invited to be present; for what reason we do not know, but they were not there. Only the twelve Apostles. He gave the bread and the cup to His disciples, and said, "Take this, and divide it among yourselves."—Matt. 26 : 26; Luke 22 : 17. He did not tell them to distribute it to others, nor invite others to come in, and partake of it. That little company in the upper chamber was substantially the incipient Church; and the Supper was with and for the Church alone.

5. *It is Commemorative*

It was designed to commemorate the death of Christ for human redemption, and to be a perpetual memorial in His churches and to His people of His sacrifice for men. The *loaf* and the *cup* represent " His broken body, and His shed blood," as sealing the covenant of grace. " This do in remembrance of me : " " This do, as oft as ye drink it, in remembrance of me."—1 Cor. 11 : 24, 25.

The paschal feast, and the slain lamb, commemorated the death of Egypt's first-born, and the deliverance of Israel from death and bondage. The Eucharist is sometimes called the Christian Passover, and is the fulfillment of that ancient and expressive type. It is when partaking of this sacred feast, the soul looks back to see the anguish of Him, who suffered as a lamb without spot and without blemish.

6. *It is Predictive*

The Supper not only points the Christian back to the sufferings of the Cross, but onward to the triumph and glory of Christ's second coming. It is a kind of mediator, a middle link, binding the shadowy past, the radiant future, and the joyous present in one. He who was dead is alive again; the sufferings of death could not hold Him. The past lays the foundation of the saint's hope, while the future holds the bright fruition. "But I say unto you, I will not drink henceforth of this fruit of the vine, until that day when I drink it new with you in my Father's Kingdom."—Matt. 26 : 29. "For as oft as ye eat this bread, and drink this cup, ye proclaim the Lord's death *till He come*."—1 Cor. 11: 26.

7. *It is Emblematic*

While it perpetuates the significance of the work of redemption by the death of Christ, the Supper is a teacher of vital Gospel doctrine. This, too, is a creed, a confession. It proclaims the love of Christ to the believer as a seal of the Covenant of grace, and a token of His faithfulness to them that trust Him. "This is the new Covenant in my blood."—Luke 22 : 20. It is not a communion of the partakers, one with the other, but of each one with Him whom it commemorates. It expressly declares their union with Him. "The cup of blessing which we bless, is it not the communion of the blood of Christ? The bread which we break, is it not the communion of the body of Christ?"—1 Cor. 10: 16. As intimate as is the relation between the loaf and the cup which we take to nourish our physical nature, so intimate is the fellowship of the partaker in the sacred rite with his remembered Lord. It expresses, inferentially indeed, a fellowship of all who partake with each other, though this is not the special object of the ordinance.

As they sit together in one place, with the same hopes, with common joys and sorrows, and a common interest in the same Lord, they, though many, constitute the one body, and Christ the one head. "For we, being many, are one bread, and one body; for we are all partakers of that one bread."—1 Cor. 10: 17. The Supper declares this vital doctrine : That the Christian's spiritual life and nourishment are derived from Christ. As natural bread and wine feed the body, so Christ, the bread of life, feeds the renewed soul. "For ye are dead, and your life is hid with Christ in God."—Col. 3: 3. "For even Christ, our passover, is sacrificed for us. Therefore let us keep the feast; not with old leaven, . . . but with the unleavened bread of sincerity and truth."—1 Cor. 5: 7, 8.

For, though the reception of the elements cannot convey grace to the soul, yet they teach the doctrine of effectual grace conveyed from Christ as the only and abounding fountain of grace. "I am the living bread which came down from heaven; if any man eat of this bread he shall live forever. And the bread that I give is my flesh, which I will give for the life of the world."—John 6: 51.

NOTE 1.—As in the case of baptism, the Supper is commonly and properly administered by the pastor, or some other ordained and accredited minister. But should occasion require, and the Church so direct, it would be just as valid if served by a private member. A deacon, or any devout member, could, with propriety, give thanks and distribute the elements. The churches should not deprive themselves of these means of grace, nor fail to remember their loving Lord for want of a clergyman. Baptists are not such sacramentarians as to suppose the ordinances invalid unless ministered and made holy by priestly hands.

NOTE 2.—The deacons usually and properly distribute the elements. But any member can be called on for that service, should occasion require, and the service would be just as lawful, valid and proper.

NOTE 3.—The doctrine taught by the Roman Church, and some other communions of the "*real presence*"—that is, that, after consecration by the priest, the bread and wine do actually become the very body and blood of Christ—is to be held as an absolute falsehood, a most pernicious error, and a monstrous absurdity.

NOTE 4.—When Jesus therefore said, "this is my body," and "this is my blood," He did not mean, and could not have intended, it in a literal sense, since His body and His blood at that moment were not in the loaf and cup, but in His corporeal person. He must, therefore, have meant what Protestant Christendom holds, generally, that He did mean, namely, that these elements *represented* His body and blood.

There is, therefore, no transubstantiation, or change of elements, and the bread and wine, when received by the communicant, are literally the same as before their use and distribution, and nothing different.

NOTE 5.—Nor is there any such thing as a *consecration* of elements in the Supper. Jesus did not bless the bread and the cup at the institution.* He blessed God, not the bread; that is, He gave thanks, as in one record it is rightly rendered.— Luke 22 : 19. The minister's part, therefore, is to thank God for the elements, and for the glorious realities they represent and ask His blessing on them as applied to a sacred use.

NOTE 6.—The "hand of fellowship" is usually given to new members at this service, just before the distribution of the elements. This act is simply a fraternal welcome, and has no other significancy; it does not make them members, but only recognizes their membership, already effected by vote of the Church.

NOTE 7.—It has been the prevailing custom for the pastor, before the ordinance, to give an invitation for "members of sister churches," or "members of churches of the same faith and order," or "members of other Baptist churches," who might be present, to remain and partake with them. But some pastors give no invitation at all. It is not, however, the right of the pastor to give or to withhold any invitation, except as the Church directs. It is the prerogative of the body to decide that question. The pastor should assume no responsibility in the matter, but let it all rest with the Church. He is their servant, not their master, in these matters.

NOTE 8.—Strictly speaking, however, the *privileges* of a Church are coextensive with the *authority* of the Church. A right to the communion, therefore, is limited to those over whom the Church exercises the right of discipline; that is.

---

* The pronoun "it" is not in the Greek text, and is improperly supplied in two of the records by the translators. This, however, is corrected in the New Version.

its own members. Consequently, if the members of sister churches are invited to partake, it is an act of courtesy proffered, and not a right allowed. This rule would of itself forbid a general, open, or free communion, since that would bring in persons whose characters the Church could not know, and whom, if they were unworthy, the Church could not discipline or exclude.

NOTE 9.—It often happens that members of Pedobaptist churches, or other persons not entitled to the privilege, being present at communion service, remain and receive the elements. No harm is done by this, and neither the pastor, nor any one else, need be disturbed by it. They were *not invited* —and could not lawfully have been—and probably knew it to be contrary to the custom of the churches. It would not be wise to ask them to retire, and thus disturb the service. But if the same individuals should often repeat the act, the pastor, or some judicious member, should take occasion privately, in a kindly way, to talk with and dissuade them from such a course, unless, indeed, they were prepared to unite with the Church in full communion.

NOTE 10.—Since the Supper is distinctively a Church ordinance, it is to be observed by churches only, and not by individuals, even though Church members; neither in private places, nor in sick-rooms, nor on social occasions, and not by companies of disciples other than churches, though composed of Church members. But a church may by appointment, and in its official capacity, meet in a private house, a sick-room, or wherever it may elect, and there observe the ordinance.

NOTE 11.—There is no Scriptural rule as to the frequency with which, nor the time or place at which, it shall be observed. The primitive Christians evidently kept this feast daily. "And they, continuing daily with one accord in the temple, and *breaking bread* from house to house, did eat their meat with gladness and singleness of heart."—Acts 2: 46. Subsequently it came to be a weekly service, at each public assembly.   By some it is still so observed.   Some churches observe it quarterly, some bi-monthly; but with our people it has come to be a general custom, especially in cities, towns and villages, to have the Communion monthly, and usually on the first Sunday in the month.   This is not so often as to impair its sanctity by frequency, and not so seldom as to allow it to pass out of mind and be forgotten.

NOTE 12.—A neglect of the Supper by Church members is a grave evil.   It betokens a decline of spirituality, and promotes it.   And it is usually without excuse.   If there be but one service in the month that a member can attend, that service should be the Communion; and if there be but one other, that should be the Covenant Meeting.   Pastors and deacons will do well to watch with jealous care this index to the churches' vital piety, and strive to inspire the absentees with a sense of its importance, and their own duty in respect to it.   To disregard it is an indignity to Christ's ordinance, a breach of good order, and a violation of covenant obligations, which the Church should endeavor promptly to correct.   Some churches, by a rule of discipline, have each member visited, who is absent twice in succession, to learn the cause of such absence.   To a devout Christian it is a sacred privilege, which he would not willingly forego.

NOTE 13.—Pastors often blame their members for a neglect of the Supper more than they instruct them as to its nature, significancy, and claims.   The people should be well taught as to the meaning of the ordinance, and its true relation to their faith and spiritual life.

NOTE 14.—The objection to the "individual communion cups," and the practice of holding the bread till all are served is, that it tends to exalt the form over the spirit and make the service ritual rather than spiritual.

CHAPTER 6

CHURCH GOVERNMENT

Is there any particular form of Church government revealed in the New Testament? And if so, what is it?

These questions will be variously answered by Christian scholars and Bible students. Some hold that no specific form can be deduced from the sacred records, and that no one form is best suited for all people and for all places; and that it was purposely left for Christian wisdom and prudence, guided by experience, to decide that question. But the greater part believe that a specific form is at least outlined in the New Testament; and, naturally enough, each one believes the form with which he is identified is that divinely given form. It may be safely allowed that no one class or company of Christians has attained to all the truth, leaving all others exclusively in error; and it is a comfort to know that, however believers may differ in opinion as to any matter of doctrine or of duty, if with loving hearts they sincerely desire to know the right and do it, they are blessed of God. As Peter said at the house of Cornelius, we may say, "Of a truth I perceive that God

142

is no respecter of persons : but in every nation he that feareth Him, and worketh righteousness, is accepted with Him."—Acts 10 : 34, 35.

If, however, there be any definite plan plainly taught or clearly deducible from the words of Christ or His inspired Apostles, we should, if possible, ascertain that fact and be guided accordingly. Or if—what would be equivalent—we can ascertain how the Apostles, under the guidance of the Spirit, organized and ordered the churches they founded, with what regulations they were instituted, and what polity was impressed upon them, our questions will be substantially, and, it should seem, satisfactorily answered. Indeed, there appears to be light on the subject in this direction ; for though no formal plan of government is detailed, yet there are numerous incidental references in the Epistles which clearly disclose formative and conclusive facts in the case.

I. THREE PRINCIPAL FORMS

of Church government are in current use among the denominations :

1. The *Prelatical ;* in which the governing power is in the hands of prelates or bishops, and the clergy generally, as in the Roman, Greek, English, and most of the Oriental communions.

2. The *Presbyterian ;* in which the governing power resides in Assemblies, Synods, Presbyteries, and Sessions ; as in the Scottish Kirk, the Lutheran, and the various Presbyterian bodies.

3   The *Independent ;* in which the governing power rests entirely with the people, *i. e.,* the body of the members of each local Church, each being entirely separate from and independent of all others, so far as authority and control are concerned ; as among Baptists, Congregationalists, Independents, and some others.

Now, is either of these forms taught in the New Testament ?   And if so, which ?   And which best accords with the genius of the gospel, and with what we know of the constitution and government of the apostolic churches ?

Baptists claim that a Christian Church is a congregation of baptized believers associated by mutual covenant, self-governing, and independent of all others ; having no ecclesiastical connection with any other, though maintaining friendly and associational intercourse with all of like faith and order. It has no power to enact laws, but only to administer those which Christ has given.

The government is administered by the body acting together, where no one possesses a preëminence, but all enjoy an equality of rights; and in deciding matters of opinion, the majority bears rule. The pastor exercises only such control over the body as his official and personal influence may allow, as their teacher and leader and the expounder of the great Lawgiver's enactments.   His influence is paramount, but not his authority.   In the decision of questions he has but his single vote. His *rule* is in the moral force of his counsels, his instruction and guidance in matters of truth and duty, and also in wisely directing the assemblies whether for worship or business. Much less have the deacons any authoritative or dictatorial control over Church affairs. Matters of administration are submitted to the *body* and by them decided.

II. CHURCH INDEPENDENCY

As has been said, each particular and individual Church is actually and absolutely independent in the exercise of all its churchly rights, privileges, and prerogatives ; independent of all other churches, individuals, and bodies of men whatever, and is under law to Christ alone. The will and law of the great Lawgiver are to be found in the New Testament, which is the only authoritative statute book for His people.

This statement is broad and comprehensive, and needs not defence, but explanation only. That Independency is the true form of Church government, as opposed to Prelacy and Presbyterianism, will not now be argued, but is assumed, as accepted by all Baptists, taught in the New Testament, verified by history, and justified by the genius of the gospel itself. But all human liberty is under limitations ; strictly speaking it is not absolute.

How is Church Independence Limited?

1. The liberty which the independence of churches exercises is limited by the laws of Christ as ex-

pressed or clearly implied in the Scriptures. A Church is not a legislative body, but administrative only. It cannot make laws, but it is the interpreter of the laws of Christ; the interpreter for itself, not for others. Nor can others interpret laws for it. The opinions of the wise and good have their weight, but no man or body of men external to itself, has the right to become authoritative interpreters of the word of God to a Church, and compel submission to their *dicta*—to a Church, or indeed to an individual, even.

Churches may perform many unwise and unjustifiable acts. They may misapply or misinterpret, or openly do violence to both the letter and spirit of law. But there is no human tribunal to which they can be brought for trial and punishment, except that of public opinion. Others, in the exercise of their personal or Church liberty, may condemn their acts and disclaim all responsibility in connection with them; may withdraw all fellowship and intercourse from them. But farther than this they cannot go, except by the moral force of their dissent and condemnation. And it is fortunate that such is the case, since to crush liberty and destroy independency in the churches of Christ would be a greater calamity than to bear all the evils which may spring from a misunderstanding of the one, or a misuse of the other.

2. The independence of the churches is limited, so far as its corporate acts are concerned, or any matters of personal rights or legal equity may be in

question, by the laws of the State in which they are located. This, however, has reference only to the temporalities of Church life, and cannot touch any question of doctrine, worship, or Christian duty. Most churches, by an organized " society," or in some other way, hold relations to civil law, in order to enjoy its protection in rights of property. To this extent they are subject to civil authority, and both as bodies and as individuals they should be law-keepers and not law-breakers. But as to all matters of spiritual concern in questions of religious faith and practice, the State and civil law have no rights of control over, or interference with the churches in any manner whatever, except to protect them in the enjoyment of all their lawful privileges.

It may also happen that in the exercise of its ecclesiastical functions in acts of discipline or exclusion, a Church or even a Council may be charged with decisions which are defamatory in their nature, calculated to injure the reputation or interfere with the secular interests of the individual, and he may seek redress at the civil courts. Such occurrences have sometimes transpired, and under stress of circumstances, are liable to take place. Civil courts usually observe this rule when appealed to in ecclesiastical matters, viz.: that the established usages of any body of Christians have a right to be followed, and if these have been carefully observed and not transcended, the courts will not interfere. But if from passion, prejudice, or ignorance, these have been disregarded, and the precedents and customs of the denomination have been violated, the court may interfere to give relief, only so far, however, as to require that the case have a new trial, in which their own established rules and precedents shall be strictly observed.

3. By some it has been held, that, while each Church is independent in theory, its liberty is somewhat abridged by its relations to other churches, and because of that fellowship and comity which exists between them. By such it is claimed that the relation of each Church to the great body of churches is similar to the relation of each member of a Church to the body of members which constitute that Church ; and, therefore, as each member relinquishes something of his personal liberty on becoming a member, and consents to be subject to the authority of the body, so the individual Church does on becoming one of the general fellowship of churches. Or, they argue, to take another figure ; as each particular State, though in a sense sovereign and independent, yet has its independency limited by being a member of the federation of States, and submits in certain matters to be subject to the general government, while represented in it, so is it with a single Church in the federation of churches.

This condition of affairs has sometimes been called the *interdependence* of churches. Precisely what that term means is not easily explained. But it is safe to pronounce it a fiction. There is no such thing as interdependence in the sense of a limitation of the self-governing right and authority of a Church. And that is the sense in which their interdependence is asserted. One Church may be poor and need help from one that is rich ; or it may be in perplexity and need advice from one supposed to be more experienced — as the Church at Antioch sought counsel of the older and more experienced Church at Jerusalem, or as the churches in Macedonia and Achaia contributed to the poor saints in Judea. But these facts do not touch the question of polity or government ; their relations to each other in these respects remain the same. Fellowship and fraternal concord may be strengthened ; the helpfulness of the one and the gratitude of the other may be increased, but the one is none the more independent, nor the other any the less so, because of these friendly interchanges.

But this whole course of argument alluded to is fallacious and misleading, and the illustrations used are unauthorized, inapplicable, and contrary to the facts. There is no such relation subsisting between the various churches constituting a general fellowship as exists between the individual members of a single Church. No hint or intimation of any such similarity is found in the New Testament, where the constitution and polity of a Church is taught. There is no other and larger organization provided for, with officers, orders, and regulations, including many smaller ones, called churches, as its units. If this similarity of relation be insisted on, then we shall have this comprehensive confederacy of churches claiming authority over the individual churches, receiving, disciplining, and excluding them, and otherwise exercising powers similar to those exercised by the individual Church over its members. Admit so much, and we have prelacy or papacy at once, in spirit and in fact.

Nor is there any relation subsisting between the separate churches, which can be fitly compared to the union of States in a federal government. If it were so we should have a *de facto* Presbyterianism. This whole course of reasoning, if carried out to its logical results, would not leave a vestige of Church independency. The only limitation, the only check upon the exercise of Christian liberty required by the Gospel, is loyalty to Christ as King in Zion, fidelity to His truth, and a constant exercise of that kindly courtesy which is innate in the Gospel and essential to the true Christian life, whether individual or organic, whether personal, social, or official. This spirit dominant will give all the fellowship which churches need or can demand ; and all which a Scriptural polity can render or allow.

4. It is sometimes objected that Baptists are too independent, and that their liberty degenerates into license. Now, on calm reflection, all this must be denied. They cannot, as churches, be too independent, using that word in a true Christian sense. Nor can liberty become license.

Ignorant and foolish men may be charged with many wrong acts. They may practise injustice and oppression in the name of liberty, and under pre-

tence of independence. But liberty and independence are, at the very most, only the occasion, and
are in no sense to be made responsible for the evils
which perverse and wrong-headed persons perpe-
trate under the shelter of their name. Church independency has its peculiar liability to misuse and
abuse, but it cannot be shown that its difficulties
are any more numerous, or any more serious than
those to which other forms of Church government
are liable. Indeed, if this be the true, the divine
plan, then it is the best plan, with the fewest evils
and the most advantages. The defects lie not in
the plan, but in those who administer the government; and, as a matter of fact, it can be shown that
churches acting under the independent polity, actually suffer from fewer and less serious difficulties
than those subject to stronger and more centralized
governments.

5. The independence of a Church is limited by
the personal rights of its individual members. That
is to say, the liberty of the body to act cannot lawfully be used to infringe the lawful liberty of its
members. A Church, as a body, has no right to
violate the rights of its members in the exercise of
its authority. These rights need to be clearly defined and well understood on both sides. If the
morals of the member do not coincide with the
morals of the Gospel, the Church has the right to
put him away from it, if he cannot be reclaimed.
But the body cannot properly interfere with the
rights of faith, or conscience, on the part of the

individual. If his faith be judged heretical, and an element of discord, they can withdraw fellowship from him; but they can neither compel uniformity nor punish dissent—except by separation.

6. And still further, the liberty of a Church is limited by the terms of the great Commission, and by its divine institution, to the pursuits and the purposes contemplated in the Gospel. Whatever its members may do in their individual capacity as citizens and members of society, the Church as such must confine itself to the mission for which it was founded—the spread of the Gospel, and the advancement of the Kingdom of God in the world. It cannot become a corporation for mercantile or manufacturing pursuits; it cannot become a political organization; it cannot become a scientific or literary association. On all moral questions, however, the Church as a body, as well as its individual members, should be plainly pronounced and clearly understood as standing for the defence of virtue, purity and good order, since these are essential elements of Christianity. Also it should have an unmistakable record as an abettor and helper of good works, charitable and benevolent endeavors, since these are inherent in, and grow out of, the gospel. The Church cannot dictate what a member shall eat or drink or wear; what shall be his business or his pleasure. But if, in any of these matters, questions of morals and religion come to be involved to the reproach of truth and the Christian profession, then the Church has the right to interpose.

III. EVIDENCE OF IT

Wherein lies the proof that the primitive Church government was an *independency* ?

In Matthew, chap. 18 : 15–17, where our Saviour for the first time, and, with one exception, the only time, in His personal conversation, speaks of the *Church* distinctively, His recognition of it as the only source of ecclesiastical authority is positive and complete. In giving directions for the adjustment of difficulties among brethren and the pacification of their social disturbances, He first expounds their personal duties; but when He speaks of authoritative action, *that* belongs to the Church. And the Church's action is *final*. That action admits of no reversal and of no review. There was to be no court beyond or above the single Church. He recognized no hierarchy, no presbytery, no synod, no assembly, no council ; but " tell it to the Church." That ends the matter of appeal. " If he neglect to hear the Church, let him be unto thee as a heathen man and a publican."

The course pursued by the Church at Antioch, in Syria is suggestive. When a difficulty arose pertaining to the engrafting of Jewish customs upon a Christian polity, respecting which they were in doubt, they sent a delegation to the Church at Jerusalem, as being not only at the seat of the Jewish *cultus*, but of the earliest Christian knowledge as well, besides having in their fellowship the apostles. From this source, therefore, they would obtain authoritative instruction.—Acts 15. This deputation, including Paul and Barnabas, on their arrival did not appeal to any select company of officials, not even to the inspired Apostles; but to the *whole Church*, inclusive of these. " And when they came to Jerusalem they were received of the Church, and of the Apostles, and elders."—v. 4. After a full statement and discussion of the case, and an expressed opinion by James, the pastor of the Church, they agreed on what reply to make to the Church at Antioch. "Then pleased it the apostles, and elders, with the whole Church, to send chosen men of their own company to Antioch, with Paul and Barnabas."— v. 22. In addition to this delegation they sent letters also conveying their judgment in the case And these letters recognized the Church in its three estates. "The apostles and elders and brethren greeting, unto the brethren which are of the Gentiles in Antioch."—v. 23. And they added : "it seemed good unto us, being assembled with one accord." And "it seemed good to the Holy Ghost, and to us."—vs. 25–28.

One independent Church, wishing advice, sought counsel of another independent Church, in whose experience and wisdom they had more confidence than in their own. And the Church appealed to, in the exercise of their independence, gave the advice sought. Nor did the Apostles, though inspired, assume to dictate in this matter, or to act without the coöperation of the elders and brethren. Nor yet did the Apostles and elders assume to act alone; "all the multitude," and "the whole Church," were present to hear and act with their leaders.

The Apostles regarded and treated the churches as independent bodies, having the rights of self-government, without subjection to any other authority. They reported their own doings to the churches, and addressed their epistles to them, as to independent bodies, and not to a confederacy, including many distinct congregations; nor yet to any official representatives of these congregations. In communicating with them the Apostles recognized their right to choose their own officers, to admit, discipline, and exclude members; primary and fundamental rights, which, being conceded, imply all other rights necessary to a self-governing community, acting under divinely enacted laws. They also enjoined upon them, as the responsible and authoritative executives of this power, the exercise of these functions, especially in the discipline and exclusion of unworthy members.

And nothing could more distinctly or more emphatically declare what is here claimed, than the fact that the Lord, in the Apocalyptic Epistles, addressed specifically the individual churches of Asia, through the angels, or pastors of these churches. The counsels, warnings, reproofs and commendations are in each case for the particular Church addressed, as responsible, censurable, or commendable. They were not addressed as a combination, or system of churches, either hierarchical or synodical ; not as " the Church of Asia," but the *churches*, individual and separate.

MOSHEIM, the Church historian, says of the first century :

"In those primitive times each Christian Church was composed of the *people*, the presiding *officers*, and the *assistants* or deacons. These must be the component parts of every society. The principal voice was that of the people, or the whole body of Christians." "The assembled people therefore elected their own rulers and teachers." Of the second century, he adds: "One president or bishop presided over each Church. He was created by the common suffrages of the whole people." "During a great part of this century all the churches continued to be, as at first, *independent* of each other. Each Church was a kind of small independent republic, governing itself by its own laws, enacted or at least sanctioned by the people."—*Eccl. Hist. Cent. I. part I. Ch. II. secs. 5, 6; Cent. II. Ch. II. secs. 1, 2.*

GIESELER, in his Church history, speaking of the changes which occurred in ecclesiastical order during the second century, says :

"Country churches, which had grown up around some city, seem, with their bishops, to have been usually, in a certain degree, under the authority of the mother Church. With this exception, all the churches were alike independent; though some were especially held in honor, on such ground as their Apostolic origin, or the importance of the city in which they were situated."—*Ch. Hist. Period I. Div. I. Ch. 3 sec. 52.*

SCHAFF, in his history, says :

Thus the Apostolic Church appears as a free, independent, and complete organization; a system of supernatural divine life, in a human body. It contains in itself all the offices and energies required for its purpose. It produces the supply of its outward wants from its own free spirit. Instead of receiving protection and support from the secular power, it suffers deadly hatred and persecution. It manages its own internal affairs with equal independence. Of union with the State, either in the way of hierarchical supremacy or of Erastian subordination, the first three centuries afford no trace."—*Ch. Hist. Vol. I. sec. 45, p. 138. N. Y., 1871.*

WADDINGTON, on this subject, says:

"It is also true that in the earliest government of the first Christian society, that of Jerusalem, not the elders only, but the whole Church, were associated with the apostles. And it is even certain that the terms *bishop* and *elder* or presbyter, were in the first instance, and for a short period, sometimes used synonymously."—*Hist. of the Ch., p. 41*

ABP. WHATELY says of the primitive churches:

"Though there was one Lord, one Faith, and one Baptism for all of these, yet they were each a distinct independent community on earth, united by the common principles on which they were founded, by their mutual agreement, affection and respect."—*Kingdom of Christ, pp. 101–156. N. Y. Ed.*

DR. BURTON says:

"Every Church had its own spiritual head, or bishop, and was independent of every other Church, with respect to its own internal regulations and laws."—*Cited by Coleman, Primitive Christianity, p. 50.*

DR. BARROW says:

"At first every Church was settled apart under its bishops and presbyters, so as independently and separately to manage its own affairs. Each was governed by its own head, and had its own laws."—*Treatise on the Pope's Suprem. Works Vol. I. p. 662.   Col. Prim. Christ.*

DR. COLEMAN says:

"These churches, wherever formed, became separate and independent bodies, competent to appoint their officers and administer their own government without reference or subordination to any central authority or foreign power.   No fact connected with the history of the primitive churches is more fully established or more generally conceded."—*Prim. Christ'y Exemp. Ch. 4, sec. 4, p. 95.*

DR. FRANCIS WAYLAND says:

"The Baptists have ever believed in the entire and absolute independence of the churches.   By this we mean that every Church of Christ—that is, every company of believers united together according to the laws of Christ—is wholly independent of every other.   That every Church is capable of self-government; and that therefore no one acknowledges any higher authority under Christ, than itself; that with the Church all ecclesiastical action commences, and with it all terminates."   "The more steadfastly we hold to the independency of the churches and abjure everything in the form of a denominational corporation, the more truly shall we be united, and the greater will be our prosperity."—*Princ's and Prac's of Bap. Chs., pp. 178, 190.*

DR. DAVID BENEDICT, the Baptist historian, says:

"The doctrine of absolute Church independence has always been a favorite one with our people.   Under it they have greatly flourished, and very few have complained of its operation."—*Fifty Years among the Baptists, p. 399.*

That the apostolical churches, therefore, were independent in their form of government, seems to be clearly proven. Many prelatists, as well as others besides those here cited, concede this point. In this respect, therefore, and so far as their independency is concerned, Baptists are manifestly founded on the New Testament order of Church building and Church life ; and, so far, are true successors of the Apostles. Nor does it avail to urge objections to this independency, or magnify the difficulties to which it is liable. It can be shown that other forms have inherent in them even greater liabilities to misuse ; while this, if it were established by divine wisdom. must be the best fitted to its purpose, and is the one to be used and preserved.

CHAPTER 7

CHURCH DISCIPLINE

EVERY organization which proposes to work smoothly, and yet efficiently, must have certain rules and regulations to be followed; certain laws for the individual members to obey. Failing in this —either without laws or with laws disregarded—all effort will go wide of the mark, and all endeavors, instead of succeeding and furthering each other, will counteract and interrupt each other; confusion will ensue, the wisest designs be frustrated, and the best-laid plans become abortive. This is true everywhere. In the State, in the family, every association whether for business, politics, scientific, literary or art research or improvement, all must be regulated by *laws* adopted for the common good, to which obedience is to be rendered by the members. And the object sought to be attained must fail unless there be conformity to the laws by which the organization is bound together, and obedience to which constitutes its vital force.

There is no society to which these remarks apply more appropriately and with more emphasis, than to that one divinely constituted organization, the

" Society of Jesus," the Church of Christ.   It has its
laws, not human enactments, but divine.   They are
few and simple, not difficult to be understood or
obeyed.   " His commandments are not grievous;"
and on conformity to them, both by the Church as
a body, and by the individual members as well, depend the peace, harmony and efficiency of the society.   When these regulations fall into disuse, and
the good order of the body is neglected, it becomes
weak and inefficient, neither commanding the confidence of its own members, nor the respect of the
world.   It is true that mere *laws* are a dead letter
without the indwelling spirit of life in Christ Jesus.
But the indwelling spirit of life becomes effectual
only as it works to its purpose in harmony with
those laws given for its guidance.   Law and life!
Life and law!   Life to energize; law to guide.
This is the philosophy and the method of the uni-
verse, both in nature and in grace.

To some the word *discipline* has an unpleasant
sound.   It seems punitive.   It savors of transgression, conflict and punishment.   But Church Discipline is not to be taken in this narrow sense alone;
nor does it develop these unlovely features, except
where, by the culpable neglect of pastors and others,
it has fallen into decay, good order and the well-be-
ing of the body have been long disregarded, and
the Church has become a lawless and disorderly
company.   Then a very hasty, and possibly an in-
temperate effort to make matters right, without sufficient prudence and precaution, may develop dif-

ficulties. As chronic disorder and disregard of lawful regulations in every society tend not only to a decay of efficient action, but to the ultimate destruction of the society itself, and prepare for conflict, if a vigorous effort be made to reëstablish good order and the reign of law; so many a Church has declined even to imbecility, if not to death, by long neglect of judicious and healthful discipline. Many a Church has found serious trouble in reëstablishing a healthful order and discipline, after long-continued neglect and disorder. But many a Church has also found that a thorough course of Christian labor, and the reëstablishment of a healthful scriptural discipline has brought back to the body order and harmony, reinvigorated its wasted energies, has produced a better tone of practical piety, and become the precursor of a revival of religion.

Discipline, in its larger sense, means training, cultivation, improvement, according to prescribed rules; subordination to law; administration of government and submission to lawfully constituted authority; from *disco*, I learn ; *disciple*, a learner, one under discipline, taught and trained. Church discipline is sometimes distinguished as *formative* and *corrective;* the former having reference to culture, training and development according to Christian law, and the latter to the management of difficulties, and the correction of offenses as they arise in Church life and practice. It is to the latter, more especially, that attention is given in discussions on the subject and the latter is usually understood to be meant when Church discipline is mentioned. To this more particularly is attention here given. But this is not because formative and cultural discipline for edification and development is less important, but these ends are largely attained by instruction from the pulpit, the various departments of worship and the general activities of Christian life.

That corrective discipline may be carried to an unwise and an injurious extent is not denied; but the prevailing tendency among our churches is in another direction. It is to too great laxity, and not to too great severity. Pastors and official members find it easier to let things drift than to attempt the unpleasant task of correcting abuses. But pastors do not wisely forecast their own comfort, nor the honor of the Church, who do not strive to preserve the purity of the body while they keep out and cast out everything that can justly become a scandal to the Christian Church, or a disgrace to the Christian profession.

The Church is the school of Christ; let the school be controlled with strict, yet wise and kindly discipline, or the pupils will learn more of evil than of good, and anarchy and confusion will supplant good government. The Church is a family; let there be law and order in the household, tempered with tenderness and discretion, otherwise the family fails of its mission, and becomes a reproach rather than a blessing to society. The Church is the organic representative of the kingdom of Christ; unless law prevail in the kingdom and order be maintained, how shall the King be honored, the kingdom be advanced, or the world be blessed by its coming and triumph?

It is therefore of the utmost importance that a correct scriptural discipline be strictly maintained. The neglect of it fills a Church with evils which check the growth of piety, hinder the success of the Gospel, and reproach the Christian name, while from an injudicious and unscriptural exercise of it, more dissensions have arisen than perhaps from any other single cause. Every well-organized society has its regulations, in which each one, on becoming a member, acquiesces, to which he pledges his support, and by which he submits to be governed, so long as he shall belong to it; and leave it, if he ever does leave it, according to its stipulated forms.

A Christian Church is the most perfectly constructed society known to men, and its system of government the most simple and complete. As each member on entering it, solemnly covenants to maintain, defend and abide by these regulations, so he should consider himself bound by the most sacred considerations to honor and keep his covenant inviolate.

I. THREE LAWS OF CHRIST'S HOUSE

There are three laws of Christ's house, royal decrees, given by Him who is "Head over all things to the Church," which stand invested with all the sanctions of divine authority, and which, could they be known, loved and obeyed, if they did not absolutely prevent all offenses, would obviate the necessity for private labor and public discipline. They would make churches "households of faith," where Christians should abide "in the unity of the Spirit, and in the bond of peace." Green pastures where the flock should rest in safety, and feed with joy. Will not every Church member make them the guide of his life?

First law : for every disciple ; the law of Love. "A new commandment I give unto you, that ye love one another ; as I have loved you, that ye also love one another."—John 13 : 34. This, if strictly obeyed, would prevent all cause of grief and offense, either personally to brethren or publicly to the Church. It would prevent cold indifference to each other's welfare, unfounded suspicions, causeless accusations, jealousies, animosities, bitterness, hatred, and strife, and cause each to love the other "with a pure heart fervently."

Second law : for the offender ; the law of Confession. "If thou bring thy gift to the altar, and there rememberest that thy brother hath aught against thee, leave there thy gift before the altar, and go thy way; first be reconciled to thy brother, and then come and offer thy gift."—Matt. 5 : 23, 24. This law makes it obligatory on every one who supposes that a brother has aught against him, to go to such an one without delay and secure, if possible, a reconciliation. And this he must do, whether there be, in his opinion, just cause or not for that brother

to be offended; whether or not he has given occasion for offense. But knowing that a brother has
grief on his account, he must go and attempt a
reconciliation. Nor must he suppose that his gift
will be acceptable to God, while he is unreconciled
to man.

*Third law : for the offended; the law of Forgive-
ness.* "If thy brother trespass against thee, rebuke
him; and if he repent forgive him. And if he trespass against thee seven times in a day and seven
times in a day turn again to thee, saying, I repent, thou
shalt forgive him."—Luke 17: 3, 4. This law enjoins a
perpetual personal forgiveness of injuries; of injuries
repented of and confessed. It does not enjoin that
the often transgressor be held in the same esteem as
before, for that might be impossible. Nor does it
require that a Church should abstain from the exercise of a needed and healthful discipline, nor that it
should discontinue a course already begun because
the individual declares his repentance. In some
cases this may be done ; but instances not unfrequently occur when it is not required. In another
form, the substance of this law was affirmed by Jesus,
when, in answer to Peter's question as to how often
he should forgive a brother, He replied, " I say not
unto thee until seven times, but until seventy times
seven."—Matt. 18: 22. That is, constantly. But this
has no reference to Church action.

NOTE 1.—It is true that Jesus did not proclaim these stat-
utes for just the occasion for which, nor in just the relation
to each other, in which they have been placed here. But

they cover all the ground of social Christian intercourse, whether in or out of Church relations, and apply with pre-eminent fitness to that intercourse which may involve matters of discipline.

NOTE 2.—Some have mistakenly inferred that because perpetual personal forgiveness is enjoined by our Lord, therefore all corrective Church discipline is needless, if not out of place. This is doing violence to common sense and plain facts. Because a father is bound constantly to forgive an erring but penitent child, is that a reason why all family government should be abrogated, and the sinning child not be called to account for his repeated offenses? Certainly not.

NOTE 3.—An erring brother may not, and probably will not, be able to regain at once the confidence forfeited by his offense, and especially if his offense be repeated. Confidence lost is slowly restored. Nevertheless, if his repentance seem sincere he should be treated with hearty good will, and not be regarded with suspicion.

NOTE 4.—It is not always satisfactory or sufficient evidence of penitence that one says he is sorry. He must "do works meet for repentance," in order that the Church should be under obligation to restore him to its favor, particularly where the offense has been grievous, or oft-repeated.

II.   THE SCOPE OF DISCIPLINE

Unhappily, offenses do come, and these *royal decrees* are not always strictly observed. Hence the nature, scope and purpose of these administrative methods need to be well understood.

1. *The Object of Discipline*

The object and purpose of discipline is to prevent, restrain, or remove the evil that may exist, to en-courage and protect the right, and cherish the good, "for the edifying of the body of Christ," that it may be "perfect in love," and without reproach. It is not to gratify personal prejudice, or secure any selfish ends, but to reclaim the wandering, guide the wayward, and secure the best spiritual interests of each member, and the purity, good order, and efficiency of the entire body. That Church is always held in higher esteem by its own members, and more respected and honored by the world, where a high standard of Christian morals is maintained, and a jealous watch-care is exercised over the faith and conduct of its members.

2. *The Spirit of Discipline*

The justification and the effectiveness of discipline depend not a little on the spirit with which it is exercised. It must not be exercised in a spirit of arrogance, nor of dictation, nor of assumed superiority, much less of vindictiveness, but of fraternal solicitude, of gentleness and love. If the impression be given to the offender that there is a disposition to condemn and punish, the whole purpose is frustrated. Paul's injunction to the Galatians was, "Brethren, if a man be overtaken in a fault, ye which are spiritual restore such a one in the spirit of meekness; considering thyself lest thou also be tempted."—Gal. 6: 1. This should be a perpetual guide to the temper of Christian labor with erring disciples, and is worthy to be inscribed in gold on the walls of every Church; or, better still, written by the Spirit of God on every Christian heart. The work of *restoration* is to be *done*, and not neglected; but it is to be done in a spirit of meekness, with a sense of one's own liability to err.

3. *The Right of Discipline*

That churches have a right to exercise a watchful supervision over their members, to reprove them when erring, and withdraw fellowship from them when incorrigible, is a necessity arising from the very constitution of their organization. The right to exercise discipline inheres in the very nature of government, whether the government be in the hands of one, the few, or the many. This right was recognized by Christ and His Apostles, and was exercised by the first churches. "But if he neglect to hear the Church, let him be unto thee as a heathen man, and a publican."—Matt. 18: 17. "Now we command you, brethren, in the name of **our** Lord Jesus Christ, that ye withdraw yourselves from every brother that walketh disorderly, and not after the tradition which he received of us."—2 Thess. 3: 6. "A man that is a heretic after the first and second admonition, reject."—Titus 3: 10.

4. *The Duty of Discipline*

Not only has a Church the right to exercise discipline, in the milder forms of fraternal labor, for the removal of evils, but to the extreme of excision it is the imperative duty of every Church to administer this needed and salutary part of government. That Church is unfaithful to itself, to its members and to its living Head, that neglects it. Not that it should seek opportunity to find faults, or to deal with the weak and the wandering, but it should be faithful to do this when occasion calls for it. "If thy brother trespass against thee, rebuke him; and if he repent, forgive him."—Luke 17: 3. "Them that sin rebuke before all, that others also may fear."—1 Tim. 5: 20. "Wherefore come out from among them."—2 Cor. 6: 17; because "Whether one member suffer, all the members suffer with it."—1 Cor. 12 : 26. "I beseech you, brethren, mark them which cause divisions and offenses contrary to the doctrine which ye have learned, and avoid them."—Rom. 16: 17. "Therefore put away from among yourselves that wicked person."—1 Cor. 5 : 13.

5. *The Limit of Discipline*

The exercise of discipline is limited in its range, by the laws of Christ as applied to Christian faith and morals, kindly and generously interpreted, in the spirit of fraternal affection, and yet with fidelity to the purity of truth, and the honor of the Gospel. Also it is limited to such matters of covenant agreement as were understood by each member on entering the Church, as forming the rules and regulations of the body. Evidently it would not be expected that such matters as were purely personal to the individual, not violations of any law of the New Testament, not transgressions of Christian morals, nor yet of covenant obligations, should be deemed offenses for which discipline should be invoked.

Personal rights are to be held sacred, and no un-authorized yoke placed upon the necks of the dis-ciples ; no yoke but His. "Now I praise you, brethren, that ye remember me in all things, and keep the ordinances, as I delivered them to you."— I Cor. 11 : 2.

6. *The Result of Discipline*

Discipline has a positive and definite purpose. It is not an aimless and vagrant administration. Its design is to heal the offense, or remove the offender; the correction of the evil, or the expulsion of the evil-doer; so far, at least, as corrective discipline is concerned. So soon as the erring one can be in-duced to turn from his evil way, making acknowl-edgment of it, with promise of a better course, the labor with him is to cease, the proper result having been attained; that is, in all ordinary cases. Some exceptions may be hereafter mentioned. "If he re-pent, forgive him."—Luke 17 : 3.   "If he neglect to hear the Church, let him be unto thee as a heathen man and a publican."—Matt. 18 : 17.   "Purge out, therefore, the old leaven, that ye may be a new lump, as ye are unleavened."—I Cor. 5 : 7.

III.   AS TO OFFENSES

Offenses are usually considered as of *two* kinds, *private* and *public;* or *personal* and *general.* These terms do not very accurately define the distinction, or indicate the nature of the offenses themselves. Nor are these classes of evils very clearly defined, since they often run into each other. There are other terms which would perhaps more accurately express the two classes; but as these are in common use, they will be retained here.

It has been already intimated, that in the social relations of Church life, personal peculiarities on the part of some may appear, which to others are unpleasant and even offensive, but which can in no sense be amenable to discipline. Such are to be endured with patience, as disagreeable things in the family are borne with, and remedied, if remedied at all, by the moulding influence of kind and genial intercourse. Not every infelicity of character or of conduct is to be regarded as an occasion for disciplinary labor. Great wisdom and discretion are needed in order to judge, both when such labor shall be attempted, and how it shall be directed.

NOTE 5.—There are in most churches certain persons with so keen a scent for defects in others, and with such a stern, almost relentless, sense of judicial orthodoxy in matters of order, that they are always finding somebody who deserves to be disciplined. These severe censors of their brethren never seem so much at home as when actively engaged in bringing to justice some offender. Then they appear at their best. They are probably honest and conscientious, and mean only to guard the purity and good name of the Church. But they need watching and moderating. Not less deplorable is the influence of those who are opposed to all disciplinary action.

NOTE 6.—In judging of the gravity of offenses, the condition in which the offender is placed, the influences under which he acts, and the peculiar provocations that affect him,

are to be considered. One man may be much more guilty
for the same act than another, since he may have had fewer
incentives to evil, and more strength to withstand temptation.
All palliations should have due weight.

IV. PRIVATE OFFENSES

A private offense has reference to the personal
relations of individual members. It may not be
an act which scandalizes the Christian name, or
injures the Church as a body; but an injury done
—or claimed to have been done—by one member
vs another, intentionally or unintentionally, by
which his feelings are pained or in some way he
believes himself to have been wronged in person,
reputation, or estate. The offense is therefore
personal, and the matter rests between those two
members alone. Except that, when it becomes
known, others may become interested in it or affected by it.

So long as such matters of difficulty are treated
as personal and kept private—that is between the
parties themselves concerned, and are not made
public, or brought to the notice of the Church,
they are reckoned as private offenses; but when,
in any case, they cannot be settled privately, they
are referred to the Church to be adjudicated, then
they become public offenses.

V. THEIR TREATMENT

The course of treatment in all cases of private
offenses is the one prescribed by our Saviour, and

to be found in Matthew 18 : 15–17. The course there prescribed is to be followed; and any departure from that rule is itself an offense deserving notice. Also any deviation from it would modify subsequent action which the Church might take if appealed to in the case. This course consists of three steps, and the final results.

First step. The one who considers himself injured must go to the offender, tell him his cause of grief, and between themselves alone adjust the matter, if possible, and settle the difficulty. "If thy brother shall trespass against thee, go and tell him his fault between thee and him alone; if he shall hear thee, thou hast gained thy brother."

NOTE 7.—It is thus made obligatory on the injured or offended one, to go to the offender, and not the reverse. This is wisely ordained, since, although the offender is bound by every consideration of justice to go to the offended brother, and confess his sin, yet possibly he may not be aware of the evil he has done, or he may be so perverse and evil-minded as to be unwilling to do justice to an injured brother. But the offended one, having done no wrong himself, would be likely to go in a kindly and forgiving temper of mind, prepared to "gain a brother." Moreover, for him to take the initiative in the movement would be likely to moderate any exasperation he might feel under a sense of wrong suffered.

NOTE 8.—This rule requires that the interview should be between themselves alone. No other persons should be present, either to help or to hinder, or to spread abroad the knowledge of the trouble. No fear or false delicacy must prevent his telling the offender his fault. He must tell it to him, but to no one else, till this step has failed to effect a reconciliation. He must not tell it in the presence of a third person ; nor must he plead that because the other is the offender, therefore the first step must be taken by him. And his object must be to "gain his brother," not to humiliate, accuse, or condemn him.

Second step. If the previous step shall fail of success, then the offended one must take one or two of the brethren with him. Seek another interview with the offender in their presence, and with the aid of their united wisdom and piety hope to succeed where he himself alone had failed. He is not to abandon the effort with the failure of the first step, nor throw the responsibility of further effort on the offender. "But if he will not hear thee, then take with thee one or two more, that in the mouth of two or three witnesses every word may be established."

NOTE 9.—The offended one must not make the matter public with the failure of the first attempt, nor must he abandon it, unless, indeed, he has "gained his brother;" nor tell it to any, except the "one or two more."

NOTE 10.—The object of taking the "one or two more," is chiefly that the Church, should the matter come before them, may have witnesses, and not depend on the complainant, whose testimony very likely would be contradicted by the defendant. They could witness to the temper and spirit of the two, and to the facts, so far as ascertained. Moreover, they could act as mediators between the parties, and possibly aid in a friendly adjustment of the trouble, without an appeal to the Church.

Third step. Should the second attempt be in like manner unsuccessful, and no reconciliation be effected, then the offended one must tell the whole matter to the Church, and leave it in their hands to be disposed of, as they shall judge best. His personal efforts failed ; his effort, with one or two for witnesses and helpers, was unsuccessful ; he has but one other appeal; that is to the Church. And this is ultimate. " And if he shall neglect to hear them, tell it unto the Church."

NOTE II.—Having gone so far, the effort to gain a brother and to remove an offense is not to be abandoned. The offended brother is not to say he is sufficiently vindicated by the witness of the " one or two more," and he will drop the matter. The end is not yet gained. The influence is not salutary on either of the brethren nor on the body, to leave it incomplete. The Church is the final arbiter, and its decision is to be invoked. The matter is not a trifle now, even if it were such at the first; let the voice of the Church be heard.

NOTE 12.—When told to the Church its *private* character disappears, and it becomes a *public* offense, to be treated as such. Both parties are then in the hands of the body, to await and abide by their decision. No further action on the part of either is to be expected, except for the offended to make his statement, and the offender to make his defense; as to both of which the " one or two more " are witnesses.

The result. The Church is to pass the final sentence, after a full and fair hearing of the whole case. There is no higher tribunal, and no further appeal. The great Head of the Church has directed what that decision shall be, if the offender be still unmoved and incorrigible. The object all the way through is to " gain a brother." Failing in this he is to be no longer a brother. As he will not show a brother's spirit, and will not act a brother's part, he is to be removed from the fellowship of the brotherhood. " And if he neglect to hear the Church, let him be unto thee as a heathen man and a publican."

NOTE 13.—Let it be borne in mind that the mere *neglect* to hear the complainant, brings it before the "one or two more," and a neglect to hear the " one or two more," brings the matter before the Church; and a *neglect* to " hear the Church" ends in exclusion. No offensive deportment, no other insubordination to authority, no vindictive spirit on the part of the accused, is necessary to secure this final sentence, but simply a " neglect to hear." That becomes a refusal to submit to lawfully constituted authority, as well as a violation of voluntarily accepted covenant obligations when admitted to its fellowship.

NOTE 14.—We have, in this language of our Lord, the only time and place where He is recorded to have spoken of Church action, a clear and explicit recognition of the authority and independency of the local Church. The case was not to be appealed to any priest or hierarch, to any bishop or presbytery, to any council or conference or any other representative body; but to " the Church," whose decree was to be final in the case.

Observe. It should be solemnly impressed on the minds of pastors, deacons, and every member of every Church that the preceding course for the treatment of personal difficulties in Church relations was prescribed by Christ as a positive law for His churches, always and everywhere ; and that it abides invested with all the sanctions of divine authority ; that it cannot be abrogated, nor departed from with impunity. If every Church would require a strict and invariable compliance with its requirements, it would greatly lessen the number of personal difficulties, and make less harmful those which are inevitable. On pastors, as the teachers and leaders of the churches, largely rests the responsibility of seeing that these positive, wise, and salutary provisions are complied with.

NOTE 15.—Let it be repeated with emphasis that to effect its best, its true results, all discipline is to be administered in love and meekness—in the spirit of the Master, with the desire and the manifest design to win an erring brother rather than to punish an offending member.

NOTE 16.—Although the divine law requires that the offended shall first seek the offender, yet any one who is at all aware that he has grieved or offended another, should without delay seek the aggrieved, and by such efforts as he may be able to make—explanations and acknowledgments—remove, if possible, the cause of grief. Let him first be reconciled to his brother, then offer his gift. Even though he may claim that he has not injured his brother, yet if that brother believes he has, let him be sure to remove, if possible, such an impression.

NOTE 17. — If a member attempts to bring before the Church, or in any other way make public, any matter of private grief or offense, before he has fully pursued the above course, according to the Gospel rule, he makes himself an offender thereby—subject to labor and discipline.

NOTE 18.—If members become involved in personal difficulties, and make no effort to settle or remove them, or if they take any other than the scriptural course, they become themselves offenders against the Church, and subject to its discipline.

NOTE 19.—When personal difficulties are known to exist, which the parties themselves cannot, or will not settle, the officers or other members should use their best endeavors to reconcile them privately, and avoid, if possible, the publicity of bringing them before the Church.

NOTE 20.—But if all private endeavor fails to heal such difficulties the case should be taken before the Church, and treated as a public offense. The continuance of such disturbing elements is greatly injurious to the prosperity of the body. The old leaven should be purged out that the body of Christ may be wholly a new lump.

NOTE 21.—There may be instances where wrongs are perpetrated, but the member who is wronged is unwilling to pursue any course of labor with the offender, or to make any complaint, or take any notice of it, yet the Church, knowing the facts and considering its own character compromised or its welfare periled by the case, may find it necessary to take it up and act upon it.

NOTE 22.—When a member refers any private difficulty to the Church, which he is unable to settle, he should then leave it entirely in their hands, and be satisfied with such disposition as they may think wise to make of it; neither complaining of the result, nor attempting to prosecute it further.

NOTE 23.—Nothing can properly be considered a reasonable cause of offense or just ground for discipline, but what is manifestly contrary to the Scriptures. Members may see many things in others which they dislike—personal idiosyncrasies perhaps offensive, but which cannot be justly considered subjects for complaint, or ecclesiastical censure. They are matters for Christian forbearance, to be endured, if they cannot be corrected in some other way.

NOTE 24.—And yet should one, on uniting with the Church, understandingly agree to covenant pledges, or administrative regulations, which afterward he may come to regard as extra-scriptural and unpleasant, he must still submit to them according to the promise, or bear the discipline which their violation imposes.

NOTE 25.—Nothing can be considered a just and reasonable cause for the withdrawal of fellowship, and exclusion from the Church, except it be clearly forbidden in, or manifestly contrary to, the Scriptures, and what would have prevented the reception of the individual into the Church had it existed at the time and been persisted in. Even these do not usually lead to disfellowship, providing they be confessed and forsaken.

VI.   PUBLIC OFFENSES

A public offense is one claimed to be a breach of Christian morals, or a violation of covenant faith or duty. It is not an offensive act committed against an individual, of which that individual might complain. It is an injury to the cause of piety, a scandal to the Christian name and profession.

In such a case, one member is no more interested in or wronged by it than another. The whole body is equally concerned and equally responsible. And while the " steps of private labor " taken by any member in such a case would be appropriate, and might be effective, yet it is obligatory on no one more than another to take them. And since there is a natural indisposition to do it, such personal effort usually goes undone, and it is left to the Church, or its official members, to move in the matter. For instance, if it be credibly reported that a member is addicted to intemperance, or profanity, or dishonesty, or if he have departed from the faith, or violated the order of the Church in some grave matter, these are considered general, or public offenses, since in no sense are they personal or private in their commission or bearing.

VII.   THEIR CHARACTER

It would be impracticable to attempt to specify all possible occasions when labor might be called for in this line of irregular Christian conduct. The Church must judge each individual case on its merits, and decide whether discipline be needed, and if so, to what extent. But in the Epistolary writings we have not only a watchful disciplinary supervision of the Church enjoined, but various occasions for the exercise of discipline specified. The following may here be mentioned as prominent :

1. *False Doctrine*

Holding and teaching doctrines fundamentally false, contrary to the law of God, as understood by the body, and subversive of their accepted faith. "If any man preach any other Gospel unto you, than that ye have received, let him be anathema." —Gal. 1 : 9. "If there come any unto you, and bring not this doctrine, receive him not into your house, neither bid him God speed."—2 John 10.

2. *Disregard of Authority*

When a member refuses to submit to the requirements of the Church, and thus becomes insubordinate to lawfully constituted authority. "But if he neglect to hear the Church, let him be unto thee as a heathen man, and a publican."—Matt. 18 : 17.

" Now we exhort you, brethren, warn them that are unruly."—1 Thess. 5 : 14.

3. *Contention and Strife*

Where a member is factious, foments discords, stirs up strife and becomes a leader of party, disturbing or destroying the peace and harmony of the body. " I beseech you, brethren, mark them which cause divisions and offenses contrary to the doctrines which ye have learned, and avoid them."—Rom. 16 : 17. " But if any man seem to be contentious, we have no such custom, neither the churches of God."—1 Cor. 11 : 16

4. *Immoral Conduct*

This takes a wide range and embraces many particulars. Such acts and practices as are inconsistent with the honor, rectitude and purity which the Gospel inculcates and requires. It is on the theory that the Christian Church must have a higher standard of moral virtue than the world holds essential. Otherwise how can it be the light of the world and the salt of the earth ? " But now I have written unto you, not to keep company, if any man that is called a brother be a fornicator, or covetous, or an idolater, or a railer, or a drunkard, or an extortioner, with such a one, no, not to eat."—1 Cor. 5 : 11.

5. *Disorderly Walk*

Such a course of conduct and habit of life as brings the Christian profession into disrepute, and becomes

subversive of the established faith and good order
of the Church.   It does not necessarily imply im-
morality of conduct.   "Withdraw yourselves from
every brother that walketh disorderly, and not after
the tradition which he received of us."—2 Thess.
3 : 6.   "There are some which walk among you
disorderly, working not at all."—2 Thess. 3 : 11.

6. *A Covetous Spirit*

Cases where members will not contribute of their
means, according to their evident ability for the
support of the gospel, or for other Christian work;
throwing heavy burdens on others, of which they
refuse to bear their proportion.   For while the
Church cannot compel liberality, nor dictate what
its members shall give, but leaves all offerings to be
free-will, yet liberality is required, and any one who
refuses to share an equality of responsibility while
enjoying an equality of benefits, exposes himself to
reproof and discipline.   "For this ye know, that no
covetous man, who is an idolater, hath any inheritance in the kingdom of Christ."—Eph. 5 : 5.   "If
any man that is called a brother, be covetous, with
such a one no, not to eat."—1 Cor. 5 : 11.

7. *Arrogant Deportment*

When a member, in a spirit of arrogance and
pride, assumes authority, and affects superiority, un-
dertaking to domineer and rule the Church.   "I
wrote unto the Church, but Diotrephes, who loveth
to have the preëminence among them, receiveth us

not; wherefore, if I come, I will remember his deeds."—3 John 9, 10.

8. *Going to Law*

The going to law with brethren "before unbelievers," and the prosecution of fellow-members at civil tribunals, instead of private and peaceable arbitration "before the saints." This was severely censured by the Apostle, and deserves to be made a cause of discipline in every Church where it takes place. "I speak to your shame; brother goeth to law with brother, and that before the unbelievers. Now, therefore there is utterly a fault among you, because ye go to law with one another. Why do ye not rather take wrong? Why do ye not rather be defrauded?"—1 Cor. 6: 5–7.

NOTE 1.—Observe: where in these Epistolary citations, the churches are enjoined, with disorderly walkers, and evil persons, "not to eat," the evident meaning is not to eat with them in the celebration of the Supper. Not to commune with them. And when it is said, "from such withdraw yourselves," reference is evidently had to Church fellowship, and not to social intercourse.

NOTE 2.—The Apostle manifestly did not purpose to give a list of disciplinable offenses, and those cited above are only such incidental cases as occurred in the churches, with respect to which he had occasion to give instruction. But they show conclusively two things. *First:* that purity of faith and doctrine, and virtue and good order in the management of Church-affairs, were matters of importance, which they needed to understand. *Second:* that each Church was to be held responsible for a faithful and earnest administration of its government, so as to keep itself true to the law and the kingdom of Christ.

NOTE 3.—Whatever may be thought of the relative importance of some of the faults of christian character mentioned above, as compared with others, and still others that might be named, they are all blemishes and defects which should, by a judicious treatment, be corrected; they constitute stumbling-blocks to unbelievers, and a dangerous example for other disciples. They be all evils. Therefore put away the evils, or the evil-doers.

VIII. THEIR TREATMENT

In the treatment of public offenses, the proper course of labor and discipline would be substantially as follows :

It must, however, be borne in mind that various cases have some peculiar features, and require peculiar treatments. The treatment of the case will therefore vary somewhat with the circumstances. Those who have the direction of them must be familiar with the general principles which apply; if beyond these some way-marks can be given, wise and prudent men need not go far astray in their arrangements.

1. The first member who has knowledge of the offense should, the same as in private cases, seek the offender, and, if possible, remove the difficulty. True, he is under no special obligation to do this simply because he chanced to be the first to learn the fact. But if he can win a brother from his evil way, and remove a reproach from the Church, such would be a work of faith and a labor of love, with which any Christian might feel

greatly satisfied.   This personal labor should be undertaken because each member of the body suffers in any wrong inflicted on the body, and because such personal efforts are often the most effectual. Should there be many individual efforts, by many members at the same time, aiming at the same end, so much the more effectual would it be.

2. But if no one can or will pursue this course of personal private labor, or if such a course should prove unsuccessful, then should the one who has knowledge of it consult the pastor and deacons—or if, as in some churches, there be a prudential committee for such purposes, refer it to them—and leave it to their judgment as to what further course should be taken.   If they will not notice the matter, this brother could bring it up at the next business Church meeting.   But even then it would be well not to give names and facts, but say a case deserved attention, and ask that a committee be appointed, to which facts would be referred.   All such cases should be kept out of the Church, and managed privately, so long as there seems hope of an effectual settlement by that means.

3. The Church, having formal knowledge of the matter, would, perhaps, as the most kindly fraternal "first step" in their movement, visit him, hear his explanation and excuse, and ascertain his purpose in the case.   They might, indeed, without transcending the limits of propriety, at once cite him before the body to answer for himself, disprove the charges, or make his defense.

But this course at the beginning seems a little more judicial and harsh than the visit of a committee, and a brother "out of the way" might not accept it too readily. But the case should ultimately come before the Church, where the offender shall know the charges, hear the witnesses, and be allowed to answer for himself.

4. If a committee act in the case, they should act in the name of the Church, and with their authority; but they should go in the spirit of meekness and love, with the desire uppermost to win a brother. If the offender will not appear before the Church, by that refusal he sets its authority at defiance, and the body must decide how long they will bear with his insubordination. If he be so situated that he cannot appear before them, they must depend on the report of a committee, and act according to their best judgment in the matter.

5. If, in any case of discipline, and at any stage of the proceedings, the accused brother disproves the charges, or, in any ordinary case, if he admits them, confesses the wrong, makes suitable acknowledgment and reparation, so far as possible, together with promise of amendment, this should be deemed sufficient, and the case be dismissed. The purity of the Church is vindicated, its authority sustained, and an erring brother is won back to Christ, and to the fellowship of His people.

6. But if, after patient, deliberate and prayerful labor, all efforts fail to reclaim the offender, then, however painful the necessity, they must withdraw

from him their fellowship. He has refused to hear them, and must be put away. With such a one, "no, not to eat." Better to lose many members than that the government and good order of the Church should be prostrated and trampled on and its good name become a by-word. When a course of discipline has been inaugurated, it must be carried on till the offender is reclaimed, or excluded.

NOTE 4.—Any one tried by a Church should be allowed every opportunity, both as to time, place and circumstance, to vindicate himself. The very justice of Christ's house should incline to mercy. It should be made manifest that the object is not to punish, but to reclaim.

NOTE 5.—Every person so tried has a right to demand and receive copies of all charges against him, the names of the accusers and witnesses, both of whom he shall have the privilege of meeting face to face, hearing their statements, bringing witness on his side, and answering for himself before the Church itself as the ultimate and authoritative tribunal.

NOTE 6.—All persons on trial, or having been excluded, have a right to receive authenticated copies of the records of all proceedings held by the Church in their cases.

NOTE 7.—It would not be proper for a member on trial to bring any person as his advocate who was not a member of the body to plead his case, without special permission from the Church to do so. The whole matter pertains to the Church alone, and outside parties have no right of interference. Moreover, it would be strange if the entire body should be so swayed from right and justice as not to give any member under accusation a reasonable hearing and an equitable treatment. Such a case might be possible, but would not be likely to occur.

NOTE 8.—In every case of exclusion the charges against the member, and the reasons for his exclusion, should be carefully and accurately written out, and entered on the records of the Church, the excluded member to receive an authentic copy if he desires it.

NOTE 9.—It is customary, also, to notify the individual that fellowship is withdrawn from him by sending him a copy of the reasons for the final action in the case, or otherwise, at the option of the clerk, as directed by the body.

NOTE 10.—The Church should not commence disciplinary proceedings, nor even entertain a charge against a member, unless the evidence be such as to make the truth of the charge highly probable, if not absolutely certain.

NOTE 11.—Offenses may, and not unfrequently do, occur, of such an aggravated character as to require, when confessed or fully proven, immediate exclusion, without the need of further labor, and notwithstanding confessions, penitence and promises; though not without a hearing. No temporizing or delay should be allowed, but the Church of Christ should show the world that it will not shelter in its bosom, nor hold in its fellowship, gross transgressors.

NOTE 12.—Should the Church at any time find that it has dealt unjustly with a member, or excluded him without sufficient cause, it should at once proceed, of its own accord, without waiting for solicitation, to repair, so far as they may be able, the wrong done, and by concession and restoration make it apparent that they are as ready to reverse their action when they see it was wrong, as they were to take it when they believed it was right.

NOTE 13.—The members of the Church should be impressed that they still owe a duty and a service of love to those "cut off." They have once been among them, members of the family and brethren beloved, now, though wayward and unworthy of fellowship because of their errors, yet may it not be hoped that, through their prayers and kindly treatment, they may come to themselves, repent of their errors and seek again their Father's house. Follow them with blessing; they may be saved.

NOTE 14.—The Church should at any time be willing to grant a rehearing of his case, if requested by an excluded member, providing he gives assurance and makes it appear probable that he can establish his innocence, show their mistake or satisfy them by his acknowledgments.

NOTE 15.—The Church should restore to its fellowship, at his request, any excluded member whenever his confession and reparation for the past are satisfactory and his present walk according to godliness.

NOTE 16.—Pastors, deacons, and all officers are subject to the same discipline, administered in the same way, as other Church members; except that unusual caution should be had in giving credence to charges that lead to discipline, according to apostolic injunction: "Against an elder receive not an accusation, except at the mouth of two or three witnesses."
—1 Tim. 5 : 19.   And also it may be added, that considering the prominent position they occupy and considering the fact that disciplinary proceedings in their case may have a more serious effect, both on themselves and on the cause, than in ordinary cases, therefore unusual caution should be used and perhaps a Council, or the advice of wise brethren be called in aid.*

NOTE 17.—In all things not contrary to his conscience, the member should submit to the Church, but in all questions of faith and conscience he should do what he honestly believes to be right, whether the Church, in the exercise of administrative function should commend, or condemn him.

NOTE 18.—While on the contrary, the Church as an executive body must not fail to exercise its legitimate and rightful authority, and discipline its members for what it regards as sufficient cause, even though such members may think the discipline unjust, and believe themselves injured by it.

* The discipline of accused ministers is treated at length in the chapters on Councils.

NOTE 19.—No one, while on trial before the Church, can properly accuse or bring charges against another member as a vindication of his own cause, or a palliation of his offense. His own case must be first decided on its merits. If his offense be proven, or confessed, no accusation of others can justify it, or should be allowed. But any legitimate evidence can be adduced in his own favor, even though such evidence may implicate others.

NOTE 20.—The relation of the pastor to persons accused, and to processes of trial before the body, is delicate and important. He is not to act the partisan for or against the accused, much less is to be the prosecutor of his erring brethren. He is to be judge and expounder of law and evidence; and whatever may be his private opinion, he is to maintain fairness and equity on all sides and to all parties. As moderator of the meeting, he is to keep all parties to good order, and just measures. It is important that he be familiar with parliamentary rules, and with the principles of scriptural discipline, so that the results reached shall commend themselves to the reasonable approval of all.

NOTE 21.—The pastor, by virtue of his office, is moderator of all business meetings. But in cases where he may himself be personally involved in the difficulty, or charged with complicity in it, he should not preside, but resign the chair and allow the meeting to elect some one else.

NOTE 22.—The pastor, by virtue of his office, is moderator of all *church* business meetings, but not of *society* business meetings, which meetings are held according to statute law, for the election of trustees and for other matters pertaining to temporalities. These meetings, even though composed of the same individuals, yet are not the same official bodies. The moderator is elected on nomination. The pastor is eligible to election the same as any other member of the society, but cannot assume the chair by right of his office.

CHAPTER 8

In the maintenance of good order, and the administration of equitable discipline in a Church, there will at times arise cases of unusual difficulty; cases which require more than ordinary wisdom and prudence to manage justly, not to say satisfactorily; not so much, perhaps, because of the gravity of the offense, as because of the persistency of those concerned, the complications which arise in the progress of the case, the party spirit which may be engendered, and possibly, worst of all, the mistakes which the Church itself may make in the treatment of the matter. These mistakes thus give the culpable parties occasion to complain at the course pursued, even when they would not have condemned the final issue itself.

I. A DIVIDED CHURCH

It is probably safe to say that two-thirds of such vexatious cases grow out of misjudged or mismanaged discipline. A wiser course pursued would, in most instances, have reached a just and a peaceful termination. But prejudice, self-will, and heated passion, make partisans contend for the mastery, and rend the body of Christ. Our churches do not have too much discipline—indeed, they have too little—but it is often so unwisely administered as to produce more evil by the method than is removed by the act. It may be too much influenced by personal animosities, by a party spirit engendered, or by ignorance of the principles according to which all true discipline should be exercised.

Such proceedings, even when instigated by sufficient provocation, may degenerate into a mere party or personal conflict for supremacy, in which leading members and related families become identified, and the pastor himself, possibly, involved. Alienations are produced, bitter feelings engendered, and discord rends the Church. The example becomes a reproach, bad men rejoice, and the good are grieved. Injustice has most likely been done to some one, if not by the final act, yet by some of the passionate and ill-advised proceedings leading to it. Unable to harmonize their difficulties, advice from outside is sought, a Council is called to extricate them from the difficulty. Each party of course believes itself to be right, and as firmly holds the other to be wrong.

All that a Council can do is to hear patiently the statements of all parties, corroborate, or disprove confused assertions, so far as possible, by collateral testimony; sift the mass of excited personalities from the vital facts and the underlying principles involved; make a careful digest of the substance of the case, what and where they judge the mistakes and the wrong to be, and advise what course they think the parties concerned should pursue. The Council has, of course, no power to enforce its decisions, to impose penalties, or to compel the performance of its recommendations. But if the advice is carefully and kindly given, and seems reasonable and wise in itself, public sentiment will sustain it, and bear with a heavy moral force against those who reject it.

One very common and very serious difficulty is, that Councils, when called for such purposes, do not usually take sufficient time to thoroughly understand the case, and to put in proper form their findings. The members have little time to devote to other people's troubles, and but little patience to unravel the confused tangle of personal contentions which have run through months and years of conflict. Hence they are likely to hurry through the examination, make a hasty and not too well-considered report, dismiss the case, and return to their homes. The report, which was kindly meant to be equitable to all parties, very likely will not be acceptable to any, and the conflict will continue.

True, a similar fruitless issue may follow the most patient and considerate action, owing to the perversity of the contestants; yet a Council, when called for advice, should give all the time and care which the gravity of the case demands. If the petty squabbles of misguided good men and women do not deserve so much, yet the peace of the Church, the cultivation of Christian virtue, and the honor of the Christian name, are worthy of such labor for their maintenance.

The Order of Proceedings

When such difficult cases are to be investigated by the aid of a Council, the order of proceedings would be substantially as follows :

1. The Council is to be organized the same as for other purposes by the election of a moderator and clerk ; by prayer for divine guidance and a right spirit ; by the preparation of a list of messengers, showing how many messengers are present, and from how many and what churches they come ; and then by a distinct statement of the object for which they are convened. This statement may be made by the moderator or by those who have called the Council. Usually it is enough to read a copy of the *letter missive*, which should set forth the object of the call. This object must be kept in view, and not departed from during the proceedings. No foreign or extraneous matters should be admitted ; nothing beyond what may be presented as evidence or for the elucidation of the main question. Of the relevancy of such matter the moderator must judge ; and if his decisions be doubted, the Council must decide by a vote.

2. Those who have called the Council will then present their case as they wish it to stand before the body. In doing this they will pursue their own

course and make such a presentation as they choose, embracing statements, documentary evidence, and the testimony of witnesses. In doing which they should not be interrupted, except that questions may be asked for explanation of matters not understood.

3. If it be a *mutual* Council the party which considers itself aggrieved and seeks redress, will present its case first ; a full statement of all the facts bearing on it, with the testimony of witnesses if desired, and documentary evidence.

4. Following such a presentation, the other party will make their statements with such collateral evidence as they desire to offer, and with such reply to the other side as they may wish to give.

5. To this, a rejoinder of the first party may be made, with explanations, refutations, and new evidence, if any be had. And to this a rejoinder by the second party is allowed.

6. If it be an *ex parte* Council, in which no second party appears, there will of course be no rejoinders, but the chairman or members will ask such questions as may elicit the fullest information, and present the whole case clearly to the minds of the members of the body.

7. The discussion should close when the Council is satisfied that all the facts, in their proper relations are before them, so that they fully understand the case on which they are to express an opinion.

8. No discussion, crimination, or contradiction between the parties themselves should be permitted. No other interruption than asking or answering

questions for information should be allowed by the moderator ; otherwise irritation will be increased rather than allayed. The moderator should protect all parties in the exercise of their rights, that the simple truth may be reached.

9. It would not be in accordance with usage, nor consistent with the principles on which such references proceed, for parties in difficulty to procure the services of *lawyers*, the more skillfully to present and defend their course. It is not a contest before a civil tribunal for a judgment, but a confidential reference to brethren for advice. There could, however, be no objection, if parties deemed themselves unable to do themselves justice in the presentation of their case, to have some member of the Council act for them in the matter. Or, did the Council agree and no party to the difficulty object, have some brother outside, whether layman, lawyer, or minister, perform this service. No person, however, outside the Council and the parties in dispute, could have any *right* to appear before the body in advocacy. If they so appear at all it would be only by permission of the Council and of the parties calling it.

10. As the single object in statement and discussion should be the attainment of truth, by the ascertainment of facts, therefore the technicalities of *legal proceedings* in secular courts need not be regarded, but parliamentary rules should be observed, and good order strictly maintained through all the proceedings.

11. When all the evidence is in, and all the facts are supposed to be understood, it is voted that the case be closed, the parties retire—spectators too, if such be present—and the Council goes into private session for deliberation. Or the Council itself may retire to some convenient place for deliberation, all others remaining if they so desire.

12. In private session there is a free and full discussion of the subject ; perhaps the moderator sums up the case by presenting in condensed form the various points which constitute its substance. If there be any forgetfulness of facts, the parties can be recalled to repeat their statements. Then a committee may be appointed to embody the results of their deliberations in certain resolutions. This expression of opinion is sometimes called the *findings* of the Council, and is twofold, as containing : 1. The substance or result of the investigation as they understand it ; 2. The opinion expressed as to the merits of the case, embracing the advice given to the parties asking counsel.

13. It would seem proper that in making up these *findings*, no statement or resolution should be adopted except by a *unanimous* vote, though of course a majority vote would carry any question.

14. When the work is completed the parties are called in and the moderator announces the result by reading the statement. This statement, when once made on the basis of facts as presented, is understood not to be subject to revision or change. And

yet it is supposable that a case might occur where facts or evidence had clearly been misapprehended, and the findings might and should, by unanimous consent, be modified accordingly. But this could not be done after the Council had finally adjourned. A Council ceases to exist on final adjournment.

15. It is usual to give the parties calling a Council authenticated copies of the proceedings and the results reached; and also, if desired, to order their publication.

16. If the proceedings be in the nature of a trial of some person or party before the Council, who may be called on to answer to an accusation, or to refute charges made, then the accused, as in all other cases of trial, must have copies of all charges, with specifications, including times and places and names of witnesses, served on him sufficiently long before the trial to allow him full opportunity for preparation to answer for and defend himself before the body.

The foregoing statements cover the ground for the treatment of difficult cases of discipline in all ordinary circumstances where outside help becomes needful. Extraordinary cases develop peculiar features, which must be judged by general principles and the good sense of advisers called to consult. It must be presumed that those called upon for advice, whether Council or Reference, are impartially disposed to ascertain the facts, and to act in kindness and equity toward all concerned.

II. AN EXCLUDED MEMBER

Another frequent occasion for dissension and strife in the churches, leading to protracted conflict, and, most likely, to the calling of a Council, is that of *excluded members.** Such disfellowshiped members very commonly, and perhaps very naturally, believe themselves to have been unfairly dealt with, and unjustly excluded. This feeling is the more likely to be entertained if they have occupied a prominent position in the Church, and if the disciplinary course, which finally led to exclusion, was protracted and exciting. Then it is likely to be regarded as the act of a hostile party, and not of the Church, as such—the result of passion, and not an act of justice.

Now, while the presumption is, that in such cases the Church was right in its action, and the individual was justly disfellowshiped, the fact *may be*, and sometimes evidently is, that the action of the Church has been ill-judged and unjust, and the individual has good cause for complaint. This is most likely to occur where the exclusion is the issue of a protracted dissension between contending factions, maintained by headstrong leaders and partisan adherents. Moreover, it is sometimes true that, while the individual justly deserved discipline, and possi-

---

* What has been already said in the preceding pages might apply to the case of excluded members as treated in this section. But in this case there arise some peculiar features not presented in the other.

bly exclusion even, on the merits of his case, yet the manner in which the case was managed, and the method by which the result was reached, were improper, ill - considered, and unjust to him.

For these reasons, if for no others, an excluded member has a right at least to lay his grievance before a Council, and ask such relief as their opinion and advice may afford. If it were not so, and if, as some have absurdly claimed, an excluded person should not be allowed the right of calling a Council, then such prohibition must be urged on the ground either that the Church could do no wrong, or else that an excluded member should have no redress for wrongs inflicted by unjust Church action; both of which suppositions are monstrous.

Church independency and personal liberty are both to be conceded and defended. If any man believes himself to have been wronged, he has the inalienable and unquestioned right to lay his grievances before any man or any number of men, and ask their opinion and advice. When a Church has excluded a member, their connection with him and control over him ceases. They have no further right to say what he shall or shall not do, nor what others shall or shall not do respecting him. And for churches or ministers to enter into a compact, formal or implied, that, because he is an excluded man, they will not even hear his statement, nor give advice, would be the most intolerable religious tyranny—especially for liberty-loving Baptists. Such a proscription would approach the anathema of papal excommunication.

A Church may exscind a member judged unworthy of further fellowship, after due process of disciplinary law; but having cut him off, they cannot continue to hold the rod in terror over him, and bar him from the counsel, and even from the sympathy of others, simply on the ground of their action. And they ought to be ashamed of themselves if in any wise they attempt to follow him with maledictions after they have cast him out.

While, therefore, the presumption is, that the action of the Church in his exclusion has been just and right, the possibility is that it may have been unjust and oppressive. And such a possibility entitles the individual to a hearing before unprejudiced brethren, should he so desire—not being able to find relief in any other way.

What Causes Invalidate Church Action ?

Since a Church may err, and invalidate its action of exclusion by irregular and unjust methods of procedure in discipline, as well as for insufficient cause in exclusion ; we may inquire, what are the more common mistakes in processes of discipline, which would invalidate such action and give a member, thus disfellowshiped, good reason to complain of injustice done to himself?

1. He might complain that his exclusion was for *insufficient cause*, even though the proceedings in the case were orderly and fair. The Church, of

course, would hold a different opinion ; therefore, those who undertook to advise him would need to know the facts as the Church understood them, in order to advise discreetly.

2. It might be claimed that no *first steps* had been taken by those whom he had offended, in case his offense was a personal one. No matter of personal difficulty should be brought before the Church until the aggrieved member, who brings the charge, shall first have faithfully pursued the course prescribed by our Saviour in the eighteenth of Matthew. Whoever fails to follow this direction, makes himself an offender and subject to discipline for so doing.

3. The Church may have acted on his case without having furnished him with a copy of the charges or having allowed him opportunity to hear the witnesses against him, or sufficient opportunity to defend himself.   All this would be unfair.

4. Final action on his case may have been taken on some unusual occasion, at some other than the proper meeting for hearing such cases, and without due notice to him that his case would be then acted on and decided.

5. There may have been refusal or failure to give full opportunity for defense before the Church, as a body, rather than before the officers or some committee, privately.   It is the right of each member, when accused, to defend himself in the presence of the whole Church before he is condemned by it.

Other irregularities might occur, but the above named are such as are most likely to take place.

What Course Shall He Pursue?

It would be a piece of very great folly for **every** excluded member, exasperated at what he thinks unfair treatment, to undertake immediately to precipitate a Council in the hope that they will right his wrongs, and antagonize the Church on his behalf. There are certain preliminary steps which good order requires him to take to justify the calling of a Council for his relief.

What Are These Preliminary Steps?

1. He should, after a little time, and when the heat of excitement has died down, make an appeal to the Church for a *re-hearing* of his case. In doing this he should give his reasons for claiming that he did not have a fair trial, and that he was unjustly judged. If a new hearing should be granted, with the opportunities he claims, then he must submit to the results. If the new hearing should be granted, but with similar irregularities as at first, then he is left in the same attitude as at the end of the first trial. If a re-hearing be refused, then :

2. He should request them to unite with him in calling a *mutual* Council to which the case may be submitted. If this request be granted, he will have the selection of one-half of the Council. Whatever the result of such a reference may be, it would be unwise for him to prosecute the matter any further. At any rate, the action of a Council so convened must be very extraordinary to justify him in any further attempts at self-vindication. If this request

for a mutual Council be *declined* by the Church, then :

3. He might present himself to some other Church and request to be received to its fellowship on his experience, as an excluded member, giving them all the facts. The Church thus appealed to might think it wise to call a Council to advise them as to the propriety of receiving a member excluded from a sister Church. Should they, however, see fit to receive him—as they would have an undoubted right to do without a Council — that would dispose of the case, giving him Church standing and fellowship again, and he would have no occasion to pursue the matter further. And should this be done, the Church which excluded him could have no just ground for complaint. One Church has the same right to take a man in as another has to put him out. But should the Church appealed to, for any reason, decline to receive him or to call a Council, then ;

4. He might with propriety—and it would be his undoubted right to do so, as the only further step toward redress — call an *ex parte* Council, before which the whole case could be laid ; both as to his trial and exclusion and as to his subsequent efforts for reconciliation. Of course he should be ready to place before the Council, when convened, all the facts and evidence needed to justify his course in having called them together.

5. Any one thus calling a Council should have a clear and definite idea of what it can and what it

cannot do. Otherwise he may be much disappointed in the result. He must not expect a Council to right all his wrongs, fancied or real, to redress all his grievances, or to punish the Church for what he believes, or even they may think, misjudged and unjust action in his case. The functions of a Council not being *judicial*, but *advisory* only, they can, at most, only express an opinion on the merits of the case, and give him advice. Even the expression of an opinion on the merits of the case they may withhold, but some *advice* they are bound to give ; it was for that purpose they were called, and accepted the invitation to sit as counselors. The moral effect of their opinion and advice constitutes the only vindication or condemnation they have the power to pronounce.

III. AN ACCUSED MINISTER

One of the most grave and difficult cases of discipline which is likely to arise to vex, and possibly to divide a Church, is that of a minister who has lost public confidence, and who, by unchristian or unministerial conduct, is believed to be unfit to discharge the functions of, or to remain in, the sacred office. No case occurs where churches more need the wise and prudent advice of others, or where a Council finds a more legitimate field for its friendly offices than this.

Great caution should be exercised, even in giving heed to unfavorable reports against a minister of the gospel. Christ's anointed ones should not be touched with unholy hands. The Apostle wisely decreed that, " Against an elder, receive not an accusation except at the mouth of two or three witnesses."—1 Tim. 5 : 19. Charges which implicate their moral or ministerial character should not be entertained, only on very strong evidence. Their position is a very delicate one. Called by professional duties into almost all sorts of company, and placed in well-nigh all kinds of positions, evil-minded persons can, if disposed, excite suspicions against them on the most trivial occasions. They themselves are bound to exercise perpetual vigilance and care, while their reputation and good character, on which their comfort and usefulness so much depend, should be sacredly guarded and defended. But their sins should not be covered when they deserve exposure, nor should they escape discipline when they merit it.

Such cases are important and difficult, because:

First—Of the high position and wide influence of a minister, and the fact that he stands before the public as an example of godliness, a religious teacher and leader of the people. If he proves himself an unworthy man his case becomes more a reproach and scandal to religion, and more an obstacle to the progress of truth than if he were a private member of the Church. The purity of the ministerial character and the honor of the Christian profession must be vindicated.

Second—A minister's character and good name

must be held sacredly and dealt with tenderly, since they are his richest possessions, and usually all he has as a means of usefulness, for the maintenance of a respectable position in society, or the continued support of himself and family with the ordinary comforts of life. When these are gone, all of worldly worth is gone. They must not be trifled with.

FACTS TO BE KEPT IN MIND

In dealing with such a case, therefore, unusual caution should be exercised ; and there are few churches so strong, so wise, so well-balanced and sclf-contained that it would be prudent to proceed to extremities without calling a Council, or in some way securing outside aid and advice.

In the calling of such a Council the following facts are to be kept in mind:

1. As in all other cases, it must be accepted that Baptist Councils are *advisory* only, and never authoritative. They are called to give advice to those who have called them—advice based on their knowledge of the merits of the case, after having carefully examined it.

2. Neither ministers nor others can organize themselves into a Council, nor can they, self-moved and unasked, call one for the trial of a minister whose presence may be unwelcome to them, and in whose character they may have no confidence. Such cases have occurred; but such an act is a gross outrage on personal rights and Church independ-

ency, as well as a violation of Baptist polity, by an unlawful assumption of authority.

3. A Council called to advise in matters relating to the trial of an accused minister can only be called by a Church; and by that Church of which such minister is a member. Any other Church could call a Council to advise them what course they ought to take in respect to the fellowship of a Church which persisted in sustaining a pastor whom they believed unworthy. A party in a Church—even a very small party — might call a Council to advise them as to their duty, if their Church were sustaining a minister in whom they had no confidence; but in neither of these cases could a Council try or pronounce judgment on the character of the man himself. They were not convened for that purpose. They could only advise those who called them, as to their duty in the premises.

4. A Council, having no ecclesiastical authority, cannot be called to *try*, and, if found guilty, to *depose* a minister. Judicial acts belong to a Church, and not to a Council; nor can a Church transfer its authority for the exercise of judicial functions to any other body. A Council, in order to express an opinion and give advice, is asked to examine all the facts, consider all the circumstances, sift and weigh the evidence on all sides, the accused having full opportunity to defend himself. In a modified, but not in a judicial sense, it may be called a *trial* of the accused: because it is a search for the merits of

the case, by an investigation of all the facts, and a sifting of all the evidence.

5. The minister on whose case his Church may call a Council, is not obliged, and cannot be *compelled*, to appear before such a Council, or in any way submit his case to them. He is amenable to the Church alone. But it is his *right* to appear before them, have copies of all charges, hear all testimony, examine witnesses, and answer for himself. And usually it is better for him to take this course than to stand upon his reserved rights, and treat a Council with disregard. The presumption is, that a company of Christian men will judge impartially on the evidence placed before them. And though this presumption may not always be justified, it is better for one to meet all charges frankly, and all accusers face to face, than to seem to evade an investigation of matters laid against him.

6. There is no absolute necessity inherent in the case itself, for the calling of a Council in the discipline or trial of a minister. If done at all, it is done for expediency, and not from necessity; for order and safety, and not for authority. But because many churches are weak as to numbers, and inexperienced in the treatment of difficult matters, because, in serious and complicated disciplinary proceedings, there is likely to be much irritation and impetuosity, when even good men are too much influenced by party zeal and prejudice—therefore it is wise to call in the experienced, prudent and impartial, for advice. Such advice will invest the

Church's final action with weight, and give the public greater assurance of its equity and justice.

7. In most cases of the kind, where a Council is resorted to, it is best to make it a *mutual* Council, by agreement between the Church and the accused. He would then have the privilege of selecting one-half the members. If this be not done, and the result be unfavorable to him, he will be almost sure, with the advice of friends—for he will have friends —to call another to counteract the influence of the first, and to place his case in a more favorable light before the public.

8. After the investigation has closed, and the Council rendered its opinion and advice, the Church will take such action as, in view of all the facts, may be deemed wise and right. They are not obliged to follow the advice given. The Council has no power to enforce its recommendations, and should have no desire to do it. The responsibility of the final action lies with the Church. But the advice given would naturally constitute an important factor in their final decision. It would require very weighty reasons to justify a Church in disregarding the judgment and advice of a Council of its own selection. Such a case would seldom occur.

The Church's Final Action

9. The final action of a Church, as to an accused minister, may take any one of the following forms:

a. That of an *acquittal;* where no fault worthy of

further consideration was proven against him; the charges were not sustained, and he is pronounced innocent.

b. That of *admonition;* indiscretions which caused reproach and hindered his usefulness, having been shown; suspicions being excited, the enemies of religion had occasion to magnify his faults to the injury of the cause of truth. To caution and admonish him to greater circumspection may be all which the case requires.

c. That of a *withdrawal of fellowship* from him as a *minister* of the Gospel, with a declaration, that in their opinion he is unworthy of, and unfit to continue in, the ministerial office. This may be done, and the man still be retained in the fellowship of the Church as a private member. There may be faults which would disqualify him for the exercise of a public ministry, which might not unfit him for private membership. Such an act of disfellowship as a minister, would virtually be an act of deposition from the sacred office, so far as any act of Church or Council could depose him.

d. That of the *withdrawal* of fellowship from him as a Church *member;* thus excluding him from the body. This, accompanied with a declaration of his unworthiness as a minister of the Gospel, constitutes the final and utmost act of the Church's disciplinary power, in such a case. They can do no more. This puts him out, and deposes him from the ministry, so far as any human power can depose him. It also clears the Church from any further responsibility as to his character or conduct. His disfellowship as a *member* adds emphasis to his disfellowship as a *minister*.

To the above-named acts a Council may advise; but the acts themselves, to be valid and of any force, must be the acts of the Church and not of the Council. It would be an impertinent assumption for a Council to attempt such an exercise of ecclesiastical authority.

Shall Another Council Follow?

10. If the final action of the Church—based on the advice of a Council—be unfavorable to the minister on trial, and result in his degradation, or exclusion, he will very likely think that still greater injustice has been done him, and seek relief by calling another Council. If the former was a *mutual* Council, in the calling of which he had part, and to which he consented to commit the case, it would be extremely unwise for him to prosecute the matter further—except, indeed, in very extraordinary circumstances. If the former were an *ex parte* Council, called by the Church without his concurrence, there would be more occasion for him to call another, especially if so advised by wise and prudent friends. It certainly would be his right to do so, should he be disposed. But the fewer Councils the better. It is quite as well to suffer for want of them as to suffer by means of them.

Should he decide to call another, *three rules* should be observed in reference to it:

a. He should invite the Church to unite with him, and make it a *mutual* Council, in whose judgment all parties might acquiesce. Nor should he hesitate to do this, because the Church had hitherto refused similar requests from him. To repeat the request would put his case in a better attitude before those who might be called to consider it.

b. Have the Council larger than the previous one, and, if possible, more marked for wisdom and experience. Some would advise that such a Council should be composed of new men entirely, since those on the previous Council had already judged the case, and could hardly re-judge it with impartiality. Others would advise that it be composed largely of the same members, with such additions as might counteract any local or personal prejudice that might previously have existed. And this would seem a wise course.

c. Such new Council, when convened, should confine its action strictly to the object for which it was called. It should not attempt to traverse the action, either of the Church, or of the previous Council, and should consider them only so far as to obtain information, in order that they may justly and wisely form an opinion and impart advice.

By such a course the action of councils will, so far as practicable, prove conservative and salutary, vindicating the right, and giving furtherance to equity and truth.

NOTE 1.—A Council possessing no ecclesiastical authority can neither make nor unmake a minister. No Council, therefore, can put a man out of the ministry. All it can do, is, to declare him, in their opinion, unfit for, and disqualified to remain in, the ministry, and that they cannot fellowship him as a minister; and they can add the advice, that the Church exclude and depose him.

NOTE 2.—Though all ecclesiastical authority resides in a Church, yet a Church cannot, in any absolute sense, depose, and put a man out of the ministry, except so far as that ministry relates to themselves. They can depose him from being *their* minister, and declare him, in their opinion, unworthy to fill the sacred office. But any other Church can have him for *their* minister, if they so desire, since each Church is entirely independent as to the choice of its pastor and the management of its internal affairs.

NOTE 3.—Such action, however, on the part of councils and of churches, though having no power to compel silence. or to enforce penalties, substantially effects the same end, through the force of public sentiment. This will, sooner or later, lead an unworthy man to retire from the ministerial calling.

NOTE 4.—A Church might declare a man unfit for the ministry, and depose him from the office, and yet retain him in its fellowship as a private member. His ministerial rather than his Christian character being involved in the discipline.

NOTE 5.—If a minister be excluded from the fellowship of a Church, such exclusion is equivalent to a deposition, so far as Church action can effect a deposition. For if he be not worthy of Church fellowship, he surely is not worthy to hold the office and discharge the functions of a Gospel minister.

CHAPTER 9

CHRISTIAN WORSHIP

RELIGIOUS faith expresses itself both in worship and in work. In such acts of religious service as may declare the soul's devotion to the Deity, and in such works as are believed to be pleasing to Him, and such as naturally grow out of the faith cherished, and correspond to the worship offered.

Worship, properly speaking, is adoration and praise offered to God. The emotion is instinctive in a devout soul and tends to exalt and magnify Him to whom all honor and glory are due. It is offered in view of the glorious excellency of the divine character; and also because of what God has done for men. Both for what He is, and for what He does. Worship is usually attended with confession for sin and with supplication for pardon and needed grace. It is an important duty and a gracious privilege. But no act of devotion can be acceptable to Him, unless it be spontaneous and sincere. If it be such, He delights in it and accepts it with pleasure from His creatures. Its influence on individual piety, on the Church's spiritual life, and on the moral sense of the community, is not sufficiently understood nor highly enough valued.

While, strictly speaking, it is defined within narrow bounds, yet in ordinary language all religious service is spoken of as worship. All recognize the Divine Presence as the inspiration of devotion and the object of veneration. The various parts of public and social worship claim brief attention.

I. THE PREACHING SERVICE

As public religious service is usually arranged by evangelical Churches generally, *preaching* holds a foremost place and the *service* is secondary. With a liturgical Church it is different. There the service rules, and preaching is largely subordinate. Preaching, strictly speaking, is not worship, though calculated to inspire and assist worship. Preaching is a proclamation of truth, not an address to the Deity. The preacher is a herald (*kerux*), a proclaimer, and his address (*kerugma*), a message delivered to an audience.

1. *The Object of Preaching*

The true object and design of preaching is the salvation of sinners and the edification of the saints by means of instruction and persuasion. Instruction may properly be said to be the first object of preaching. Most emphatically it is not to entertain or recreate an audience; nor to crowd the house with hearers, nor to build up wealthy and fashionable congregations; nor to rent pews and replenish the treasury; nor to teach literature, science, or art; but to save and sanctify souls by an exhibition of Christ crucified. All preaching which fails of this, fails of its chief design. For this purpose our Lord "gave some to be pastors and teachers, for the perfecting of the saints, for the work of the ministry, for the edifying of the body of Christ."—Eph. 4 : 11, 12.

And the Apostle's ministry was, "Warning every man, and teaching every man, in all wisdom, that we may present every man perfect in Christ Jesus," —Col. 1 : 28. There are occasions which press the minister of the cross very sorely to diverge from, if not altogether to forget, this high aim of his calling, and adapt his efforts to draw admiring and curious crowds to his ministry. And for this purpose, themes not Gospel and not even strictly religious, may be resorted to. But viewed from the low ground of expediency even, this is a mistake. Preachers who hold, longest and strongest, the consciences and the confidence of the community, and who command the most respectful attention of the people, are those who are loyal to the truth as it is in Jesus.

2. *The Character of Preaching*

All preaching to be profitable should be plain and simple in style, spiritual in tone, experimental and practical in substance. The very basis and foundation of every sermon should be *instruction*. In the arrangement of the matter, order should be so manifest that the parts will follow each other by a natural sequence, so that the minds of the hearers will easily comprehend their relations. As to the style, *clearness* is of the first importance. The speaker is not preaching in an unknown tongue, and every sentence and word should be so transparent in its meaning that none can misunderstand. A mere jumble of words, a heap of figures and of flowers are as chaff compared with these qualities. All the arts of oratory and the adornments of rhetoric poorly compensate for the absence of transparent clearness.

Nevertheless, with these qualities possessed, the more interesting and attractive the preaching, in style, matter, and manner, the more welcome and useful it is likely to prove. And every preacher should strive to become as attractive and useful to the people as possible. There would be poor comfort in saying a sermon was good, if the style were such as to make it incomprehensible, or the manner of its delivery such as to make it repulsive. With these drawbacks it certainly would not be good for its purpose. Every preacher should " study to show himself approved unto God, a workman that needeth not to be ashamed."—2 Tim. 2 : 15. Many sermons, in themselves really good, would be far more effective were the manner of their delivery more intelligible, animated, and impressive.

3. *The Frequency of Preaching*

According to established customs in religious society, it is expected that in our places of public worship, two sermons will be regularly preached on each Sunday.   Formerly it was customary to have a lecture — a somewhat informal sermon — on some evening during the week.   Special and protracted preaching services, daily or nightly, are often held during seasons of unusual religious interest or to produce unusual interest.

In primitive times, as now on mission fields, preaching was less formal and more pervasive. It was "daily, from house to house," "instant in season and out of season," that people might by any means hear the glad tidings of salvation.   Now, congregations ordinarily require too much preaching in proportion to the more social services of religion.   So far as the Church members and the stated congregation are concerned, it is questionable if any better arrangement for Sunday service than the following could be devised ; viz., a sermon in the morning, the very best the preacher is able to produce ; a Bible class, and Sunday-school service in the afternoon, and a prayer and conference meeting in the evening, so arranged as to be animated and attractive.

In our cities, towns, and larger villages, the Sunday evening congregation is largely different from that of the morning, consisting to a great extent, of a floating population, with but few of the Church families, and to a considerable extent made up of young people.   Of course it is not thought best to abandon preaching for that service.   To meet this tendency, not a few preachers have held very loosely the evangelical character of their evening services, and instead of Gospel themes, have treated semi-secular and otherwise alien subjects to catch the drifting current. This is a great mistake ; for no subjects can be so attractive in a Church service as simple Gospel themes, if rightly presented. It would seem that music should have a larger place in evening than in morning worship.

Considering the necessities of the world, and that men perish perpetually without the gospel, those called to that sacred work should " Preach the word ; be instant in season, out of season ; reprove, rebuke, exhort, with all longsuffering and doctrine." —2 Tim. 4 : 2.

NOTE 1.—Though no fixed rule can be adopted for the length of sermons, yet when the Sunday is crowded with services, as it usually is, that should not be protracted. Ministers are not usually complained of for long sermons unless they be uniformly long. If it be only occasional it is borne. Some discourses require more time than others, and some will be listened to with more interest and patience than others. Seldom, however, should one consume more than *forty minutes*, and the entire service should be something less than an hour and a half on all ordinary occasions.

NOTE 2.—Very unreasonable objections are at times made to *doctrinal* preaching. It is a little doubtful whether those who object really know what doctrinal preaching is. In fact, doctrine is the very essence and marrow of the Gospel, and little instruction in godliness can be imparted without doctrine. It is the framework of the building where edification —upbuilding—is enjoined as the special duty of the religious teacher. No doubt doctrine can be preached so abstractly and uninterestingly as to be a burden to the hearers.

NOTE 3.—Should manuscripts be used in the pulpit, or should sermons be *extemporaneous* in manner, are questions which the preacher must decide for himself.   Opinions differ. The excellency or usefulness of a sermon does not largely depend on either method.   Some subjects cannot be accurately treated without writing.   Moreover, writing is an important aid, and an invaluable mental discipline to the preacher.   It helps him to think systematically and to express himself concisely and forcibly.   But for all ordinary occasions of preaching it cannot be doubted that an extemporaneous style of address is most in accordance with the spirit of the Gospel, and more agreeable, forcible, and profitable to the congregation.

NOTE 4.—The great temptation, however, to extemporaneous preachers—especially if they have large facility in the use of language—is to neglect the *preparation* of their sermons and depend on the inspiration of the occasion.   This temptation, if yielded to, becomes fatal to both the reputation and the usefulness of the preacher.

NOTE 5.—Sermons need not be *read* even though they be written.   Nor, if a manuscript be used, need the manner of address be servile and lifeless.   Some ministers are as free, animated, and vigorous in using a written sermon as others are who never wrote one.   The trouble is not with the manuscript, but with the manner of using it.

NOTE 6.—Perhaps no better advice could be given on this subject than that one written and one extemporaneous sermon should be prepared and preached each Sunday.   Two well-prepared and well-written sermons each week, with the many pastoral duties and the many interruptions incident to a minister's position, will prove a severe tax on his time and energies, or an utter impossibility.

NOTE 7.—Probably no more effective method could be adopted than for the preacher to write his sermon carefully, then make a brief abstract or skeleton for use in the pulpit, leaving his manuscript at home.   He would thus largely combine the advantages of a written style with the freedon and force of an *extemporaneous delivery*.

NOTE 8.—Above all things, let the preacher have something to say ; know what it is ; be thoroughly penetrated with the importance and the spirit of it ; then say it earnestly and devoutly as an ambassador of Christ, to do the people good. The Spirit will help his infirmities.

II. THE PRAYER SERVICE

Prayer is an important element in all religious service. Not only is it vital to the individual Christian life, its importance in social religion is scarcely less important. " Ask, and it shall be given you ; seek, and ye shall find ; knock, and it shall be opened unto you," was the positive declaration of our Lord to His disciples.—Matt. 6 : 7.

There are special blessings promised to united prayer, as well as to personal prayer. " If two of you shall agree on earth, as touching anything that they shall ask, it shall be done for them of my Father which is in heaven."—Matt. 18 : 19. Secret prayer, and personal communion alone with God, is essential to the soul's spiritual life, and is encouraged by the promise of special blessing. " But thou, when thou prayest, enter into thy closet, and when thou hast shut thy door, pray to thy Father which is in secret; and thy Father which seeth in secret shall reward thee openly."—Matt. 6 : 6.

Prayer adjusts itself in form to the various occasions which demand its exercise, but in spirit it is essentially everywhere the same. The pastor's prayer before his congregation would speak for them as well as for himself. and would be different from his prayer in his own study, at the family altar, in the sick-room, with a penitent sinner, or with a dying saint. An intelligent faith will adjust its form to the peculiar circumstances in which it is called forth. The prayer before the sermon would naturally be somewhat different from that at its close. If the petitioner have the true spirit of supplication, the petition will take on suitable language for its expression. The form will need to give no anxiety.

1. *The motive of prayer*—Prayer includes worship in its strictest sense. He who prays is supposed to shut out the world, and become insensible to aught else, while he communes with God. It includes adoration, confession, thanksgiving and petition. In its narrower sense prayer is supplication (*precari*—to beseech, to supplicate); making request for needed blessings on behalf of the worshiper, and other objects of divine clemency. The *intercession* of Christ must evermore be recognized as the only prevailing influence with, and cause of blessing from, the Father. "Whatsoever ye shall ask the Father in my name, He will give it you."—John 16 : 23. While the office of the Holy Spirit must be relied on as the only means of communication with the Throne of Grace by the merits of Christ. "For we know not what we should pray for as we ought; but the Spirit Himself maketh intercession for us, with groanings which cannot be uttered."—Rom. 8 : 26.

2. *Preparation for Prayer*—There needs to be a preparation for prayer, in order to lead profitably

the devotions of others in addresses to the mercy seat. Not a preparation of words, but of the heart; not a forethought of phrases for that particular occasion, but a spirit in harmony with the divine fulness and a *felt* necessity for the blessings sought. He who would have the preparation, when in the pulpit, must obtain it before he goes there. " He that cometh to God must believe that He is, and that He is a rewarder of them who diligently seek Him."— Heb. 11 : 6. " But let him ask in faith, nothing wavering."—James 1 : 6. "Praying in the Holy Ghost."—Jude 20.

To *make* prayers and to *pray*, are very different things. Anyone can make a prayer, who can command the use of language; but to pray, the soul must commune with God. There is constant danger that prayers offered in the pulpit will become stereotyped and monotonous, so constantly are they repeated, and under circumstances so almost exactly similar. The best preventive is a fervent spirit, and a deep sense of the need of divine assistance.

3. *Style of Prayer* —While prayer is not to be measured and meted out by mechanical rules, nor subjected to the rigid canons of logic or rhetoric, yet the petitioner is not—ordinarily, at least—beyond a self-conscious sense of certain proprieties, which even prayer, as a public or social exercise, should not transgress. Nor need it dampen the spirit, or interrupt the flow of devotion, to regard those proprieties. Prayer should be simple, direct, and brief. It should be so simple in style that all

in the assembly can intelligently unite in it. It should be direct as to what is prayed for, and not wander over all possible subjects, seeking nothing in particular, and expecting nothing in particular. It often seems as if prayer was offered in public worship, not because there was a felt need of it, but because it is the prevailing custom to pray in that particular part of the service.

Prayers should be *brief :* of course, in some cases more so than in others. There is no excuse for the painful length of what is called "the long prayer" preceding the sermon in the case of many clergymen. In fact, the "long prayer" is a calamity, to both the minister and the people. It is often difficult to perform it, and painful to endure it. Very largely it is not prayer at all, but a religious address, the rather, discursive in style and promiscuous in matter. If it could be confined to three or five minutes, the "long prayer" would be no more, and public worship would gain immensely. But the tyranny of established usage still preserves and inflicts it on preacher and people alike without compensation.

Prayers should be distinctly uttered, so that all can understand and unite in them; nor should there be anything, in manner or expression, so peculiar as to divert the thoughts of hearers from the devotion. Especially should not the petitioner "use vain repetition as the heathen do; for they think they shall be heard for their much speaking."—Matt. 6 : 7. Besides which, the whole style and manner of address should be penitential, reverential, and dignified withal, savoring of meekness and humility, as is becoming in sinful, helpless creatures when approaching a holy God. All flippant familiarity with the sacred names, which seems an affectation of unusual piety, should be avoided, as most offensive to sensible minds.

4. *Faults in Prayer.*—It may seem a most ungracious thing to criticise so sacred an exercise as prayer ought to be, and point out defects which not unfrequently mar its excellencies. The one prevailing defect, no doubt, is want of faith, spirituality, and the influences of the Holy Spirit. But these attach to all Christian exercises. There are, however, certain defects in the drift of prayer — more particularly prayers in the social meetings — into which the pious sometimes unconsciously fall, which deserve attention and correction.

Preaching Prayers, in which Scripture is explained, doctrine expounded, and instruction offered to the audience.

Exhorting Prayers, where warnings, rebukes, and exhortations seem addressed to classes, or individuals, and possibly personal sins are pointed out.

Historical Prayers, in which facts and incidents are related, from which inferences and arguments are adduced. Not to be commended, though David, Solomon, and Ezra indulged in them on very special occasions.

Oratorical Prayers, which seem framed with special regard to the language, as if intended for critical ears.

Complimentary Prayers, where the excellencies of persons present or absent are effectively dwelt on, as if individuals were flattered, rather than the Deity worshiped.   Clergymen in praying for each other, on public occasions, often use flattering speech.

Fault-finding Prayers, which make prominent the real or fancied faults of the Church or of individuals, existing difficulties deplored, advice given, remedies suggested, or rebukes administered.

All such things should be avoided.

THE PRAYER-MEETING.

The Prayer-meeting is emphatically a Christian institution. For while prayer, as a religious exercise, or form of religious service, is by no means confined to Christian assemblies, nor indeed to Christian life, yet gatherings for social worship, chiefly for thanksgiving, supplication and song, are peculiarly the outgrowth of the Gospel of Christ. In saying this, the fact is not overlooked that among idolatrous and barbarous races, even, there are assemblies for worship constantly recurring, largely and enthusiastically attended. But the prayer-meeting idea does not enter into the purpose or conception of such assemblies. The disposition to pray, to petition the Supreme Being for benefits needed, and for defense against impending evils, is instinct in the human mind. But the idea of worship, in its strict sense, of fellowship with the spiritual, and communion with the unseen, seems never to have entered into the idea of prayer, except to those illuminated by a divine revelation.

The teachings of Jesus revealed to men the fact that God is a father interested in human affairs, caring for the welfare of His creatures, and that He is pleased to have them approach Him, and make known their requests with prayer and supplication. Indeed, under the old dispensation, God declared Himself to be a praying-hearing, and a prayer-answering God. But Jesus brought the divine presence nearer to believing souls, and gave assurance of the Eternal Father's loving care, which even a weak faith could not question. "Ask, and ye shall receive; seek, and ye shall find; knock, and it shall be opened." And He further assured His disciples, that God was more willing to give the Spirit to those who asked, than parents were to give good things to their children.

In the Old Testament much is said of prayer, many remarkable instances of which are narrated, with equally remarkable answers to them. But nothing is said of prayer-meetings for worship. The temple services contained nothing equivalent to it. During the captivity the Jews had their assemblies for mourning and lamentation over the desolations of Zion. They may have mingled prayers for the promised restoration. Of this we do not know. It is certain that the jubilant spirit of social worship could not have inspired their assemblies without song, for they hanged their harps on the willows, and refused to sing the Lord's songs in a strange land. In the triumphs of a Christian faith, Paul and Silas beguiled the midnight hours, in the Philippian jail, with prayer and singing, though their feet were held fast in the stocks of the innermost prison. After the captivity it appears that the synagogue service, in some cases at least, did approach the social worship of the prayer-meeting. Pious Jews, not numerous enough, or not rich enough to build and sustain a synagogue in heathen cities, were accustomed to have *oratories*, places of prayer, cheap and temporary resorts for worship. In one of these the Apostle found Lydia and her associates, out of the city of Philippi, by the riverside, where they were accustomed to pray.

It does not appear that even Jesus and His disciples held seasons of social prayer together. He prayed much, and taught them how to pray, as John also taught his disciples. But immediately after the ascension, the spirit of the new life took possession of the disciples, even before the baptism of the Pentecost, and they resorted to "an upper room," where " these all continued, with one accord in prayer and supplication, with the women, and Mary, the mother of Jesus, and His brethren." There was born the prayer-meeting of the Christian dispensation, which has, through all the generations continued, with non-liturgical churches, a component, and a most important part of Christian worship —in theory at least, however much it may be neglected in practice.

As the services of evangelical churches generally

are arranged, the principal prayer-meeting, or, as it is sometimes distinguished, "the Church prayer-meeting," comes in the middle of the week. As a rule it is not numerously attended. But the most spiritual and devout members attend; and those who do habitually attend become the devout and spiritually minded, if they were not such before. This service not only reveals, but nourishes and develops the religious vitality of the Church, and the importance of the service as a spiritual force cannot well be overestimated. The pastor who is wise unto righteousness for the good of his people, will cultivate this part of worship with the most painstaking assiduity. Those pastors who have been most successful in edifying their churches, have most magnified the prayer-meeting. Those ministers who have been most successful in winning souls, have most magnified the functions and the efficacy of prayer. And those churches which most devoutly pray for the success of the gospel among them, are the most likely to realize that their work is not in vain in the Lord.

Some Suggestions

Doubtless every pastor believes himself fully capable of so ordering this service as to produce the best results, without advice from any one. And yet it is probably safe to say, that not one minister in ten knows how to make a prayer-meeting efficient, and about one in twenty would kill the best one that could be put into his hands. By many it is considered a very unimportant affair, that will care for itself, or, if not cared for at all, it matters little. No wise pastor will make such a mistake.

The following suggestions—a few out of many— may be helpful to some.*

1. The success and utility of the prayer-meeting depends on the *leader*, more than on any other one thing, save the presence of the Holy Spirit. The leader will presumably be the pastor. He certainly ought not to commit the management of so important a matter to other hands, as a rule. And he ought to give diligence and prayerful study to bring this department of worship to the highest possible state of interest and efficiency.

2. The success of the service does not depend on the numbers who attend. Though a full meeting is desirable, yet a very full meeting may be a very poor one, and a very small meeting may be a very good one. And all attempts to crowd the service by introducing other than legitimate topics, is a mistake. The prayer-meeting has its special mission. Diverted from that, it ceases to be the true prayer-meeting, though it may prove an interesting service of some other kind.

3. The prayer-meeting is not a " teaching service." Though its exercises will convey instruction, yet instruction is not its special function. That belongs

---

* For a more extended discussion of the subject see " The Star Book on Prayer-Meetings," published by Ward & Drummond, New York.

to the pulpit, the Bible class, and other similar exercises. This is for the heart rather than for the intellect. To feed the spiritual hunger of the soul. To cheer, inspire, comfort. Many keep silent because they say they cannot *instruct*. But that is not the peculiar vocation of the service. They can console, sympathize, encourage.

4. The opening exercises should be brief. So should they all. Many pastors talk to death the service, by long, dull, dreary harangues, just to "start the meeting!" Give a desultory discourse, a kind of pointless lecture, of a promiscuous character, confusing rather than illuminating the minds of the people, giving them nothing in particular to think about, to speak on, or to pray for. Then the leader sits down, telling them to occupy the time and be very brief! Is it a wonder that no one feels like moving, and that the meeting expires after a few ineffectual struggles for animation?

5. Singing should have a large place in the prayer-meeting. Not so much as to absorb and cover up, or exclude prayer and exhortation, or degenerate into a singing-school. The hymns should be wisely adjusted to the service and the temper of the occasion. After the meeting is fairly opened, one stanza at a time is all that should ordinarily be used. The hymns should be so familiar that all can use them. At the opening and closing of the service an instrument is of special use. But during the progress of the meeting, it is rather preferable, as being more free and less formal, for some one to strike a

familiar verse, without waiting to look it up in the book, or for the instrument to lead.

6. Begin the meeting *on time*. That will help the attendants to be prompt. If the leader waits for the people, the people will be all the later. Train them to habits of punctuality. Close on time, except that, on occasion, the interest may justify protracting the exercises somewhat. But do not continue so long as to exhaust the interest, and have to stop on a falling tide.

7. Have the place of meeting *pleasant* and *attractive*. This can be done, however plain and poor it may be, by those little arts of handicraft and good taste which people anywhere can exercise. By the use of flowers, inexpensive pictures and mottoes, you can make a barn look pretty. Worshipers, especially the young, should associate beauty, purity and good order with religion.

8. Be sure to have a plenty of *pure air* and *good light* in the prayer room. Few buildings are so badly ventilated as our church buildings. On Sunday people can better bear to be poisoned with a noxious atmosphere, when they have nothing to do but listen to the preacher—or not listen, as the case may be. But in the conference meeting, where they are expected to take some part, it is absolutely essential that they shall not be put to sleep, made drowsy, or given a headache by vitiated air.

9. As the chief value and potency of the social meeting lies in its *spiritual unction* and power, therefore one of the chief subjects of prayer should

be the implored presence and aid of the Holy Spirit. And those persons are best prepared for it, and the most useful in it, who do the most to live in and walk by the Spirit. No intellectual or literary qualifications can meet this demand. Here, the spiritually minded bear the palm, though in all else they may be quite behind.

10. As the fabric of the prayer and conference meeting consists of this threefold texture, *prayer*, *exhortation* and *song*, does not assume the functions of teaching, and relates largely to personal Christian experience, therefore all, old and young, male and female, learned and unlearned, can take part in its service, be benefited, and benefit others. All who have a personal experience of divine grace in their own hearts and lives, are fitted to do good and to receive a blessing in this sacred service.

OTHER PRAYER-MEETINGS

Besides the mid-week general prayer-meeting of the Church, many other occasions for special or stated prayer are observed by most Christian congregations.

The women's prayer-meeting In very many churches Christian women have a weekly service of this sort, conducted by themselves, where they can feel more freedom than in the general meetings. These services, sometimes inaptly called " female prayer-meeting," give occasion for those to exercise their gifts who lack the courage, or possibly doubt the propriety of females speaking in promiscuous assemblies, as in some communities they do.

Young people's prayer-meeting   Within recent years, the organization of *classes*, especially women and young people, for religious and benevolent work, has assumed proportions not formerly dreamed of. Great good has resulted, and greater good, we may hope, will yet result, notwithstanding some doubts and drawbacks as to the evils of class divisions in Church life and work, as imperiling the unity of the body.   The young people's prayer-meeting is now almost everywhere in the churches.   The only objection that seems valid, as against them, is, that having done their part in their own prayer-meeting, they may either feel at liberty to absent themselves from the Church prayer-meeting, or, if present, to take no part.   Where this does happen it is a serious misfortune, and overbalances any good their separate service may produce.   The Church should not be broken up into sections and segments of old people and young people, male and female, but be as one family, a sacred unity, as the body of Christ.   But these unfortunate results do not always follow.

The missionary prayer-meeting   The concert of prayer for missionaries, and the success of the Gospel in heathen lands, held once each month, seems falling into neglect.   Formerly it was generally observed by all Evangelical churches.   " The week of prayer," for the same object, and for the universal revival of religion, is still generally observed on the first week in the year.   Usually very gracious re-

sults follow in the churches which observe it. They
that water others shall themselves be watered.

The temperance prayer-meeting This is not so
generally observed as it should be. For if there be
anything that appeals to Christian faith, and which
should lead Christian people to appeal to God, the
righteous judge, for help, it is this cause,—that the
gigantic iniquity of the saloon, and the drink habit,
which cause more suffering than war, pestilence and
famine combined, may be checked and destroyed.
With churches so apathetic, and good people on
every hand so indifferent, the rum power rides riot
over all that is fairest and best in society, destroying homes, impoverishing nations, and invading the
sacred altars of our holy religion. Appeals need to
be made to Him who is able to hear and save, for
who else can avail?

The mothers' prayer-meeting There is fitness in
the gatherings of mothers for special prayer for their
children, that they may escape the snares of sin and
the temptations of the world, be early converted,
and make honorable and useful Christians. Such
meetings, persisted in, have often been followed by
the most manifest blessing of God in answers to
prayer. But mothers who pray for the conversion
of their children must constantly strive to answer
their own prayers, by training them in the nurture
and admonition of the Lord.

The Sunday-school prayer-meeting It is quite
natural for Christian workers in any department of
service to feel specially interested in that depart-

ment, and to implore the divine favor to attend and give success to their endeavors. Sunday-school work has become so wide-spread, so vital as a religious agency, and so efficient among the young, that it rightly holds a large place in the sympathies and the prayers of the churches. It is most commendable, therefore, that special prayer, and special seasons of prayer be designated for the success of this line of Christian endeavor.

For colleges and schools of learning   An annual "week of prayer" is now generally observed for educational institutions, especially schools for higher learning, that they may be made subservient to virtue, truth and piety. For the conversion of students, and the sanctification of all intellectual acquisitions to the best interest of true religion. This is a matter of the gravest importance, especially as nearly all of our colleges and high schools were founded, and are largely supported by the benevolence of Christian men and women.

III   THE SERVICE OF SONG

The power and influence of sacred song in worship are not understood and appreciated as they ought to be.

Even where music is highly cultivated in Christian congregations, it is rather for æsthetic effect and popular attraction, than for spiritual uses ; rather as an appeal to the intellect than to the heart ; rather to gratify the taste than to answer the cravings of a devout spirit. Music may become high art in the house of God, but that does not make it worship. Of course it should be artistic in the best sense of that term, but only that it may be the more devout. In the old temple service of the Hebrews, music, conjoined with sacrifices and offerings, constituted almost their only worship.

Indeed in our less pretentious Christian services, singing constitutes almost the only act that can be called *worship* in the strictest sense. Like prayer, the service of song may express adoration, confession, supplication and praise. But, unlike prayer, all can vocally unite in this act of worship. Now, as in the primitive churches, the saints can mitigate their sorrows, beguile their griefs, elevate their affections, and gird themselves with strength, " Speaking to themselves in psalms and hymns, and spiritual songs, singing and making melody in their hearts to the Lord."—Eph. 5 : 19.

Being performed in concert, **where many unite, it** prevents an unpleasant sense of individual responsibility, and becomes a pleasant privilege, instead of a burdensome duty. It animates the dull, and soothes the agitated spirit. While it comforts and inspires the saints, it, more than any other part of religious service, attracts the unconverted and the unbelieving. It is the act of worship in which all occupy a common attitude, and mutually bear a part. It is not, therefore, strange that sacred song has occupied so large a place in the history of Christian worship, and that the affections of the renewed heart cherish it so fondly, and resort to it so constantly. Christianity has sung its triumphs through the ages, and around the world.

1. *The Character of Song-Worship*

It should be the united expression of the assembly —the worship of all uttered in song. It is not to be a performance by a company of musicians, for the entertainment of the congregation, but an act of worship *by* the congregation itself. It is not to be an act of worship, performed by others, to which the people are to listen, but an act of worship which they themselves are to offer. "Let the people praise thee, O God: let all the people praise thee."—Ps. 67 : 5.

Therefore singing should be congregational; that is, the people should sing; all the assembly should praise God in song. Singing is the people's worship. The chant, the anthem, the oratorio are rather for the cathedral and the temple. Though beautiful and grand, and potent with a savor of worship, they should be sparingly used in the Christian congregation. They may incite an audience to worship, but the assembly does not to any considerable extent worship in them. The genius of the Gospel requires chiefly the *chorus*, where the people shall not simply listen, and have devotion excited, but where they shall sing, and express devotion.

2. *The Style of Music*

Since the true idea of sacred song is that the people shall worship, not witness a performance, there fore the style of music should be such as the people can perform. But the mass of worshipers can never go beyond the simplest elements of any art or science; therefore the music for Christian service should be of the simplest kind, in structure and execution, and limited to a small number of tunes. Music more complicated in structure, and more artistic in execution, a few could perform, and perhaps more highly enjoy; but it could not express the devotion of the great majority of worshipers because they could not unite in it. Devotion seeks plain choral harmonies in which to utter its worship.

The leaders of Church music will be constantly endeavoring to treat the congregation to a greater variety in style and execution; but this will be a departure from the true idea of worship. As our religious services are usually arranged it may be very well to introduce them with an anthem, a chant, or a sentence by the choir; and possibly a short set piece somewhere before the sermon; perhaps immediately following the " long prayer," before the notices, and the second hymn. But the hymns—and prevailing custom calls for *three*—should be sung to simple music, so familiar that the people can sing them, without an effort to remember the tune, and without danger of losing it, all thought being given to the sentiment and spirit of the words.

3. *The Leader of Music*

It makes little difference whether the leader be an organ, or a single voice, a quartette, or a choir.

Either of these would harmonize with the spirit and design of worship, so long as it be simply a *leader*, and not a performer. If the singing is to be done for the people, and they take no part in it, it matters little whether that part be performed by an instrument, a single voice, or several voices. But a Christian congregation should not omit so important a duty, nor deprive itself of so sacred a privilege as that of singing the praises of God in His house of worship.

NOTE 1.—The too common custom, in our large and wealthy congregations, in cities and towns, of hiring a company of professional musicians, operatic or otherwise, carnal, worldly minded, and irreverent persons, destitute of religious sentiment, to perform this important part of religious service for the Church, is a shameful perversion, which outrages every sentiment of a pure spiritual worship, violates the proprieties of a simple Gospel service, and ought not to be tolerated by a Christian assembly. For while it is proper for unconverted persons to sing in worship, and even to be members of the choir if reverent, and while it is proper for persons who devote valuable time and service to music to receive appropriate compensation, yet to give up to a company of paid performers the most important part of worship, simply because they possess musical taste and culture, is an offense to the spirit of devotion, and it must seem to the Spirit of grace as well.

NOTE 2.—While it is as proper for unconverted persons to sing, as it is for them to read the Scriptures, or to pray, yet it is altogether inconsistent for one not truly a Christian to lead, have charge of and control the music for Church service; as inconsistent as it would be for an unconverted man to take charge of the prayer-meeting. The choir *leader* should be a thoroughly Christian man.

NOTE 3.—Since the music is a part of Church service, and a principal part of its worship, the right and obligation to engage, dismiss and manage those connected with it, belongs to the *Church* distinctively, as pertaining to its spiritualities, and not to the *trustees*, whose duties are confined to the temporalities; though so far as the payment of salaries is concerned, that falls to the trustees. Sometimes the Church by a special act gives up the entire management of this department to the trustees, to the deacons, to a music committee, or places it in the hands of the chorister, making him responsible. Either of these courses the Church has the right to take, judging for itself which is the wisest and best way.

NOTE 4.—It must be remembered that Church music is a part of worship, and since the conducting of worship devolves on the *pastor*, and is his by right, so the management of the singing should be only on consultation with him, and with his approval. And while he has not the right to overrule or reverse the action of the Church, they should not attempt to force on him musical adjustments which are unwelcome, or repugnant to his sense of propriety. The pulpit and the orchestra must be in accord, if worship is to be pleasant and profitable.

NOTE 5.—All levity and irreverence on the part of singers during the time of service should be strictly avoided, and if need be, absolutely forbidden and prohibited. All whispering, trifling, leaving the gallery during the sermon, returning in time for the closing hymn, with all other marks of indifference and disrespect, are painfully incongruous in scenes of devotion, especially on the part of those who occupy so prominent a place in worship as do the musicians. The same respectful attention to all the services should be demanded from them, as is expected from others of the congregation.

NOTE 6.—In order to realize the full advantage of congregational singing as an aid to worship, some churches have weekly meetings, especially of the young people, for the purpose of practising, and becoming familiar with the hymns and tunes used on the Lord's Day.

NOTE 7.—Every Church should provide for the instruction of the young in the congregation and Sunday-school, in the elements of vocal music. Such instruction, during six, or at least three months of the year, with a weekly exercise, would soon make congregational singing practicable and successful.

NOTE 8.—It certainly would seem that every Christian congregation should be able to recruit a volunteer chorus choir from its own members, without the necessity of hiring professional artists from abroad. This would better harmonize with the true idea of devotion. And if Church music were sustained purely for worship, as it should be, and not as a special entertainment or attraction, this might be realized more frequently than it now is.

IV. THE WORD OF EXHORTATION

Whether the gift of exhortation were one of the special *charisms* bestowed by the Spirit on the primitive Church, as many believe, and as would seem to be implied in the eighth of Romans, where it is mentioned as one of the *gifts*, and classed with prophecy, the ministry, teaching and ruling, we do not undertake to decide. Certain it is that it has always been developed among the spiritually minded as a powerful auxiliary to the preaching of the Gospel, and other means of grace. It constitutes a considerable part of worship in social religious meetings, where God's people " exhort one another daily," and each " suffer the word of exhortation."—Heb. 3 : 13; 13 : 22. The meaning of the original word (*parakaleo*) is significant of the importance of the exercise. It means to call for, or upon, and especially to call upon in the sense of cheering, encouraging, comforting, inspiring, those addressed.

There are persons in every Church who have a depth and richness of Christian experience far beyond the common average, whose remarks are attended by a peculiar unction and power unknown to the ordinary Christian life. This is, doubtless, largely owing to their closer fellowship and more intimate communion with God. But, aside from such special cases, every saint can speak of his experience in the life of faith, and by a recital of both his sorrows and his joys, exhort and encourage others. They are not called upon to expound the Scriptures, nor to conduct public meetings, but they can tell of the love of God and the grace of Christ as revealed to them.

The exhortations of God's children form one of the most effectual means of spiritual improvement and edification to the churches, " Or he that exhorteth on exhortation."—Rom. 12 : 8.

1. *Who should exhort* —All who have the spirit. It is the privilege, and, doubtless, at times, the duty of all who know the grace of God, without distinction of age, sex or condition, to speak of their experience in the divine life, and thus encourage others. This is an exercise specially fitted for the social meetings. There, where the greater freedom of " the household of faith " prevails, they should " exhort one another, and so much the more as they see the day approaching."—Heb. 10 : 25.

2. *The gift of exhortation* —Whether there be a special *gift* for this exercise, and whether some are called to it as others are called to preach, it is clear that some are specially gifted in it, as some are in prayer and some in the ministry of the word. But every one who has an experience in godliness can speak to edification, and the deeper and more constant is that experience the more gracious and edifying will be the exhortation. Ordinary abilities, sanctified by the Spirit, cannot fail to be profitable. Those who speak the most fluently and the most eloquently do not always speak the most profitably; but those who speak with the Spirit never fail to edify those who walk in the Spirit.

3. *Faults in exhortation* —Christians sometimes fall unconsciously into faulty habits in this exercise, which hinder their usefulness and mar the pleasure of spiritual fellowship.

Gloomy and despondent expressions should be avoided. Comforting, inspiring, stimulating utterances befit the meaning of the word and the wants of the saints.

A preaching style should be avoided, though passages of Scripture will often be mentioned, suggesting reflections of great interest and profit.

Prolix exhortations should never be indulged in, since they become wearisome and unprofitable, and deprive others of their privileges.

One's self should not be too often mentioned, lest it might appear boastful and egotistic.

Fault-finding and complaining should be most

carefully shunned. It closes the ears and hearts of the hearers, and casts a pall over the spirit of the meeting.

Denunciation and a censorious spirit is, if possible, still worse. It exhibits a spirit opposed to the Gospel, and never fails to do harm.

Hobbies are unprofitable. Some dwell on hackneyed themes until both themselves and their subjects are distasteful to the audience.

Foreign subjects should not be often introduced, except as illustrations, or from which to draw lessons of instruction. Experimental religion furnishes the fittest themes for exhortations.

Adulation and excessive praise of individuals are as unwise and offensive as harsh criticism and denunciation; though commendation and approval, when called for, are praiseworthy.

Confessing one's self a very great sinner, parading his shortcomings, will be understood as an affectation of unusual piety. This is not wise exhortation.

V. THE COVENANT MEETING

The Covenant Meeting is an order of religious service, very generally, though not universally observed among Baptists. Its observance, however, is extending, and becoming more general. In form, it is a usage peculiar to our people, but in spirit and purpose, it has its counterpart in some of the other denominations. Somewhat like the " class-meeting," it aims to secure some expression of Christian experience from each Church member present; and somewhat like the "preparatory lecture," it proposes to become a fitting preparation for the communion of the Lord's Supper, to be observed on the following Sunday.

The origin of this service, in its present form, is not known. It was peculiarly valued by the old New England Baptists, and traveled West and Northwest with the tide of their emigration, more than South and Southwest. Its spirit is instinct in the fellowship of the Gospel, and the spiritual sympathy of the Christian brotherhood. The saint, at conversion, enters into joyous covenant with Christ, and with His people. Whether formally expressed or not, every Christian does, on being baptized and received to the fellowship of the Church, covenant to walk together with the other members, in all sincerity and godliness, as common heirs of the grace of life. This pledge, to love, pray for, and help each other, shunning all ungodliness, and living soberly and righteously before the world, is the renewed assurance of fellowship, in the bonds of a common faith, and the love of a common Saviour, from time to time renewed. These covenants of mutual sympathy and help, had a significancy amidst the persecutions of the early martyr age of Christianity, which they have not now. The same may be said as to the times of persecution, when the early Baptists of New England endured much cruel opposition and suffering inflicted by their fellow-Christians, for conscience' sake, and for Christ's sake patiently borne. The renewal of this covenant is with both Christ as the Head of the Church, and with the members of the body.

In favor of the covenant meeting, as a means of spiritual help and culture, much may be said. If a member could attend but one service of the Church during the month, that one should undoubtedly be the Communion of the Lord's Supper. This is the highest expression of piety, and brings the soul into most immediate fellowship with its exalted and living Lord. If there be but one other service which the member can attend, that other one should be the covenant meeting, which anticipates the near approach of the commemorative Supper, and reviews the vital relationship of the disciple to His Saviour on the one hand, and to his fellow-disciples on the other. And where the service is so conducted as to realize its true ideal, it becomes the most endeared to those who attend, and the most spiritually stimulating and helpful of all occasions of social worship.

But the covenant meeting, in order to realize its benefits, must be made distinctive, and kept true to its purpose. The service is unique. It is not a prayer-meeting, it is not a lecture service, it is not a teacher's meeting. It is for each member. So far as all are willing—for there is no compulsion—to speak briefly of his religious estate and experience, especially during the past month, and in view of the approaching Communion. After the usual opening exercises, and brief remarks from the pastor, along the special line of the meeting's purpose, calculated to be helpful to what follows, the members are expected "to speak to their covenant," or in more common phrase, "to renew their covenant." This is done in few words by each in turn, by a renewed declaration of their interest in, and fellowship with, the Church and the Christian life, with mention of any peculiar experience of joy or sorrow, during the previous month. The whole area of Christian experience comes under review, as each one's meditations may be led.

It is not always an easy task to induce an assembly of Christian people to speak readily and freely concerning their own religious experiences. Some have so little experience in godliness; some are so little accustomed to speaking before others; some shrink with such timidity from speaking of themselves, that there is probably more difficulty in reaching a satisfactory attainment in this service, than in any other social meeting. No one is called on personally. But some pastors, to save so large a loss of time, and to secure a larger number of testimonies, have the speaking begin at a particular part of the room, and go in order through one row of seats after another, till the whole is completed. Each one speaks, or declines, as he chooses, when the turn reaches him. This plan is a little more formal, but a much larger number of testimonies will in this way be secured, and usually the effect of the meeting is better. Many will have something to say when their turn comes, and others immediately about them have spoken, who otherwise would remain silent. And those who are thus induced to bear their part in the service find themselves to have enjoyed it vastly more on that account. The covenant meeting is held monthly, on the week preceding the communion Sunday. In cities, towns and villages, it usually takes the place of the prayer-meeting for that week, notice being given on Sunday, that it may be kept in mind. In frontier districts, and sparsely settled country neighborhoods, it is common to hold it on Saturday afternoon, as more convenient for attendance. In such cases it is usual for them, in addition to the covenant service, to transact any Church business, needful to be done.

NOTE 1.—To the Articles of Faith, which the churches use, there is generally attached a form of Church Covenant. This, some pastors are accustomed to read to the Church when assembled at the Supper, and to which they give assent by standing while it is being read, Some read it at the Covenant Meeting, as a partial substitute for, or supplement to, the meeting.

NOTE 2.—It will be understood that with our churches no formal pledge, creed or covenant is made compulsory on members, either on being received to their fellowship or subsequently. On making application for membership, copies of the articles of faith and covenant are put into their hands —or should be—and they are asked to examine them carefully. A general concurrence in these is expected, but no pledged conformity is ever exacted.

CHAPTER 10

THE CHURCH'S MISSION

CHURCHES are Heaven's appointed agencies for the salvation of men. For, though it would be false and profane to say that men could not be saved outside the churches, and without their aid, yet, as a matter of fact, but few are converted and saved aside from associated Christian effort, as represented by the churches, or the zeal of personal piety, as nourished and stimulated by them.

The mission of a Christian Church, therefore, is to a " world lying in wickedness," to men " dead in trespasses and sins," as the bearer of glad tidings to " prisoners of hope," and herald of the great salvation to lost men. In order to accomplish this, the Church must sustain a suitable spiritual condition, and maintain itself in the faith and discipline, the order and ordinances of the Gospel. Indeed, for this cause Christ gave Himself for the Church, "that He might present it to Himself a glorious Church, not having spot or wrinkle, or any such thing; but that it should be holy and without blemish."—Eph. 5 : 27. A carnal, selfish, worldly minded Church can never perform this holy mission ; indeed, is neither worthy of it, nor fitted for it.

The responsibility of a Church is both corporate and personal. As a *body* it is bound to make its influence felt far and near. But the body is what the individual units which compose it make it to be. Each member, therefore, should strive to be and to do what the entire Church ought to be and to do, " the light of the world and the salt of the earth," " a city set on a hill, that cannot be hid." There is work for all, and work adapted to the condition and ability and capacity of each, however weak and humble. Old and young, great and small, male and female, have something to do, and something that each can do—if there be a heart to do it. The efficiency and usefulness of a Church depend on each member's filling his own place, and doing his own work, so as neither to attempt the work of others, nor yet to stand idly by while others serve. In nothing, perhaps, are the wisdom and skill of the pastor and officers more apparent than in finding work for all, and giving something fit and adapted for each to do.

It is a sad and somewhat humiliating reflection that so many churches clustered together in communities with all the appointments and means of grace at their command, and yet that they exert so small an influence on these communities — make such trifling inroads on the domain of sin, and win so few trophies for the truth. The moral influence of these institutions of Christianity ought to do more to repress iniquity, and to increase righteousness. The results of Church life and action are often more apparent in heathen than in Christian lands. Doubtless the explanation of this is to be found in a lack of vital godliness, and for want of a higher standard of Christian living among us.

The common and ordinary means of doing good, and the methods of Christian work as now usually organized, are as follows :

I. GOSPEL MINISTRATIONS

The preaching of the Gospel, the proclamation of pardon and eternal life through faith in Christ, is the foremost and the most effective instrumentality for the salvation of the world.

It is divinely ordained, and divinely sanctioned and **sustained.** The command is, " Go ye into all the world, and preach the Gospel to every creature. And lo, I am with you alway, unto the end of the world."—Mark 16 : 15 ; Matt. 28 : 20. The promise is, " My word shall not return unto me void, but it shall accomplish that which I please, and it shall prosper in the thing whereto I sent it."—Isaiah 55:11. Though an apparently feeble, even an obnoxious agency, yet it is "mighty to the pulling down of strongholds." " We preach Christ crucified, unto the Jews a stumbling-block, and unto the Greeks foolishness; but unto them which are called, both Jews and Greeks, Christ the power of God, and the wisdom of God."—1 Cor. 1 : 23, 24.

1. It is taken for granted, as a matter of course, that every Church will support a faithful and an

evangelical ministry among them, for *ordinary service* in the house of God. This is for the edification of the Church itself, and for the instruction and conversion of all, old and young, who may be attracted to it. A home ministry should be able and faithful, and generously sustained. If the nations are to be fed, the family at home must be built up and instructed in the purposes of grace. The more the saints know and taste of the word of life, the more liberally and earnestly will they send living bread to the perishing nations.

2. But there come times in the history of every Church, when *extraordinary services* seem demanded, special occasions indicated by the Spirit's movement, and an unusual disposition on the part of the people to give heed to spiritual and eternal concerns. While all times are times of favor from the Lord, and truly times of need with men, yet it is clearly manifest that there are times which are more hopeful for sowing, and more abundant in reaping than others. Such should be specially improved.

3. Within the range of every Church, and within the parish lines of every pastor's field, there are certain peculiarly *destitute places*, which are generally very much neglected, and to which few, if any, means of grace are furnished. The people cannot, or do not attend the churches. If they have the Gospel it must be carried to them. And often they are more ready and eager hearers of the word than stated congregations, surfeited with its abundance. Under

faithful spiritual cultivation such destitute communities often become fruitful as the garden of the Lord.

4. But the world is the field, whose bounds extend beyond home, and country and kindred. Begin at Jerusalem, but do not stop till *all nations* are reached, and every creature taught the way of life through Christ crucified. Each Church and each individual should feel his obligation to aid in sending the Gospel to the destitute *the world over*. That was Christ's purpose and design. For that He died. And those who have His spirit will strive to carry forward the work He began; and "if any man have not the spirit of Christ, he is none of His."

Note 1.—In some of these destitute fields, pastors will find some of their most pleasant hours of labor, and some of their richest rewards. In such services there will be a sincerity and a simplicity hardly expected in the more formal, and often perfunctory services of the sanctuary. The hearty welcome given to simple truth, instead of cool reserve, or critical hesitancy, is quite refreshing to the spirit of a true minister of Christ.

Note 2.—Some churches do, and many more might—and ought—sustain a colporteur, or missionary, to labor a part, or all of the time in such destitute neighborhoods. Not a few able churches support a pastor's assistant to aid in work too large and laborious for one man to do in addition to pulpit ministrations. Most churches could accomplish tenfold more in such ways than they do.

Note 3.—Great good has been effected by a few churches, in developing and putting to use lay-preaching. In almost every Church are brethren who possess more than ordinary gifts for exhortation, expounding the Scriptures, addressing congregations, and conducting religious meetings. Why should such abilities lie dormant, and find no appropriate exercise? They will not push themselves to the front; but they can be encouraged to assume responsibilities. It would be a great blessing to the churches themselves if such capable members should be called into requisition for holding meetings in destitute places, and bearing the gospel to those beyond the ordinary means of grace.

II. SUNDAY-SCHOOL WORK

In their spirit and purpose, Sunday-schools are in harmony with gospel methods of doing good ; though, unlike the Church, there is no scriptural precept or precedent for their separate and independent organization.

The churches should provide religious instruction for the children and youth of their own families, and for the children and youth of other families who may be disposed to avail themselves of the privilege, quite as much. Particularly should this instruction make prominent a study of the Bible. This is the one text-book for, and the one purpose of, Sunday-school and Bible-class study. It is likely that, so far as the local congregation is concerned, next to the preaching of the Gospel, the Sunday-school is to be ranked in importance as an evangelical agency. To what extent its object is realized depends largely on the course pursued by the superintendent, officers and teachers.

The influence of Sunday-school work is *threefold*: The *direct* influence on the pupils in storing their minds with religious knowledge, forming their characters to virtue and moulding their hearts to good morals. The *indirect* influence on the homes of the pupils, to which they carry their impressions from the school; their books and papers to be read, and the songs they had learned to sing, to be repeated in their own families. The *reflex* influence on officers and teachers, and all who are interested in, and work or make effort for, the school. Those who are engaged in doing good are benefited as much by the effort as those to whom the good is done. Hence, those who stand aloof from any Christian service are the chief losers.

The religious training of the young, both in the household and in the Church, is undervalued, and too much neglected. The character of men and women, and their influence for good or evil in subsequent life, depend largely on their moral and religious training in childhood. Divine wisdom has foreseen and provided for this, and has enjoined that: " These words which I command thee this day shall be in thine heart; and thou shalt teach them diligently unto thy children, and shalt talk of them when thou sittest in thine house, and when thou walkest in the way, and when thou liest down, and when thou risest up."—Deut. 6 : 6, 7. Aside from the direct beneficial influence on the young themselves, no greater boon can be conferred on posterity than to train the rising generation to virtue, honor and integrity; and this is most effectually done by Christian culture. In accomplishing this, the Sunday-school is a potent agency.

1. *The Relation of the School to the Church*

There are in the main three prevailing theories of Sunday-school control, somewhat diverse, and not a little at variance with each other, each of which for the greater part works smoothly, because of the good disposition of those concerned in the work.

First—That the school is created by, dependent on, and controlled by the Church, as a part of its legitimate work. In this case the Church appoints its officers, with or without instructions, as it would appoint a committee for any other service. Of course these appointments would be on consultation with the workers, and not in an arbitrary manner. The Church is responsible for all expenses incurred, and for the general management of the body. The pastor is the official head of this, as of all other Church work, even though not practically engaged in its details. Undoubtedly this is the true normal relation of the school to the Church.

Second—That the school is a benevolent association, like any other organized for a specific purpose, not created by, dependent on, or subject to the authority of the Church. On this theory, individuals interested in the work, from the same or from different churches, form themselves into a society, appoint their own officers, make their own laws, meet their own expenses, and manage their own affairs. The Church sympathizes in the work, aids it, if so disposed, but assumes no responsibility in connection with it.

Third—That the school adopt its methods, appoint its officers, and administer its government, subject to the approval of the Church, which holds a veto power, and the right of ultimate control in all matters of authority. The school is allowed independence with non interference, so long as its management meets the approval of the Church, but when they differ, the Church rules. This method is a modification of the two preceding.

NOTE 1.—In the case of a " home school "—that is, one growing out of a given Church, and occupying the Church's premises for its service, the *first* of these plans is the only consistent one; although many home schools are organized on the second plan, where the pastor and Church have no more authority or control than if it were a temperance society or a literary club. This is all wrong, and the wonder is that troubles do not more frequently arise.

NOTE 2.—Where schools are organized in destitute regions, and sustained by persons from different churches, constituting distinctively mission schools, the *second* method is perhaps the only practicable one, since they are the outgrowth not of Church activity, but of individual zeal.

NOTE 3.—Every Church should feel obligated to provide religious instruction, under its own inspection, for its own children, and should know what kind of instructors they have, and what kind of instructions they receive, in this most important part of their education. In such a service the pastor should lead the way, and insist on its being done, and being properly done.

2. *The Continuance of School Service*

In city schools, formerly, two sessions were commonly or frequently held on Sunday. In a few instances this practice is continued, but is of doubtful expediency. Certainly it is of doubtful expediency in home schools, whatever may be said of mission schools. In many thinly populated neighborhoods and frontier settlements school exercises are wholly intermitted during the rigors of winter weather. In not a few this is inevitable, but in many others, no doubt, with a little more energy and perseverance, they might be continued throughout the year, though possibly with a diminished attendance.

3. *Character of the Government*

A Sunday-school cannot be governed quite like other schools. The government must be paternal and kind. Corporeal punishments and ordinary penalties are not resorted to, but moral forces and the power of love must rule. Neither should the promise of rewards be too freely used. Presents, picnics and festivals, held out to the pupils as an inducement to attend, present a wrong and selfish motive. Once in a while these have a good effect, not as a promise beforehand made, but as a pleasant enjoyment afterward granted.

4. *Exercises Should be Diversified*

The exercises should be greatly diversified, in which singing should have a large place. Singing pleases children, and they readily learn to unite in it. It instructs and elevates the sentiments, while it softens and subdues the ruder traits and rougher passions. Children soon weary of protracted application, therefore the exercises should not be long continued in any one direction. It requires all the versatility of superintendent and teachers to sustain the interest of the school and the classes. Of course this should not be carried to any such an extent as to dissipate serious interest, and make the school seem a play resort instead of a place for learning.

5. *Books for the Library*

The books furnished for the children to read and take to their homes deserve very special attention. It is no easy task to make a judicious selection of books for such a use. Good books are one of the best appliances for Sunday-school work. But the practice of admitting to these libraries so large a portion of fiction, even if it have a weak flavor of religion, is to be severely condemned. The sickly, sentimental love stories, with a little prayer-meeting talk interspersed, fifth or sixth rate in literary quality, will counteract a large part of the good the school will otherwise accomplish. But good books are greatly to be commended. For some years past periodicals adapted to this use have come largely into vogue, and to a considerable extent have displaced the libraries. Papers are cheap, and being pictorial, are attractive and pleasing. Good, sound books will, however, hold their places.

6. *Bible-Class Study*

This is a similar, not a separate, department of religious instruction. These classes contain the older and more advanced portions of the youth, together with adults, associated for mutual study of the Word of God. The formation and support of such classes should be encouraged for the great advantage to those who compose them, and also as a place for the members of lower classes when they suppose they have outgrown the proper dimensions of their own.

As this is not a manual on methods of study and plans of management, the subject need here be no further pursued.

NOTE 4.—Since the study of the word of God is the one specific object of Bible-school work, the one thing which justifies its existence and gives it importance, therefore nothing should be allowed to obscure that one thing, or interfere with its successful prosecution. All the arrangements of the school should make prominent the *lesson*, illustrate its meaning, and enforce its teaching.

NOTE 5.—Nor is it enough that the letter of the lesson be comprehended. Teachers should never be satisfied until the *spirit* and power of the truth shall savingly affect the hearts of the pupils. An intellectual mastery of the Bible will effect but little unless the salvation of the soul be secured. To this result should all the labor tend.

NOTE 6.—In this field of Christian endeavor the *pastor* has great responsibility and great opportunity. He should exercise a constant, watchful care and guardianship over it. He may, or he may not, become statedly identified with its exercises, but he should often visit it, speaking such words of cheer and making such suggestions as may seem wise. It will make him familiar with the children, and give him influence with all.

NOTE 7.—Very little should be said in the school, even by way of notices, calculated to divert the minds from the one purpose for which they are assembled. And the custom in some schools, of circulating tickets for fairs, festivals, picnics, suppers, with elaborate notices and explanations, cannot be too severely condemned. All religious impressions are prevented or obliterated by these captivating devices. They should not be permitted ; other opportunities may be allowed for them.

NOTE 8.—It is to be feared that the Bible itself is becoming too much a stranger in the Sunday-school classes. So much dependence is had on "lesson leaves" and other "helps," while the Bible is overlooked as the constant handbook and text-book of the service. In a study of the Scriptures there is a vast advantage in each teacher and each pupil having *his own Bible*, in searching that, and becoming familiar with it. It serves a purpose, but not the same purpose nor one equally important, to read a text or a lesson from a slip of paper as from the book itself.

NOTE 9.—The school deserves and should receive the prayers, sympathies, and sustaining help of the entire Church. Parents and other members, not engaged in it, should often visit it, and thereby show their interest. It is the least they can do, and workers will be cheered by their presence.

NOTE 10.—A school may be full of vital activity, while all the Church besides may be very dull or very dead. And yet it is very foolish and very absurd to say the school is as important as the Church, and doing more good. A Church may be degenerate, and false to its mission, but still it is a divine institution. Even the life of the school is the Church's life transferred to, and centered in, that particular department of service. Unreasoning enthusiasts make a great mistake when they exalt the school at the expense of the Church.

III. RELIGIOUS VISITATION

Religious *visitation* is an effective means by which the churches can further their mission among the families of their own immediate field of Christian work; at least, such families as are supposed to have no Church relations, and to be under no definite religious influence.

It is presumed the minister will visit such households, and afford them religious instruction and consolation. But the point here is, that the Church, under the leadership of the pastor, should adopt some plan for systematic religious visitation carried on by private members. The purpose is to hold religious conversation with the inmates, read the Scriptures, and have prayer; invite them to the house of God, and bring the children into the Sunday-school. If in sickness, want, or other misfortune, report them to the Church, and furnish such relief as may be practicable; especially, as in more needy homes, suitable raiment may not be possessed, to furnish it. And in any other way that may be open, to relieve temporal necessities to those found to be really deserving.

In no other way can Christians more effectually imitate their Lord and Master, who " went about doing good," mitigating and removing the temporal sufferings of men, that He might the more effectually reach their souls with spiritual food. There is no more Christly mission for the churches than this, and every member can bear some part in it, if there only be a willing and ready mind. Hearts oppressed with sorrow hunger for sympathy, and welcome the counsels of those who will give it.

This ministry of Christian faith and love cannot well be overestimated in its value, both to those who perform it, and to those who receive it. James was right: "Pure religion and undefiled before God and the Father is this, to visit the fatherless and widows in their affliction, and to keep himself unspotted from the world."—James 1 : 27. And yet how few of God's people appreciate this work, or are anxious to imitate this most notable feature of the life and character of Jesus!

As to the *method* for this service:

1. Let the whole field, which the Church is supposed to occupy, be divided into districts, and a certain number of families be apportioned to each member, male or female, who is willing to undertake the service; or, let them go "two and two," which is better, and according to the apostolic plan. Let these visitors report the results of their mission, from time to time, in the social meetings of the Church, or at specially designated times, and at the end of the year make a full report of the work done, and the realized results. Such reports will not only be interesting, but cannot fail to stimulate Christian activity through the entire body.

2. But if the Church as a whole cannot be moved to such a service, then let the few who are willing, agree among themselves to attempt it. The Lord will bless the endeavor, and their success will stimulate others. Should there be but one or two who are willing to make so noble an endeavor, let them try the blessed service, and spread the result before the Church. The Lord can work by few, as well as by many, "And he that reapeth

receiveth wages, and gathereth fruit unto life eternal."—John 4 : 36.

NOTE 1.—Such visits, to serve their purpose, should be strictly *religious*, and not merely social and friendly. Conversation should be had, so far as practicable, with the various members of the family, as to their personal religious welfare, with reading a brief portion of the Scriptures, and prayer, unless circumstances make these exercises inconsistent or impracticable.

NOTE 2.—The distribution of tracts and other *religious reading* should accompany such visits, and will prove greatly beneficial, providing such reading be wisely selected, and adapted to their conditions. Bibles should be furnished for homes destitute of them. A tract or book left at one visit, to be replaced by another at the next, will both interest and profit those disposed to read. This is substantially the work which tract missionaries, Bible readers, and colporteurs perform with so much success.

NOTE 3.—The most needy and the most hopeful subjects for such a ministry are the *afflicted*—the sick, the bereaved, those in want, and otherwise the children of misfortune. To such, sympathy and help are no empty compliments, but blessed realities, and those who bring them will be welcomed as ministers of mercy. Temporal mercies bestowed open the heart for the reception of spiritual grace to be welcomed.

NOTE 4.—Since so large a part of poverty, affliction, and distress in social life arises directly or indirectly from *intemperance*, constant endeavors should be made in all Christian work to suppress this fearful evil, and to promote temperance ; to win the inebriate from his destructive habits, and save his home and household from this terrible curse—a curse which falls on women and children with fearful and appalling severity.

NOTE 5.—Cases of sickness and want should be reported to the Church, both to stir them to sympathetic coöperation, and to secure the means of relief, and the Church should, according to its ability, furnish temporal aid and relief, thus conferring blessings on both the bodies and souls of the unfortunate.

NOTE 6.—Such visitation should aim to secure the habitual attendance of adults on Church services, and of the children at Sunday-school, wherever the preferences of the people may lead them ; most naturally, though not necessarily, where the visitors themselves worship.

NOTE 7.—These visits are most profitable if made *statedly*, usually once each month. Then they will be expected, and probably will be more impressive. In cases of sickness, destitution, or religious seriousness, or for other reasons, where special need demands, or special good is promised, more frequent calls will be required. When Christians with devout spirits become interested in such a work, they will find great pleasure, and an abundant reward in it.

IV. CHRISTIAN LITERATURE

Another practicable and effective means for bringing religious truth in contact with human minds is in the use of the printed page; by disseminating a sound and salutary Christian literature in the houses of the people. Both for the quickening and edification of Christians, and for the profiting of the unconverted, religious reading is of the greatest importance. Every good book or periodical put into circulation is a personal and a public blessing. And this means of grace is so accessible that none need be without it. Aside from the periodical religious press, there are numerous societies with abundant capital for the purpose, whose only business is the publication and circulation of religious reading; and that, too, at prices so low as to bring it within the reach of all. Our own, as well as other Christian denominations, has its publication society, doing nobly and well this work, and deserving the utmost confidence and the largest patronage.

1. *A few good books* should be in every home. Many are not needed, and a few can be obtained. A few, read over and over until the mind is thoroughly imbued with their spirit, are better than many carelessly read, or not read at all. Many families, and many Christian families, it is a pity to say, have masses of romances, novels, light and injurious reading, to pervert the taste and poison the minds of the children, and few or none of an instructive and devotional character.

2. *Church libraries*, composed of sound and substantial works of general as well as of religious literature, are an excellent means for intellectual and religious instruction. These serve for adults what Sunday-school libraries do for the young. They can be entirely free to the congregation, or used at a trifling fee, which may go to replenish the list.

3. *Religious periodicals* are, if possible, still more important than books, not in their intrinsic worth, indeed, but because they are so much more easily obtained, and so much more likely to be read. The cost of a weekly religious paper is so small that few are too poor to obtain one, while its value in the family is very great. Few things could become so efficient an auxiliary to a pastor in his pulpit and pastoral work as a really good religious paper in

every family.   And a wise pastor will see to it that
his people are well supplied with such helpers; helpers both for them and him.   A reliable denominational paper should be in the home of every Church
family.   It is certainly a shame for Baptists not to
know what is going on among their own people.

NOTE 1.—An easy and effective method of scattering religious truth in a community is by *lending* good books and
periodicals from house to house, among those destitute of
them.   Few persons would refuse, or neglect to read what
was kindly loaned, though they did not care to purchase, or
even to read, if it were their own.

NOTE 2.—If churches, or benevolent individuals would
pay for copies of papers to be sent *gratuitously* to those unable to buy—as some do—they would do a good service, and
one becoming Christian philanthropy.   A small fund could
be raised for this purpose.   Such seed-sowing would be
blessed.

NOTE 3.—Denominational periodicals should be generously sustained, and widely circulated.   They are maintained
as the advocates of evangelical truth in general, but especially of those distinctive truths, which are denominationally
cherished, and held as vitally important, and which in this
way are effectually defended and propagated.

V.   DISTINCTIVE MISSION WORK

Christianity is the most emphatic missionary force
in the world, and every Christian Church is a
divinely appointed missionary society, of the primitive type.   If every Church were instinct with the
life of its Divine Head, and true to the purpose for
which it was instituted, no other missionary organiz-

ations would be needed to send the Gospel of the blessed God to the ends of the earth. In apostolic history, no others were known, and yet they went everywhere preaching Christ, and filled the world with the Gospel of His salvation.

What has thus far been said as to the *mission* of the churches, has had principal reference to their specific but limited work, in the fields where they are located. Every Church and every disciple, however, is under bonds to Christ to aid in carrying out, and fulfilling the great commission, "Go into *all the world,* and preach the Gospel to *every creature.*" No Church can hope for prosperity at home unless it strives to give the means of salvation to all men. He that waters others shall himself be watered. And they that withhold more than is meet will find it tending to poverty.

It is a fallacy with which many curse themselves, to say that they have hard work to sustain their own Church, and therefore cannot help others. They that withhold from others who need, dry up the fountains of their benevolence, and have less for themselves, instead of more. He who alone can give the increase, prospers those who trust and honor Him. The churches that do not sympathize with, and aid missionary endeavor, are never very flourishing or prosperous. The missionary churches are uniformly the most honored and useful, whether rich or poor, large or small.

We have our missionary societies, for both home and foreign Christian service, in their various departments doing grand and most effective work, having a long and honorable history of good deeds, and noble successes. They possess all the appliances for the most effective and economical prosecution of their gracious enterprises. Their service commands our confidence, and we know their work is in harmony with gospel purposes. The churches are bound to give these societies their sympathies, their prayers, and their generous pecuniary support. Thereby they help to give the knowledge of salvation to those beyond the reach of their individual endeavors. The success which has attended the missionary work of American Baptists, through these societies, both in our own country, and in foreign lands, is most amazing, and testifies unmistakably to God's blessing on the work, and the favor with which He regards the methods pursued.

In all that is said or may be said it must be constantly borne in mind that a very large responsibility does and necessarily must rest on the *pastors*. For such purposes is the pastor made *overseer* of the flock, to instruct in duty as well as in privilege, and lead on to the discharge of every obligation. Few churches will be missionary churches if the pastors feel no interest in such work, and do not stimulate them, propose plans, impart information, and lead the people forward. With a pastor to do this faithfully, few churches would fail or fall short of a good degree of effectiveness.

NOTE I.—In most of our churches there are missionary and other benevolent societies of various kinds, acting in

concert with larger external societies. The wisdom and expediency of this course may well be questioned. Indeed, it
is a humiliating confession that it is the *apathy* of the
churches touching the objects contemplated, which at all
justifies the existence of such organization within them.
They, at times, accomplish great good, and their intention is
always good. But the Church was instituted by Divine Wisdom for these very purposes, and is an organization better
fitted for their accomplishment than any other can be.

NOTE 2.—It is to be feared that the churches find relief
from a sense of their legitimate obligation, and throw the responsibility of benevolent action on supplementary organizations. This should not be done. In such a case, "let every
man bear his own burden." A Church cannot alienate its
duties any more than its privileges, nor transfer to others its
obligations, and still be guiltless.

NOTE 3.—In some churches there are so many interior
organizations that the Church proper is well-nigh lost sight
of, covered up and submerged by these secondary circles.
This cannot be wise, nor according to the Founder's plan.
They abstract the vitality of the parent body, and concen-
trate the active energy of the whole around their specific
parts ; they, therefore, leave the remainder of the Church in
apathetic inactivity, as but the segments of a circle, of which
these societies are the vital centre.

NOTE 4.—Another difficulty, possible in such circumstances, is that these specific circles tend to restrict and localize
benevolence, by confining all their endeavors each to one
special department, overlooking for the time all others. It
makes specialists in good works of the members of each
separate society. No doubt more work is done, and more
money is raised for that one object by making it special.
But whether that is the best training, particularly for young
Christians, is a question. The benevolence of the gospel,
and the impulses of the new life are as broad and varied as
the wants of humanity, and the opportunities offered for do-

ing good. The including *whole* should be regarded, while the included *parts* may be held in special remembrance.

NOTE 5.—Is there not, for all this energy and working power—which certainly should not be repressed nor discouraged—a *better way?* If a Church will do nothing for missions, or any other Christian work, except poorly to sustain its own languid life, let those who feel impelled to do more, instead of forming a separate organization for the purpose, labor to inspire the pastor and other members with their own enthusiasm, and if they cannot be moved, then let them go to work personally, with agreement but without organization ; do what they can to stimulate others ; raise what money they can for the purpose ; make a report of their doings, at the close of a prayer-meeting ; seek the coöperation of others, and continue this course for a while. It would not be long before the whole body, instead of a fraction of it, would be interested and moved to recognize the need, and work for it.

VI.   MORAL REFORM SOCIETIES

What relation does a Church sustain to the various reformatory movements, supported by organizations which contemplate the suppression of specific vices, and the confirmation of specific virtues, but which are not expressly religious in their purpose ? Such societies exist for the suppression of intemperance, Sabbath-breaking, gambling, licentiousness, and other vicious and corrupting practices.

A Church is a society emphatically for the suppression of *all* vice and for the encouragement of all virtue. And no person should be admitted to, or retained in, its fellowship who will not both agree to, and walk by, this rule. If the churches were loyal to their duty, and true to their mission, they could do more for the suppression of immoralities than any other organization. But, as it is, no doubt some forms of moral evil can be better antagonized by distinct organizations, where all are of one mind concerning the object to be accomplished. The confession must be made, however mortifying, that in some churches there are members, who, for personal reasons, do not like to hear much said on the temperance question, and some ministers there are who lack courage to say much on it; while the souls of others burn with zeal to do something to suppress the fearful evils of intemperance.

Since churches, as such, cannot identify themselves organically with other societies, they should in every consistent way give their moral support to encourage such endeavors, as well as pray for their success. All that any moral society professes, the Church professes; and the Church professes more —not only to conserve the morals of society, but to save the souls of men. Only let them be true to their profession. They can well give their " God speed " to every individual, and to every organization which honestly strives to do good in the world.

NOTE 1.—It is often a serious question, how far a Church member may consistently identify himself with societies whose object is the suppression of prevailing moral evils. Certain it is that every Christian should encourage, and, so far as practicable, aid every good enterprise. It is equally certain that no Church member should favor any alliance with outside associations, however good their intent, which will interfere with his most faithful performance of duty in the Church. There his first service is due. The claims of the Church are paramount and imperative. The man who can be false to his Church, while he is faithful to other fraternities, shows how unworthy he is to bear the Christian name.

NOTE 2.—The moral reform societies are not inimical to Christianity or to the churches ; certainly not so far as their objects are concerned, whatever unwise and fanatical members may sometimes affect to be. With many mistakes they have done great good, and will do much more. With the prevailing indifference, on the part of churches, to these moral issues, Christian men can often work more hopefully through them, than in any other way.

NOTE 3.—As to the propriety of Church members connecting themselves with *secret societies*, this is to be said : that whether such societies be good or bad in themselves, all the advantages they propose can be obtained in less objectionable ways, since on the part of many there are strong objections to them. It is not a Christian act to grieve brethren for the sake of some slight personal gratification. To ministers of Christ this reason applies with double force. Why they should wish to be identified with secret organizations it is impossible to see. Such a step seems quite beneath the dignity of the high office of the heralds of salvation. Their company is, of course, earnestly sought for to grace these secret conclaves, but why should men in such positions desire to hold offices with high-sounding titles though with empty honors, or with childish vanity wish to be decked out with tinsel and showy trappings ? Christian ministers should possess a holier ambition. Oath-bound societies of all kinds should be greatly deprecated by Christian men.

CHAPTER 11

THE CHRISTIAN MINISTRY

FEW questions can be so vitally important to any Church, whether as relates to its own peace and prosperity, or to the success of the work it is appointed to do, as that of the kind of *ministry* which shall serve and lead it.

No greater blessing can be granted of Heaven to a Church than a capable, judicious, pious pastor; and no greater calamity can befall one than to have an incompetent, unfaithful, secularized, and worldly minded minister. The people naturally contemplate the office with feelings of reverence, and consequently regard the incumbent with very great deference, to say the least. The young, in a special manner, consider what he says as true, and what he does as right. The position commands high regard, for the minister is looked upon not only as a teacher, but as an example. He is, therefore, accepted as the one who is to illustrate, by his private walk and public deportment, the doctrines and morals which he inculcates from the pulpit.

The old prophet's declaration, "like people, like priest," is as true now as when Hosea uttered it.

For where the people have freedom of choice, and select their own pastors, they will choose them on the plane of their own religious thinking and acting. Moreover, there is a constant tendency, on the part of the preacher, to keep somewhere near the standard of the people. It requires a heroic effort for the pulpit to rise far above the level of the pews, as to Christian teaching and consecration, and he who long sustains himself in that position may expect, sooner or later, to hear the mutterings of discontent. But then, contradictory as it may seem to be, the converse of the prophet's epigram is equally true: "like priest, like people." Indeed, this is the form in which the proverb is usually quoted by the laity, as a salient thrust at an unfaithful or incompetent pastor, supposing they are quoting Scripture. The implication is, that if the Church is not right, it is the fault of the pastor. To a large extent this may be true, and the censure just. For, to a large extent, by faithful, judicious, and persistent endeavor, a godly pastor can mould and win the Church to a higher standard. To that extent will the spirit of all-powerful grace work with him and for him, while an unworthy and carnally minded man in the pulpit will surely degrade and lower the standard of piety among his people to somewhere near his own.

The old prophets—notably Jeremiah—represented the people of Israel under the similitude of a flock, led, and fed, and guarded by shepherds, called pastors. It was a promise of peculiar favor by Jehovah, that He would give them pastors after His own heart; while the lamentation over some of their heaviest calamities was, that the shepherds destroyed the flock, and fed themselves instead. The same figure Jesus used when He declared Himself to be the Good Shepherd that gave His life for the sheep. The relationship between pastor and people is intimate, vital, and sacred. Woe to the churches and the cause of Christian truth, when they have not a faithful, capable, and spiritual ministry!

Christian congregations under the control of State-churchism, or subject to ecclesiastical domination, cannot choose their own pastors, but receive such as are sent them. All the currents of religious life stagnate under such a system. It is one of the first and most important fruits of religious liberty and Church independency, that congregations of Christian worshipers can elect their own religious teachers. They may make mistakes, but they insist on the right, and they will not willingly submit to the dictation or control of others in this regard, either from civil or ecclesiastical authority. This is a point Baptists have always emphasized, maintaining this as well as other expressions of religious freedom for the individual Church.

The ministry is of divine appointment, and its purpose is to instruct and edify the Church, and to bear the knowledge of salvation abroad to the world. As a means and medium of spiritual good to men, the Gospel ministry stands preëminent; it is without a parallel among beneficent agencies.

Every true disciple is under obligation to preach the Gospel according to his ability and opportunity; but the economy of grace anticipated the need of special leaders and teachers for the congregations of the saints, and the Spirit of God moves on and fits certain men for the work, while the providence of God develops and calls forth their ministry. It is all under the direction of the chief Shepherd and Bishop of souls, who sends among His people the under-shepherds.

This work He began while among men. He "ordained twelve, that they should be with Him, and that He might send them forth to preach."—Mark 3 : 14. Also, " After these things, the Lord appointed other seventy also, and sent them two and two before His face into every city and place, whither He Himself would come."—Luke 10 : 1. And His final instructions, as He was about leaving them, were: " Go ye, therefore, and teach all nations, baptizing them in the name of the Father and the Son and of the Holy Ghost; teaching them to observe all things whatsoever I have commanded you, and lo, I am with you alway, even unto the end of the world. Amen."—Matt. 28 : 19, 20.

I. HOW THE MINISTRY ORIGINATES

Does the ministry grow out of the churches, or the churches out of the ministry ? These are questions which require thoughtful care to answer correctly. Which is first in the order of time, and according to the genius of the Gospel ?

Where the Gospel is proclaimed, converts will be made and churches will arise. Converts will associate, will assimilate, will aggregate, and so become churches. These are the sheaves brought together on the harvest field, and bound in bundles for the Master's use; the fruit of the seed-sowing. Also, where there are churches a ministry will be developed Jesus preached the Gospel of the kingdom, and disciples were gathered—gathered and assimilated, and held together as a band by the attraction of His personal presence and influence. A Church, we may say, inchoate and unorganized; but still, to all intents and purposes, an *ekklesia*, called out from the world and concentred about Himself. The centripetal force of their fellowship did not die with His removal from among them. They kept together after His death, and especially after His resurrection. At the Pentecost the number of converts increased, under the preaching of Peter, by the power of the Spirit; the Church became more clearly developed, and more definitely organized. With the increase of the Church the ministers increased, until, not very long after, on the breaking out of persecution, they went everywhere, preaching Christ. Heralds of the glad tidings were multiplied; they were begotten of the Spirit and born of the Church in such abundance as the occasion required.

Thus has it ever been, and thus must it ever be. Our ascended Christ furnishes for the churches, and from the churches, the only true Gospel ministry. They are not by natural descent of one appointed lineage, as was the Aaronic priesthood, from the loins of Levi—born with a prescriptive right to the sacred office.   They are not to be assigned by either civil or ecclesiastical establishments to the " cure of souls," with only a perfunctory knowledge of, and fitness for, the place.   " When He ascended on high He led captivity captive, and gave gifts to men. He gave some apostles, and some prophets, and some evangelists, and some pastors and teachers."—Eph. 4 : 8, 11.   These were Christ's " ascension gifts " to His churches, and these He continues to bestow, in one form or another, on the churches and the world.

II. CLERGY AND LAITY NOT PRIMITIVE

It is well to bear in mind that the distinction which has for ages prevailed in Christian society between *clergy* and *laity* is not primitive; was not known in the apostolic age.   There was an apostleship and a discipleship, but no clerical caste, separated by a wide gulf of sacramental ordination from the common people.   The Holy Spirit working in each believer developed those gracious qualities which were profitable to the edifying of the body of Christ.   All alike constituted a holy and a royal priesthood, " ordained to offer spiritual sacrifices unto God."   The churches chose for their pastors and teachers such of their own members as exhibited the needed qualities which fitted them for the positions.

DR. BLOOMFIELD says :

"But when, in the next generation [after the first], it was thought expedient that presbyters should be confined to their sacred duties, and kept apart from all secular occupations—which, by the way, occasioned the two classes of *clergy* and *laity*—then ordination would become a much more solemn affair."—*Com. on Acts, 14 : 23.*

DEAN STANLEY says :

"In the first beginnings of Christianity there was no such institution as the *clergy;* and it is conceivable there may be a time when they shall cease to be."—*Christian Institutions, p. 175. N. Y., ed. 1881.*

DR. COLEMAN says :

"There was then no such distinction between clergymen and laymen." "They were all equally the priests of God." "The first instance of the distinction of the clergy and laity, as separate orders of men in the Christian Church, occurs in Tertullian, at the beginning of the third century."—*Ancient Christ. Ex., pp. 93-107*

GIESELER says :

"There was yet [in the apostolic age] no distinct order of clergy, for the whole society of Christians was a royal priesthood."—*Ch. Hist., Vol. I., p. 58.*

SCHAFF says :

"The Jewish and the Catholic antithesis of clergy and laity has no place in the apostolic age."—*Hist. Christ. Ch., Vol. I., p. 131.*

FISHER says :

"The basis of ecclesiastical organization was the fraternal equality of believers. 'All ye are brethren.' Instead of a sacerdotal order, there was a universal priesthood."—*Hist. Ch. Church, p. 35.*

RIGALTIUS, SALMASIUS, SELDEN, and others,

assert the same as cited by Bingham, who finds the earliest historical evidence of the distinction of clergy and laity in the third century after Christ.—*Ancient Christ. Ch., B. I., chap. 5.*

III. THE PURPOSE OF THE MINISTRY

The general purpose contemplated by the appointment and sustenance of an official ministry in the churches is clearly enough defined in the popular mind, and well enough understood by the prevailing customs of religious society : to shepherd the flock, to instruct congregations in religious truth, and guide the churches as to internal order and the practical activities of Christian life. But, to be more specific, it may be said the ministerial purpose is *twofold :* the edification of saints and the conversion of sinners. Or, to reverse, and perhaps make more natural the order, the conversion of men, and then their instruction and upbuilding in the faith of the Gospel. Thus did Jesus, in His farewell injunction, command His disciples to go forth, preach the Gospel, disciple men, baptize them, and then teach them to observe all things whatsoever He had commanded them.

Not infrequently extremists are heard to say that there is nothing comparable to the conversion of souls; that is *the* one great object of preaching. It is allowed to be *one* great object, but not the only one to the exclusion of the other. Both should be constantly sought, and devotion to one does not exclude the other. It is quite supposable that God may be as much glorified and the world as much blessed by the development of character, the enlargement of graces, and the increase of good works on the part of believers, as by the addition of converts. Read the epistles to the churches, and see how much is said about edifying the body of Christ; about growth in grace; about perfecting the saints in holiness; about being filled with the Spirit. The truth is, when Christians are living in the fullness of the blessing of the Gospel, and exhibiting the life of Christ, sinners will be converted. The ministry will be crowned with divine success.

There is a passage in Paul's Epistle to the Ephesians on this subject, the force and comprehensiveness of which is only equaled by the beauty of its diction, and the vivid imagery employed. After saying that Christ gave gifts, some to be apostles, prophets, evangelists, pastors and teachers, he states for what purpose these gifts were bestowed; namely, " For the perfecting of the saints, for the work of the ministry, for the edifying of the body of Christ : till we attain unto the unity of the faith, and of the knowledge of the Son of God, unto a full-grown man, unto the measure of the stature of the fullness of Christ."—Eph. 4 : 12, 13. How grand the conception of an advancing Christian growth, under the culture of pastors and teachers, even to the attainment of a "perfect man;" not a perfect angel, but a perfected humanity in Christ! How sublime the upward sweep of Christian development, from the inchoate believer in the infancy of his new life, along all the planes of development, until finally the full purpose is realized in the "measure of the stature of the *fullness* of Christ!"

IV.   A CALL TO THE MINISTRY

If the spiritual life of the churches is to be maintained, and the power of godliness to be preserved, a *divine call* to the work of the ministry must be insisted on by the Churches.

It is not enough that a man—young or old—has piety, and ability, and education; that he possesses a facility in the use of language, and can address a congregation with ease and interest, both to himself and to them.   Nor is it enough that he has an earnest desire to do good. All this may be, and yet he may not be called to the sacred office. All these are important, but not of themselves sufficient. It must not be the mere choice of a profession; nor the dictate of an ambition which looks to the pulpit as a desirable arena for achieving distinction, nor even as the best field for usefulness. Nor must it be a yielding to the opinions or persuasions of over-partial, but, it may be, injudicious friends. A true *call* to the work of the ministry must rest on more solid ground than any or all of these evidences.

"No man taketh this honor unto himself; but he

that is called of God, as was Aaron."—Heb. 5 : 4.
He that would lawfully enter upon this work must
do it from a deep, abiding and unalterable conviction,
wrought into his soul by the Holy Spirit, that such
is the will of God concerning him; and that nothing else is, or can be, the work of his life, whether it
may bring joy or sorrow, prosperity or adversity.
He that can follow any other pursuit or profession
with a peaceful mind, and a conscience void of offense, should never enter the ministry. This inward
movement and monition of the Spirit does not cease
with a single impression, nor subside with a single
occasion; but it continues usually through weeks
and months, and perhaps years, holding the mind
to this one conviction; not always continuously, but
from time to time, calling it back from all other purposes and plans to this conviction of duty.

As this conviction of duty is slowly working its
way into the soul, various emotions are excited.
Not unfrequently the mind revolts at what seems
the inevitable conclusion, and sometimes violently
rebels against it. The thoughts of unfitness for the
work; the apparent impossibility of being able to
secure the proper qualifications; the fact that many
cherished plans for life, which seem to promise
more of pleasure and of profit, must be abandoned;
and, what to some minds with noble instincts is
most of all humiliating and painful, that if one enters the ministry he must become dependent on
others, in a certain sense, for his living, and subject
to their caprices in many ways for his comfort:

the temptation to sink his personal independence, so as not to antagonize the opinions of his hearers, and to modify messages of truth, rather than offend the ignorance or the prejudices of those on whom he is dependent, to an over-sensitive nature become difficulties of no ordinary magnitude. But through it all the Spirit holds the mind true to its destiny, until at length it submits, silences every objection, sacrifices every consideration, accepts every condition, and yields implicit obedience to the *divine call.* Then a new peace fills the soul, and light from a new horizon irradiates all its sphere.

The *evidences* of this divine call are various. The most convincing is that just named, where the Spirit works the ever-deepening conviction into the soul, that it must be so. Another sign is that the mind is being led into a fruitful contemplation of the Scriptures, whose spirit and meaning, whose deep and rich treasures of truth are unfolded and made plain to an unusual degree. An increasing facility of utterance in addressing religious meetings, especially when attempting to explain and enforce particular portions of the word, is another evidence. This, however, is not uniform, owing to many causes. For sometimes, instead of joyous liberty, every thing seems dark and confined. Particular cases, either on the one side or the other, are not so much to influence the judgment as the general trend and current of these tokens. Still more, if one has been divinely called to this work, there will soon rise a conviction of the fact in the minds of pious and prayerful people. All truly spiritual saints are, in a sense, prophets to discern spiritual things. If they be interested in, and profited by, the exercise of such gifts, that fact itself goes far to establish the call.

And further: if one be divinely called to preach the Gospel, Providence will open such ways of needed preparation for the work, as may be best in the circumstances. Precisely what that fitting preparation may be, it is impossible here to tell. It should be *the best that can be secured*. But there is a great variety of fields, and of conditions of work, and an equal variety of ability, and of intellectual preparation is needed to fill them. There may be difficulties in the way; but let not the young man who believes himself called to this service, be impatient, nor too hasty. Let him "wait on the Lord," observe the indications of Providence, and not run before he is sent. Our Lord Himself waited in patient preparation till He was thirty years of age, before entering upon His public ministry; and that, too, when He was to have but three short years of active service afterward. Let the young man improve his gifts as occasion offers, and wait; sooner or later he will become satisfied, as will also his brethren, whether or not he is called to preach.

NOTE 1.—It is not an evidence of a *call* to the ministry, that the heart sets itself in persistent rebellion against the monitions of the Spirit. So commonly is this resistance to the gracious movement felt, that some seem to think they lack good evidence of such a call. unless they stoutly fight against

God. On the other hand, some of the most devout and useful men in the ministry did most earnestly desire the sacred office, though feeling themselves unworthy of it, and unfitted for it. Paul said, "If a man desire the office of a bishop, he desireth a good work."

NOTE 2.—Any man whom God has not called to that work, will find the pulpit the most difficult and disastrous of all positions, and the work of the ministry the most irksome and uncongenial. No hope of gratifying a carnal ambition, no expectation of praise for learning or eloquence can mitigate the uncongenial burden of a service in which the heart is not enlisted.

NOTE 3.—Young men exercised on this point, as to the choice of the ministry, should not attach too much importance to the flattering encouragements of ardent, and over-partial friends, whose judgments may not be as sound as their impulses are generous. Nor, on the other hand, should they be too much discouraged, if any throw stumbling-blocks in their way. Let them carefully weigh all things, pray for divine direction, and decide the question according to their best light.

V. THE PERPETUITY OF ITS OBLIGATIONS

Is the obligation involved in a divine call of perpetual force? Or may a man called to that work leave it for some other profession or calling at his option? Is a man "once a priest, always a priest"? Or may there be a demission of sacerdotal functions?

This is a question in which our churches have not so much interest as men already in, and candidates for, the office most naturally have. It is, however, admitted almost universally by evangelical Christians, that such a call is of *perpetual obligation*. It is manifest that if divine authority puts a man into the ministry, the same authority is requisite to direct, or give permission for him to leave it and enter upon some other work. There are, no doubt, men in the ministry who never ought to have entered it, and who would confer the greatest possible benefit on the churches and the cause by leaving it. There are doubtless many instances in which men are incapacitated by sickness, or other causes, for a discharge of its duties. Providence clearly indicates that such should seek some other sphere of service, where they can still be useful, and yet secure support for a dependent family. In such cases of manifest necessity, temporary diversion from exclusive ministerial labor would be not only permissible but commendable, and perhaps even imperative.

But young men, looking to this calling, should regard it as a life-long service, and not consider a change to a more lucrative or less laborious pursuit as a possible contingency. Providential causes may arise where temporarily the active duties of the ministry —especially of the pastorate—may be remitted, to be resumed when the obstacles are removed. But how one, who believes himself called of God to preach the Gospel, can quietly and conscientiously devote himself to other callings, secular or semi-secular, without such providential compulsion, it is difficult to understand. And there are many of our ministers, men of sound health, and ability for usefulness, who have abandoned pastoral service for these side issues; positions for which laymen would be quite as competent, and often better fitted. It is not a sufficient answer to say that these posts are important and useful spheres of service. All that may be true, and they may have peculiar qualifications for the places, but it was not for these, or such as these, they professed to have been called, and to which they were ordained and set apart. If they were mistaken in their original purpose, it is well they have made a change.

NOTE 4.—The question may arise, How far is it allowable for a minister to engage in outside work for the sake of added gain, while holding a pastorate and receiving a salary from the people? Though no general answer can be given that would meet every case, yet it is safe to say that no outside work should be engaged in that will in any way interfere with a full and faithful discharge of his duties to the Church and congregation of his charge. If they give him a respectable support he should devote his best energies to them.

NOTE 5.—But it often happens in small and feeble congregations, especially in frontier settlements and rural districts, that congregations cannot—or think they cannot—support a pastor, and he is obliged to supplement a scanty salary from other sources. This is right not only, but most commendable in such cases. It should, however, be done not for *gain*, but for *godliness*, that he may be the better enabled to preach the Gospel, and give his family the comforts of life. Paul worked at his trade of tent-making, that he might the better be able to preach Christ.

VI   THE SPHERE OF MINISTERIAL LABOR

A minister is not necessarily a pastor. If a minister have not a pastoral charge, to whatever field he may be designated, there lies his first and chief obligation for service. If he be a pastor, his Church, and congregation, and the community about him constitute his principal sphere of ministerial labor. To neglect them would be disloyalty to his Church, and to his Lord. Unless that be cultivated with fidelity, zeal, and a good degree of devotion, he need not expect any great amount of success. Nor yet need he expect that his work will be greatly appreciated, or widely demanded. He should, however, countenance and aid, to the extent of his ability, every good word and work, consistently with his duties to his own people. His nature should vibrate in sympathy with all endeavors made to ameliorate the sufferings of humanity, to suppress vice, and elevate virtue everywhere. He should stand the friend and abettor of missions, temperance, and of every virtue which the Gospel inculcates and promotes. He would be unfaithful to his holy trust, should he stand quietly by, without a hand to help in giving the means of salvation to the world, for which Christ died; should he remain unmoved amidst the ravages of sin, and not strive to withstand them; should he be indifferent to the ignorance of a world lying in wickedness, and not labor for its enlightenment.

It sometimes happens that pastors can, in special emergencies, render needed and valuable aid to other pastors in times of great discouragement or of special religious interest. Other occasions will arise when incidental aid can be rendered a good cause outside the limits of his ordinary duties, without injury to other interests. And yet the apostolic injunction must continue to be the pastor's guide: "Take heed unto yourselves, and to all the flock, over which the Holy Spirit hath made you overseers; to feed the Church of God, which He hath purchased with His own blood."—Acts 20 : 28.

VII. THE SOURCE OF MINISTERIAL AUTHORITY

Whence does the minister derive his *authority* for the exercise of ministerial functions? For preaching, administering the ordinances, and other prerogatives? "For no man taketh this honor unto himself."—Heb. 5 : 4.

Whence is it then? Not from the Church, for no Church holds in itself any such authority to bestow. Not from a Council, since councils possess no ecclesiastical authority. Not from the State, for the State has no right of interference in matters of faith and conscience, and possesses no control over, or authority in, ecclesiastical affairs. The minister, therefore, derives his credentials as a preacher of righteousness, and the right to minister as a priest in spiritual services from no human source, but directly from Christ, the great Head of the Church, by the witness and endowment of the Holy Spirit; He who calls, endows and authorizes. He sends forth His heralds with authority to preach the Gospel to the end of the age.

All that a Church or a Council can properly do is to recognize, and express approval of a man's entering the ministry. The force of ordination is simply a recognition and sanction, in a public and impressive manner, of what is believed to be the divine appointment of the candidate to the sacred office. The object of Church and Council action is not to impart either ability or authority to preach the Gospel, for these they cannot give; but to ascertain if such ability and authority have been divinely given, and if so, to approve their public exercise. If not in so remarkable a manner, yet probably just as really is every true minister called and invested as was Paul: " But when it pleased God, who separated me from my mother's womb, and called me by His grace to reveal His Son in me, that I might preach Him among the heathen; immediately I conferred not with flesh and blood."—Gal. 1 : 15, 16.

NOTE 6.—Any one who believes himself called and authorized of God to preach the Gospel, as one under law to Christ, and ultimately accountable to Him alone, has a right to preach the Gospel, though churches and councils should oppose his course. But he would not have the right to preach in any congregation without their consent.

NOTE 7.—The right of any man to be the minister and pastor of any particular Church is derived from that Church itself. No man, no body of men can make him a minister to *them* without their consent. While on the other hand, if they so determine and choose him, he is a minister to them though councils and churches should forbid it. Others are not obliged to recognize or fellowship them or him, but they cannot interfere with them. A man's right to preach the Gospel, and administer the ordinances comes from God alone ; a man's right to do this in any particular Church comes from that Church alone.

Note 8.—But suppose a man believes himself called to preach, and insists on the exercise of that right, while the Church of which he is a member, after long and careful consideration, is convinced that he is mistaken in his convictions, and that he ought not to undertake the work. The Church has its *authority*, as well as the individual his *rights*. In such a case, while the Church should be careful not to infringe on the individual's rights of conscience, or freedom of action, they may, in the exercise of their lawful and legitimate authority, labor with, admonish, and, if need be, rebuke such a one, he being a member in covenant relations with them ; and if he will not hear them, and they judge the occasion calls for it, discipline, and even withdraw fellowship from him. They possess that right.

VIII.   QUALIFICATIONS FOR THE MINISTRY

It is not to be expected that of all men the minister alone will be perfect. And yet in no other man is a near approach to perfection so imperative as in him. Of all men, he should prayerfully strive to have as few faults and as many excellencies as possible. For in no other man do they count for so much, either for or against truth and righteousness as in him.

He should be a man of good physical health. This counts for vastly more, even in a spiritual point of view, than is usually supposed. And if, by hereditary taint, or for any other reason, he may lack physical vigor, he should, by careful self-training in regard to diet, exercise, and otherwise, strive to reinvigorate his energies. This is a duty as sacred and imperative as prayer, the study of the Bible, or other spiritual exercise. He will find that an enfeebled body impairs his best endeavors. He should also avoid all of those habits which tend to enervate and undermine his health. Irregularity of life, late hours, heavy suppers, and the like; while the use of tobacco, opium and alcohol should be regarded as an abomination, not to be tolerated by one who preaches a gospel of purity, and who himself should be pure.

It must not, however, be understood as saying that a man manifestly called of God to the work, should not undertake it because he does not enjoy robust health, and has not been favored with a vigorous constitution. Some of the most godly and useful ministers who have ever blessed the world and the churches, have been life-long invalids and sufferers. And sometimes the active and varied duties of the pastorate, especially in rural fields, have been highly conducive to physical health and longevity. Still, "a sound mind in a sound body" must be insisted on as of the greatest importance, for the possession of which no prudent or persistent effort is too great a price to pay.

Moreover, the minister should be a Christian gentleman in the best sense of that term. Not a technical gentleman, flippant and finical, according to the standard of so-called genteel society, but far better and higher than this—a true gentleman at heart, courteous, considerate, gentle, generous, and kind to all. There is no excuse for a minister's being rude, boorish, inconsiderate of the proprieties of so-

ciety, and indifferent to the feelings or comfort of
others. He who is such, no matter what amount of
talent he may possess, will drive people from him,
and his life will be largely unfruitful of good. Some
ministers seem to think it a mark of superiority to
be rude and supercilious toward others. It is simply
a mark of superior boorishness, and a disgrace to
the profession.

But those special qualifications named by the
Apostle, and detailed in the epistles to Timothy and
Titus (1 Tim., chap. 3; Titus, chap. 1), should be
insisted on by both churches and ordaining councils. They are such as all who aspire to that sacred
office can possess, and such as, if possessed, may
give assurance to the most humble and timid that
their work and labor of love will not be in vain in
the Lord. According to these inspired specifications, the bishop or pastor should be " blameless,
the husband of one wife, vigilant, sober, of good
behavior, given to hospitality, apt to teach, not
given to much wine, no striker, not greedy of filthy
lucre, patient, not a brawler, not covetous, one that
ruleth well his own house, having his children in
subjection; not a novice, having a good report of
them that are without, not self-willed, not soon an-
gry." Such qualifications, quickened and sanctified
by the Spirit, could not fail to make good ministers
of Jesus Christ. There is no impossible endowment
enjoined, and the morality of the Gospel, so largely
prominent in these qualities, should be conspicuous
in a religious teacher and leader of the people.

NOTE 7.—As to those qualifications which are purely *scholastic*, whether literary or theological, as a preparation for the work of the ministry, no certain amount or given standard can be fixed. The importance and difficulties of the profession make it necessary that the divinity student should avail himself of the largest and most liberal culture possible in the circumstances. The indications of Providence, his own convictions of duty, and the advice of wise and judicious friends must decide that question.

NOTE 8.—The wide field over which our churches are scattered, the vast variety of social conditions which mark the different congregations, not only make possible, but demand all types and varieties of ministerial gifts. Certain it is, that many a field would welcome the man without the culture of the schools, but with a knowledge of men and a deep insight into the Gospel, much more readily, and find him much more useful, than the scholar from the seminary, thoroughly versed in books, but ignorant of men and practical life.

NOTE 9.—It is desirable that every young man preparing for the ministry should, if possible, be able to read intelligently the Scriptures in the original Greek and Hebrew. This, and all other linguistic knowledge, will be to him of great value, if rightly used. But of all " book knowledge " that can be named, none can compare with a deep, thorough knowledge of the *English Bible*. The importance of this to the minister of Christ outranks all others, and does more than any other literary attainment to make a man an able minister of the New Testament. And this qualification is within the reach of all—even the plainest and the poorest.

NOTE 10.—It is of great practical advantage to the student that, during his preparatory studies, he should not unfrequently exercise his gifts in preaching, as occasion offers. It will give him opportunity for developing his capabilities, testing his theories and correcting his faults under the most favorable circumstances. But this should be done with caution, and not to any such extent as seriously to interfere with his studies, which for the time constitute his principal business.

NOTE 11.—Let no young man deem the time wasted that confines him to the class-room in mental training, and the acquisition of knowledge preparatory to the great work. He *serves* his Master best who patiently and faithfully *prepares* best to serve Him. That foolish enthusiasm for the work which hurries one into the field only half fitted, when a better preparation was possible, will always after be deeply regretted.

IX. THE LICENSING OF MINISTERS

It is one of the prevailing customs of our churches to grant a *license* to young men believing themselves, and believed by others, to have been called to preach the Gospel, but not yet prepared to enter upon the work of the ministry.* This is simply an approval by the Church of the course which the candidate is pursuing. It confers no rights and imparts no authority, but expresses the conviction that the bearer possesses gifts and capabilities which indicate a call to the ministry, and a promise of usefulness in it. The giving of licenses is not universal in such cases. Theological schools usually require them of students entering, as an evidence that they have the approval and confidence of their churches. Churches should be very careful not to grant licenses without sufficient evidence of a divine call, and not till they have had

---

* The form of a license may be found in the Appendix to this volume.

sufficient opportunity to judge wisely in the case. And where there is good evidence of a call, the Church should be as ready as they are careful to encourage the candidate in his chosen course.

NOTE 12.—Ordination does not necessarily follow the granting of a license, though usually it does. The Church may have occasion to change their opinion of the case, and may, for sufficient cause, *revoke* the license.

NOTE 13.—A license should never be granted simply because it is sought, nor to gratify the candidate or his friends, nor because they dislike to refuse. It is a serious and an important matter, and should be acted on with kindly feeling, but with conscientious care.

NOTE 14.—A letter of *commendation* is sometimes given a young man, approving of his entering upon a course of study, with the ministry in view, but deferring a license until better opportunities are offered to judge of his gifts and calling.

NOTE 15.—It is, of course, understood that the practice of *licensing* is merely a cautionary measure, a custom not essential and not uniform, but salutary, and tending to good order.

X. THE ORDINATION OF MINISTERS

The importance of selecting and placing over the churches the right kind of men as pastors and teachers cannot be overestimated. But the high regard, the almost sanctity, in which our churches hold the *ceremony* of setting apart, of the inauguration of the clergy, finds no parallel and no sanction in the New Testament, and is derived directly from sacramentarian communions, remotely from the

Romish Church, which holds ordination as one of the seven sacraments.

The New Testament meaning of the word *ordination* is choosing, electing, appointing a man to the office of bishop or pastor, and has no reference to a ceremonial setting apart, or investiture with the functions of the office. A president is elected —that is, *ordained*—to the presidency by the votes of the people; but the ceremony of his inauguration is quite a different thing; very proper, becoming and impressive, but not essential. He is as really president without it as with it: president by virtue of his election, not of his inauguration.* Our churches, unfortunately, have come to apply the term " ordination " exclusively to the ceremonial induction, and not to the election, which was its primitive and is its proper meaning. Thus laying all the stress on the ceremony, they have come to insist on certain ritual observances as essential to its validity. All the more notable is this since Baptists contend so earnestly for following the New Testament in all things. And however appropriate such forms of induction may be, they find no warrant for them in the Scriptures. Therefore they should be urged, if

---

* As the question of ordination holds an important place among the usages of our Church life, and as not a little misapprehension and perplexity often arise from the diversity of views entertained by our people respecting it, and its relation to primitive Church practice, it has seemed wise to devote a separate chapter in this work to a somewhat full discussion of the subject. See page 344.

urged at all, as matters of *order*, and not matters of *authority;* as appropriate and becoming, but not essential.

No reasonable objection can be made to our usual forms of ordination service, providing these forms be rightly understood and held at their right value. But no instance can be found in the New Testament where any man was set apart to the work of the Gospel ministry, at his first entrance upon it, by any ceremony whatever. The seven deacons were ceremonially inducted into their office, but not the preachers of the Gospel—or if they were, we do not know it.

The Order of Proceedings :

The usual course of proceedings in ordinations is as follows :

The Church which calls for the ordination—and of, which Church the candidate should be a member —invites a Council, by sending letters to such other churches (and individuals) as they may desire to have present, requesting them to send their pastor and brethren (usually two) to consider and advise them as to the propriety of setting apart the candidate to the work of the Gospel ministry. In some parts, particularly at the South, a Presbytery is called instead of a Council; that is, a number of ministers personally invited without the presence of laymen. So far as the validity of the action is concerned, there is no choice in the methods.

The Council, when convened and organized, listens to a statement from the Church calling them, through a committee appointed for the purpose, and then proceeds to the examination of the candidate. This examination usually traverses *three* principal lines of inquiry, but may go beyond them, viz. :

1. His Christian experience.
2. His call to the ministry.
3. His views of Christian doctrine.

Other topics than these may appropriately be made subjects for inquiry, providing they be germane to the occasion, but remote subjects and profitless discussion should be avoided; especially such subjects as those on which members of the Council themselves may be divided.

When the Council is satisfied with the examination, the candidate is allowed to *retire*, while the body proceeds to discuss the matter, and the action to be taken. If there be any particular dissatisfaction in the case, such matters are considered; and if desired, the candidate can be recalled to give his views more fully on doubtful points. If not, on motion duly made, the Council votes its satisfaction on each of the above three distinct topics of inquiry. Then a final vote to this effect is passed : "*Resolved :* that being satisfied with the result of our examination, we approve the setting apart of the candidate, and recommend the Church to proceed to the public services of ordination." As the Council was called to *advise* the Church, this is the advice they give. The committee of the Church acting for them, request the Council to take charge of the services, and assign the several parts, with the concurrence of the candidate, as they may think desirable.

What these various parts shall be, and who shall perform them, is a matter of no importance beyond the wishes of the candidate, and the Church. Usually they are as follows:

1. Preliminary services, consisting of music, reading the Scriptures, and an introductory prayer.

2. Sermon: preached usually by some one previously selected by the candidate.

3. The ordaining prayer: during which the candidate kneels, and near the close of which he who offers the prayer, and some others, lay their hands on his head.

4. The hand of fellowship: in a short address welcoming the candidate to the fellowship and fraternity of the ministry, and to all the pleasures and toils of the sacred service.

5. A charge to the candidate: in an address, usually by some older minister, reminding him of the various duties and responsibilities the ministry imposes.

6. A charge to the Church: in an address enjoining on them their reciprocal duties and responsibilities, in consequence of his settlement among them; duties to him, to themselves, and to the community.

7. This closes the service, and the *benediction* is usually pronounced by the candidate; before which the minutes of the proceedings are read and ap-

proved, and a copy voted for the candidate, as his certificate of ordination — and perhaps notices ordered sent to the papers.

NOTE 16.—The Church which calls the Council usually appoints a committee to represent it before the Council in giving information, answering questions, or making suggestions, but such a committee is no part of the Council, and cannot vote on any question.

NOTE 17.—Should the Council decide against the propriety of ordaining the candidate, still the Church can have him as their minister if they choose to do so, and none can prevent. The independence of churches cannot be questioned. This, however, in ordinary circumstances would be highly inexpedient. Neither the Church nor candidate would be likely to command the approval or confidence of other churches, or of the community, should they utterly ignore the judgment and advice of a Council of their own calling.

NOTE 18.—A call to the ministry does not necessarily involve an immediate entrance upon its duties. Hence a Church or a Council may agree that a man is called, but on account of his inexperience, ignorance of doctrines o. of duties, or for other reason, may decide against immediate ordination, and advise to defer that step until he shall be better qualified, and more thoroughly instructed in the ways of the Lord. Quite often, no doubt, this would be a wise course to take.

NOTE 19.—Since the peace and prosperity of a Church so vitally depend on the knowledge, discretion, and experience of a pastor, and his ability to guide its affairs, as well as his gift in preaching the Gospel, therefore the utmost caution and prudence should be used on the part of the churches in calling men to ordination. The Council that examines the candidate, also, should give a wide range to their investigations, and thoroughly ascertain the candidate's general competency for the work.

NOTE 20.—It will be clearly inferred from statements already made, that the *right* of ordination inheres in the *Church*, and not in the *Council*. This must be so, if, as is universally conceded in our churches, all ecclesiastical authority resides in a Church. And also since the Church is of divine appointment and authority, while the Council is not.*

NOTE 21.—The practice of "laying on of hands," is an Oriental custom of immemorial usage, as a form of blessing conferred by the old upon the young, and by superiors upon inferiors. In the ritualism of the Mosaic economy it was a symbolical act. Jesus laid His hands on the sick to heal them, and on little children to bless them. With the pentecostal gift of the Holy Spirit, miraculous effects followed the laying on of the Apostles' hands. Some of the Baptist fathers laid hands on the head of each candidate baptized, pronouncing a brief blessing; a few continue the practice. Since the original significancy of the act is no longer realized, and since no gifts, either common or extraordinary, are pretended to be conferred, the act should no longer be deemed essential as a part of ordination services, nor as affecting the completeness of ministerial character, or the validity of ministerial acts.

XI. RECOGNITION, INSTALLATION REORDINATION

Services bearing these designations are sometimes, though with no considerable degree of uniformity, resorted to. Nor does any considerable importance attach to them, except that *reordination* from time to time becomes a question of perplexity and of controversy among our people.

---

* For a more exhaustive discussion of the subject of *Councils*, their nature, prerogatives, and uses, see the chapter on that subject. Also "Star Book on Baptist Councils."

Recognition. When a pastor changes his field, and takes a new one, he is at times welcomed by some special services to celebrate the event, and introduce him to the community. Neighboring clergymen and others, are invited in; a sermon is preached by some personal friend of the pastor, or by some other one selected, or several addresses are made instead; attractive music is had; the pastor is congratulated on his field, the Church on its pastor, and a pleasant time is enjoyed. There can be no objection to such a service—and it is difficult to see how any marked benefit can arise from it, especially as the pastor may change his field again in a year, and some one else take his place—when the service will be repeated.

Installation. This term has no proper use in the customs of Baptists; though it is sometimes used by accommodation to indicate a recognition service, where a minister takes possession of a new pastorate. The word is properly used to designate the service by which a minister is placed over a new charge, with appropriate ceremonies by his ecclesiastical superiors. To *install* is to place in a stall or seat, indicative of official duties and functions, by which the incumbent is invested with official authority. The term is appropriate only where a minister is placed in a charge by superior ecclesiastical functionaries, acquiring new rights and prerogatives thereby.

Reordination. The question of reordination arises when a minister of some other denomination unites with us, and wishes to become a pastor among us. He has professed conformity to our denominational views, and has been baptized into our fellowship. But that gives him only the standing of a private member and not that of a minister. He was, however, an accredited minister in an evangelical denomination before, regularly set apart to the sacred office. Now, the question is, in order to become a Baptist minister, will his previous ordination suffice, or should he be ordained again as though he had never been a clergyman? On this point opinions somewhat differ.

Some answer in the affirmative and some in the negative. But really it makes very little difference which course is pursued. Either would be *valid*, and neither is *essential*. Considering what ordination is, and what use it is intended to serve, in the case supposed, a recognition would be as good as an ordination; and the reverse would be true. In case of a minister coming from some other communion, before he should be admitted to ministerial functions among our churches, it would be every way desirable that a Council or a Presbytery should be called by the Church which proposes to have him as pastor, to examine and ascertain his views as to Baptist doctrine and Church order. If satisfied, some public services would be proper and desirable. Call it a recognition or a reordination; the difference is slight. Indeed, the only difference in ceremony is, that in the latter the laying on of hands is practised, but omitted in the former. Let the wish of the candidate, or the Church, or the Council—if they have a preference—be gratified.   A man is a minister none the more with the imposition of hands, and none the less without it. *

* On the discipline of unworthy ministers, see Chapter on Discipline, page 206.

CHAPTER 12

BAPTIST COUNCILS

COUNCILS for consultation and advice in ecclesiastical affairs are an established usage among American Baptists, especially at the North, East, and West. With the Southern churches there is a prejudice existing against them lest their action should come to be considered authoritative, and threaten a domination of the churches. For this reason they are seldom resorted to in that section.

Indeed, through the whole extent of our denomination their doings have been watched with jealousy and regarded with not a little of suspicion, for fear they might grow to an interference with the independence of the churches; this doctrine of Church independency being held by them with great tenacity, both because they believe it taught in the New Testament and also because of the wrongs perpetrated on the true people of God during past ages, by acts of Councils and papal decrees in the name of ecclesiastical authority.

Hence Baptists watch with commendable vigilance against every combination of men, and every form of action which by any possibility may threaten an assumption of power over, or interference with, the free and independent action of the local churches. Thus it has come to pass that Associations, when appealed to to decide disputes which vexed the churches, or to settle perplexing questions which disturbed their peace, have either declined to respond altogether, lest they might come to be regarded as a court of appeals, or if they did reply, did it with the distinct avowal that they could not dictate to, nor interfere with their internal order in any wise. It is just and proper jealousy.

It is indisputable that Councils have, at times, done great good both to churches and to individuals, by prudent and well-considered advice in cases of great perplexity. It is equally evident that at times they have been the occasion of much harm, even of manifest injustice, by decisions hastily reached, or based on false assumptions. Whether, on the whole, they have been productive of more good than evil, is still an unsettled question with those who have known them the longest, and watched them the most carefully. The danger lies in a constant tendency to recognize them, in some sense, as a court of appeal and of arbitration—in effect if not in form. And this danger is the greater, because there will always be among us some who think they see the need of a stronger government for the control of virulent disorders than the independency of the churches furnishes. They desire some more speedy and more effectual method of removing rank offenses than the slow and uncertain process of

Church discipline. They would therefore welcome a *quasi* authority in the action of Councils, which should make an end of all controversy with the contentious and the perverse.

But such tendencies, fortunately, have thus far been counteracted by that innate apprehension with which the Baptist mind regards any possible approach to dictation, and stands guard against the interference of any external authority whatever, beyond the simple act of giving advice, when advice is asked.

I. THE ORIGIN OF COUNCILS

It has generally been taken for granted, by both Protestant and Papal authorities, that all Church Councils had their origin and find their sanction in the conference held in Jerusalem (Acts, fifteenth chapter), convened to consider questions which disturbed the Gentile churches, as to the reception of Jewish customs.

That meeting, it is claimed, was a Council somewhat within the accepted meaning of that term. And it is quite notable, not to say remarkable, that all men, and all classes of men, have with an easy liberality of interpretation, explained that primitive conference to meet their own peculiar views of Council need, and of Council action. Whether Papal or Protestant, ultra-Prelatical or moderately Congregational, every man who desires to find some central authority, some Church court to settle disputed questions, and to coerce or control Church action, claims to find a warrant for his particular theory in " the Council held in Jerusalem." That is declared to have been apostolic ; and an appeal to the fifteenth of Acts is assumed to be the end of all controversy.

It has been made the warrant and justification for ages of spiritual tyranny exercised over the churches of Christ and over the freedom of Christian thought and action, by men ambitious to lord it over God's heritage.   By this means Christian liberty and spiritual life almost have been crushed out of Christ's free churches, and the flock of God has been made a prey to the rapacity of men whose spiritual pride blinded them to the true methods of the Gospel.

The Syrian Christians had been disturbed by certain Jewish teachers who insisted they must observe the law of Moses ; especially must they be circumcised.   Against this they rebelled, and Paul who had planted these churches, refused to impose on the Gentile converts such a yoke.   To settle the matter, therefore, the Church at Antioch sent Paul with certain others to Jerusalem, to ask the opinion and advice of the mother-Church in reference to the matter.   This mother-Church would be more likely to understand the genius of the Gospel, especially in its relation to Judaism ; and moreover they had the Apostles with them, whose inspired judgment in such a case could not go amiss.   When the messengers from Antioch arrived, the Church at Jerusalem had a meeting to consider the matter.

It was no Council, no Synod, no Consociation, but a *church-meeting* simply. Just that, and nothing more. It consisted of the *Apostles*, and *elders*, and *brethren*. That is, the entire Church. And the Church, with just this composition, heard the case, deliberated, and, under the guidance of the Holy Ghost, gave a decision. This is the view taken of the matter by Hackett, Alford, Schaff, Waddington, and indeed nearly all Church authorities.

MOSHEIM, in his Church history, says:

"To call it a Council is a perversion. For that meeting was a conference of only a single Church, collected together for deliberation; and if such meetings may be called ecclesiastical Councils, a multitude of them were held in those primitive times. An ecclesiastical Council is a meeting of delegates from a number of confederate churches."—*Eccl. Hist., Vol. I., p. 72, sec. 14, note 17.*

Councils are of *human*, not of *divine* origin. They cannot therefore take precedence of, nor claim authority over, churches, which are divinely instituted. Nor were Councils known during the first age, and not until Christianity began to be corrupted. And to organize combinations of ecclesiastics to govern and dominate the churches, was one of the early corruptions which afflicted the kingdom of Christ.

DR. COLEMAN says:

"The apostolic churches were entirely independent of each other." "But in the *second* century this primitive liberty and independence began to be relinquished, and merged in a confederation of the churches of a province, or country, into a larger association." "They [Councils] were appointed by merely human authority, and were regarded as being instituted neither by Christ nor by His Apostles."—*Ancient Christ. Exemp., pp. 475, 476.*

DR. MOSHEIM further says:

"Nor does there appear in this first century any vestige of that *consociation* of the churches of the same province which gave rise to ecclesiastical Councils. But rather, as is manifest, it was not till the second century that the custom of holding ecclesiastical Councils first began, in Greece, and thence extended into other provinces."—*Eccl. Hist. B. 1., Cent. 1, part 2, ch. 2, sec. 14.*

DR. EMMONS, one of the fathers of New England Congregationalism, says:

"All the present disputes about Councils, *mutual* or *ex parte*, in respect to their *authority*, are vain and useless, be-cause they have no divine authority at all." "The human device of giving power to Associations, Consociations, or Councils, to decide in ecclesiastical causes, has been a fruit-ful source of ecclesiastical injustice, tyranny and persecu-tion."—*Emmons's Works, Vol. III., pp. 584, 586.*

There is, however, a sense in which the Church conference at Jerusalem may be said to have con-tained the germ of subsequent Councils—Councils in their better form. It is the dictate of common sense, and of Christian prudence as well, for those called to deal with grave and difficult matters, espe-cially if such matters be new and unfamiliar, to seek advice from those supposed to be better informed, whose counsel can instruct their minds and guide their action more wisely. In a multitude of counselors, also, there may be safety. A large number of wise and pious men, viewing a question from different points, with unbiased judgments, will be more likely to reach a safe and just conclusion, than a smaller number, less experienced, who are personally interested in it. And therefore it is natural and wise to *ask advice* in cases of moment and of doubt, in order to be helped by the wisdom and the experience of others. This explains the philosophy of Councils, committees of reference, and Presbyteries, as used by Baptists. The fellowship of individuals, and the fraternity of churches, lead Christian men to desire concurrence in matters of local interest, and so far as may be, to secure uniformity in matters of general concern.

But uniformity would be purchased at too great a cost if the rights or the liberties of the churches should be imperiled. When *usage* becomes *uniform*, it is not difficult to have it considered as *essential;* and when it is conceded to be essential, it has already become *authoritative.* Councils may be desirable and beneficent, but they are not essential for any purpose for which their advice is usually invoked; nor are they authoritative in any opinion they may express, or in any decisions they may render. Their possible perversions should not wholly condemn them, nor their probable benefits unduly magnify them.

II. GENERAL PROPOSITIONS

The principles on which, and rules by which—according to common usage and general consent—Baptist Councils are constituted, and their action governed, may be stated in the following propositions :

1. It must be accepted as a rule without exception, that such Councils are *advisory* only, always and everywhere ; they neither have, nor can have, any ecclesiastical *authority*. They bind individuals and churches so far, only, as they may choose to submit to their judgment and advice. Their province is simply *counsel*—what the name implies. Never, and in no sense, are they Church courts for authoritative decrees ; much less are they legislative bodies for the enactment of laws for the churches.

2. Councils have no original authority for action, and, indeed, no antecedent right of existence. Their existence depends on those who call them into being, and their right to act is derived from the same source. No company of persons, not a Church, has the right to convene, organize and take action on ecclesiastical matters which have not been submitted to them.

3. A Council is composed of delegates or messengers—either laic or cleric—appointed by the churches of which they are members, at the request of those calling it. A committee of reference is composed of individuals personally asked to advise, but with-

out any Church action as to their appointment. A Presbytery, in the Baptist sense, is a company of ministers personally invited to assist in ordination, or to advise in any Church matter.

4. Councils may be convened by *churches* or *individuals*—more commonly by churches—to consult and advise touching questions to be submitted to them. Individuals in difficulty with their churches, or persons excluded from them, may call a Council, if the Church will not, in circumstances hereafter explained.

5. But individuals in difficulty among themselves in the same Church, could not with propriety call a Council to settle their difficulties. Such difficulties would constitute a case of discipline which the Church would be under obligation to see adjusted. But the Church might feel the need of advice, and call a Council on the ground that it could not effect a settlement of the trouble without such assistance.

6. The usual and proper method for convening a Council, is by sending letters to such churches as may be selected, a majority of which should be those located in the vicinity, asking them to appoint their pastor, and one or more—usually two—brethren, to sit in consultation with them. These letters are called *letters missive*, and constitute the only authority for the assembling of the body, and the charter under which it must act when assembled.

7. The *letters missive* should be uniform, their statements identical, distinctively announcing when

and where the body is to convene, and what churches and individuals are invited as members.

8. The *letters missive* should also distinctly state what matters they will be asked to consider, and respecting which they are to advise. It is an admitted rule, sanctioned by common consent, that a Council cannot be convened under a *roving commission*, to act on any subject that may chance to be presented, but must confine its deliberations to such matters as were specified in the letters by which it was convened.

9. The delegates, or messengers, who compose the Council, are in no proper sense *representatives* of the churches which appoint them. They cannot therefore act for their churches, to bind them by their action. *A Baptist Church cannot be represented in any other body;* nor can it transfer its authority or its functions to any persons either within, or external to itself, to act for it. It can send messages by messengers, but cannot delegate its power to act.

10. A Council, when duly organized, is an *independent body* within its own sphere of action. It cannot be coerced, dictated to, or controlled by the churches from which its members come, nor by those who called it. Its acts are the result of the judgment of a majority of its members, and have the weight and force which such opinions may command—simply that, and nothing more.

11. It is somewhat common for those calling Councils, to invite, in addition to Church messen-

gers, certain *individuals* whose presence and counsels they may desire. To this custom, though it constitutes a somewhat mixed commission, there seems to be no reasonable objection. They are members by invitation, not by appointment.

12. Parties cannot properly convoke a Council to investigate or pass judgment on the case of persons with whom they hold *no ecclesiastical connection*—such as a member or pastor of another Church than that of which those convoking the Council are connected. But one Church may call a Council and ask advice as to their duty in respect to some other Church with which they are in fellowship.

13. The messengers, when convened, at the hour named in the call, *organize* by the election of a chairman and a clerk. These elections are usually on nomination ; and any one may call the meeting to order and ask for a nomination. But sometimes, in very important and difficult cases, a temporary chairman and clerk are chosen, and a committee is appointed to recommend permanent officers. After this the credentials of messengers are called for, and the clerk makes an accurate list of members, and of their churches. Then the object for which the Council was called, is stated—usually by reading a copy of the *letter missive*. By this the body understands what it is desired to do, and what it will be lawful for it to attempt. Further explanations, the presentation of evidence, and a discussion of the subject follow, concluding with such action as the body may agree to take. The usual parlia-

mentary rules govern in order and debate, unless different rules are adopted at the beginning of the session.

14. A Council is composed of all the persons present in response to the invitations sent out. This number of members can neither be increased nor diminished. Its composition is fixed by those who call it, and cannot be changed by its own action, nor by the authority of any other body. It cannot, therefore, admit others to membership, nor exclude those who are members by appointment.

15. But, as an *exception* to this rule, all deliberative bodies have the primal and inherent right to protect themselves against insult, disgrace, and such interruptions as would frustrate the object of their deliberations. Such conduct, therefore, on the part of any member during the proceedings, would make him liable to censure or expulsion.

16. If, however, any member be dissatisfied with the presence of any other member or with the proceedings of the body, he can refuse to act, and withdraw. He has no other remedy.

17. Usage has not decided that any specified number of messengers appointed shall be necessary to constitute a *quorum* for doing business. Any considerable number, or even a small portion of them, usually proceed to act, especially if the case be one involving no great difficulty. If, however, the matter be important and complicated, action should not be taken without a full attendance of members. In all important cases, it would be a

salutary rule, that no action should be had unless a *majority* of those called to constitute the Council, were present ; **or** unless a majority of the churches invited had responded by messengers present. But so diverse are the views of those who convene Councils, as well as those who act on them, that no rule on this point, fitted to all occasions, has thus far been established.

18. A Council may *adjourn* from time to time, if necessary, to accomplish the purpose for which it was convened. But it cannot perpetuate a continued existence as a *standing court of appeals*. When its object is accomplished it expires by limitation ; but a formal vote to dissolve or to adjourn, *sine die*, is usually passed.

19. If a Council adjourns, it must retain the *same composition* when it subsequently meets as at its first session. It cannot have new members added to it, except by mutual consent of the body and all parties interested in its action. Nor can it be diminished, except that the absence of some members would not vitiate its action.

20. Before the final adjournment, the minutes of the proceedings are read, corrected, and approved, and a certified copy is ordered to be given to the parties by whom it was called, as containing the results of the deliberations, and the Council's answer to the request for advice.

21. When finally adjourned or dissolved, the Council ceases to exist, and cannot reconvene at its own option, or by the authority of its members. If con-

vened at all, it must be by process similar to that which brought it into being at first. It would, in fact, be a new Council, though composed of the same individuals.

22. It is not proper for one Council to sit in judgment on, or review the action of, a previous Council. But a matter not satisfactorily disposed of by one may be referred to a second. Such a second should so far, only, canvass the proceedings of the first as to ascertain the facts they had before them, and the ground of their decision.

23. When a second is called to consider some matter submitted to a previous one, the second should contain, so far as practicable, all or most of the members of the previous one, with such additions, however, as will be likely to counterbalance any local or personal bias or prejudice, or any want of information or experience, which may have prevented satisfactory results in the former case.

24. In the calling of a Council no *packing* process should ever be resorted to, seeking to compose it of such persons only as would be likely to favor the object of those who called it. Such a course may be a device of worldly policy, but is unworthy of Christian men, who in all honesty should act on higher principles, and seek not simply the endorsement of a man or a cause, but equity and justice, truth and right. For this, and not for the furtherance of personal or of party ends, should they ask counsel of their brethren.

25. A Council may be called by a single Church, or

by several churches united; by a single individual, or by several persons acting in concert. The *letters missive* should distinctly state by whom the call is issued, as well as the object for which it is issued.

26. Councils called to adjust and settle difficulties are usually designated as either *mutual* or *ex parte*. A *mutual* Council is one in which the several parties to the difficulty unite in the call and reference. An *ex parte* Council is called by one party to the difficulty.

27. In the calling of a *mutual* Council, each party uniting in the call—whether an individual, several persons, or a Church—has the selection of *one-half* the members; otherwise there might be a want of fairness in the composition of the body. While the parties may confer together as to the churches or individuals to be invited, yet neither has the right to *object* to those selected by the other, provided they be all reputable members, in good and regular standing in Baptist churches.

28. An *ex parte* Council should not be called until all proper efforts have been made for, and have failed to secure, a *mutual* Council. The reason is obvious. General harmony and agreement are desirable, and are more likely to be secured in a mutual representation, where all parties can be heard.

29. Parties not uniting in the call can have *no rights* or standing in the Council when convened. But as a matter of courtesy, or for the sake of obtaining all possible information, other persons who have knowledge of the case may be heard by consent of the body and those who convened it.

30. Parties calling a Council *cannot be members of it*, and have no vote or right of action in it, except to place before the body all the information they possess, through persons chosen by them for that purpose; otherwise they would sit as judges of their own cause.

31. An *ex parte* Council *cannot*, by its own act, transform itself into a *mutual* Council. Such a change can be effected only by the consent and agreement of the various parties involved in the difficulty.

32. When a *mutual* Council is to be called, to adjust difficulties between a Church and some of its members, the *letters missive* should be sent out by, and in the name of, the Church, and not of the individuals. But the fact of its being by mutual agreement of the parties should be stated in the letters.

33. A Council *cannot review* and pass judgment on the conduct of any other Church than that which has called it and submitted its case; nor can a Council properly be called for such a purpose. No body of men holds the right to try and pass judgment on an independent Church, except by its own request; nor review its acts of internal order and discipline. Such a body would thereby become judicial—a Church court; which Councils are not.

34. But either churches or individuals may call a Council *to advise them* what is their duty in relation to a Church deemed heretical in doctrine or irregular in practice; or for other reasons thought important. In such a case matters pertaining to that

other Church would necessarily come under review, so far, and so far only, as the facts were concerned regarding which advice had been asked, and so far as might be needful to enable the Council to advise intelligently and discreetly in the case.

35. Members, if aggrieved by the attitude of their own Church, believed by them to be heretical or disorderly, having failed in efforts at adjustment, and in efforts for a *mutual* Council as well, before proceeding to call an *ex parte* Council, would do well to lay the case before some neighboring Church or churches, as a matter in which such churches have an equal interest with themselves. Churches thus appealed to could, with propriety, ask a Council to advise *them* as to their duty in regard to the matter, or to advise the aggrieved members as to *their* duty in the case. Should such churches decline, as not deeming the occasion sufficient, or not wishing to become involved in controversy, then the individuals may proceed to call one to give them advice. The call should state what efforts had already been made for the adjustment of the difficulty.

36. Councils, when convened to aid in settling difficulties, should take sufficient time to understand the case thoroughly, and then act heroically in expressing their opinions as to where the blame rests, and in giving their advice as to what should be done. Aim to be *right*, rather than try to *please*. It is usually a vain thing to attempt a compromise. As a rule, this pleases neither party. Whatever is decided, almost certainly one party, and very

likely both, will be dissatisfied. Too much must not be expected from Councils; they can give advice and express opinions; beyond this they cannot vindicate the right or punish the wrong.

37. When persons, excluded, as they believe, unjustly, resolve to call a Council *ex parte*, they cannot be expected to ask the *excluding Church* to send delegates to sit in the Council. It would be contrary to a natural sense of justice for those who had prejudged the case, and decided against the plaintiff, unfairly, as he believed, to be asked to sit again on its decision. Such persons could not be regarded as unbiased or impartial judges. But the excluding Church should be asked to send some one to the Council to give any information to the body, and to present their version of the case.

38. If those who are invited to sit with councils do *not approve* the object of the call , and decline to act, they should at once *notify* those inviting them to that effect, giving their reasons for non-concurrence. Such communications should be laid before the body when convened. But it is better to respond to the call—unless the circumstances be very remarkable—and by one's presence and influence, prevent unfortunate action, rather than permit it by their absence.

39. It is a course of questionable propriety for a Council to require the parties to a difficulty to *pledge themselves* at the beginning to abide by whatever decision the body may reach. This is sometimes done with the commendable purpose of putting an

end to the controversy. But it seems hardly consistent with freedom of conscience to pledge agreement beforehand to a course of action at the time unknown, and contingent on future and unforeseen events. As a matter of fact, such pledges when made are seldom kept.

40. Councils for the adjustment of difficulties involving Church action should not be called, unless the need seems imperative. Churches *should administer their own affairs*, exercising their own prerogatives, and discharging their own responsibilities, without external aid, so far as possible. They may make some mistakes, but that is inevitable in all human affairs, and the aid of Councils will not absolutely obviate that misfortune. But against all tendency to relieve the churches of their appropriate duties, to intrude into the sphere of their just authority, or to undermine their rightful independence—against all this Councils should constantly and sacredly guard.*

* For further and more specific application of Council action, especially in difficult cases of Church discipline, and the trials of unworthy ministers, see chaps. 6 and 7, pp. 193–214.

CHAPTER 13

RELATED SOCIETIES

WHILE the churches are the only Christian socie
ties provided for by the New Testament economy,
and, therefore, the only ones really essential to the
accomplishment of the purposes contemplated by
the Gospel, yet combinations of individual and local
efforts have been found convenient for the carrying
on of Christian work on wider areas and more distant fields than could well be cared for by individual
service. These combinations have grown into vast
systems of organized endeavor, making societies
almost innumerable for Christian and benevolent
service of many kinds. It may well be questioned
if there be not quite too many such. Some of the
more common, which have grown into established
usage with our churches, are the following:

I. ASSOCIATIONS

There is at times no little confusion of thought
occasioned by want of a clear understanding as to
the true nature and real purpose of *Associations;*
and that, too, by ministers themselves, who ought

to be able expounders of Baptist polity and usage
Especially as to the relation which these bodies
sustain to the churches; whether they can act *for*
the associated churches, and in some sense *bind*
them by their action.

It is customary for churches occupying a given
extent of territory—usually less than a State, perhaps limited portions of contiguous States, not
so widely extended as to make it difficult, because
of distance, to meet in one place, nor yet embracing so many churches as to make the meetings
inconveniently large — by common agreement to
organize on some simple basis of association for
mutual helpfulness and counsel.

These churches agree to coöperate in the Association, and meet yearly with some one of them, by
their pastors, and a certain number of members,
appointed as *messengers**. These meetings usually
hold two days, sometimes more, and the time is
occupied in hearing reports from the various churches
—each one sending with the messengers a letter,
setting forth their condition as to anything of special interest to themselves or to the body. Sermons
are preached, prayer-meetings held, and various
matters pertaining to the prosperity of the cause

* The term *representative* is sometimes used, and *delegate* more
frequently.   Both terms are liable to be misunderstood, as imply-
ing that an Association is a representative body, and that the
messengers bear delegated authority to represent their churches
and act for them.   The term *messenger* was commonly used by
the earlier Associations, is least objectionable, and most accu
rately characterizes the purpose for which they are appointed.

come under consideration. Missionary work on their field is fostered, new churches are planted, and weak ones aided. If any of the churches have peculiar difficulties to encounter, and choose to ask advice and help, such matters are considered, and help rendered, if practicable.

When the body meets to observe its anniversary, the moderator of the previous year calls the meeting to order at the appointed time, and presides until a new moderator is elected, with clerk and treasurer; then the body is fully organized for business. Thence its services proceed according to its by-laws, or a prearranged programme. It is customary to hear, during the sessions, appeals with important information from the representatives of various missionary and benevolent bodies, for the sake of instructing and stimulating the members in reference to such causes.

These annual gatherings constitute not only favorable opportunities for projecting plans for missionary work within the bounds of the Association, but they also give occasion for pleasant fraternal intercourse on the part of members of the various churches, who, at these Christian festivals, form and foster personal friendships of a most pleasant and profitable character. This is particularly true in rural districts, where they have few opportunities for personal intercourse.

Observe the Following Facts

1. The term *Association* is used in *two* distinct

and quite dissimilar senses; by not observing which fact much confusion, and at times no small difficulty, arises in the minds of people.

First, the organized body which meets annually for the transaction of business, is called the *Association*. This body corporate consists of *pastors* and *messengers*, as its constituent elements and active *members*. It has its constitution, by-laws, its order of business, meets and adjourns, publishes its proceedings, enrolling the names of its pastors and messengers, who alone have the rights of membership in its sessions.

Second, in a somewhat vague and ideal sense all the associated churches, and the geographical limits over which they are scattered, are called the *Association*. Thus we speak of the dearth or the prosperity which prevails in this or that Association, or we say that revivals have, or have not been extensive in such or such an Association. No reference is here had to the organic body which meets annually for business, but to the territorial field, and the local churches, from which the pastors and messengers come.

2. An Association — the organized body that meets for business—is *not* composed of churches, but of individuals, the pastors and messengers. It is a common way of speaking, but a very loose and misleading way, to say it is composed of churches. This arises from a misapprehension, and perpetuates a misunderstanding. A Baptist Church cannot be a member of any other body whatever. It would

violate its sacred charter, and lose its identity as the body of Christ, to attempt such a union. And if many churches should enter into organic relations, and constitute an ecclesiastical confederation, the local churches would be absorbed, losing largely their individuality and their independence. Also, in that case, the confederate body would possess legislative and judicial control over the separate congregations. This is the actual *status* of most Christian denominations. But our polity and our traditions repudiate both the inference, and the hypothesis on which it rests.

3. But it may be asked, How is it, if churches are not *members* of the body, that the Associations uniformly receive new churches to their number, or dismiss, or drop churches from it? The reply is this: Churches are not received to *membership*, though such expressions are often, and indeed ordinarily used; but they are received to *fellowship* and *co-operation;* which fact is evinced, by their pastors and messengers being admitted to *membership*, thus composing its constituent elements.

4. An Association is not a *representative* body, in the ordinary acceptation of that term. A Baptist Church cannot appoint persons with delegated authority to act for it, so as to bind it by their action. It cannot transfer its authority and responsibility to any person, or persons whatever. It can appoint persons as committees to perform service for it, and report their doings. If it be still insisted, for the sake of terms, that the churches do meet in the As-

sociation, by their representatives, the pastors and messengers, the reply must be—such is not the case, and cannot be, either actually or constructively, for a Baptist Church cannot be *represented* by delegates authorized to act for it in any other organization whatever.

5. An Association is a *voluntary* society formed and maintained for mutual help among the churches associated, and for the religious welfare of the field it occupies. It is of human, not of divine authority; it grows out of the sympathies of Christian fellowship, and the need of mutual help. No Church is under obligation to affiliate with it; and any connected Church can withdraw coöperation, at any time, for any reasons which seem to itself sufficient, without prejudice to either its evangelical or its denominational reputation and standing. But while it continues associated, it must abide by the rules and regulations, mutually agreed upon, by which the body is governed.

6. Because an Association is not a representative body, and because a Church cannot be represented in any other organization, and because a Church cannot, even if it would, alienate, or transfer its powers and responsibilities to any man, or body of men, *therefore* an Association cannot legislate for the churches, exercise any authority over them, or bind them in any way by its own action. Whatever is done while in session, is of authority only to those who do it; that is, the members—pastors and delegates. They may make suggestions to the churches, or

present appeals, and lay requests before them; to all of which the churches will give such attention as may seem to them right and proper.

7. The fact that the messengers are appointed by their respective churches argues nothing as to their being invested with delegated power. This appointment is made at the request of the Association, and according to its constitutional provisions, as the most convenient and equitable method of constituting the body, not because the appointment carries any ecclesiastical authority with it. These messengers bear the letters and salutations of their churches, and consult with the other members as to the objects for the interest of which they meet.

8. An Association is an *independent* body, not subject to the authority or control of the churches any more than the churches are subject to its authority and control. It frames its own constitution, makes its own by-laws, elects its own officers, and manages its own business, without dictation from any one. Within its own sphere of action it is just as independent as a Church is within its sphere of action. It fixes the terms of membership and the conditions on which the churches may associate; designates the number of messengers to be sent from each Church, orders its own exercises, meets and adjourns at its own pleasure. If any Church does not approve the proceedings it can refuse to affiliate, and withdraw at any time from the Association, if it thinks best.

9. In the exercise of its independence, also, the

Association can refuse to receive its messengers, and drop from its fellowship any Church that has violated the constitution and the original compact, or that has, in any matter deemed vital, departed from the faith and practice of the associated churches and the denomination. Provisions for such emergencies are made in the constitutions of all Associations; also, the process of fraternal labor to be pursued with the recusant Church before final excision shall be decreed is likewise prescribed.

NOTE 1.—Should one of the associated churches be commonly reported to have become unsound in the faith, or irregular in practice, to have violated the constitutional provisions, or broken the compact accepted at the union, and these reports seem credible, it would be the right and the duty of the Association to inquire into the case, by committee or otherwise, and ascertain the facts. The Association would have no right to call the Church to account, to exercise any authority on it, reprimand or censure it; but only to *ascertain the facts* in the case, and then to take such action as their mutual relations warranted. Such action might result in the Church being disfellowshiped, dropped from the minutes, and all intercourse with it discontinued. That would be the extent of an exercise of disciplinary power on a Church by an Association.

NOTE 2.—If an Association should disfellowship a Church and drop it from its minutes, that act would not interrupt the intercourse and fellowship of said Church in its relation to other churches. An Association cannot act for the churches, but only for itself; nor can it exercise disciplinary power beyond its own corporate limits. Such an act of disfellowship would indeed be presumptive evidence that something was wrong in the Church dropped. But if the fellowship of other churches is to be interrupted, or withdrawn, it must be by their own act; the Association cannot do it; it acts for itself alone, not for the churches.

NOTE 3.—Should the pastor of one of the associated churches be known, or believed, to be a disreputable and unworthy man, the Association would not be obliged to accept him as a member of the body, or allow his name to appear on their minutes—to do which would give him a *quasi* endorsement and recommendation. They could refuse to do this, and thereby free themselves from all responsibility as to his standing. Such an act, however, could not affect his relation to the Church of which he was the pastor, nor yet to other churches. If those relations are to be interrupted, it must be by the action of the Church, or the churches themselves. No one else can act for them.

NOTE 4.—If an associated Church persists in retaining and supporting for its pastor a man of bad reputation, generally believed to be unfit for the ministry, and unworthy of confidence, the Association can refuse to receive the *man*, and they can disfellowship and drop the *Church*, should the case become serious. They possess this right; but such disfellowship does not carry with it the disfellowship of the other churches. Their intercourse with the dropped Church or man is not interrupted until they interrupt it by their own action. The Association acts for itself, not for the churches. Such action may at times become necessary, in order to free the body from apparent complicity with evil, and to relieve other pastors and messengers from all responsibility in sustaining and giving currency to an unworthy man or an unworthy Church.

NOTE 5.—Many of the larger Associations—especially those that centre in cities and towns—became *incorporated*, with a board of legally elected trustees, for the purpose of holding and managing real estate, not for speculative uses, but to aid mission stations and feeble churches to houses of worship. These trustees act for, and under the direction of, the body, while the churches furnishing funds for the purpose. Thus the Association becomes an efficient missionary organization within its own bounds.

NOTE 6.—In former times, when churches were less numerous, and obtaining counsel in perplexing matters was more difficult, it was no uncommon thing for them, vexed with divisive questions of doctrine, order or discipline, to send up *queries* to the Associations at their annual meetings, and thereby seek advice from the assembled wisdom, which might dispel their doubts. These queries were considered warily, and answered with caution; usually protesting that they could not meddle with the internal affairs of the churches, and that the Association was not a legislative body to enact laws, nor an ecclesiastical court to settle questions judicially for them. They could express an opinion, or give advice—nothing more. They were very jealous for the *independency* of the churches. So it is now, and should ever continue to be.

II. STATE CONVENTIONS

As a single Association covers a limited extent of territory, and the various Associations, whose boundaries touch, hold no organic relation to each other, but each working for the same end, in a similar way, it has been thought wise to have a more general organization, extending over and embracing the fields of all the Associations in the State. This is called a *Baptist State Convention*, or, as in many States it is termed, a *General Association*. This latter designation is by some supposed more accurately to express its relation to the local or district Associations.

The Convention is a missionary organization, to

operate in extending evangelical religion within the bounds of the State, in connection with the Associations and churches. It works by sustaining feeble interests and supporting missionaries in destitute neighborhoods. This is done either in coöperation with the Associations within their bounds, or else in fields which they cannot cultivate. Sometimes the Associations work under the general direction of the Convention, and report to it and through it. But all this is according to mutual agreement, since each is equally independent in its own sphere. In addition to the strictly spiritual culture of their fields, State Conventions not unfrequently plant and foster educational institutions, especially denominational academies and schools for higher learning.

The composition of State Conventions is varied and indefinite. Associations are uniformly constituted by the pastors and delegates or messengers from the churches. The membership of Conventions, according to their mutually arranged and voluntary constitutional provisions, is composed of persons appointed by contributing churches, delegates sent by cooperating Associations, individuals who make themselves annual or life members by the payment of a specified sum, and perhaps still other classes, as may be provided; while no person can be a member, unless he be a member in good standing of some regular Baptist Church, yet, to a large extent, a money qualification is insisted on, the better to stimulate liberality and secure funds to the treasury.

The meetings are held annually for two or three days—one day being usually given to a State pastors' conference. Reports are made by the Associations, addresses by missionaries and others, plans projected for enlarged endeavors—special time and attention being given to the Sunday-school cause. The anniversaries alternate between different sections of the State, and are held chiefly in the larger communities, the smaller churches finding it difficult to accommodate the numbers which attend, for whose entertainment gratuitous provision is usually, though not always made.

III. MINISTERS' MEETINGS

In nearly all compact communities, and, indeed, in many rural and scattered neighborhoods, the Baptist pastors form associations for mutual intercourse and improvement, called *Ministers' Meetings*, *Pastors' Conferences*, or other similar names. They organize with a simple constitution and by-laws, and constitute a voluntary and independent society for the purpose set forth. They have no organic connection with the churches, and possess no ecclesiastical character or significancy. Essays are read for criticism on assigned topics, plans of sermons presented, sermons preached also for criticism, and discussions held on subjects germane to ministerial culture and service.

These meetings are held monthly, or, in larger communities, weekly. They are composed mostly of pastors, but in some, ministers without a charge, and even deacons, are admitted. These meetings have no right of interference with the churches, and no action they can take with reference to any pastor who is a member, can affect that pastor's relation to his Church. They have the right to admit, dismiss, or expel their own members, but cannot interfere with the relations the various pastors sustain outside the conference itself.

IV.   OTHER SOCIETIES

There are other denominational societies, well known to all, sustained for Christian service in connection with our denominational activities. The Missionary Union, for conducting Baptist missions in foreign lands; the Home Mission Society, performing a similar service in our own country ; the Publication Society, for disseminating a denominational literature; an Education Society—indeed, many of them, one general, and many local—for the establishment and support of schools of learning; a Historical Society, for the collection and preservation of denominational records. The Southern Baptist Convention represents the mission work of Baptists in the Southern States, both home and foreign.*

These various missionary organizations are so many voluntary and independent societies, sustain-

---

* See Appendix for a historical sketch of our various mission-ary organizations.

ing no organic connection with the churches; are not controlled by them, and cannot control them. They derive their financial support from the churches, to which churches they make appeals, and to which appeals they respond as they may feel inclined. Membership in these various organizations is largely secured by the payment of a stipulated sum of money. Usually they are incorporated societies, holding property devoted exclusively to the purposes of their work. Many other societies not here named, exist, operating on local fields for various beneficent purposes connected with our denominational work and welfare.

CHAPTER 14

ORDINATION

ORDINATION, in its popular sense, is that form of service by which men are admitted to the ranks of the Christian ministry, and to the exercise of its functions. So important a relation does this service sustain to the character of the men who fill their pulpits and become the instructors and guides of the churches, that ritualistic communions hold it as a sacrament. While *ordination* is but one of the avenues by which worthy men can be admitted to, and unworthy men excluded from, the sacred office, yet it is one, and should be sedulously guarded by watchful churches and conscientious Councils and Presbyteries—that the ministry be kept pure and true to its high calling. For, while neither churches nor Councils can prevent a man from preaching, if he desires to do it, and can secure hearers, they can refuse him recognition and fellowship in such a course, and ought to do it, if they believe him unfit or unworthy.

Ordination, therefore, as the act by which men are admitted to the rank and functions of religious teachers among our people, and pastors of the flock of Christ, becomes a matter of serious moment, and should be well considered. Its motive, its purpose and its effect should be clearly understood.

To do this in the light of Baptist Church polity, the following questions must be asked and answered:

1. What is ordination? 2. By whom is ordination? 3. What is the effect of ordination? 4. Is ordination to be repeated?

Primary Propositions

The discussion which follows will maintain, and it is believed will establish, the following propositions:

PROP. I. That the ordination of the New Testament was an *election*, or appointment, to the ministerial office, and not a ceremonial *setting apart*, or consecration to that office.

PROP. II. That there is no proof in the New Testament that persons chosen to the office of elder, pastor or bishop in the apostolic churches were designated for, or inducted into, that office by any formal service or ceremony whatever.

PROP. III. That, though the laying on of hands was common on many occasions, as an ancient Oriental Jewish and early Christian form of blessing, especially in the bestowment of the gifts of the Spirit, yet there is neither precept nor precedent in the New Testament to require its use in the ordination of Christian ministers.

PROP. IV. That, while some public service of inauguration and designation for one who first enters the ministry, or at any subsequent entrance upon a new field of labor, would be very appropriate and becoming as expressing the approval and fellowship of other ministers and the churches, yet such service is not of divine authority, and cannot be made obligatory or essential, either to the lawfulness of ministerial standing or to the validity of ministerial acts.

PROP. V. That if such ordination or recognition services be held, their form and order are matters of liberty and choice with those concerned in them, since they are prescribed by no Scriptural authority.

PROP. VI. That, since all ecclesiastical authority resides in the local, visible Church according to the New Testament polity, therefore the right to set apart, as well as to elect, belongs to the Church alone, and the only sphere of Council or Presbytery action is that of advice to, and cooperation with, the Church, being in no sense authoritative or essential.

PROP. VII. That while, for the sake of order and propriety it is becoming for accredited ministers to conduct all public religious services on ordinary occasions, yet ceremonial ordination is not essential to the ministry of the Word, nor to the administration of the ordinances; therefore, a Church without an ordained minister may, with the strictest propriety, direct a private member to administer the ordinances, conduct its services, and preside in its assemblies; and, indeed, this should be done for the edification of the body.

PROP. VIII. That reordination, in the case of ministers who come to us from other evangelical denominations, is a matter of Christian liberty, optional
with those concerned, but cannot be made essential to ministerial character or the validity of ministerial acts, though it may with propriety be made
to conform to prevailing custom, for the sake of
uniformity in usage.

Our space will admit of little more than a statement of positions deemed true and tenable ; while
many of the arguments, and most of the authorities
by which these positions are maintained must be
omitted.

I. WHAT IS ORDINATION ?

This question, to be clearly answered, needs
definition and limitation. Ordination means different things to different minds, and according to different ecclesiastical standards.

It is defined to be the act and form of setting one
apart to the work of the Christian ministry; or induction into the sacred office. Or, in a little more
formal and churchly language it is " the act of conferring holy orders, with prayer, and the imposition
of hands." If, however, a more comprehensible explanation be desired, as to both the form and substance of it, we must keep in mind the point of view
from which it is contemplated.

First, there is the ordination of present usage
as held and practised by the various Christian de-

nominations, with great diversity of subjective import and ceremonial observance.

Second, there is the ordination of history which found its highest conception and most complete expression in the mediæval Latin and Greek churches, which held it as a sacrament, invested it with the sanctity of inspiration and surrounded it with the pageantry of an imposing ritualism.

Third, there is the ordination of the New Testament, which differs from both the others, and which alone need command the regard or research of those churches who claim to draw both the form and spirit of all life from that sacred fountain of ecclesiastical order and authority.

Our inquiry, then, is narrowed to this question, What is the "ordination" of the New Testament?

The English words *ordain* and *ordained*, are used with some frequency in the sacred writings, and render several Greek words, but constitute, as every careful reader knows, no argument for ceremonial ordination, as now or formerly practised.

In Mark 3 : 14 it is said Jesus " ordained (*epoieese*) twelve, that they should be with Him." It implies no " setting apart," but simply an appointment, a choice.

In Luke 10 : 1 it is said, " the Lord appointed (*anedeixen*) other seventy also." The word means to point out, to declare, to appoint. Has no reference to formal induction into office.

In 1 Tim. 2 : 7, Paul says, " Whereunto I am ordained (*etetheen*) a preacher, and an apostle." Here the word means to set, to constitute, to appoint, and has no reference to ceremonial ordination.

In Acts 1 : 22 Peter declares that one must be ordained (*genesthai*) to be a witness of the resurrection of Jesus, to fill the place of Judas. Here the word means to select, elect, appoint, to bring about, cause to be.

In Acts 14 : 23 it is said of Paul and Barnabas, " when they had ordained (*cheirotoneesantes*) them elders in every city," etc. This much-quoted word, which has been relied on to prove a ritualistic ordination, by the " laying on of hands," the best scholarship decides to mean the stretching out of the hand or the lifting up of the hand as in voting. The meaning of which here is, that the Apostles secured the election of elders by the vote of the churches, with no reference to ceremonial induction into office.*

The word used in Titus 1 : 5, "ordain elders in every city," is *katasteesees*, which means to set, to

---

* This word, *Cheirotoneoo, Robinson*, in his N. T. Lexicon, defines, " to stretch out the hand, to hold up the hand, as in voting; hence to vote; to give one's vote. In N. T. to choose by vote, to appoint." *Green*, in his N. T. Lexicon, defines it, " to stretch out the hand; to constitute by voting; to appoint." *Donnegan*, in his Greek Lexicon, defines, " to stretch forth the hand; to vote in an assembly by extending the hand; to elect, to choose." The only places where this word is used in the N. T. are that already named, Acts 14: 23, and 2 Cor. 8: 19, where Paul speaks of the brother " who was chosen (*Cheirotoneetheis*) of the churches to travel with us." Here the choice or appointment of the brother is the only thing indicated.

place, to constitute, to set over.   And which Robinson defines, "to constitute, to make;" and Green, " to place, constitute, set, appoint."

I. *The Testimony of Scholars*

DR. DEXTER, with reference to these cases, says :

" There being no hint in either case of any thing of a character like what is commonly called ordination in our time."   " Fairly translated, and unmodified by any coloring from subsequent unscriptural ecclesiastical usage, these texts would never have suggested any such act as that which is called ' *ordination* ' by the common speech of men."—*Congregationalism, pp. 138, 139.*

DEAN ALFORD says :

" The word (*Cheirotoneesantes*) will not bear Jerome's and Chrysostom's sense of ' laying on of hands,' adopted by Roman Catholic expositors.   Nor is there any reason for departing from the usual meaning of electing by show of hands."—*Comments on Acts 14 : 23.*

DR. HACKETT renders the phrase :

" Now having appointed for them elders in every Church, " which he interprets thus; "having appointed for them by their outstretched hand."—*Comment in loco.*

DEAN ALFORD renders the passage, Titus I : 5,

"And mightest appoint, city by city, elders. "   He sees no ceremonial ordination in it.

CONYBEARE renders it :

" Mightest appoint presbyters in every city."—*Com. in loco.*

BLOOMFIELD says:

" There is indeed no point on which the most learned have been so much agreed, as this, that *Cheirotoneesantes* here simply denotes having selected, constituted, appointed."— *Com. on Acts 14: 23.*

DR. LYMAN COLEMAN says:

" This conclusion is sustained by the most approved authorities. According to Suicer, the primary and appropriate signification of the term is to denote an election made by the uplifted hand, and particularly denotes the election of a bishop by vote." " In this sense it continued for a long time to be used in the Church, denoting not an ordination or consecration, but an election. Grotius, Meyer, and De Wette so interpret the passage, to say nothing of Beza, Böhmer, Rothe, and others."—*Prim. Christ., p. 64.*

MATTHEW TINDALE says:

" We read only of the Apostles constituting elders by the suffrages of the people, Acts 14 : 23, which is the genuine signification of the Greek word, *Cheirotoneesantes*, so it is accordingly interpreted by Erasmus, Beza, Diodoti, and those who translated the Swiss, French, Italian, Belgic, and even English Bibles, till the Episcopal correction, which leaves out the words, ' by election,' as well as the marginal notes which affirm that the Apostles did not thrust pastors into the churches through a lordly superiority, but chose and placed them there by the voice of the congregation."—*Rights of a Christian Church, p. 358.*

DR. VICTOR LECHLER (in Lange), says:

" *Cheirotonein* signifies to raise the hands, to vote, to elect by stretching out the hands. The expression, accordingly, suggests the thought that the Apostles may have appointed and superintended a congregational election. And this view is supported by the circumstances related in chap. 6:2, when the Twelve directed that the election of the Seven should be held."—*Com. on Acts 14: 23.*

DR. GILL says :

" The election and call of them [pastors] with their acceptance, is ordination. Election and ordination are spoken of as the same." " Though there was a *stretching out* of the hands, there was no *imposition* of hands in ordination." " No instance can be given of hands being laid on any ordinary minister, pastor, or elder at his ordination."—*Body of Divinity, pp. 525-6. Phil. Ed., 1810.*

A want of space forbids further citation of authorities. Nor is it needful. New Testament ordination was an election, an appointment to office, and had no reference whatever to any formal induction into office ; did not imply any ceremonial investiture, or setting apart to the functions of that office. The New Testament calls an election to office, ordination ; we call the setting apart of those elected, ordination. Those who are jealous for New Testament models, should correct their phraseologies by the New Testament standard.

It may be fairly asked—admitting that ordination in the New Testament sense was an election, an appointment—Were not those, thus elected, set apart by formal ceremonies to the discharge of their official duties ? This we can neither affirm nor deny. We simply do not know. There is neither precept, example, nor manifest inference to decide the question. It has usually been taken for granted that the primitive ministry was inducted into office by formal services, and that " prayer with the laying on of hands," was the essential part of such ordination. But this has been accepted as scriptural, not because it is found in the Scriptures, but because Prelatical and Presbyterial authorities have interpreted the Scriptures by their own ecclesiastical usages, rather than adjusted their usages to the New Testament teaching. They have seen Episcopal and Presbyterian ordination in the New Testament because they saw it in their Church standards and practices. Their scholars have largely so interpreted the text, and Baptists have accepted their conclusions without even their justification.

2. *The Laying on of Hands*

But does not Paul expressly declare to Timothy that he was ordained and set apart to the work of the ministry by the laying on of his hands and the hands of the Presbytery ? No ; he makes no such declaration. Does he not enjoin Timothy not to ordain any man hastily by suddenly laying hands on him ? No ; he makes no such declaration, as we shall see.

The subject of " the laying on of hands " must be treated very briefly in this place. It was an old Jewish and common Oriental custom, by which benedictions were conferred or invoked, and other symbolical acts performed. Our Lord laid His hands on the sick to heal them ; on the little children to bless them. The Apostles did the same. But in the apostolic church this act was chiefly associated with the special impartation of the Holy Spirit. The *Charismata* was thus conferred. Peter and John laid hands on the converts at Samaria, and they received the Holy Ghost. So did Paul on the twelve disciples at Ephesus. Ananias laid his hands on Saul at Damascus that he might receive his sight, and be filled with the Holy Ghost. Jesus, after the resurrection, conferred the Holy Ghost by breathing on His disciples. And His farewell blessing, when He ascended, was conferred by the lifting up of His hands.

Now, the apostolic precedents relied on to enforce ceremonial ordination by the laying on of hands, are the following :

1. The ordination of the Seven as related in Acts 6 : 1-6. The true ordination, *i. e.*, the election in this case was by the " whole multitude," " the multitude of the disciples."

But this case is not in point, and constitutes no argument ; since this setting apart was to a secular office and not to a spiritual ministry ; to the serving of tables and not to preaching of the Word. An induction into the Diaconate and not into the Episcopate. Moreover, this act was by inspired Apostles, who have no successors. Neither the Diaconate, the Episcopate, nor the Presbyterate can claim to be the official successors of the Apostolate. Presumably this act was for their especial endowment by the *Charismata.* It has no authority unless it be in the ordination of deacons.

2. The next precedent relied on is the case of Barnabas and Saul, sent forth to the Gentiles by the Church at Antioch, Acts 13 : 1-3.

But this was not an ordination in any technical sense. Both these men had been engaged in the active work of the ministry for years—not less than eight or nine, possibly twelve, according to the best chronological data. They were not here *inducted* into the ministry, but *designated* to a new field of work. Moreover, this designation was by the special and express dictation of the Holy Ghost, showing that it was not a common and customary, but an extraordinary and wholly exceptional thing, and therefore not an imitable example. Also, it is wholly undetermined who laid hands on them, whether the prophets, the elders, or the disciples generally.

DR. HACKETT says :

" Paul was already a minister and an Apostle, and by this service he and Barnabas were now merely set apart for the accomplishment of a specific work."—*Com. in loco.*

3. The next case usually quoted to the same end, is Paul's injunctions to Timothy ; " Neglect not the gift that is in thee, which was given thee by prophecy, with the laying on of the hands of the Presbytery."—1 Tim. 4 : 14. Also, " Wherefore, I put thee in remembrance that thou stir up the gift of

God, which is in thee, by the putting on of my hands."—2 Tim. 1 : 6.

These passages are held to prove primitive ordination by the laying on of hands. This inferential reasoning is quite of a piece with that which proves primitive infant baptisms from the fact of household baptisms. The fact is, the Apostle makes not the least allusion to ordination in these citations. He speaks expressly and only of "the gift of God" (*to Charisma tou Theou*), which had been bestowed by the laying on of hands. It would do no more violence to the text to infer that Paul laid his hands on the disciples to ordain them, or that Peter laid his hands on the converts at Samaria for the same purpose, than to say that the above texts refer to Timothy's ordination.

DR. VAN OOSTERZEE, in *Lange*, says :

" There is here absolutely no mention of ordination in the later hierarchical sense."—*Com. on 2 Tim. 1: 6.*

DR. EBRARD, the continuator of Olshausen, says :

" Ordination, in its later sense, is in no way referred to." —*Com. on 2 Tim. 1: 6.*

DR. OLSHAUSEN says :

" In these passages, indeed, it is the laying on of hands for the communication of the Spirit that is spoken of, not, however, for a definite sphere of duty or a special calling, but for the general calling of the Christian."—*Com. on 1 Tim. 4: 14.*

Dr. Van Oosterzee, in *Lange*, says :

" Laying on of hands. This was of old a symbol of the communication of the Holy Spirit."—*Com. 1 Tim. 4: 14.*

Dr. Whitby says :

" The *Charisma*, or gift here mentioned, being the gift of the Holy Ghost, was usually conferred by the laying on of the hands of an Apostle."—*Com. on 2 Tim. 1: 6.*

Dr. Gill says :

" And since gifts have ceased being conveyed this way, the rite of laying on of hands in ordination seems useless and of no avail."—*Com. on 1 Tim. 4: 14.*

Dr. Conybeare says:

" The grace of God required for any particular office in the early Church was conferred after prayer and the laying on of hands. This imposition of hands was repeated whenever one was appointed to a new office or commission."—*Com. on 2 Tim. 1: 6, Note 6.*

To say the very most for those who insist that these passages refer to ordination, it must be confessed the foundation is too slender and uncertain to allow of resting on them any doctrine, or imposing any ceremony that shall be regarded as essential to the validity of ministerial acts. It is not strange that many interpreters, looking at these passages through their own standards and usages, should see ordination recognized where the Apostle seemed to see nothing but extraordinary spiritual gifts imparted by the imposition of hands.

4. We come lastly to mention the text much relied on to prove ceremonial ordination as existing in the apostolic Church; and while it fails to substantiate that doctrine, it is undoubtedly the strongest citation for that purpose that can be made from the New Testament. It is I Tim. 5:22.—" Lay hands suddenly on no man." This is interpreted to mean, " do not ordain and put into the ministry any man, hastily." If it does refer to ordination, the inference would be strong—though not conclusive— that a custom prevailed, of inducting men into the sacred office by the imposition of hands. But does it refer to ordination ? It has generally been so interpreted. But we learn to distrust the scholarship which interprets the word of God under the bias of ecclesiastical prepossession.

This passage stands near the end of a chapter composed of a variety of preceptive injunctions, in which Timothy is advised how he shall conduct the various matters referred to among the churches. The injunction immediately preceding is, " Do nothing through partiality." That immediately following is, " Neither be partakers of other men's sins." The connection gives us no clew to its proper application.

DEAN ALFORD, while he believes that it refers to ordination, cites DeWette, Wiesenger, Huther, Hammond and Ellicott, who interpret it of receiving back into the Church excommunicated persons, as from the later testimony of Cyprian, the Nicene Council, and other sources, is proved to have been the early practice ; except as Luther regards it as simply a form of expressing an ecclesiastical bene-diction.

DR. EBRARD says:

"It should be understood of receiving into the Christian fellowship in general, or of restoring to this fellowship those that had fallen." He adds, "I prefer the latter view, with DeWette, from regard to v. 20." "Baur explains the passage principally of the restoration of heretics, of which he adduces examples from a later period." This is also his opinion, though he does not regard the evidence as decisive.—*Com. in loco.*

DR. HAMMOND says:

"This belongs to the laying on of bishop's hands in ab-solving penitents."—*Com. in loco.*

DR. VAN OOSTERZEE, in *Lange,* while he does not feel sure as to the interpretation and application of the words, says:

"But the question is, 'To what laying on of hands does the Apostle here refer?' According to DeWette he means the admission of such as had been excluded from the Church fellowship. Without doubt the connection favors this opin-ion. And already, at an early day, the laying on of hands was practiced as a sign of absolution for excommunicated or heretical persons, restored into the pale of the Church."—*Com., 1 Tim. 5: 22.*

DR. ELLICOTT says:

"The preceding warning, however, and still more the de-cided language of the following clause, appears to point so very clearly to some disciplinary functions, that it seems best, with Hammond (so also DeWette and Wiesenger) to refer these words to the *Cheirothesia*, on the absolution of penitents and their re-admission to Church fellowship."—*Comment. 1 Tim. 5: 22.*

McKNIGHT says:

"Lay hands suddenly on no man. Appoint no one to any sacred office, hastily, without inquiry into his character and qualifications."—*Com. in loco.*

DR. WM. B. JOHNSON, one of the most honored of American Baptists, says:

"As there is not a solitary case in the New Testament of ordination to the ministry by imposition of hands, I cannot suppose that the direction of Paul to Timothy, to lay hands suddenly on no man, does refer to imposition of hands in ordination."—*The Gospel Developed, pp. 155, 156.*

DR. J. B. JETER, a man acute, discriminating and conservative, says:

"In the primitive age very little stress was laid on the ceremonies attending the induction into office. The Apostles laid on their hands several times to confer the gift of the Holy Ghost; but *never* in confirmation of an appointment to office—except in the case of the Seven." "There is no scriptural proof that any elder or bishop of any Church was ordained by the laying on of the hands of an Apostle, or of any Christian minister." "In the apostolic times ordination was simply an appointment to office." "A formal ordination service is not essential to the performance of ministerial duties; but it is eminently becoming and useful. The appointment of a Church is the essence of ordination." *Religious Herald, editorial of May 25, 1876.*

An attempt to extort apostolic authority for a ceremony deemed important, if not absolutely essential, from a text so variously understood, in which, with its contexts, Schleiermacher found " an extraordinary confusion," and which the best scholars find it difficult to construe with satisfaction, would be something more than absurd.

NOTE 1.—Ordination, therefore, by the laying on of hands, since not taught in the New Testament, by either precept, example, or clear inference, is not essential nor obligatory.

NOTE 2.—While, however, it is not a matter of obligation, it is also not contrary to the letter or spirit of the Scriptures, and as a matter of Christian liberty, is permissible.

NOTE 3.—As a matter of liberty, also, the form and manner of induction into the ministerial office is optional with the churches and candidates for orders.

NOTE 4.—Uniformity in order among the churches is desirable. But if uniformity be demanded as essential to orthodoxy, or to validity, in any thing not clearly taught in the New Testament, then the demand should be resisted. Christ is the only lawgiver for the churches.

3. Its Place among the Churches

Our most orthodox Baptist churches formerly practiced the laying on of hands upon persons baptized. Some still practise it; not a few believe it of apostolic origin. Dr. David Benedict, the historian, declares, " This was a practice of high authority in our denomination in other countries, and in this country it formerly prevailed much more extensively than at the present time."* When the

* Fifty Years Among the Baptists, p. 160.

Philadelphia Association adopted the London Baptist Confession of 1689, they added, Sept. 15, 1742, an article (the 35th) beginning, " We believe that laying on hands with prayer, upon baptized believers, is an ordinance of Christ, and ought to be submitted unto by all such persons that are admitted to partake of the Lord's supper."* This article, however, was afterward omitted.

In the modern Roman Church imposition of hands is deemed essential in the sacraments of ordination, confirmation, and baptism. Also in the Anglican and other Episcopal churches it is similarly used. In other Protestant churches, our own included, it retains its place only in ordination, in all of which it is insisted on with a tendency to sacramental effect.

Ordination, therefore, by public prayer and the imposition of hands by other ministers, is not essential to the genuineness of ministerial character or the validity of ministerial acts. It does not make a minister any more than inauguration makes the president. He is president, *de jure* and *de facto*, by virtue of his election, with all the rights, powers and privileges which belong to the office, with or without an inauguration. Such is the relation of ordination to the ministry. It is their inauguration, making public the election, with the approval and commendation of those who take part in the services. And this only.

The fathers of New England orthodoxy took this

* See Cutting's Historical Vindications, p. 189.

view of the matter; even the rigid leaders of the
Standing Order

COTTON MATHER said:

" Our fathers reckoned ordination not to be essential unto
the vocation of a minister, any more than coronation to the
being of a king; but that it is only a consequent and convenient adjunct of his vocation, and a solemn acknowledgment of it, with a useful and proper benediction of him in
it."—*Magnalia, Vol. III., pp. 242-3.*

THOMAS HOOKER said:

"It is plain that ordination presupposes an office constituted; does not constitute.   Therefore it is not an act of
power, but of order."—*Right and Power of Ordination.*

THE CAMBRIDGE PLATFORM says:

" Ordination we account nothing else but the solemnly
putting a man into his place and office in the Church, whereto he had right before by his election; being like the installing of a magistrate in the commonwealth."—*Chapter 9,
secs. 2, 4.*

ISAAC BACKUS, *clarum et venerabile nomen* among
Baptists, said:

" And ordination of ministers is no more than swearing
them to be faithful in that office.   Their being furnished
with grace and gifts for it is the most essential thing in the
affair."—*Hist. N. E. Churches. p. 111. Phil ed., 1853.*

DR. KNAPP says:

" That a religious teacher should be solemnly consecrated
to his office, or ordained, is indeed useful, both to the teacher

himself and to the Church.   But in itself considered it is not a matter *juris divino.*   It is nowhere expressly commanded of God, and contributes nothing, considered as an external ceremony, to efficiency and activity in the sacred office."— *Christ. Theol., p. 477, 21st Am. ed.*

To induct a minister into the sacred office to which he has been chosen by some public service, though required by no scriptural authority, is therefore, nevertheless, becoming, appropriate and impressive.   The kind of service and the form of the ceremony may well be left to those directly interested to decide.*

II. BY WHOM IS ORDINATION?

Admitting that, for the sake of order, ceremonial ordination should be continued, where resides the right and the power to set men apart to this service? Is it in a Church, or in a Council or Presbytery?

The answer is brief, and should be conclusive. The right of ordination is inherent in the *Church;* and in no other body of men whatever.   This conclusion is inevitable to those who hold to Church

* It would be difficult to conceive of a more impressive ordination service than that of the celebrated Robert Hall, by the Church of which he was a member, and of which his father was pastor, at Arnsby, England.   Of this we have an account in his memoirs by Dr. Olinthus Gregory, copied from the Church records. After a careful examination of the candidate by his father and the Church, and an appropriate sermon preached by his father, the Church set him apart " by lifting up their right hands, and solemn prayer."—*Hall's Works, Vol. III., p. 8.*

independency, and repudiate sacramental ordination and hierarchical assumptions, as Baptists do. The contrary claim, that the right inheres in a Council or Presbytery, and that the ceremony must be performed by those who have had hands laid on them, in order to be valid, is so preposterous, that no man should make it unless he be prepared to defend holy orders by Episcopal hands as a sacrament, with an uninterrupted apostolical succession. For to that he must be finally driven.

That the right of ordination resides in the local, visible Church—though ministers may be called upon to advise in the matter, and to perform the public services—will be evident from the following considerations:

1. Because all ecclesiastical authority resides in the local Church. This is the only organic form of Christian life divinely appointed. Christ instituted no society but the Church, and to it He committed authority to administer His laws. This is the Baptist doctrine, held, taught and defended, always and everywhere. Councils and Presbyteries, as organized bodies, are of human, not of divine origin or authority, and cannot be essential to, much less supersede, the Church in the performance of any ecclesiastical functions.

DR. FRANCIS WAYLAND says:

"While we believe that men are to be set apart for the duties of the ministry, in whom we see the evidence of ministerial gifts, yet, that it is the Church itself—by which I

mean, not the clergy, but the whole body of Christians—
which sets them apart; and that when thus appointed to this
work, they are, by this act, rendered no better or holier than
their brethren."—*Principles and Practices, p. 131.*

A Council is created by the Church which con-
venes it. Now to suppose that a Church has not
power to ordain, while a Council has, is to suppose
that the body created has more power than that
which created it. Moreover, the Council has no inherent power, and possesses only what the Church
which called it has conferred upon it. It is, therefore absurd to suppose the Council can do more
than the Church.

And further, Christ gave to the churches pastors
and teachers. But if Councils hold the right to ordain, the churches cannot enjoy these most important gifts of ministerial service divinely bestowed,
without the consent of a Council, a body of men
for which the great Head of the Church made no
provision.

2. Because a Church is a body complete in itself
as to authority, though without officers. It has
power to create officers out of its own members, and
set them apart to the service for which they may be
chosen, by any form or ceremony it may choose, or
without any ceremony, at its option. The right to
choose and enjoy the ministry of its own religious
teachers, without let or hindrance from any, is one
of the primary rights with which Christ has invested
His churches.*

* See chapter on Councils.

HAYNES says:

" The Church is competent to make her own ministers, as far as man can make them, and this she always does among the Baptists. She authorizes him to preach by her own license, which is granted or withheld, as she thinks best. The *essential act* in ordination is her election of him for the purpose, and he may become a minister or a pastor without the agency of the Presbytery."—*Baptist Denomination, p. 250.*

3. Because that in the primitive churches, though there was an apostleship and a discipleship, there was such division into *clergy* and *laity* as afterward sprang up and now prevails. There was no official caste or class, save as the Holy Spirit, working in each, developed certain gracious capabilities, which the churches used for the edification of the body. It was neither *cleric* nor *laic*, but a common discipleship. All alike constituted a holy priesthood, ordained to offer spiritual sacrifices unto God. And the churches selected and elected teachers and leaders, as the fitting qualifications were developed which commended the individuals.*

Dean Stanley said:

" The Church, the Christian society, existed in those faithful followers, even from the beginning, and will doubtless last unto the end." " But even for years after the Lord's departure such a society existed without a separate order of clergy." —*Christ. Institutions, p. 179.*

It is indisputable that after the primitive age the common discipleship was divided by this class-dis-

* See chapters on the Ministry for other authorities.

tinction into clergy and laity. Then developed the hierarchical tendency to wrest ecclesiastical authority from the churches and vest it in an ambitious clergy. Especially did this tendency show itself in the claim that the right of ordination belonged exclusively to the clergy. For in no other way could they so effectually dominate the churches as by holding in their own hands the exclusive right to consecrate and invest their pastors. This right conceded, the churches were powerless in the grasp of their despotic spiritual rulers. The demand now for an exclusive clerical ordination has this same hierarchical tendency for its germ and life.

DR. CROWELL said:

"It is evident that the right to consecrate is involved in the right to elect; and this right, as we have seen, the Lord Jesus Christ has vested in each Church." "The choice or election of a man to the ministry is a greater act than that of consecration or induction into office. Consequently, the Church, which is competent to do the greater, must possess in itself the power essential to the valid performance of the less."—*Ch. Members' Manual, pp. 106–7.*

DR. DEXTER says:

"If ordination is the mere solemn installing of a functionary, previously appointed, in the place to which he has been chosen, since the putting in the place is a lesser act than the electing to the place, and since the Church has done the greater, it must follow that the power must rest with it to do the less. So that, if a Church may elect its pastor, it may ordain him—which is but the carrying out of that election to its full completion and result."—*Congregationalism, p. 141.*

DR. WM. B. JOHNSON said:

"The sole power of ordaining to the pastorate or bish-opric is lodged with the churches."—*Gospel Developed, pp. 133, 144.*

DR. STRONG says:

"It is always to be remembered, however, that the power to ordain rests with the Church; and that the Church may proceed without a Council, or even against the decisions of a Council. Such ordination, of course, would give authority only within the bounds of the individual Church."—*Systematic Theology, p. 514.*

DR. WELLMAN said:

"It should not only be understood, but it should be more distinctly and formally acknowledged than it usually is, both by the ordaining Council and the members of the Church, that the ordaining power is vested in the Church, and not in the Council."—*Church Polity of the Pilgrims, p. 114. Cited by Dexter, p. 61, note.*

4. Because the claim made by some, that while a Church may have the right to ordain or set apart a minister for themselves, ordination by a Council makes one a minister for the *whole denomination*, is false, illogical and absurd. A Church cannot, indeed, make a man a minister to any but themselves. The fact that they had chosen him and approved his ministry, would to that extent give him credit with other churches. Nor yet can a Council do any more than give a man the credit of their approval and commendation. They cannot make him a minister for any Church save that one which

asked their advice and coöperation in his ordination.

It is preposterous to claim that a Council can assure the confidence and fellowship of the entire denomination to any man on whom they may lay their hands. What is the denomination? It is not an organic entity; it has no corporate existence; it is not an ecclesiastical body; it has neither organization, laws nor officers, and has no means of expressing approval or dissent. It is a mere conception of the aggregate of all the churches. The ministers who lead and direct its activities are not the denomination; the journals that speak to and for it are not the denomination; and in the sense in which it is so often appealed to, or spoken for, it is a fiction.

When, therefore, did the denomination authorize a Council or Presbytery to ordain a man into its ministry, or give him the credit of its fellowship throughout the land? What havoc it makes with our theory of Church life, to claim that a Council sitting in Maine or Vermont can make a man an accredited minister for all the churches in Mississippi or Texas or Montana; or that a Presbytery acting in New York can give a man the fellowship of the churches in Chicago, St. Louis or San Francisco, and elsewhere and everywhere.

And since it is by this same theory claimed that a Council is necessary to depose an unworthy man, because a Church can neither make nor unmake a minister, we have such inconsistency and confusion as this. A Council in Massachusetts ordains a man and makes a minister of him for the whole denomination, it is said; while a Council in Virginia, for cause, deposes him, and thereby unmakes a minister of him for the whole denomination! And neither Council knew what the other had done, or that it existed; and the *denomination*—that mythical something—was ignorant of what both had done, while trading on its credit and acting without its authority. This whole theory of Council authority is false, untenable and pernicious. There is no such discrimination to be made in favor of the power of a Council, and against the power of a Church in the ordination and deposition of ministers. All that a Council can do is to examine, advise and assist a Church when called upon to do so.

It is right, however, for the sake of order, courtesy, and prudence, that the churches consult and coöperate with each other. But if this be insisted upon as a matter of *necessity*, then we protest, and fall back on what the fathers called " the power of the keys," committed by Christ to the *churches*. Uniformity in order is greatly desirable. But when uniformity is made compulsory by making it essential in things not vital, then nonconformity becomes a virtue and is to be commended.

JOHN COTTON said:

" The warrant by which each particular Church doth depute some of their own body, though not presbyters, to lay their hands on those whom they have chosen to be their presbyters, is grounded upon 'the power of the keys' which the Lord Jesus Christ hath given to the churches."—*Way of the Churches, p. 43.*

John Robinson, John Davenport, Thomas Hooker, Samuel Mather, and the other fathers of New England Congregationalism, held the same opinion. Usually, and orderly, of course, they held that the elders, when present, or easily accessible, should perform this service, just as when present they should conduct other religious services; but their presence and assistance was not *imperative.* The power was in the churches.

THE CAMBRIDGE PLATFORM, their standard of Church order, says:

"In such churches where there are no elders, imposition of hands may be performed by some of the brethren, orderly chosen by the Church thereto. For if the people may elect officers, which is the greater, and wherein the substance of the office consists, they may much more (occasion and need so requiring), impose hands in ordination, which is less, and but the accomplishment of the other."

DR. FRANCIS WAYLAND, on methods of admitting to the ministry, says:

"I believe that our mode is not only as good as any other, but that it is more nearly than any other conformed to the principles of the New Testament. Let our churches, then, never surrender the authority to single ministers, or to Councils, or to any other organization whatever. I believe that Christ has placed it in their hands, and they have no right to delegate it. Let them use it in the manner required by the Master, and it can be placed in no safer hands."—*Principles and Prac. of Bapt. Chs., p. 100.*

III. WHAT IS THE EFFECT OF ORDINATION?

What does ordination do for a man? What is he different after it, from what he was before? Does it impart any new rights, powers, privileges or qualifications to him?

It is not usually claimed—certainly not among Baptists—that ordination endows the candidate with any intellectual, moral, or spiritual grace which he did not before possess. To claim that it did would place them in the ranks of sacramentarians, who see, in the imposition of hands, the pledge of special spiritual gifts, as in apostolic times. But this question is answered by prevailing custom and current Christian sentiment thus: the ordained minister can lawfully solemnize marriage, administer the ordinances, and lay hands on others, which the unordained cannot lawfully do. Is this true?

Marriage is held by law to be a civil contract, and its conditions prescribed by statute. The various classes of persons permitted to take the acknowledgments of the contracting parties, are specified. Among these are accredited clergymen of the various denominations, so recognized by the usages of their own churches. An unordained person, in the eyes of the law, is not a clergyman, and therefore is not legally qualified to solemnize marriage, although the marriage contract is not invalidated by such defect, when so performed; but he who marries the parties, being thus disqualified, is subject to complaint and fine. A licentiate is not, in a legal sense, a qualified minister.

As to imposition of hands in the ordination of ministers, any one whom the Church may select is competent for this service. It is customary and proper for ministers to do it, if such be present, just as it is proper for them to read the Scriptures, give out the hymns, and make the addresses. But as to its validity and lawfulness, the one is just as good as the other.

This question then remains, Is it right and proper for an unordained man to administer the ordinances ? The prevailing opinion is, that he has no such right until the hands of the Presbytery have been laid on him—an opinion that finds no warrant in the New Testament. It is every way proper and becoming for an accredited minister to baptize, and preside at the observance of the Lord's Supper, just as it is proper for him to preside at any other religious service. But it is a notable inconsistency that current religious opinion will welcome almost any man into the pulpit, who can talk, even though his talk be little more than a travesty of Gospel preaching, and yet insist that the administration of the ordinances is too holy a service for any unordained man to perform.

Paul made it a strong point that he did not baptize, except in a very few cases.* His call was to the higher office of preaching the Gospel. The

* 1 Cor. 1 : 14, 15.

ordinances were committed to the disciples. And this arose from no depreciation of the ordinances, but from the fact that higher spiritual qualifications had been imparted to him, as an ambassador of Christ, for the work of the ministry. Any of the " royal priesthood " of the discipleship could baptize converts, and break the loaf and fill the cup at the Supper; preaching the Gospel was a higher function.

There is no evidence in the New Testament that any Apostle presided at the " breaking of bread," and scanty evidence that they baptized converts— beyond the few baptized by Paul. They may have done it, but if so, we lack the evidence. The beauty and impressiveness of these sacred symbols do not depend on the administration—only so that they be decently and reverently served—but on the inherent sanctity of the ordinances themselves. Many small and feeble churches go without the ordinances for months, or years, because no or- dained minister is accessible to serve them. This is all wrong. Let them select some deacon, or private member to serve in this capacity, as they would choose one to lead a prayer-meeting. The ordinances were committed to the churches; and Christ's institutions should not be neglected. The neglect of these by the pastorless churches is one cause of their long-continued weakness and decline.

TERTULLIAN said:

" In itself considered, the laity also have also the right to administer the sacraments, and to teach in the community.

The Word of God and the sacraments were communicated to all, and may therefore be communicated by all Christians, as instruments of Divine grace." " If we look at the order necessary to be maintained in the Church, the laity are to exercise their priestly rights of administering the sacraments only when the time and the circumstances require it."—*Baptism, chap. 17. Cited by Neander, Ch. Hist., Vol. I., p. 796.*

MOSHEIM says:

" At first, all who were engaged in propagating Christianity, administered this ordinance [baptism] nor can it be called in question that whoever persuaded any person to embrace Christianity, could baptize his own disciple."—*Eccl. Hist., Cent. I., part II., chap. 4, sec. 8.*

DR. JACOBS says :

" There are positively no sacred rites or acts which it is declared in the New Testament *must* be administered by men ordained or in any way separated from the general body of Christians. The two sacraments are justly considered the most solemn of Christian ordinances. But even of *them* such administration is nowhere commanded."—*Eccl. Polity of the New Testament, p. 144.*

DR. PRESSENSÉ declares :

" That the words of St. Paul to the Corinthians imply that all Christians might break the bread and bless the cup at the Lord's Supper, and not an officiating minister only. For he says: 'The bread which *we* break, and the cup of blessing which *we* bless.' "—*Vol. II., p. 224.*

PROF. CURTIS says:

" Originally every Church member, as such, was an evangelist wherever he could be. As Neander has shown, and all

Church history proves, the distinction between the clergy and laity was much less marked at first. In regard to the administration of baptism, this was quite as much the case as in teaching. It belonged to the original priesthood of all, at first, or was, at least, committed to them, except as limited by the Church."—*Prog. Bap. Principles, pp. 298–99.*

DR. CHARLES HODGE, while he believes that the common and orderly way of serving the ordinances is by an ordained minister, yet says:

"If baptism be a washing with water, in the name of the Holy Ghost to signify and seal the ingrafting into Christ, does it cease to do this, if not administered by an ordained minister? Does not the man thus baptized make a profession of his faith?" "Can it therefore be any more invalid than the Gospel preached by a layman?"—*Systematic Theology, Vol. III., p. 525. Ed. 1875.*

DR. DAVIDSON says:

"Thus when a Church has no elders, the members may legitimately partake of the Supper. An elder's presence is not essential to the validity of it. It is desirable, because the presumption is, that such an one is better qualified to lead the devotions of the brethren than an individual selected from among themselves." "But it is certainly unnecessary to send for the elders of another Church; for such an one bears no official relation to any society except his own." "When a Church, therefore, is without an elder or pastor, let them by all means partake of the Supper. It is their duty and privilege to do so. To neglect it is culpable." "A deacon selected by the brethren may preside." "There is no one passage in the New Testament which proves that it is the exclusive right of the elders to baptize. And yet the notion is tenaciously held. Coming as it does from the Church of Rome, and received from that source by the Protestant Episcopal Church it has taken hold of other denominations."—*Eccl. Polity of the N. T., pp. 280, 283–86.*

DR. LYMAN COLEMAN says:

"The duty of administering the ordinance [baptism] does not appear to have been restricted to any office in the Church." "Lay baptism, of which frequent mention is made in the early history of the Church, was undoubtedly treated as valid by the laws and usages of the ancient Church." Of the Supper he says: "Nothing is said in the New Testament respecting the person whose prerogative it is to administer this sacrament."—*Ancient Christ. Exemp., pp. 390, 2–427.*

DR. HENRY M. DEXTER says:

"The supposed need in the case of evangelists and missionaries grows out of the assumption that only an ordained person has the right to administer baptism and the Lord's Supper. But that assumption is a legacy of Popery which Congregationalism will do well to decline; since the Bible does neither affirm nor endorse it. Scripturally one of the deacons, or any brother of the Church whom it may authorize for the purpose, is competent—in the absence of the pastor—to baptize, or preside at the remembrance of Christ at the Lord's Supper."—*Congregationalism, pp. 155–57.*

DR. LEONARD BACON says:

"I have found nothing in the Bible, and nothing in what I have seen of the earliest Christian writers, which implies that it was the peculiar duty, or the peculiar honor of this or that officer, to administer baptism."—*Manual of Ch. Polity, p. 58.*

DR. DANIEL CURRY, than whom there has been no abler man in the Methodist Episcopal Church, says:

"The sum of the whole matter is, that whosoever is called

of God is thereby invested with all the essential characteristics and prerogatives of a Gospel minister; and whether inducted by one form or another, or without any form, and acknowledged by no fellow-minister, he has an indefeasible right, *de iure divino*, to administer the sacraments and ordinances, and feed the flock of Christ. And if occasion requires, he may recognize other ministers by solemn forms, and appropriate ceremonies."—*Editorial, Christian Advocate, Nov. 11, 1875.*

ANDREW FULLER said:

" It appears to me that every approved teacher of God's Word, whether ordained the pastor of a particular Church or not, is authorized to baptize." " I see nothing objectionable, if, when a Church is destitute of a pastor, it [the Supper] was administered by a deacon, or an aged brother. I know of no Scripture authority for confining it to ministers. Nay, I do not recall any mention in the Scriptures of a minister being employed in it, unless we reckon our Lord one."—*Works, Vol. III., p. 494. Phil. Ed., 1845.*

DR. FRANCIS WAYLAND says :

"I know that we restrict to the ministry the administration of the ordinances; and to this rule I think there can be no objection. But we all know that for this restriction we have no example in the New Testament."—*Sermons to the Churches, p. 35. Ed. 1858.*

DR. RICHARD FULLER, while he approves the present usage, yet says :

" Suppose, however, there is a Church that has no ordained pastor; I grieve to say that there is so much popery among us that some churches in remote places go without the Supper for years because they cannot get a Baptist priest to consecrate the elements." "As to the abstract question whether an ordained minister is necessary for the ordinances, I answer, no. Andrew Fuller, Robert Hall, and all our eminent men were of one sentiment here."—*Autograph letter to the author, Sept. 12, 1876.*

DR. HOWARD MALCOM says :

"I cannot see that baptism can only be rightly performed by an ordained minister. It would be just as valid if done by any private member. The qualification belongs only to the candidate. Hence, a Church without a pastor may designate any member to baptize, or break bread at the Lord's Supper."—*Autograph letter to the author, Sept. 7, 1876.*

DR. GALUSHA ANDERSON says :

"There is not a scrap of evidence in the New Testament that either baptism or the Lord's Supper was administered by the elders, or bishops, or pastors of the churches. That they did administer the ordinances I think quite probable, but there is no record of it in the Scriptures." "Churches may not only authorize unordained persons to administer the ordinances, but I think they are bound so to do, rather than suffer them to be neglected. The idea that the humblest band of believers cannot baptize converts to Christ, nor remember their Savior by breaking bread, is, to a New Testament student, absurd."—*Autograph letter to the author, dated Feb. 16, 1877.*

THE BAPTIST CONFESSION OF FAITH, issued in London, 1643, by seven congregations, as a vindication against the aspersions of their enemies, says :

"The person designed by Christ to dispense baptism, the Scripture holds forth to be a *disciple*, it being nowhere tied to a particular Church officer, or person extraordinarily sent, the commission enjoining the administration being given to them as considered disciples, being men able to preach the Gospel."—*Article 41.   See Neal's Hist. Puritans, Ap., and Cutting's Hist. Vindications.*

More need not be said on this point.   Ordination does this for a man—this, and nothing more—it accredits him to the churches and the public by the moral force which the approval and commendation of the men engaged in the ordination service carries with it.   Their certificate is a testimonial to the Church and to the religious community.   Nor do I think much of the claim that Councils protect the churches against unworthy men, who otherwise would force themselves into the ministry.   I do not see but Councils are about as easily deceived by impostors as are the churches themselves.   Probably all the clerical cheats and rascals who deceive and destroy the churches have successfully passed the examination of Councils, received their commendation, had hands laid upon their heads, and gone out with their letters of credit in their pockets. Presbyteries are a bulwark of gossamer against the inroads of wolves in sheep's clothing intent to prey upon the flock.   Councils usually do what they are asked to do.   Churches should themselves be more wary and cautious, and, perhaps, would be if they had no Council upon whom to throw the responsibility which they themselves should bear.

IV.   IS ORDINATION TO BE REPEATED?

There is but this other question that needs here

to be considered, viz., Is the effect of ordination permanent or transient?

Does it confer an indelible ministerial character? Or, does it need to be repeated? If the minister should lapse from the faith, be deposed, or leave the sacred for a secular calling, and be restored, or return, would ordination need to be repeated? Or, if he pass from one denomination to another, is he to be reordained by new forms? or will his old investiture be deemed sufficient and accepted as valid? The former aspects of the question, as to the character *indelibilis*, have occupied a large place in the polemical disputations of past centuries. In these, however, we have small interest, and on them we need not dwell. The only aspect of the case with which we have much concern is that of *re*-ordination or recognition.

Should a minister, who comes among us from another denomination, be *ordained*, or simply *recognized*? Do we accept his former ordination, if among evangelical Churches, or do we not? To this, Baptist sentiment answers *Yes*, and *No*. Some do; others do not. And it is perfectly immaterial which side of the question one accepts and defends. Both are equally orthodox, and whichever the candidate, and the Church of which he is to be pastor, should prefer would be safe to adopt. Just at present the tide sets rather in favor of reordination; and perhaps this, on the whole, is the wiser course, since each Christian communion has its own method of induction into office. Baptists may well make theirs uniform in all cases of men set apart to the ministry among them. It can be no reflection on the sanctity of methods in other churches for us to pursue our own.

The difference between ordination and recognition lies mair'y in this, that in the former there is an examination of the candidate, and the imposition of hands; in the latter these are omitted. But if a Council be called, there is no good reason why they should not examine the candidate sufficiently to satisfy them of his fitness for the ministry—and, indeed, for the *Baptist* ministry. And the imposition of hands would be quite as appropriate in this as in any other case, and would be sanctioned by the setting apart of Barnabas and Saul at Antioch, on whom hands were laid after having been many years in the ministry; they were thus sent forth to a new field of labor with fraternal benedictions.

Let the question, therefore, be answered as follows:

1. Reordination is not necessary. For the substance of the first ordination—if it were to an evangelical ministry—was to recognize a divine call to, and a fitness for, that ministry, and to send the man forth with commendation to the work. His "setting apart" was not, presumably, to a ministry of denominational specialties, but to a dispensation of the word first; the other followed, of consequence, from his position. To insist that ordination is essential, is to insist that he was not set apart to an evangelical service. Moreover, to demand reordination on

the ground that it makes him an accredited and lawful minister to the whole denomination, proceeds on the assumption that a Council called by one Church can give a minister credit with all other churches, an assumption somewhat too lofty for the characteristic modesty of Baptists. That assumption has already been discussed.

2. Reordination, or recognition, whichever the Church and the candidate may prefer, is equally effective, and a matter of indifference. The purpose and the effect of both are the same. Some public service would be appropriate; and an examination of the candidate, on points which distinguished his former ecclesiastical relations from those which he has now assumed, would perhaps be needful. Otherwise they could not give him their fellowship and commendation in his new position.

3. To insist on the invalidity of all except denominational ordination is to enter the list for a defense of sacramentarianism, and to stand challenged before the Christian world for the proof of an unbroken succession of sacred orders. This would be as impossible to prove, as it would be useless if proven. We cannot accept the baptism of other denominations because it is *not baptism*, but *sprinkling*. It is defective both in substance and in form. It is quite otherwise with ordination, since both the form and the substance in the various communions are virtually the same. And if they be not, there is no authoritative Scriptural standard by which to be guided, as in the case of baptism.

4. Whether ordination be supposed to represent the verity of a divine call, or the validity of ministerial acts, in either case recognition and ordination stand on the same ground. The one is as effectual in ascertaining his call, and declaring his authority, as the other, if what has heretofore been shown is to be accepted, since ordination is not to empower, but to approve.

5. The claim that the action of a Council or a Presbytery can accredit a minister to the whole denomination is to be emphatically denied. With other denominations, which consist of a confederation of churches, or societies, bound together in one general ecclesiastical system, represented and controlled by a central legislative body, with Church judicatories, it is different. They put men into the ministry by established laws and usages, which are authoritative to all, and command the recognition of all the churches. No central body is empowered to act for our denomination in anything. Common usage is to be respected, but is not authoritative.

6. In the absence of special and weighty reasons in favor of recognition it would, perhaps, on the whole, be wise and prudent to reordain ministers who come to us from other denominations, and thus, so far as may be, unify the order of our Churches. This course would probably harmonize with the current drift of sentiment on this subject, while no valid objection could ordinarily be urged against it.

CHAPTER 15

CHRISTIAN BAPTISM

BAPTISMAL PROPOSITIONS

THE subject of *baptism* constitutes one of the primary and fundamental discussions between Baptists and other Christian denominations, and has reference to the form and uses of that ordinance. The following propositions set forth the nature and extent of the controversy, the proof of which propositions will amply justify the Baptist position on that subject.

PROP. I.—That the baptism which John administered, which Jesus received and enjoined, and which the Apostles practised, was an *immersion*, a dipping, an entire submergence of the person baptized, in water, on a profession of repentance and faith in Christ.

PROP. II.—That this same baptism of immersion was used by the Apostles and disciples of our Lord, and by the primitive churches, without any known exception, for more than *two hundred years* after Christ.

PROP. III.—That the first recorded departure from the practice of *immersion* in baptism was, about A. D. 250, in the case of Novatian, *affused* on his sickbed, being, as was supposed, incapable of baptism. No earlier instance is known to history.

PROP. IV.—That from this time *pouring*, or *sprinkling*, for baptism, was occasionally resorted to as substitutes, in cases of sick persons, called *clinics ;* hence clinic baptism came into use in emergencies.

PROP. V.—That for more than *thirteen hundred years* immersion was the prevailing practice of Christian churches throughout the world in the administration of baptism.

PROP. VI.—That the Greek and other Oriental churches have never abandoned the primitive mode, but still practise *dipping*, whether in the case of adults or of infants, in all climates, and at all seasons of the year.

PROP. VII.—That the substitution of *aspersion* for immersion was one of the corruptions of the Papal Church, transmitted to, and accepted by, the Protestant Christians in later times.

PROP. VIII.—That, after the Reformation, *sprinkling* for baptism came into general use among Protestant Christians in Europe, by whom it was transmitted to Protestant churches in America.

PROP. IX.—That the leading scholarship of the world declares that the meaning of the Greek word *baptizo* is to *immerse*, and that immersion was the original Scriptural baptism; while sprinkling and pouring are conceded substitutes, used for convenience only, and are without divine authority.

PROP. X.—That more than half the nominal Christians in the world still practise *immersion* in baptism, denying the validity of any other form, while all Christians, the world over, hold such baptism to be *valid*, primitive and Scriptural.

If these propositions be proven, it ought to end the controversy—certainly, with candid and unbiased minds. But the force of education, social relations and religious predilections are often more powerful to influence conduct than the combined energies of truth, judgment, and conscience. The injunction of our Lord was and still is: " If ye love me, keep my commandments." Cotton Mather's words could not have a more appropriate or emphatic application than to such a case: " Let a precept be never so difficult to obey, or never so distasteful to flesh and blood, yet if I see it is God's command, my soul says, it is good; let me obey it till I die."

Let it be distinctly understood, however, that all the eminent and learned authorities hereafter cited are Pedobaptists. Baptist witnesses are wholly omitted, not because they are less learned, or less valuable, but because we prefer to allow our opponents in this controversy to bear witness for us, rather than to testify in our own behalf. Possibly, also, the testimony of their own scholars may have more weight with our Pedobaptist brethren than would the testimony of ours, who might be thought interested witnesses in such a case.

WHAT IS CHRISTIAN BAPTISM?

This is the greatest question that enters into the baptismal controversy, and the one in which Baptists take sides against the Pedobaptist world, both Papal and Protestant, so far, at least, as their practice is concerned. Other questions of moment arise in connection with this sacred rite; questions as to its mode, its purpose, and its efficacy. They have their importance, and a legitimate sphere of discussion. What shall precede baptism, or accompany it, or follow it? Whether salt or oil shall be used; whether a black robe or a white robe, or no robe at all shall be worn, by candidate or administrant; whether the candidate shall be dipped once, twice, or thrice, forward or backward, standing or kneeling—all these, and many others, which burdened mediæval polemics, are mere accidents, having reference to *mode*, in which we have no special interest. But it is of primary importance to know what constitutes baptism itself. That point, once settled, will decide the form of its administration. To say it is a ceremony in which water is the element used, and by which persons are admitted to the Christian Church, does not answer the question. What *is* baptism? As a Gospel ordinance, the New Testament must define it.

Baptists answer the question by saying that baptism is the immersion or dipping of a candidate in water, on a profession of faith in Christ, administered in the name of the Father, Son and Spirit.

Pedobaptists answer the question by saying it is either the sprinkling or pouring of water upon the person, touching the forehead with a wet finger, or the dipping of the candidate into water, in either case in the name of the Father, Son and Spirit; and that it may be administered to one on his own profession of faith, or to an unconscious infant on the professed faith of some other person. This would make four forms of the ordinance, administered to two classes of subjects.

Baptists hold to a unity in the ordinance, as in the faith, believing that as there is but one Lord and one Faith, so there is but one Baptism, and not four. And the one baptism is the immersion in water, in, or into the name of the Father, Son and Spirit. Neither pouring nor sprinkling water upon, nor any other application of water to a person, is baptism, though it may be called such ever so often, and ever so earnestly.

MEANING OF BAPTIZO

The word "*baptize*" is, properly speaking, a Greek word (*baptizo*), adapted to the English language by a change in its termination. This is the word used by the sacred writers to express and define the ordinance. What does this word mean as originally used ? For it is certain that Divine Wisdom, in commanding an ordinance to be observed by believers of all classes, in all lands, and through all ages, would use a word of positive and definite import, and one whose meaning would admit of no reasonable doubt.

What, then, does "*baptizo*" mean? Let us ask Greek scholars—men familiar with and skilled in the use of Greek words. How do the dictionaries define it? What do lexicographers and scholars say?

SCAPULA says:

"To *dip*, to immerse, as we do anything for the purpose of dyeing it."

SCHLEUSNER says:

"Properly, it signifies to *dip*, to immerse, to immerse in water."

SCHREVELIUS says:

"To baptize, to *merge*, to bathe."

PARKHURST says:

"To *dip*, immerse, or plunge in water."

GREENFIELD says:

"To *immerse*, immerge, submerge, sink."

GREEN says:

"To dip, *immerse*, to cleanse or purify by washing."

DONNEGAN says:

"To *immerse* repeatedly into liquid, to submerge, to soak thoroughly, to saturate."

STEVENS says:

"To merge or *immerse*, to submerge, or bury in the water."

ALSTIDIUS says:

"To baptize signifies only to *immerse*, not to wash, except by consequence."

PASSOW says:

"To *immerse* often and repeatedly, to submerge."

SCHÖTTGEN says:

"To merge, *immerse*, to wash, to bathe."

STOCKIUS says:

"Properly, it means to *dip*, or immerse in water."

ROBINSON says:

"To *immerse*, to sink."

LIDDELL AND SCOTT say:

"To *dip* repeatedly."

SOPHOCLES says:

"*Baptizo*, to dip, to *immerse*, to sink."

ANTHON says:

"The primary meaning of the word is to *dip*, to immerse."

CREMER says:

"*Baptizo*, immersion, submersion, for a religious purpose."

GRIMM'S LEXICON of the New Testament, which in Europe and America stands confessedly at the head of Greek lexicography, as translated and edited by Prof. Thayer of Harvard University, thus defines *baptizo:*

"(1.) To dip repeatedly, to immerse, submerge. (2.) To cleanse by dipping or submerging. (3.) To overwhelm. In the New Testament it is used particularly of the rite of sacred ablution; first instituted by John the Baptist, afterward by Christ's command received by Christians and adjusted to the nature and contents of their religion, viz., an *immersion* in water performed as a sign of the removal of sin, and administered to those who, impelled by a desire for salvation, sought admission to the benefits of the Messiah's kingdom. With *eis* to mark the element into which the immersion is made; *en* with the dative of the thing in which one is immersed."

The noun *baptisma,* the only other word used in the New Testament to denote the rite, this lexicon thus defines: " A word peculiar to the New Testament and ecclesiastical writers; used (1) of John's baptism; (2) of Christian baptism. This, according to the view of the Apostles, is a rite of sacred *immersion* commanded by Christ."

MOSES STUART, one of the ablest scholars America has produced, says:

" *Baptizo* means to *dip*, plunge, or immerse into any liquid. All lexicographers and critics of any note are agreed in this."—*Essay on Baptism, p. 51; Bib. Repos., 1833, p. 298.*

ROSENMÜLLER says:

" To baptize is to *immerse* or dip, the body, or part of the body which is to be baptized, going under the water. — *Scholia, Matt. 3:6.*

WETSTEIN says:

" To baptize is to plunge, to *dip*. The body, or part of the body being under water is said to be baptized."—*Com. on Matt. 3:6.*

LEIGH says:

" The native and proper signification of it is, to *dip* into water, or to plunge under water."—*Critica Sacra.*

TURRETIN says:

" The word 'baptism' is of Greek origin, which signifies to baptize, to *dip* into, to immerse."—*Inst. loc. 19, quest. 11.*

BEZA says:

" Christ commanded us to be baptized, by which word it is certain *immersion* is signified."—*Annot. on Matt. 7:4; Acts 19:3; Matt. 3:2.*

CALVIN says:

" The word baptize signifies to *immerse;* and the rite of immersion was observed by the ancient Church."—*Institutes, B. IV., ch. 15, sec. 19.*

WITSIUS says:

" It cannot be denied that the native signification of the word *baptism*, is to plunge, to *dip*."—*Econ. Cove., B. IV., ch. 16, sec. 13.*

LUTHER says:

" The term *baptism* is a Greek word. It may be rendered *a dipping*, when we dip something in water, that it may be entirely covered with water."—*Cited by Du Veile on Acts 8:38.*

Vossius says:

"To baptize signifies to *plunge*."—*Discourses on Baptism Dis. 1.*

Wilson says:

"To baptize, to *dip* one into water, to plunge one into the water."—*Christ. Dict., Art. Baptism.*

Campbell says:

"The word *baptizein*, both in sacred authors and in classical, signifies to *dip*, to plunge, to immerse; and was rendered by Tertullian, the oldest of the Latin fathers, *tingere*, the term used for dyeing cloth, which was by immersion."
—*Translation Gospels. Note on Matt. 3: 16.*

Very many other competent scholars and critics familiar with the Greek language, might be cited to the same effect. Can there be any reasonable question that the true, indeed the only proper, meaning of *baptizo* is to dip, plunge, immerse, or bury in water? And if at any time it may have the secondary meaning of wash, cleanse, saturate, or dye, it is in consequence, and by reason of, the manner in which these acts are performed by immersion. As to the meaning of the word there can be no dispute. Both classic and sacred Greek are in harmony as to that. The New Testament decides its meaning as an ecclesiastical term applied to a Gospel ordinance.

SIGNIFICANT USE OF THE WORD

Our Lord in commanding baptism, evidently used such words as conveyed His meaning in no doubtful terms. And the sacred writers in transmitting His command to posterity, as well as His Apostles in preaching His Gospel to the nations, chose from all the words of the Greek language that one which accurately and truthfully conveyed His meaning to those who should believe upon His name. The Greek language is rich in terms to express all positive ideas, and all varying shades of thought. Why was this one word, and *no other*, selected to describe an ordinance of great significancy, intended to be observed by all believers, to the end of the world ?

Baptizo is found *eighty* times in the New Testament, and is a derivative from *bapto*. In nearly all it is used to designate this ordinance—and no other word is ever used for that purpose. *Baptisma*, a baptism, an immersion, is found twenty-two times, and *baptismos*, the act of baptizing, or immersing, four times, both formed from *baptizo*. Dr. Carson, Professor Stuart, and others, have abundantly proven that this word means to *dip*, plunge, or immerse; and that, primarily and properly, it means *nothing else*. Our Saviour, in leaving a command universally binding on His disciples, meant doubtless to express it so plainly and so positively, that none could misunderstand Him. Therefore, this particular word and no other has been used, because it means just what He intended, and nothing else.

Bapto is found *three* times in the New Testament, and also means to *dip*, but is never used to describe baptism. Why not ? Because it has other meanings, as well as that of dipping; and with this word the nature of the ordinance might be misunderstood.

Louo is found *six* times, and means to wash; to wash the whole body; to bathe. If baptism means to wash, as some hold, here was just the word to express it. But this word is never applied to the ordinance; because washing is not baptism, and baptism is not washing.

Nipto is found *seventeen* times, and means also to *wash*, to wash the extremities, as the face, hands, or feet, as distinguished from bathing the entire body. But this word is never used to express baptism. Why not, if a little water applied to the face may be baptism, as some teach?

Breko is found *seven* times, and means to wet, to moisten, to rain upon, but is never used to designate the rite of baptism; therefore to touch or moisten the forehead with wet fingers is not baptism, though frequently declared to be such.

Rantizo is found *four* times, and means to *sprinkle*. If baptism could have been performed by sprinkling, as is at present so widely believed, this would have been the word above all others to describe the ordinance. But this word is in no case so used; simply because sprinkling is not baptism.

Keo is found many times in its various combinations, and means to *pour*, but is never used to designate baptism. But if baptism may be performed by pouring water on a candidate, why was not this word sometimes used to indicate the act?

Katharizo is found *thirty* times, and means to

purify, but is never used to signify the act of baptizing. If the ordinance means to purify, as some claim, this word would have expressed it much better than the one used.

We again ask, why did the sacred writers, from all the words in the Greek language, select only and always that one which strictly means to *dip* or *immerse*, to express the act by which the sacred ordinance which Christ had commanded, and which His disciples administered, should be performed? The only consistent answer is, because baptism means immersion, and nothing else—and nothing but immersion is baptism.

THE BAPTISM OF CHRIST

Of the baptism of Jesus in the Jordan, it is said: "And Jesus, when He was baptized, went up straightway out of the water."—Matt. 3: 16. Again it is recorded that Jesus, "was baptized of John in the Jordan; and straightway coming up out of the water."—Mark 1: **9, 10.**

Does not the very fact of His going down into the water, so as to come up out of the water, show, if not positively, yet presumptively, that His baptism was an immersion, or burial in the water? For to say He went down into the river for the purpose of having a small quantity of water poured, or a few drops sprinkled on Him, is quite too trifling to have weight with candid minds.

BP. TAYLOR says:

"The custom of the ancient churches was not *sprinkling*.

but *immersion;* in pursuance of the sense of the word in the commandment, and the example of our blessed Savior."— *Com. Matt. 3: 16.*

DR. CAMPBELL says:

"Jesus being baptized, no sooner rose out of the water, than heaven was open to Him."—*Trans. Gospels, Matt. 3: 16.*

MACKNIGHT says:

"Christ submitted to be baptized, that is, to be *buried* under water, and to be raised out of it again, as an emblem of His future death and resurrection."—*Epist. Rom. 6: 3, 4.*

LIGHTFOOT, the most distinguished and influential member of the Westminster Assembly, says:

"That the baptism of John was the *immersion* of the body, in which manner both the ablutions of unclean persons and the baptism of proselytes was performed, seems evident from those things which are related of it; namely, that he baptized in the Jordan, and in Enon, because there was much water; and that Christ, being baptized, went up out of the water."—*On Matt. 3: 6.*

POOLE says:

"A great part of those who went out to hear John were baptized, that is, *dipped* in the Jordan."—*Annot. on Matt. 3: 6.*

OLSHAUSEN, on the baptism of Jesus, says:

"The one part of the action—the *submersion*—represents the negative aspect, the taking away of the old man; the other—the *emersion*—denotes its positive aspect, the appearance of the new man."—*Com. Rom, 6: 3, 4.*

DEAN STANLEY says:

"The mode of John's baptism has been, and still is much

discussed, but the practice of the Eastern Church, and the very meaning of the word [*baptizo*] leave no sufficient ground for questioning that the original form of baptism was *complete immersion* in the deep baptismal waters."—*Hist. Eastern Church, p. 34.*

GEIKIE says of John's converts:

"He led them in groups to the Jordan, and *immersed* each singly in the waters, after earnest and full confession of their sins."—*Life and Words of Christ, Vol. I., p. 405.*

DR. DÖLLINGER says:

"The Baptists are, however, from the Protestant point of view, unassailable, since, for their demand of baptism by submersion, they have the clear text of the Bible; and the authority of the Church and of her testimony is not regarded by either party."—*Kirche und Kirchen, 337.*

PROF. HARNACK says:

"*Baptizein* undoubtedly signifies *immersion*. No proof can be found that it signifies any thing else in the New Testament, and in the most ancient Christian literature. The suggestion regarding a 'sacred sense,' is out of the question."—*In Independent, Feb. 19, 1885.*

MUCH WATER FOR BAPTISM.

"Then cometh Jesus from Galilee to Jordan, unto John, to be baptized of him."—Matt. 3: 13. "And John also was baptizing in Enon, near to Salim, because there was much water there."—John 3: 23.

Thoughtful persons will ask why should they have resorted to places expresssly because these furnished large supplies of water, if baptism was performed by sprinkling? A very small quantity would have answered the purpose in that case. Let Pedobaptist scholars themselves answer the question as follows:

CALVIN, whom Scaliger pronunced the most learned man in Europe, says:

"From these words of John (ch. 3:23) it may be inferred that baptism was administered, by John and Christ, by *plunging* the whole body under the water."—*Comment. John 3:23.*

BENGEL says:

"Many waters; so the rite of *immersion* required."—*Comment on John 3:23.*

POOLE says:

"It is apparent that both Christ and John baptized by *dipping* the body in the water, else they need not have sought places where had been a great plenty of water."—*Annot. John 3:23.*

CURCELLÆUS says:

"Baptism was performed by *plunging* the whole body into water, and not by sprinkling a few drops, as is now the practice. For John was baptizing in Enon, near to Salim, because there was *much* water there."—*Relig. Ch. Inst., cited, Booth, Ped. Ex. ch. 4, p. 50.*

WHITBY says:

"Because there was much water there, in which their whole bodies might be *dipped*."—*Crit. Com. John 3:23.*

ADAM CLARK says:

"As the Jewish custom required the persons to stand in

the water, and having been instructed, and entered into a covenant to renounce all idolatry, and take the God of Israel for their God, then *plunged* themseives under the water, it is probable that the rite was thus performed."—*Com. on John 3 : 23.*

GEIKIE says:

" John had to leave the Jordan as too shallow at its accessible parts for baptism, and go to another place—Enon near Salim—an unknown locality, where pools more suitable were yet to be had."—*Life and Words of Christ, p. 410.*

PHILIP AND THE EUNUCH

Why should Philip and the eunuch, or either of them, have gone down into the water, if a mere sprinkling or pouring of water, and not immersion in water, was to be used ? " And they went down both into the water, both Philip and the eunuch, and he baptized him. And when they were come up out of the water, the Spirit of the Lord caught away Philip."—Acts 8 : 38, 39.

CALVIN says:

" Here we perceive how baptism was administered among the ancients; for they *immersed* the whole body in water."—*On baptism, ch. 3, p. 56.*

Dr. TOWERSON says:

" For what need would there have been of Philip and the eunuch going *into* this [the water], were it not that the baptism was to be performed by *immersion*."—*Com. Acts 8 : 38.*

GROTIUS, whom his biographer declared one of

the most illustrious names in literature, politics and theology, says:

"But that this customary rite was performed by *immersion*, and not by pouring, is indicated both by the proper signification of the word, and the places chosen for the rite."
—*Annot. Matt. 3 : 6.*

VENEMA says:

"It is without controversy, that baptism in the primitive Church was administered by *immersion* into water, and not by sprinkling, seeing that John is said to have baptized in Jordan, and where there was *much water*, as Christ also did by His disciples in the neighborhood of those places. Philip, also, going down into the water, baptized the eunuch."—*Eccl. Hist., ch. 1, sec. 138. See Booth, Ped. Ex., ch. 4, sec. 76.*

THE TESTIMONY OF EXPOSITORS

The great question with every candid mind should be, "What is truth? What is right?" But as the Scriptures are our only and sufficient standard in matters of religious faith and practice, we ask, what do the Scriptures teach? In order to ascertain this point, we inquire of those pious men, eminent for learning and a devout study of the Bible, who have prepared able commentaries on the sacred text, as to what they understand to be the nature of baptism, and the form of its original administration. What do expositors say?

ZANCHIUS, whose opinion, De Courcy declares, "is worth a thousand others," says:

"The proper signification of *baptizo* is to *immerse*, plunge under, to overwhelm in water."—*Works, Vol. VI., p. 217. Geneva, 1619.*

WITSIUS says:

"It cannot be denied that the native signification of the word *baptein*, and *baptizein*, is to plunge or dip."—*Econ. Covenants, p. 1213.*

BP. TAYLOR says:

"The custom of the ancient churches was not sprinkling, but *immersion*."—*Duct. Dubit, B. III., ch. 4, R. 15.*

LUTHER, the great German reformer, says:

"The term *baptism* is Greek; in Latin it may be translated *immersio;* since we *immerse* anything into water, that the whole may be covered with the water."—*Works, Vol. I., p. 74. Wit. Ed., 1582.*

MELANCTHON says:

"Baptism is *immersion* into water, which is made with this admirable benediction."—*Melanct. Catec., Wit., 1580.*

CAVE, in his able work on Christian Antiquities, says:

"The party to be baptized was *wholly immersed*, or put under water."—*Prim. Chris., P. I., ch. 10, p. 320.*

BP. SHERLOCK says:

"Baptism, or an *immersion* into water, according to the ancient rite of administering it, is a figure of our burial with Christ, and of our conformity to His death."—*See Bloom. Crit. Dig., Vol. V., p. 537.*

BEZA says:

"Christ commanded us to be baptized; by which word it

is certain *immersion* is signified."—*Epis. ad. Thom. Tillium, Annot. on Mark 7 : 4.*

POOLE says :

" He seems here to allude to the manner of baptizing in those warm Eastern countries, which was to *dip* or plunge the party baptized, and, as it were, to bury him for a while under water."—*Annot. on Romans 6 : 4.*

MEDE says :

" There was no such thing as *sprinkling* used in the Apostles' days, nor for many ages after them."—*Discourse on Titus 3 : 5.*

VITRINGA says :

" The act of baptizing is the *immersion* of believers in water. This expresses the force of the word."—*Aphorism 884.*

GROTIUS says :

" That baptism used to be performed by *immersion*, and not pouring, appears by the proper signification of the word, and by the places chosen for the administration of this rite." —*Annot. Matt. 3 : 6; John 3 : 23.*

BP. BOSSUET says :

" To baptize signifies to *plunge*, as is granted by all the world."—*Stennett against Russen, p. 174.*

DIODATI says :

" Baptized—that is to say, *ducked* in the water, for a sacred sign and seal of the expiation and remission of sins."— *Annot. on Matt. 3 : 6.*

CALVIN says :

" The word baptize signifies to *immerse ;* and it is certain

that immersion was the practice of the ancient Church."—
Institutes, B. IV., ch. 15, sec. 19.

SAMUEL CLARKE says:

" In the primitive times the manner of baptizing was by
immersion, or dipping the whole body into water."—*Exp.
Ch. Catec., p. 294. Ed. 6.*

STORR and FLATT say:

" The disciples of our Lord could understand His command in no other way than as enjoining *immersion*, for the
baptism of John, to which Jesus Himself submitted, and also
the earlier baptism of the disciples of Jesus, were performed
by *dipping* the subject into cold water."—*Bib. Theol., B. IV.,
sec. 109, par. 4.*

ADAM CLARK says:

" Alluding to the *immersions* practiced in the case of
adults, wherein the person appeared to be buried under the
water, as Christ was buried in the heart of the earth."—*Comment on Col. 2:12.*

BLOOMFIELD says:

" There is here plainly a reference to the ancient mode of
baptism by immersion."—*Greek New Test. Exp. Rom. 6:4.*

SCHOLZ says:

" Baptism consists in the *immersion* of the whole body in
water."—*Comment on Matt. 3:6.*

SCHAFF says:

" *Immersion*, and not sprinkling, was unquestionably the
original form.　This is shown by the very meaning of the
words *baptizo, baptisma* and *baptismos*, used to designate the

rite."—*Hist. Apos. Ch., p 488. Merc. ed., 1851. See also Noel on Bap., ch. 3, sec. 8.*

PROF. BROWNE says:

" The language of the New Testament and of the primitive Fathers sufficiently point to *immersion* as the common mode of baptism."—*Smith's Bib. Dict., Art. Bap. Sup.*

DR. JACOBS says:

"It only remains to be observed that baptism, in the primitive Church, was evidently administered by *immersion* of the body in water—a mode which added to the significancy of the rite, and gave a peculiar force to some of the allusions to it."—*Eccl. Polity of the N. T., p. 258.*

NEANDER says:

" The usual form of *submersion* at baptism, practiced by the Jews, was passed over to the Gentile Christians. Indeed, this form was the most suitable to signify that which Christ intended to render an object of contemplation by such a symbol: the *immersion* of the whole man in the spirit of a new life."—*Planting and Training, p. 161.*

To the same effect might be adduced many others from among the most able and distinguished of biblical scholars and commentators connected with the Pedobaptist communions.

APOSTOLIC ALLUSIONS.

The idea which Paul had of both the form and purpose of baptism is very manifest from the manner in which he refers to it in his Epistles. To the Romans he says: " Therefore we are *buried* with Him by baptism into death."—Rom. 6 : 4. To the

Colossians, using nearly the same language, he says: "*Buried* with Him in baptism."—Col. 2 : 12.

His conception must have been that of a burying, a covering of the subject entirely in the water, by a sinking into it. No other form could have been true to the figure here used. And this fact has been generally acknowledged.

ABP. TILLOTSON, on these passages, says:

"Anciently those who were baptized were *immersed*, and *buried* in the water, to represent their death to sin; and then did rise up out of the water to signify their entrance upon a new life. And to these customs the Apostle alludes."—*Works, Vol. I., p. 179.*

BENSON says:

"Buried with Him by baptism—alluding to the ancient manner of baptizing by *immersion*."—*Comment on Rom. 4: 4.*

DIODATI says:

"In baptism being *dipped* in water according to the ancient ceremony; it is a sacred sign unto us, that sin ought to be drowned in us by God's Spirit."—*Annot. Rom. 4: 4.*

TURRETIN says:

"And indeed baptism was performed in that age, and in those countries, by *immersion* of the whole body into water." —*Comment on Rom. 6: 3, 4.*

ZWINGLE says:

"When ye were *immersed* into the water by baptism, ye were ingrafted into the death of Christ."—*Annot. Rom. 4: 4. See Conant's Append. to Matt.*

WHITBY says:

"It being so expressly declared that we are *buried* with Christ in baptism, by being buried under water."—*Comment on Rom. 4:4.*

JOHN WESLEY says:

"Buried with Him—alluding to the ancient manner of baptizing by *immersion*."—*Note on Romans 4:4.*

CONYBEARE says:

"This passage cannot be understood, unless it be borne in mind that the primitive baptism was by *immersion*."—*Life and Epist. St. Paul, Rom. 4:4.*

BLOOMFIELD says:

"Here is a plain allusion to the ancient custom of baptizing by *immersion;* and I agree with Koppe and Rosenmüller, that there is reason to regret it should ever have been abandoned in most Christian churches, especially as it has so evident a reference to the mystic sense of baptism."—*Recens. Synop. on Rom. 4:4.*

SAMUEL CLARKE says:

"In the primitive times, the manner of baptizing was by *immersion*, or dipping the whole body into water. And this manner of doing it was a very significant emblem of the dying and rising again, referred to by St. Paul, in the above-mentioned similitude."—*Expos. Church Cate., 294, ed. 6.*

OLSHAUSEN says:

"Particularly Paul (Rom. 6:4) treats of baptism in the twofold reference of that ordinance to *immersion* and *emersion*, as symbolizing the death and resurrection of Christ."—*Comment Matt. 18:1-15.*

FRITZSCHE says :

" But that, in accordance with the nature of the word, baptism was then performed not by sprinkling upon, but by *submerging*, is proved especially by Rom. 4 : 4."—*Com. on Matt., Vol. I., p. 120. See Conant's Append. to Matt., p. 103.*

ESTIUS says :

" For *immersion* represents to us Christ's burial, and so also His death; since none but the dead are buried. Moreover, the *emersion* which follows the *immersion* has a resemblance to the resurrection."—*Com. on Rom. 6 : 3. Cited by Conant, Append. to Matt., p. 100.*

MALDONATUS says :

" For in Greek to be baptized is the same as to be *submerged*."—*Com. on Matt. 20 : 22 ; Luke 12 : 50.*

WHITEFIELD says :

" It is certain that in the words of our text (Rom. 6 : 3, 4) there is an allusion to the manner of baptism, which was by *immersion*."—*Eighteen Sermons, p. 297.*

ADAM CLARK says :

" It is probable that the Apostle here alludes to the mode of administering baptism by *immersion*, the whole body being put under water."—*Comment on Rom. 6 : 4.*

BISHOP FELL says :

" The primitive fashion of *immersion* under the water, representing our death, and elevation again out of it, our resurrection or regeneration."—*Note on Rom. 6 : 4.*

DR. DODDRIDGE says :

" It seems the part of candor to confess, that here (Rom.

6 : 4) is an allusion to the manner of baptizing by *immersion*, as most usual in those early times."—*Fam. Expos. on Rom. 6 : 4.*

ASSEMBLY OF DIVINES say:

" In this phrase (Col. 2 : 12) the Apostle seemeth to allude to the ancient manner of baptism, which was to *dip* the parties baptized, and, as it were, to bury them under the water for a while, and then to draw them out of it, and lift them up, to represent the burial of our old man, and our resurrection to newness of life."—*Annot. on Matt. 3 : 6; Rom. 6 : 4.*

Such opinions, expressed by these learned and pious men, do not surprise us. It is difficult to see how they could have expressed any others.

HISTORICAL EVIDENCE

Many learned men have studied with care the early records of Christianity; have written histories of the doctrines and ceremonies of the churches during the times immediately succeeding the apostolic age. What do they say of the practice as to baptism in the first centuries of Christian history ?

BARNABAS, the companion of St. Paul, in an epistle ascribed to him, and which must have been written very early, whoever was the real author, speaks of baptism as a " going down into the water." He says:

" We go down into the water full of sin and filth, but we come up bearing fruits in our hands."—*Cath. Epist., sec. 9., cited by Broughton, Hist. Dict., Art. Baptism.*

HERMAS, writing about A. D. 95, in the "Shepherd," a work ascribed to him, speaks of the Apostles as having gone "down into the water with those they baptized," and "come up again."—*Stennett against Russen, p. 143.*

JUSTIN MARTYR, writing about A. D. 140, speaks of those baptized as "washed in the water, in the name of the Father, Son and Spirit."—*Apology, secs. 79, 85, 86. Reeve's Trans.; Orchard's Hist. Bapt., secs. 1, 2, 3, 4.*

TERTULLIAN, about A. D. 204, says the person to be baptized "is let down into the water, and, with a few words said, is *dipped*."—*De Bapt., ch. 2.*

HIPPOLYTUS, about A. D. 225, says:

"For he who goes down with faith into the bath of regeneration, is arrayed against the evil one, and on the side of Christ. He comes up from the baptism bright as the sun, flashing forth the rays of righteousness."—*Dis. on the Theoph., 10. See Conant's Append. to Matt.*

GREGORY, A. D. 360, says:

"We are *buried* with Christ by baptism, that we may also rise with him."—*Stennett's Reply, p. 144.*

BASIL, A. D. 360, says:

"By three *immersions* the great mystery of baptism is accomplished;" referring to *trine* baptism.—*Baronius' Annals, V.; Bingham's Antiq., B. XI., ch. 11.*

AMBROSE, A. D. 374, says:

"Thou saidst, I do believe, and wast *immersed* in water;

that in thou wast buried."—*Bing. Ant., B. II., ch. 2. Stennett's Reply to Russen, p. 144.*

CYRIL, A. D. 374, says:

"Candidates are first anointed with consecrated oils; they are then conducted to the laver, and asked three times if they believe in the Father, Son, and Holy Ghost; then they are *dipped* three times into the water, and retire by three distinct efforts."—*Dupin's Eccl. Hist., ch. 6., sec. 2; Orchard's Hist. Bap., p. 43. Nash. ed., 1855.*

CHRYSOSTOM, A. D. 398, says:

" To be baptized and *plunged* in the water, and then emerge and rise again, is a symbol of our descent into the grave, and our ascent out of it."—*Hom. 40, on 1 Cor., p. 186; Bing. Christ. Antiq., B. XI., ch. 11. See also on all the Fathers, Conant's Append. to Matt.*

SALMASIUS says:

"Baptism is *immersion*, and was formerly celebrated according to the force and meaning of the name. Now it is only *rantism*, or sprinkling, not immersion nor dipping."—*Wolf. Crit. Matt. 28:19; De Caes. Viro., p. 669*

BINGHAM says:

" The ancients thought that *immersion*, or burying under water, did more lively represent the death, burial, and resurrection of Christ, as well as our own death to sin, and rising again into righteousness."—*Christ. Antiq., B. XI., ch. 11.*

MOSHEIM says:

"In this century [the first] baptism was administered in convenient places, without the public assemblies, and by *immersing* the candidate wholly in water."—*Eccl. Hist.. B. I., Cent. 1.. part II., ch. 4.*

NEANDER says:

" In respect to the form of baptism, it was, in conformity with the original institution, and the original import of the symbol, performed by *immersion*, as a sign of entire baptism into the Holy Spirit, of being entirely penetrated by the same."—*Ch. Hist. Vol. I., p. 310. Also Hist. Plant. and Train., Vol. I., p. 222.*

WADDINGTON says:

" The sacraments of the primitive Church were two: that of Baptism and the Lord's Supper. The ceremony of *immersion*, the oldest form of baptism, was performed in the name of the three persons of the Trinity."—*Church Hist., ch. 2., sec. 3.*

SCHAFF says:

" Finally, so far as it respects the mode and manner of outward baptizing, there can be no doubt that *immersion*, and not sprinkling, was the original normal form."—*Hist. Christ. Ch., p. 488, Mercer. ed.*

FOR THIRTEEN CENTURIES

Not only was immersion the original normal form of baptism, as received by Christ, administered by His Apostles, and practiced by the earliest Christians, but it was that form which was retained in use by all Christian churches, with few exceptions, for *many centuries*. Indeed, with a large portion of the so-called Christian world, it retains its position to this day.

DR. WHITBY says:

" And this *immersion* being religiously observed *by all*

Christians for *thirteen centuries*, and approved by our Church "—referring to the Church of England.—*Annotations on Rom. 6 : 4.*

DR. STACKHOUSE says:

" Several authors have shown and proved that this manner of *immersion* continued, as much as possible, to be used for *thirteen hundred years* after Christ."—*History of the Bible, B. VIII., ch. 1.*

BISHOP BOSSUET says:

" We are able to make it appear, by the acts of Councils, and by ancient rituals, that for *thirteen hundred years* baptism was thus administered [by immersion] throughout the whole Church, as far as possible." —*Stennett ad. Russen, p. 176; Booth's Pedo. Ex., ch. 4.*

DR. BRENNER says:

" *Thirteen hundred years* was baptism generally and orderly performed by the *immersion* of the person under water, and only in extraordinary cases was sprinkling, or affusion, permitted. These later methods of baptism were called in question, and even prohibited."—*Hist. Exhibit. Bapt., p. 306.*

VON CÖLLN says:

" *Immersion* in water was general until the *thirteenth century* among the Latins; it was then displaced by sprinkling, but retained by the Greeks."—*Hist. Doct., Vol. II., p. 303.*

HAGENBACH says:

" From the *thirteenth century* sprinkling came into more general use in the West. The Greek Church, however, and the Church of Milano still retained the practice of *immersion.*"—*Hist. Doct., Vol. II., p. 84, note 1.*

WINER says:

" Affusion was first applied to the sick, but was gradually introduced for others after the *seventh century*, and in the *thirteenth* became the prevailing practice in the West."— *Lects. Christ. Antiquity.*

AUGUSTI says :

" *Immersion* in water was general until the *thirteenth century*, among the Latins ; it was then displaced by sprinkling, but retained by the Greeks."—*Archæ.*, *Vol. V., p. 5 ; Vol. VII., p. 229.*

BINGHAM says :

" As this [*dipping*] was the original apostolical practice, so it continued the universal practice of the Church for *many ages*."—*Antiq. Christ. Church, B. XI., ch. 11.*

VAN OOSTERZEE says :

" This *sprinkling*, which seems to have first come generally into use in the *thirteenth century*, in place of the entire immersion of the body, in imitation of the previous baptism of the sick, has certainly this imperfection, that the symbolical character of the act is expressed by it much less conspicuously than by complete immersion and burial under water."—*Christian Dogmatics, p.* 749. *N. Y. ed.*

COLEMAN says :

" The practice of *immersion* continued even until the *thirteenth* or *fourteenth century*. Indeed, it has never been formally abandoned."—*Ancient Christianity, ch. 19, sec. 12.*

ENCYCLOPÆDIA ECCLESIASTICA says :

" Whatever weight, however, may be in those reasons, as a defense for the present practice of sprinkling, it is evident that during the first ages of the Church, and for *many centuries* afterwards, the practice of *immersion* prevailed."—*Ency. Eccl., Art. Baptism.*

While these testimonials do not exhaust historical evidence on this point, they are sufficient to satisfy unbiased minds as to the primitive and long-continued use of immersion for baptism, in the Christian world.

These Pedobaptist scholars concede that for *thirteen hundred years* immersion was the prevailing form of baptism, departed from only in special and extraordinary cases. And that even when abandoned by the Latin, or Romish Church, it was retained by the Greek, and other Oriental churches, which do to this day preserve the original form of that sacred rite.

USAGE OF THE GREEK CHURCH

While it may not be an unanswerable argument in favor of the position taken by Baptists, that the Greek Church has always practised, and does still practise immersion, yet the fact is too significant to be overlooked. It constitutes collateral evidence of no mean character.

The Greek Church extends over Greece, Russia, Egypt, Arabia, Palestine, Abyssinia, and other Oriental countries. Like the Romish Church, it has corrupted the primitive purity of Gospel doctrine and practice with many absurd glosses and superstitious rites. But as to the form of baptism, it holds the primitive custom of *dipping* the candidates.

STOURDZA, the Russian scholar and diplomat, says :

"The Church of the West [Rome] has, then, departed from the example of Jesus Christ ; she has obliterated the whole sublimity of the exterior sign. *Baptism* and *immersion* are identical. Baptism by aspersion is as if one should say, *immersion* by *aspersion ;* or any other absurdity of the same nature."—*Consid. Orthodox Ch., p. 87; Conant's Append., p. 99.*

DEYLINGIUS says :

"The Greeks retain the rite of *immersion* to this day ; as Jeremiah, the patriarch of Constantinople, declares."—*De Prud. Past., P. III., ch. 3., sec. 26.*

BUDDEUS says :

"That the Greeks defend *immersion* is manifest, and has been frequently observed by learned men ; which Ludolphus informs us is the practice of the Ethiopians."—*Theol. Dogmat., B. V., ch. 1., sec. 5.*

RICAUT says :

"Thrice *dipping*, or plunging, this Church holds to be as necessary to the form of baptism, as water is to the matter." —*State of Greek Church, p. 163.*

DR. WALL, whose learned and laborious researches into the history of baptism left little for others to discover, says :

"The Greek Church in all its branches does still use *immersion*, and so do all other Christians in the world, except the Latins. All those nations that do now, or formerly did submit to the authority of the Bishop of Rome, do ordinarily baptize their infants by pouring or sprinkling. But *all other Christians in the world,* who never owned the Pope's usurped power, do, and ever did, *dip* their infants in the ordinary use. All the Christians in Asia, all in Africa, and about one-third in Europe, are of the last sort."—*Hist. Inf. Bap., Vol. II., p. 376; ed. 3.*

DR. WHITBY says:

"The observation of the Greek Church is this, that he who ascended out of the water must first descend into it; baptism, therefore, is to be performed, not by *sprinkling*, but by washing the body, and, indeed, it can be only from ignorance of the Jewish rites that this can be questioned."—*Critical Com. on Matt. 3:16.*

DR. KING says:

"The Greek Church uniformly practices the *trine immersion*, undoubtedly the most primitive manner."—*Rites and Cerem. Greek Church, p. 192.*

COLEMAN says:

"The Eastern Church has uniformly retained the form of *immersion* as indispensable to the validity of the ordinance; and repeat the rite whenever they have received to their communion persons who have been baptized in another manner."—*Ancient Christ. Exemp., ch. 19., sec. 12.*

BROUGHTON says:

"The Greek Church differs from the Romish, as to the rite of baptism, chiefly in performing it by *immersion*, or plunging the infant all over in the water."—*Hist. Dict., Art. Bap. Also Ricaut's Greek Church.*

THE PANTALOGIA says:

The Greek Church is "that part of the Christian Church which was first established in Greece, and is now spread over a larger extent of country than any other established Church.

Amid all their trifling rites, they practice *trine immersion*, which is unquestionably the original manner."—*Article Greek Church*.

THE ENCYCLOPÆDIA BRITANNICA says :

"The Greek Church differs from the Romish, as to the rite of baptism, chiefly in performing it by *immersion*, or plunging the infant all over in the water."—*Article Baptism*.

The Greek Church, like the Latin, has departed from scriptural usage in baptizing unconscious infants, and in many other matters ; but has retained the true form of baptism. The Romish Church claims the right to change and abolish ordinances. For that reason, and on that ground alone, they have abolished immersion, and use aspersion in its stead. And this aspersion the Protestant Pedobaptist churches have accepted, with other ecclesiastical perversions, from that corrupt source. Why will they not go back to primitive purity, and scripture teaching ? Would they but discard *rantism*, and adopt *baptism* according to the command of Christ and the practice of the Apostles, it would do more to secure Christian unity among Protestants than all other proposed schemes combined.

THE TESTIMONY OF BAPTISTERIES

It will cast some further light on this subject to know what places were resorted to for a convenient administration of this ordinance during the early ages of Christianity. They never would have frequented rivers, pools, cisterns, and other large bodies of water, for the mere purpose of sprinkling the candidates.

We know that John the Baptist and the disciples of Jesus resorted to the Jordan for the purpose of baptizing, and to Enon, near to Salim, "*because* there was much water there."

TERTULLIAN says :

"There is no difference whether one is baptized in the sea or in a lake, in a river or in a fountain; neither was there any difference between those whom John baptized in Jordan, and those whom Peter baptized in the Tiber.—*De Bapt., ch. 4; Bing. Antiq., B. VIII., ch. 8, sec. 1.*

DR. DODDRIDGE says :

"John was also at the same time baptizing at Enon; and he particularly chose that place because there was a great quantity of water there, which made it very convenient for his purpose."—*Fam. Expositor on Matt. 3: 16.*

As Christianity spread and converts multiplied, in many places, especially in large cities, there were few opportunities for the convenient and agreeable administration of the ordinance. Other cities were not so well supplied with pools as was Jerusalem. Then began to be erected *baptisteries*, expressly designed for this use. These, at first, were constructed in the simplest manner; but, in process of time, large, costly and imposing edifices were built for this purpose.

MOSHEIM says :

"For the more convenient administration of baptism,

sacred fonts, or *baptisteria*, were erected in the porches of the temples.   This was in the fourth century."—*Eccl. Hist. Cent. 4, B. II., p. II., ch. 4, sec. 7.*

BROUGHTON says :

"The place of baptism was at first unlimited, being some pond or lake, some spring or river, but always as near as possible to the place of public worship.   Afterward they had their *baptisteries*, or (as we call them) fonts, built at first near the church, then in the church porch, and, at last, in the church itself." "The baptistery was, properly speaking, the whole house or building in which the font stood, which latter was only the fountain or pool of water in which the *immersion* was performed."—*Hist. Dict., Arts. Baptism and Baptistery.*

DR. MURDOCK says :

"The baptisteries were, properly, buildings adjacent to the churches, in which the catechumens were instructed, and where were a sort of cistern, into which water was let at the time of baptism, and in which the candidates were baptized by *immersion*."—*Mosh. Eccl. Hist., Vol. I., p. 281, note 15.*

DR. SCHAFF says :

"In the fourth century special buildings for this holy ordinance (baptism) began to appear, either entirely separate, or connected with the main church by a covered passage. The need of them arose partly from the still prevalent custom of *immersion*."—*Hist. Chr. Ch., Vol. II., p. 558-9, sec. 208.*

CAVE says :

"These baptisteries were usually very large and capacious, not only that they might comport with the general custom of those times—of persons baptized being *immersed* or put under water; but because the stated times of baptism returning so seldom, great multitudes were usually baptized at the same time."—*Prim. Christ., P. I., ch. 10, p. 312.*

BINGHAM says :

"In the apostolic age, and some time after, before churches and baptisteries were generally erected, they baptized in any place where they had convenience, as John baptized in Jordan, Philip baptized the eunuch in the wilderness, and Paul, the jailor, in his own house."—*Christ. Antiq., B. XI., ch. 6, sec. 11.*

HAGENBACH says :

"That baptism in the beginning was administered in the open air, in rivers and pools, and that it was by *immersion* we know from the narratives of the New Testament. In later times there were prepared great baptismal fonts or chapels. The person to be baptized descended several steps into the reservoir of water, and then the whole body was *immersed* under the water."—*Hist. Christ. Church, ch. 19, p. 324.*

COLEMAN says :

"The first baptistery, or place appropriated to baptism, of which any mention is made, occurs in a biography in the fourth century, and this was prepared in a private house."—*Ancient Christ. Exemplified, ch. 19, sec 10.*

The term "baptistery" was applied properly to the pool or font of water, but was also used to designate the building in which the pool was placed.

BRANDE says :

"A building destined for the purpose of administering the rite of baptism. The baptistery was entirely distinct from the church up to the end of the sixth century; after which period the interior of the church received it."—*Dict. Arts, Sci., and Lit., Art. Baptistery.*

THE ENCYCLOPÆDIA BRITANNICA says :

"In the ancient Church it was one of the *exedra*, or buildings distinct from the church itself. Thus it continued till the sixth century, when the baptisteries began to be taken into the church porch, and afterward into the church itself." —*Article Baptistery*.

Some of these structures are still preserved, and others are well known to have existed—as that of Florence, Venice, Pisa, Naples, Bologna, and Ravenna. That of the Lateran, at Rome, is considered the oldest now existing, having been erected A.D. 324.

That at Pisa was completed A.D. 1160, the entire structure being one hundred and fifteen feet in diameter, by one hundred and seventy-two feet in height, and of a circular form. That at Florence is an octagonal building, ninety feet in diameter, with a lofty dome. That of St. Sophia, at Constantinople, erected by Constantine, A.D. 337, was capable of accommodating a numerous Council, whose sessions were held in it. Most of these structures are large, elaborate, and costly edifices.

The baptistery proper, or pool for baptizing, was an open cistern in the center of the large hall, or main part of the building.

Can any one suppose these buildings would have been provided if sprinkling and not immersion had been the manner of administering baptism ?*

* For a full account of Baptisteries, see Robinson's History of Baptism, ch. 12, where, with much labor, the author has collected a large amount of information on the subject. Also Duncan's Hist. Baptists, ch. 5, sec. 3. Also Crystal's History of the Mode of Baptism.

THE DESIGN OF BAPTISM

What was baptism intended to represent and teach? As an outward rite, it must be a type, or sign, of some religious truth, or spiritual fact, meant to be taught or enforced by its observance. And the form of the rite, the manner of its administration, must be such as properly to express its design and meaning. If the form be so changed that its symbolic force is lost, and its design no longer seen in its administration, then, manifestly, it is no longer baptism in form or fact; its teaching is not understood, and its chief purpose fails.

Now, it is not difficult to ascertain from the New Testament what was intended by baptism. It was clearly this: to show forth the death, burial, and resurrection of Christ, who died for our sins, and rose again for our justification. And every candidate who receives the ordinance professes thereby faith in the merits of Christ's death as the ground of his own hope and salvation, fellowship also with His sufferings, and a declaration of his own death to sin, and a rising to newness of life in Christ. It also typifies the washing of regeneration, and the renewing of the Holy Ghost, and declares the candidate's hope of a resurrection from the dead, even as Christ, into the likeness of whose death he is buried, was raised up by the glory of the Father.

That immersion alone can teach this is evident; which view the following testimonies abundantly confirm:

TYNDALE says:

"The plunging into the water signifieth that we die and are buried with Christ, as concerning the old life of sin. And the pulling out again signifieth that we rise again with Christ in a new life full of the Holy Ghost."—*Obedience of a Christ. Man, 143, cited by Conant, Append., p. 93.*

ADAM CLARK says:

"But as they received baptism as an emblem of death, in voluntarily going under the water, so they receive it as an emblem of the resurrection unto eternal life, in coming up out of the water."—*Bap. for the dead, Com. on 1 Cor. 15: 29.*

BP. NEWTON says:

"Baptism was usually performed by immersion, or dipping the whole body under water, to represent the death, burial, and resurrection of Christ together, and therewith signify the person's own dying to sin, the destruction of its power, and his resurrection to a new life."—*Prac. Expos. Catechism. p. 297.*

FRANKIUS says:

"The baptism of Christ represented His sufferings, and His coming up out of the water His resurrection from the dead."—*Programme, 14, p. 343.*

PICTETUS says:

"That immersion into and emersion out of the water, practiced by the ancients, signify the death of the old man, and the resurrection of the new man."—*Theol. Christ., B. XIV., ch. 4, sec. 13.*

BUDDEUS says:

"Immersion, which was used in former times, was a sym-

bol and an image of the death and the burial of Christ."—
Dogmatic Theol., B. V., ch. 1, sec. 8.

SAURIN says:

" The ceremony of wholly immersing us in water, when
we were baptized, signified that we died to sin."—*Sermons,
Vol. III., p. 171.   Robinson's Trans.*

GROTIUS says:

" There was in baptism, as administered in former times,
an image both of a burial and a resurrection, which in regard to Christ was external, in regard to Christians internal."
—*Annot. Rom. 4: 4.   Col. 2: 12.*

OLSHAUSEN says:

" As believers are in Christ's death dead with Him, and in
baptism buried with Him, so they are now also risen with
Him in His resurrection."—*Comment on Col. 2: 12.*

MACKNIGHT says:

" He submitted to be baptized, that is, to be buried under the water by John, and to be raised up out of it again,
as an emblem of His future death and resurrection."—*Comment on Rom. 6: 4.*

BAXTER says:

" In our baptism we are dipped under the water, as signifying our covenant profession, that as He was buried for sin,
we are dead and buried to sin."—*Para. Rom. 6: 4. Col. 2: 12.*

ABP. LEIGHTON says:

" Buried with Christ . . . . where the dipping into water
is referred to as representing our dying with Christ, and the

return thence, as expressive of our rising with Him."—*Com. 1 Pet. 3: 21.*

DR. BARROW says:

" The action is baptizing, or immersing into water." "The mersion also in water, and emersion thence, doth figure our death to the former, and our reviving to a new life."—*Doct. Sacra. Works, Vol. III., p. 43.*

Dr. Cave says:

" As in immersion there are, in a manner, three several acts—the putting the person into water, his abiding there for a little time, and his rising up again—so by these were represented Christ's death, burial, and resurrection; and in conformity thereunto our dying unto sin, the destruction of its power, and our resurrection to a new course of life."—*Prim. Christ., p. I., ch. 10, p. 320.*

Dr. HAMMOND says:

" It is a thing that every Christian knows, that the immersion in baptism refers to the death of Christ. The putting the person into the water denotes and proclaims the death and burial of Christ."—*Comment. on Rom. 6: 3.*

DR. WALL says:

" The immersion of the person, whether infant or adult, in the posture of one that is buried and raised up again, is much more solemn, and expresses the design of the sacrament and the mystery of the spiritual washing much better than pouring a small quantity on the face."—*Hist. Inf. Bap., pp. 404–408.*

DR. SCHAFF says:

" All commentators of note (except Stuart and Hodge) expressly admit, or take it for granted, that in this verse the ancient prevailing mode of baptism by *immersion* and *emersion* is implied, as giving additional force to the idea of the going down of the old and the rising up of the new man."— *Note in Lange on Rom. 6 : 4.*

BP. BLOOMFIELD says:

" There may also be (as the ancient commentators think) an allusion to the ancient mode of baptism by immersion; which, while typifying a death unto sin, and a new birth unto righteousness, also had reference to the Christian's communion with his Lord, both in death and resurrection from the dead."—*Greek N. Test. on 1 Cor. 15 : 29. Bap. for the dead.*

DR. TOWERSON says:

" Therefore, as there is so much the more reason to represent the rite of immersion, as the *only legitimate* rite of baptism, because the *only one* that can answer the end of its institution, and those things which were to be signified by it; so, especially, if, as is well known, and undoubtedly of great force, the general practice of the Primitive Church was agreeable thereto, and the practice of the Greek Church to this very day. For who can think that either one or the other would have been so tenacious of so troublesome a rite, were it not that they were well assured, as they of the Primitive Church might well be, of its being *the only instituted and legitimate one?*"—*On Sacra. Bapt., Part III., pp. 51–58.*

CANON LIDDON, on the likeness to Christ's resurrection, said:

" Of this, the Apostle traced the token in the ceremony, at that time universal, of baptism by *immersion*. The baptismal waters were the grave of the old nature, while through those waters Christ bestowed the gift of the new nature. As Jesus, crucified and dead, was laid in the grave, so the Christian, crucified to the world through the body of Christ, descends, as into the tomb, into the baptismal waters. He was buried beneath them; they closed for a moment over him; he was 'planted,' not only in the likeness of Christ's death, but of His burial. But the immersion is over; the Christian is lifted from the flood, and this is evidently as correspondent to the resurrection of Christ, as the descent had been to His burial. Buried with Him in baptism, wherein also ye are risen with Him."—*Easter Sermon in St Paul's, June, 1889.*

Such are the opinions of candid Pedobaptist divines, as to the design of baptism. Immersion alone can meet this demand, and serve its purpose. Sprinkling, or pouring water on a candidate, has no force in the direction of this sacred symbolism. It cannot show the death, burial, or the resurrection of Christ; nor the disciple's death to sin, and his rising to a new life. If immersion, therefore, be abandoned, the entire force of the ordinance will be destroyed, and its design obliterated.

Sprinkling sets forth no great doctrine of the Gospel. Only when the disciple is buried beneath the water, and raised up again, do the beauty, force, and meaning, which divine wisdom intended, appear in that sacred ordinance.

THE WATER SUPPLY

Among the weak arguments used, and the indefensible positions assumed by the advocates of sprinkling, is this—one of the weakest, and least defensible—that the Jordan had not sufficient depth of water for immersing the multitudes said to have been baptized by John and the disciples of Jesus; and that there were no conveniences in Jerusalem for immersing the large number of early converts who were baptized there. Consequently, they say, those converts must have had water sprinkled on them instead.

Puerile as may seem this objection, it has been seriously put forth by not a few of the advocates of aspersion, even in the face of Scripture testimony, and against scholarship and history. Such assertions indicate the ignorance or the recklessness of those who make them, and show how prejudice may unfit even good men for a just discussion of grave subjects. The objection is too trifling to merit serious regard; and yet the testimony on this point is so abundant, and so conclusive—and that, too, from Pedobaptist sources—as to make it both pleasant and fitting to adduce some of it in this connection.

PROF. EDWARD ROBINSON, in 1840, made a careful survey of Palestine, including the Jordan river. His statements corroborate those of others, as to the abundant supply of water both in the Jordan and in the city of Jerusalem itself. He cites the earlier but well-known travelers whose published works are familiar to the reading public: Seetzen, who visited the country in 1806; Burckhardt, who explored it in 1812; Irby and Mangles, in 1818, and Buckingham, who traveled through it at about the same time. These distinguished explorers published the results of their travels, which can be consulted.—*Rob. Bib. Resear., Vol. II., pp. 257-267.*

LIEUT. LYNCH, of the United States navy, was, in 1848, sent out by his government in charge of an expedition to explore the river Jordan and the Dead Sea. This, of course, had no connection with polemic discussions, and least of all was it to settle the baptismal question. It was done for antiquarian research, and for the advancement of science.

The expedition passed down the entire length of the Jordan, in boats, from the Sea of Galilee to the Dead Sea; made frequent and careful surveys, which were accurately recorded and officially published.

The river was found to vary in width from seventy-five to two hundred feet; and in *depth* from *three* to *twelve feet*. At Bethabara, where tradition has fixed the place of our Saviour's baptism, and where John baptized the multitudes, Lieut. Lynch gives the *width* as *one hundred and twenty feet*, and the greatest *depth* as *twelve feet*. There certainly is no lack of water there, since one quarter of twelve feet would be sufficient for burying converts in baptism.

It is a well-known fact that thousands of Christian pilgrims from adjacent countries visit this spot at a certain season annually to bathe in the waters, held sacred by them because of Christ's baptism there. The expedition witnessed one of these scenes, and had their boats in readiness to prevent accidents, which it was feared might occur in so great a crowd of fanatical devotees, in so great a depth of water. Had the advocates of sprinkling been present they might have found an argument as perilous as it would have been convincing for a sufficient depth of water for the immersion of Christian believers. Scarcely an occasion of this kind transpires without some fatal accidents by drowning in the deep and rapid current.—*Lynch, chs. 10, 11.*

DEAN STANLEY, a distinguished divine and scholar of the English Church, made the tour of the Holy Land in 1853, explored the Jordan valley, witnessed the bathing of the pilgrims, and recorded this remark touching the baptism of John:

" He came baptizing, that is, signifying to those who came to him, as he *plunged* them under the rapid torrent, the forgiveness and forsaking of their sins." " There began that sacred rite which has since spread throughout the world; through the vast baptisteries of the Southern and Oriental churches, gradually dwindling to the little fonts of the North and West."—*Stanley's Syria and Palestine, ch. 7, pp. 306–7.*

DR. THOMSON, for a quarter of a century missionary in Syria and Palestine, and very familiar with the Holy Land, traversed it in 1857, visited the Jordan in the vicinity of Jericho, and witnessed the bathing of the Greek pilgrims, as described by Lieut. Lynch and others. Of this singular and exciting scene he gives a graphic description. He says:

" The men *ducked* the women somewhat as the farmers do their sheep, while the little children were carried and *plunged* under water, trembling like so many lambs."

Being Pedobaptists, these Oriental fanatics may not have performed their rites with becoming propriety. But there was an abundance of water, and they believed in a thorough immersion.   He adds:

" The current is astonishingly rapid, and at least *ten feet deep*."   " Two Christians and a Turk, who ventured too far, were drowned without the possibility of a rescue."   A perilous depth of water certainly.   " At the bathing-place it was twenty rods wide."   " Boats could do nothing in such a current, and it is too deep to ford."—*The Land and the Book*, *Vol. II., pp. 445-446.*

PROF. OSBORNE, who in 1857 made the tour of Palestine for scientific research, makes this note of a bath taken in the Jordan:

"The current was too strong to permit of swimming across, though washing in its waters completely freed me from the clammy sensation which was the consequence of my previous bath in the Dead Sea."—*Palestine, Past and Present, p. 476.*

LORD NUGENT says of the Jordan:

" Its general breadth is between fifty and sixty yards, perhaps a little wider; and in most parts it is too deep, within a few feet out (when thus high), to allow any but swimmers to trust themselves out of arm's reach of the brink, and its drooping branches and tall reeds.   The pilgrims who come thither in crowds at Easter, bathe in this way.   Some of us tried to make way against the current, but were carried several yards down before reaching even the full strength of it." —*Travels, Vol. II., p. 100.*

The city of Jerusalem was abundantly supplied with water, to a large **extent** by pools and cisterns, many of which were of great size. Outside, but near the city, were others of still larger dimensions. These were constructed in part for the purpose of furnishing water for the ordinary uses of life, and in part to supply conveniences for the many ablutions enjoined by the Mosaic law.

These pools were abundant in our Savior's time, and some of them still remain, containing water, and even now affording admirable conveniences for the administration of baptism in its primitive form. Others, now in a ruined state, distinctly reveal their original form and magnitude. The greater part of them were in good repair, and continued to be used for hundreds of years after Christ.

DR. EDWARD ROBINSON visited Jerusalem in the prosecution of his researches, and made careful and extensive investigations touching the topography and antiquities of the Holy City. The results, published in his " Researches " in 1841, have been fully corroborated by other and more recent surveys. They are as follows:*

The Pool of Bethesda is three hundred and sixty (360) feet long, one hundred and thirty (130) feet wide, and seventy-five (75) feet deep. When full, it was a considerable pond, covering more than an acre of ground.

The Pool of Siloam is fifty-three (53) feet long, eighteen (18) feet wide, and nineteen (19) feet deep; it now holds two

*Robinson's Biblical Researches, Vol. I., pp. 480–515. See also. Thomson's Land and Book, Vol. II., pp. 64 and 446.

or three feet of water, which can readily be increased to a much greater depth.

The Upper Pool is three hundred and sixteen (316) feet long, two hundred and eighteen (218) feet wide, and eighteen (18) feet deep, covering an acre and a half of ground.

The Pool of Hezekiah is two hundred and forty (240) feet long, and one hundred and forty-four (144) feet wide, and is partly filled with water.

The Lower Pool, or Pool of Gihon, is five hundred and ninety-two (592) feet long, two hundred and sixty (260) feet wide, and forty (40) feet deep, covering more than three and a half acres of ground. This pool is now dry; but so lately as the time of the Crusaders was fully supplied with water, and free to the use of all.

Several other pools existed, either in or in the immediate vicinity of the city. They were all constructed with sides gradually sloping inward and downward, so as to make a descent into the water to any required depth safe and easy, and were, doubtless, in daily use for purposes of ablution, as constantly practised by the Jews.

DR. BARCLAY, who spent many years in missionary labor in Jerusalem, and who, so far as that city is concerned, is perhaps the most competent and reliable of all authorities, substantiates the above statements by his own testimony.—*City of the Great King. See, also, Prof. Chase's Design of Baptism, with Dr. Sampson's Article, p. 115.*

DR. THOMSON, in his efforts to identify the place where Philip baptized the eunuch, says:

"He would then have met the chariot somewhere southwest of Latron. There is a fine stream of water, called Murubbah, deep enough even in June to satisfy the utmost wishes of our Baptist friends."—*The Land and the Book, Vol. II., p. 310.*

Good testimony that is, from a most competent and reliable source, and from one who did not think immersion essential to baptism.

How fully such testimony from well-informed sources vindicates the views held by Baptists, let any one judge. And how futile are all objections urged against immersion as the scriptural mode of baptism, on the ground of an insufficient supply of water for such a purpose, is manifest. And this testimony comes from those who have no doctrinal sympathy with Baptists.

ASPERSION FOR IMMERSION

We may now properly inquire when and why was sprinkling introduced and accepted as a substitute for the original scriptural form of dipping in baptism? Why and when did a human device supersede a divine institution? The question has its interest and its importance, and is fully and satisfactorily answered by Pedobaptists themselves. We accept their testimony as a complete justification of our position in respect to this ordinance.

For *two hundred and fifty years* after Christ we have no evidence of any departure from the primitive practice of immersion—the first authenticated instance of such a departure being about the middle of the third century, or A. D. 250. This was in the case of *Novatian.* Eusebius, the historian, gives this case, and no earlier instance could be found by Dr. Wall in his laborious researches. Good evidence that none earlier existed. What he failed in this direction to discover, it would be difficult for any other one to find.

Novatian was dangerously ill, and believing himself about to die, he greatly desired to be baptized, not having as yet received that ordinance. As the case seemed urgent, and he was thought too feeble to be immersed, it was decided to try a substitute as nearly resembling baptism as possible. Water was poured profusely over him as he lay on his bed, so as to resemble as much as possible a submersion. The word used to describe this action (*perichutheis*, *perfusus*) has usually been rendered, *besprinkle;* it rather means, to pour round about, or upon and over one. This was, doubtless, the action in the case of Novatian, and such a profuse overwhelming with water, it was thought, might serve the purpose, especially as the necessity was so great.—*See this case treated in Dr. Chase's Design of Baptism, p. 53.*

EUSEBIUS, in his history, quoting from Cornelius, bishop of Rome, gives the following accounts of this case—a case which claims the more regard as being the first recorded departure from apostolic usage in the matter of baptism:

" He fell into a grievous distemper, and, it being supposed that he would die immediately, he received baptism—being besprinkled with water on the bed whereon he lay, if that can be termed baptism."—*Eccl. Hist., B. VI., ch. 43. Cambridge ed. 1683. Also Bing. Christ. Antiq., B. XI., ch. 11, sec. 5. Also B. IV., ch. 3, sec. 11.*

The historian himself seemed doubtful as to the validity of such a rite.

VALESIUS makes the following comment on the passage:

"This word, *perichutheis*, Rufinus very well renders *besprinkled (perfusus)*. For people who were sick, and baptized on their beds, could not be dipped in water by the priest, but were besprinkled by him. This baptism was thought imperfect, and not solemn, for several reasons. Also, they who were thus baptized were called ever afterward *Clinici;* and by the twelfth canon of the Council of Neocesarea, these Clinici were prohibited priesthood."—*Cited by Booth, Pedo-ex. ch. 7, ref 2. Also, Chase's Design of Baptism, p. 53. Bing. Antiq., B. IV., ch. 3, sec. 11.*

DR. WALL, the able historian and defender of infant baptism, makes the following statement respecting the case of Novatian :

"Anno Domini 251 Novatian was, by one part of the clergy and people of Rome, chosen Bishop of that Church, in opposition to Cornelius, who had before been chosen by the major part, and was already ordained. Cornelius does, in a letter to Fabius, Bishop of Antioch, vindicate his right, showing that Novatian came not canonically to his orders of priesthood, much less was capable of being chosen Bishop; for that all the clergy, and a great many of the laity, were against his being ordained presbyter; because it was not lawful, they said, for one that had been baptized in his bed in time of sickness, as he had been, to be admitted to any order of the clergy."—*Euseb. Eccl. Hist., B. VI., ch. 43. Wall's Hist. Inf. Bap., p. II., ch. 9, p. 463.*

It is evident that such a substitute for baptism was, at the time, generally considered as unscriptural and improper. But, having been introduced, and by some accepted, from that time the practice of affusion or aspersion was resorted to in cases of sickness; hence, denominated "clinic baptism," from *clina*, a couch or bed, on which it was received.

BISHOP TAYLOR says:

"It was a formal and solemn question made by Magnus to Cyprian whether they are to be esteemed right Christians, who are only sprinkled with water, and not washed or dipped."—*Duct. Dubit., B. III., ch. 4, r. 15.*

DR. TOWERSON says:

"The first mention we find of aspersion in the baptism of the elder sort, was in the case of the *Clinici*, or men who received baptism upon their sick beds."—*Sacra. Bap., p. III., p. 59.*

VENEMA says:

"Sprinkling was used in the last moments of life, on such as were called *Clinics*."—*Eccl. Hist., Vol. IV., ch. 4, sec 110.*

SALMASIUS says:

"The Clinics only, because they were confined to their beds, were baptized in a manner of which they were capable; thus Novatian, when sick, received baptism, being *besprinkled*, not *baptized*."—*De Vita Martini, ch. 15. Cited by Witsius, B. IV., ch. 16, sec. 13.*

GROTIUS says:

"The custom of pouring or sprinkling seems to have prevailed in favor of those that were dangerously ill, and were desirous of giving up themselves to Christ, whom others called *Clinics.*"—*Comment on Matt. 3. 6.*

SPRINKLING PREVAILED.

IN the Roman Church pouring for baptism was tolerated in the eighth century, and in the sixteenth century generally adopted as a matter of convenience, that hierarchy presumptuously arrogating the right to change ordinances.

DR. WALL says :

"France seems to have been the first country in the world where baptism by affusion was used ordinarily to persons in health, and in the public way of administering it."—*Hist. Inf. Bap., p. II., ch. 9, p. 470.*

The same learned author states that Calvin prepared for the Genevan Church, and afterward published to the world, "a form of administering the sacraments," in respect to which he adds, "for an office, or liturgy of any Church, this is, I believe, the first in the world that prescribes *aspersion* absolutely."—*Hist. Inf. Bap. See above.*

DR. WALL adds :

"And for sprinkling, properly called, it seems it was, at A.D. 1645, just then beginning, and used by very few." "But sprinkling for the common use of baptizing was really introduced (in France first, and then in other popish countries) in times of popery."—*Hist. Inf. Bap., p. II., ch. 9, p. 470.*

Of England, he says :

"The offices and liturgies did all along enjoin *dipping*, without any mention of pouring or sprinkling." About 1550, however, aspersion began to prevail, being used first in the case of "weak children," and "within the space of half a century, from 1550 to 1600, prevailed to be the more general." The English Churches finally came to imitate the Genevan, and casting off the dominion of the pope, bowed to the authority of Calvin, and adopted pouring in the place of dipping.—*Wall's Hist. Inf. Bap., p. II., ch. 9, pp. 463-475.*

THE ASSEMBLY OF DIVINES, in Convocation in 1643, voted by one majority, mainly through the influence of Dr. Lightfoot, probably the most influential member of the Assembly, against baptizing by immersion, and the year following Parliament sanctioned their decision, and decreed that sprinkling should be the legal mode of administering baptism. Both immersion and sprinkling had been in common use. This action ruled out immersion and made sprinkling sufficient. The following is the form finally decided and fixed by the Assembly for the minister to use in baptism:

" He is to baptize the child with water, which, for the manner of doing, is not only lawful, but also sufficient and most expedient to be by pouring or sprinkling water on the face of the child without any other ceremony."—*Pittman and Lightfoot's Works, Vol. XIII., p. 300. Cited in Debates of Camp. and Rice, pp. 241-2.*

THE EDINBURGH ENCYCLOPEDIA gives the following account of the rise of sprinkling :

"The first law to sanction aspersion as a mode of baptism was by Pope Stephen II., A. D. 753. But it was not till the year 1311 that a Council held at Ravenna declared immersion or sprinkling to be indifferent. In this country

(Scotland), however, sprinkling was never practiced in ordinary cases till after the Reformation; and in England, even in the reign of Edward VI. (about 1550), immersion was commonly observed."—*Article Baptism.*

But during the reign of the Catholic Mary, who succeeded to the throne on the death of Edward VI., 1553, persecution drove many of the Protestants from their homes, not a few of whom, especially the Scotch, found an asylum in Geneva, where, under the influence of John Calvin, they imbibed a preference for sprinkling.—*Edinb. Ency., Art. Baptism.*

"These Scottish exiles," says the last-quoted authority, "who had renounced the authority of the pope, implicitly acknowledged the authority of Calvin; and returning to their own country, with John Knox at their head, in 1559 established sprinkling in Scotland. From Scotland, this practice made its way into England in the reign of Elizabeth, but was not authorized by the established Church."

It was not authorized in England until, as above stated, the action of the Westminster Assembly in 1643, and confirmed by Parliament in 1644.

THE ENCYCLOPÆDIA BRITANNICA states the case, much to the same effect, as follows :

"What principally tended to confirm the practice of affusion or sprinkling, was that several of our Protestant divines, flying into Germany and Switzerland during the bloody reign of Queen Mary, and coming home when Queen Elizabeth came to the crown, brought back with them a great zeal for the Protestant churches beyond the sea, where they had been received and sheltered. And having observed that at

Geneva, and some other places, baptism was administered by sprinkling, they thought they could not do the Church of England a greater service than by introducing a practice dictated by so great an oracle as Calvin."—*Ency. Britan., Article Baptism.*

Thus we have given, briefly, but accurately, the rise, progress, and final prevalence of this perversion—the substitution of sprinkling for immersion, in the administration of Christian baptism.

CHAPTER 16

THE LORD'S SUPPER

THE Lord's Supper in its institution, and also as to its symbolic import, as well as in its relation to Christian life and doctrine, has already been considered. It would be useless, in this place, to attempt a history of the rite, especially a detail of the perversions of its uses, the bitter controversies concerning it, or the false claims set up for its sacramental efficacy in working grace in its subjects.

The one question with which we are now concerned is a purely denominational one, having reference to the proper subjects of the ordinance, and the spiritual and ritual qualifications of those who partake of it. Also as to the proper and rightful authority of the Church in restricting its use, and judging of the qualifications of the participants.

EUCHARISTIC PROPOSITIONS

The following propositions may be stated :

PROP. 1.—The Gospel calls on all men, everywhere, to repent and believe on the Lord Jesus Christ unto salvation. This is the first act of submission to divine authority required of men.

PROP. 2.—Such as have exercised saving faith in

Christ, and are thus born of the Spirit, are commanded to be baptized, as a declaration of that change, and a profession of the inward washing of regeneration, which has transpired in them. And no one is required to be, or properly can be, baptized till he has believed.

PROP. 3.—All persons, having savingly believed on Christ, and having been baptized into His name on a profession of that faith, are expected, and required, to unite themselves thereby with the company of disciples as members, in fellowship with a Church which is Christ's visible body. And no one can properly become a member of a Church till he has believed and been baptized.

PROP. 4.—It becomes the privilege and the duty of all who have thus been regenerated by the Spirit, baptized on a profession of faith, and are walking in fellowship with the Church, to celebrate the death of Christ in the Supper. Moreover, it is the duty of all who believe they love the Lord to be baptized, and unite with His Church, in order that they may obey His command, " This do in remembrance of me." No true disciple should neglect it.

PROP. 5.—It becomes the imperative duty of the churches, to whom the ordinances are committed, to see to it, as faithful guardians of so sacred a trust, that these regulations be faithfully observed, according to the will of the Master, by all who are members, and by all who desire to become members with them.

PROP. 6.—The pastor, as " the chief executive officer" of the Church, acts as its representative under instructions in his sphere of service. But it is not his prerogative to determine who shall be baptized into its fellowship, or who shall enjoy its privileges, including a right to the Supper. The right and responsibility of deciding those questions belong to the Church itself, and not to its officers.

PROP. 7.—The pastor, in the exercise of his Christian liberty, is not under obligation to baptize any, though the Church may approve, unless he believes they are fit and suitable subjects. Nor can he baptize any into the fellowship of the Church without its consent.

I. OPEN AND CLOSE COMMUNION

The difference between Baptists and other Christian denominations on this question has principal reference to what is usually known as *open* and *close communion*. These terms do not very accurately define the distinction, but they are in common use in popular discussions on the subject, and are quite well understood.

Open, free, or mixed communion, is, strictly speaking, that which permits any one who desires, and believes himself qualified, to come to the Lord's table, without any questions being asked, or conditions imposed, by the Church where the communion is observed. But ordinarily the term *open communion* is applied to the practice of the greater part of Pedobaptist churches, in which they permit and invite, not *all* persons, but the members of other evangelical churches to their Communion, whatever may be their views of doctrine, or Church order, in other respects.

Close, strict, or restricted communion is properly that which does not invite all, indiscriminately, who may choose to come to the Lord's table, but restricts the invitation to a particular class. But ordinarily the term *close communion* is applied to the practice of Baptist churches, which invite to it only baptized believers, walking in orderly fellowship in their own churches. And by baptized believers, they mean, of course, *immersed* believers; since they hold that nothing but immersion is baptism.

Nearly all Baptists in the United States, and a large part of those in foreign lands, are *strict* communion in practice, as are also a few smaller denominations; while the Latin, Greek, and Oriental churches, and the greater part of Protestant churches practise *free* communion. Which are right? Let us compare them by the infallible standard.

II.   THE OPEN COMMUNION VIEW

Those who favor and practice *open* or *free* communion justify their course by various and somewhat divergent reasons. The following constitute, in the main, the arguments they use:

1.   *Sprinkling Held to be Baptism*

The *first* class of *open-communionists* are those who hold that none but baptized persons should be invited to the Lord's table, and that the Church is the rightful judge of the fitness of persons to be received to its privileges; yet they assert that *sprinkling* is lawful baptism, and that persons sprinkled only, and not immersed, should, therefore, be admitted to the Supper. This Baptists deny, and have, as they believe, proven the contrary—that sprinkling is not scriptural baptism.

2. *Baptism not Prerequisite*

The *second* class of *open-communionists* assert that the ordinances sustain no necessary relation to each other; that baptism can claim no priority over the Supper, and, therefore, it is not a condition, nor prerequisite to it. Consequently, unbaptized persons, if believers—for they do make *faith* a condition— may partake of the Supper as lawfully as baptized persons. Therefore immersion or sprinkling, either or neither, is equally indifferent. This theory virtually denies the memorial and symbolic character of the ordinance, and regards it chiefly as a sign and service of Christian fellowship. This course of argument, however plausible, is rejected and condemned by the great body of Christians the world over, both Baptist and Pedobaptists.

3. *The Church is not to Judge*

The *third* class of *open-communionists* are those who claim that the privilege of the Supper is based on no ground of prescribed conditions, on no ritual preparation, but entirely upon one's own sense of fitness and duty That the Church has no right of judgment in the case, and no responsibility concerning it, but is simply to " set the table," and leave it to each and all to take or to refrain; whoever wishes, and judges himself fit, may eat and drink in that holy service without hindrance or question.

To this attitude as to the ordinances, and to this mode of reasoning, Baptists strenuously object; as do the great majority of Pedobaptists themselves It is not only the right, but the duty of each Church to guard the sacred trusts committed to it, and to judge whether candidates for its privileges are, or are not, scripturally qualified to receive them. Each Church must be its own interpreter of truth and duty. It would be absurd to claim that the convictions of an individual must be the authoritative standard by which the body is bound to act.

If the judgment of the Church must yield to the convictions of individuals in one thing, it may in all, and then all order, government, and discipline would be prostrated before an anarchy of conflicting personal opinions. If the privilege of the Supper becomes common, all others may be, since this is the highest and most sacred of all. It would be a criminal indifference to the Master of the household to allow the safeguards with which He has surrounded the sanctity of His institutions to be broken down.

III.   THE BAPTIST VIEW

The following will express with general accuracy the view held by Baptists as to the conditions of the communion, and the qualifications of the communicants.

1. Baptists hold that there are *three* scriptural conditions to the privileges of the Lord's Supper, which are imperative on the part of the Church to be observed:

a. Regeneration; being born of the Spirit, and thus becoming a new creature in Christ Jesus. Without this, no one can be a member of His spiritual body, or can rightfully be a member of His visible body, the Church.

b. Baptism; being buried with Christ in water, on a profession of faith in Him. This act must precede Church membership, and of course Church privileges, including the Supper.

c. Godliness; an upright Christian life, orderly walk, and godly conversation as a Church member. For though one may have been truly converted, and rightly baptized, if he be a disorderly walker, violating his covenant obligations, living in sin, and openly disobeying his Lord, he has no claim on the Lord's Table.

2. Baptists claim that the Communion, strictly speaking, is a Church ordinance to be observed by churches only. That it cannot be administered, or received by those outside the Church; that members, in their individual capacity, cannot administer or receive it. Nor can the Church authorize individuals to administer, or receive it. The body must act in its organic character in the use of it; and persons must be within the Church, legitimately to enjoy it.

3. Baptists insist that they neither may, nor ought to, invite to the Supper any except persons converted, baptized, and walking orderly according to gospel rule. They believe the Church is bound to judge of the fitness of those admitted to its ordinances as well as those admitted to its membership. To invite, or permit persons to receive the Communion without conditions, is to allow the vile and the profane, the carnal and the impure, to mingle with God's spiritual people, and eat and drink, unworthily, the symbolic flesh and blood of Christ. For, if the rule be allowed, to this extent will the abuse be sure to go.

4. Baptists are firmly convinced, that, to maintain the purity and spirituality of the churches, it is absolutely needful to restrict the Communion to regenerated persons, baptized on a profession of faith, and walking orderly Christian lives in Church fellowship. To adopt any other rule, or allow any larger liberty, would break down the distinction between the Church and the world; would bring in a carnal and unconverted membership, with which to overshadow the spiritual, and control the household of faith; would virtually transfer the Communion from the house of God to the temple of Belial. To keep the churches pure, the ordinances must be kept pure and unperverted, both as to their substance and their form.

5. Baptists give the following reasons in justification of their course in the following cases :

a. They do not invite Pedobaptists to their Communion, because they do not regard such persons as baptized; they having been only sprinkled. The fact that they think themselves baptized, does not make it so. If they desire to commune, let them be baptized according to Christ's command.

b. They do not accept invitations from Pedobaptists to commune with them, for the same reason; they do not consider them baptized Christians. Therefore their churches are irregular churches according to the New Testament standard, both in the misuse of the ordinances, and in the admission of infant Church membership. Therefore to commune with them would be disorderly walking, and would encourage them in disorderly walking, by upholding a perversion of the ordinances.

c. They do not invite the immersed members of Pedobaptist churches to their Communion, because, though such persons may be truly converted and properly baptized, they are walking disorderly as disciples, by remaining in churches which hold and practise serious errors as to the ordinances, as such persons themselves judge. These churches use sprinkling for baptism, and administer the ordinance to infants; both of which are contrary to Scripture, as such persons themselves allow. And yet, by remaining in these churches, they give their countenance and support to uphold and perpetuate what they confess to be errors, and thus help to impose on others what they will not accept for themselves. This is not an orderly and consistent course for Christians to pursue.

IV.   BAPTISM IS PREREQUISITE

If the Supper was intended to be limited to those converted, baptized, and brought into the fellowship of the churches, it may be asked, Why was not this fact made plain and explicitly stated in some command or precept of Christ or His Apostles? Why was not this command as positively given as that which enjoined baptism? The reply must be, It was plainly and explicitly enjoined. The *form* of the ordinance was exhibited when instituted by Jesus; the *command* enjoining its observance was, "This do, in remembrance of me;" the qualified *subjects* were those before Him; baptized believers.

But note the following considerations.

1. The example of our Saviour at the institution of the Supper. Whom did He invite to partake of the symbols of His body and blood? Not an indiscriminate company; not all who deemed themselves fit, and chose to come; not all of His professed disciples even. But a small and very select company, who had received John's baptism, or His own, not even including His own mother, brethren, and other family connections. That first Communion service, at the close of or during the paschal supper, was a very restricted one. Certainly no unbaptized persons were present in that upper chamber to receive the elements.

2. The language of Christ in the Great Commission, and other similar forms of speech, if not conclusive proof, are very little short of it, in favor of

the necessary priority of baptism to the Supper. He commanded to *teach* all nations, *baptizing* them; His promise is to those who *believe* and are *baptized*. This order is uniform; *teaching*, *believing*, *baptizing*. Where does the Supper come in? Baptists say, after the teaching, believing, baptizing, and thus being "added to the Church." There is no room for it before. But if it comes before—then *where* before? Before the teaching, and before the believing? Why not? If the divine order is to be changed, then why not have the Supper come before the teaching and believing, and be given, as Pedobaptists give baptism, to infants incapable of either instruction or faith. Infant communion, as practised from the third to the ninth century by the Latin Church, and still practised by the Greek Church, is equally scriptural with infant baptism, as now practised by all Pedobaptists, whether Catholics or Protestants. Nor would infant communion after baptism be any more inconsistent than adult communion before baptism.

3. The New Testament history affords no instance which can be supposed to favor the theory of communion without baptism. But abundant evidence is furnished, in facts and circumstances mentioned, to show that all communicants were baptized persons. Apostolic instruction, with reference to the Supper and reproofs administered for an abuse of that sacred ordinance, all are addressed to churches and Church members. Those who *believed*, and gladly *received the Word*, were *baptized*, then

added to the Church; then they continued *steadfast* in the Apostles' *doctrine*, and in the *breaking of bread*, and of *prayer*.

4. The almost unvarying testimony of Christian history through all its ages should be accepted as important evidence in this case. Both Catholics and Protestants, Baptists and Pedobaptists, with singular unanimity, declare baptism to be *prerequisite* to the Communion.

JUSTIN MARTYR, one of the early Christian Fathers, about A. D. 140, says of the Supper:

"This food is called by us the Eucharist, of which it is not lawful for any one to partake, but such as believe the things taught by us to be true, and have been baptized."— *Apol. I. C., 65, 66. See Schaff's Ch. Hist., II., 516.*

MOSHEIM, in his Church History, says:

"Neither those doing penance, nor those not yet baptized, were allowed to be present at the celebration of this ordinance." "The sacred mystery of the service was deemed so great as to exclude the unbaptized from the place."—*Eccl. Hist., Cent. II., part II., chap. 4, sec. 3.*

NEANDER, the great Church historian, says:

"At this celebration, as may be easily concluded, no one could be present who was not a member of the Christian Church, and incorporated into it by the rite of baptism."— *Ch. Hist., Vol. I., p. 327.*

CAVE, one of the most reliable writers on Christian antiquities, says the communicants in the primitive Church were those

"That had embraced the doctrine of the Gospel, and had

been baptized into the faith of Christ. For, looking upon the Lord's Supper as the highest and most solemn act of religion, they thought they could never take care enough in dispensing it."—*Prim. Christ., ch. 11, p. 333.*

BINGHAM, in his able work on the antiquities of the Christian Church, says of the early Christians:

" As soon as a man was baptized he was communicated," that is, admitted to the Communion. Baptism, therefore, preceded the Supper.—*Christ. Antiq., B. XII., ch. 4, sec. 9; B. XV., ch. 3.*

WALL, who searched the records of antiquity for facts illustrating the history of the ordinances, says:

" No Church ever gave the Communion to any before they were baptized. Among all the absurdities that were ever held, none ever maintained that any person should partake of the Communion before he was baptized."—*Hist. Inf. Bap., part II., ch. 9.*

DODDRIDGE says:

" It is certain that, so far as our knowledge of primitive antiquity reaches, no unbaptized person received the Lord's Supper."—*Lectures, pp. 511, 512.*

BAXTER says:

" What man dares go in a way which hath neither precept nor example to warrant it, from a way that hath full consent of both? Yet they that will admit members into the visible Church without baptism do so."—*Plain Scrip. Proof, 24.*

DICK says:

" An uncircumcised man was not permitted to eat the passover; and an unbaptized man should not be permitted to partake of the Eucharist."—*Theol., Vol. II., p. 220.*

DWIGHT says:

"It is an indispensable qualification for this ordinance, that the candidate for communion be a member of the visible Church, in full standing. By this I intend that he should be a man of piety; that he should have made a public profession of religion, and that he should have been baptized."
—*Syst. Theol. Ser. 160, B. VIII., ch. 4, sec. 7.*

SCHAFF says:

"The Communion was a regular part, and, in fact, the most important and solemn part of the Sunday worship, . . . in which none but full members of the Church could engage."
—*Ch. Hist., Vol. I., p. 392. N. Y., 1871.*

COLEMAN says:

"None, indeed, but believers, in full communion with the Church, were permitted to be present." "But agreeably to all the laws and customs of the Church, baptism constituted membership with the Church. All baptized persons were legitimately numbered among the communicants as members of the Church."—*Ancient Christ. Ex., ch. 21, sec. 8.*

These witnesses to our position, not being Baptists, may command the more regard from those who do not agree with us. Other similar testimonies need not be cited.

V.   ONE AND THE SAME RULE

Here observe, that Baptists and Pedobaptists have one and the same rule as to the conditions of the Communion, viz.: they all hold baptism to be prerequisite, and that unbaptized persons have no lawful right to it.

For though there may be a few ministers, and possibly a few churches, that would invite anybody and everybody, yet such a course would be contrary to the standards, and opposed to the usages of their churches generally. They all practise a restricted or *close* communion, since they restrict the privilige to *baptized believers*. But inasmuch as they hold that *sprinkling* as well as *immersion* is baptism, their communion is more *open*, and that of Baptists is more *close*, by the difference between their views of baptism and ours, and by that difference only. Therefore the question in debate is one, after all, not of communion, but of baptism. Let them *prove* that sprinkling *is* baptism, or *admit* that it is *not*, and the communion controversy will cease.

DR. GRIFFIN, one of the fathers of New England Congregationalism, said:

"I agree with the advocates of close communion in *two* points: 1. That baptism is the initiatory ordinance which introduces us into the visible Church—of course, where there is no baptism there are no visible churches. 2. That we ought not to commune with those who are not baptized, and of course not Church members, even if we regard them as Christians."—*Letter on Baptism, 1829. See Curtis on Com., p. 125.*

BISHOP COXE, of the Episcopal Diocese of Western New York, says:

" The Baptists hold that we have never been baptized, and they must exclude us from their communion table, if we were disposed to go there. Are we offended? No; we call it *principle*, and we respect it. To say that we have never become members of Christ by baptism seems severe, but it is conscientious adherence to duty, as they regard it. I should be the bigot, and not they, if I should ask them to violate their discipline in this or in any other particular."—*On Christ, Unity, in Church Union, July, 1891.*

DR. HIBBARD, a leading Methodist scholar and divine, says:

"In one principle Baptist and Pedobaptist churches agree. They both agree in rejecting from communion at the table of the Lord, and in denying the rights of Church fellowship to all who have not been baptized;" and with admirable frankness he adds: "The charge of *close communion* is no more applicable to the Baptists than to us [Pedobaptists], insomuch as the question of Church fellowship with them is determined by as liberal principles as it is with any other Protestant churches—so far, I mean, as the present subject is concerned: *i. e., it is determined by valid baptism.*"—*Hibbard on Christ. Bap., p. II., p. 174.*

DR. BULLOCK, another Methodist divine, says:

"Close communion, as it is generally termed, is the only logical and consistent course for Baptist churches to pursue. If their premises are right, their conclusion is surely just as it should be." And he commends the firmness of Baptists in not inviting to the communion those whom they regard as unbaptized. He says: "They do not feel willing to countenance such laxity in Christian discipline. Let us honor them for their steadfastness in maintaining what they believe to be a Bible precept, rather than criticise and censure because they differ with us concerning the intent and mode of Christian baptism, and believe it to be an irrepealable condition of coming to the Lord's table."—*What Christians Believe.*

THE INDEPENDENT, the most widely circulated

and perhaps the most influential Pedobaptist paper in the country, in an editorial, says:

"Leading writers of all denominations declare that converts must be baptized before they can be invited to the communion table. This is the position generally taken. But Baptists regarding sprinkling as a nullity—no baptism at all —look upon Presbyterians, Methodists and others as unbaptized persons." "The other churches cannot urge the Baptists to become open communicants till they themselves take the position that all who love our Lord Jesus Christ, the unbaptized as well as the baptized, may be invited to the communion table."—*Editorial, July, 1879.*

THE CONGREGATIONALIST, the organ of the New England Congregational Churches, in an editorial, says:

"Congregationalists have uniformly, until here and there an exception has arisen of late years, required baptism and Church membership as the prerequisite of a seat at the table of the Lord. It is a part of the false 'liberality' which now prevails in certain quarters, to welcome everybody 'who thinks he loves Christ' to commune in His body and blood. Such a course is the first step in breaking down that distinction between the Church and the world which our Saviour emphasized; and it seems to us it is an unwise and mistaken act for which no Scripture warrant exists."—*Editorial, July 9, 1879.*

THE OBSERVER of New York, the oldest and leading Presbyterian journal of this country, said:

"It is not a want of charity which compels the Baptist to restrict his invitation. He has no hesitation in admitting the personal piety of his unimmersed brethren. Presbyterians do not invite the unbaptized, however pious they may be. It is not uncharitable. It is not bigotry on the part of Baptists to confine their communion to those whom they consider the baptized."

THE INTERIOR of Chicago, organ of the Western Presbyterians, said :

"The difference between our Baptist brethren and ourselves is an important difference. We agree with them, however, in saying that unbaptized persons should not partake of the Lord's Supper. Their views compel them to think that we are not baptized, and shuts them up to close Communion. Close Communion is, in our judgment, a more defensible position than open Communion, which is justified on the ground that baptism is not a prerequisite to the Lord's Supper. To chide Baptists with bigotry, because they abide by the logical consequences of their system, is absurd."

THE EPISCOPAL RECORDER said :

"The close Communion of the Baptist Church is but the necessary sequence of the fundamental idea out of which their existence has grown. No Christian Church would willingly receive to its Communion even the humblest and truest believer in Christ who had not been baptized. With the Baptist, immersion, only, is baptism, and he therefore, of necessity, excludes from the Lord's table all who have not been immersed. It is an essential part of the system—the legitimate carrying out of this creed."

THE CHRISTIAN ADVOCATE of New York, said :

"The regular Baptist churches in the United States may be considered to-day as practically a unit on three points : the non-use of infant baptism, the immersion of believers only upon profession of faith, and the administration of the holy Communion to such only as have been immersed by ministers holding these views. In our opinion the Baptist

Church owes its *amazing prosperity* largely to its adherence to these views. In doctrine and government, in other respects, it is the same as the Congregationalists. In numbers the regular Baptists are more than six times as great as the Congregationalists. It is not bigotry to adhere to one's convictions, provided the spirit of Christian love prevails."

Many other similar concessions from candid Christian men, who differ from us, might be adduced, but are unnecessary.

Thus, leading Pedobaptists themselves sustain the position of Baptists, so far as the principle is concerned on which close communion is based. They hold, as we do, that unbaptized persons should not be invited to the Lord's table; and that it is a false liberalism which would admit everybody there, and thus obliterate the distinction between the Church and the world, in this the most sacred service of religion. Of course, they hold that sprinkling is baptism, and therefore, that sprinkled persons have a right to the Communion.

VI. THE SYMBOLISM OF THE ORDINANCES

The *design* of Baptism was to show the death of Christ for our offenses, and His resurrection for our justification. Thus, in the two acts, the *immersion* signifies *burial*, and the *emersion* signifies *resurrection*. In baptism the believer professes his death to sin, his burial with Christ, and his resurrection to newness of life in Him—Rom. 6 : 4; Col. 2 : 12 ; the coming forth from the baptismal wave, therefore, proclaims a new spiritual life in Christ begun.

The *design* of the Supper is to show that this new spiritual life, thus begun, is to be nourished and maintained by feeding on Christ. Eating and drinking indicate sustenance and support. They show the saint's dependence on Christ, who is the bread of God, and the abundant supply of grace represented by the loaf and the cup.

Now, as life must begin before it can be nourished, so baptism, which symbolizes its beginning, comes before the Supper, which symbolizes its nourishment and support. Thus it was in the apostolic age. They *believed* and were *baptized;* then they were *added to the Church;* then they continued in the Apostles' *doctrine* and *fellowship*, and in *breaking of bread*, and of *prayers*.—Acts 2 : 41 42.

VII. BUT ONE ARGUMENT

Open communion has but one argument to sustain it, viz., *sympathy;* that, with some kindly minds, outweighs all others. It has neither Scripture, logic, expediency, nor the concurrent practice of Christendom, either past or present, in its favor. But to some it seems kind and brotherly to invite all who say they love our Lord Jesus Christ, to unite in commemorating His death at the Supper. And to exclude any, or fail to invite all, seems to those sentimental natures harsh, cold, and unchristian. To them, the Supper is rather a love-feast for Christian fellowship than a personal commemoration of Christ's love by those who have believed upon His name, and been baptized into the likeness of His death. But sympathy should not control in matters of faith, and in acts of conscience.

VIII.   OBJECTIONS ANSWERED

1. It is sometimes objected that we make too much of baptism; that we make it a saving ordinance; that it is not essential to salvation.

We reply: That baptism is not essential to salvation; but it is essential to obedience, since Christ has commanded it; and no one has a right to be called His disciple, who, knowing His command, deliberately refuses to obey.

2. Our Pedobaptist friends say they invite us to their Communion, why should we not in like manner invite them?

We answer: They can well afford to invite us, since they acknowledge that our baptism is valid and scriptural; but we do not acknowledge theirs to be either scriptural or valid.

3. Again, they say: It is the Lord's table, and we should not exclude any of the Lord's people.

To this we reply: It is the Lord's table, and not ours; therefore we have no right to invite any but such as the Lord has designated. If it were our table we could invite whomsoever we would. As it is, we must obey the Lord at His own table.

4. They also ask: If the Lord has received us, why should not you?

We reply: The Lord has received you to a spiritual fellowship; so do we. But the Lord has not received you to His visible ordinances unless you have obeyed His direction. He receives pardoned souls to His spiritual Communion, but not to the outward Communion of His Church, till they have obeyed Him in baptism.

5. But they say: We hope that all will commune in heaven together; why then should we not on earth?

This objection is based on the assumption that all who will commune together in heaven should come to the Lord's Supper here. But this is fallacious. There will be no baptism or Supper in heaven. There the communion will be spiritual, and in spiritual communion all of God's people do unite now. But Pedobaptists do not themselves invite to the Lord's table all they hope to meet in heaven, children, and many other unprofessed and unknown, but true, disciples. Christ has given His churches laws and ordinances for their earthly state, none of which will be needed in the heavenly state.

6. And when they say that they do not object to our *baptism*, but they do to our *close communion*, we reply, as has been shown, that the difficulty is not with the communion really at all, but altogether with the baptism. And in order to remove the difficulty, they must either show that sprinkling is true scriptural baptism, or else that unbaptized persons may properly be invited to the Lord's Supper.

7. In one respect, Pedobaptists are more close in their Communion than Baptists, viz., in that they

exclude a large class of their own members from the Lord's table; that is, baptized infants. Baptists do not exclude their own members against whom no charge is made. If unconscious infants can receive baptism on the faith of sponsors, they are certainly competent to receive the Supper in like manner, as they did in the earlier ages, after the introduction of infant baptism, from the third to the ninth century, according to Church historians, and as is still the practice of the Greek Church. Both are alike contrary to reason and the Scriptures.

DR. COLEMAN says :

" After the general introduction of infant baptism, in the *second and third centuries*, the sacrament continued to be administered to all who had been baptized, whether infants or adults. The reason alleged by Cyprian and others for this practice was, that age was no impediment. Augustine strongly advocates the practice. The custom continued for several centuries. It is mentioned in the third Council of Tours, A. D. 813; and even the Council of Trent, A. D. 1545, only decreed that it should not be considered essential to salvation. It is still scrupulously observed by the Greek Church."—*Anc. Christ. Exemp.*, *ch. 22, sec. 8; Bing. Orig., B. XV., ch. 4, sec. 7; Cave, 335-349; Giesseler, Vol. II., p. 332. Many other writers bear the same testimony.*

CHAPTER 17

INFANT BAPTISM

THE baptism of unconverted children and unconscious infants has become common through the Christian world. The Romish Church, the Greek Church, and most of the Protestant churches practise it. Yet Baptists condemn it as unscriptural, unreasonable and pernicious. They believe that *repentance* and *faith* should always *precede* baptism. Without these baptism has no significancy, and serves no religious purpose. Whenever these gracious exercises have been experienced, whether in young or old, the subject may be admitted to the holy ordinance of baptism. But never till he has *believed*. Infants incapable of faith are, therefore, unfit for baptism.

Manifest Propositions

Baptists make and defend the following propositions respecting this practice:

PROP. I.—That there is in the New Testament neither precept nor example found to authorize or sanction infant baptism. Nor, indeed, is there even an allusion to it in the Scriptures—very naturally, because it did not exist when the New Testament was written.

PROP. 2.—That Christ did not institute it, nor did either the Apostles or early Christians practise it.

PROP. 3.—That it arose with, and was a part of, the corruption which in subsequent ages crept into the churches, having its origin in the belief of a sacramental efficacy possessed, and a saving power exerted, by baptism on the soul of the child.

PROP. 4.—That the practice is unauthorized, presumptuous and censurable on the part of parents, sponsors and administrators, and productive of evil both to the child that receives it and the Church that allows and practises it.

PROP. 5.—That it perverts the design and falsifies the profession of the Church as the spiritual body of Christ by introducing to its membership a carnal element of unconverted persons.

PROP. 6.—That it originated with the unscriptural dogma of baptismal regeneration, so it must still be held by its advocates to have some saving or sanctifying power on the child, or else it can have no significancy, and be of no avail.

If these statements be true—and their truth will be shown—how can the custom be defended and continued by intelligent Christians?

I. NOT OF SCRIPTURAL AUTHORITY

Nearly all the learned and scholarly supporters of infant baptism have, with commendable candor admitted that it was not instituted by Christ, nor practised either by His Apostles or their immediate successors.

DR. WALL, of the English Church, who wrote a History of Infant Baptism, a work so thorough and able that the clergy, assembled in convocation, gave him a vote of thanks for his learned defence of this custom, nevertheless says:

" Among all the persons that are recorded as baptized by the Apostles, there is no express mention of infants."—*Hist. Inf. Bap., Introd., pp. 1, 55.*

FULLER, the historian, says:

" We do freely confess there is neither express precept nor precedent in the New Testament for the baptizing of infants." —*Infant's Advoc., pp. 71, 150.*

BISHOP BURNETT says:

" There is no express precept or rule given in the New Testament for the baptism of infants."—*Expos. 39 Articles, 27 Art.*

BAXTER says:

" I conclude that all examples of baptism in Scripture do mention only the administration of it to the professors of saving faith; and the precepts give us no other direction."— *Disput. of Right to the Sacra., p. 156.*

PROF. LINDNER says:

"Christian baptism can be given only to adults, not to infants. The Holy Spirit, which is given only to believers, was a prerequisite to baptism."—*On Lord's Supper, p. 123.*

GOODWIN says:

" Baptism supposeth regeneration sure in itself first. Sacraments are never administered to begin or to work grace. You suppose children to *believe* before you baptize them. Read all the Acts: still it is said, ' They *believed*, and were baptized.' "—*Works, Vol. I., part I., p. 200.*

CELLARIUS says:

" Infant baptism is neither commanded in the sacred Scriptures, nor is it confirmed by apostolic examples."—*Shyn Hist. Mennonites, p. 168.*

LIMBORCH says:

" There is no instance can be produced from which it may indisputably be inferred that any child was baptized by the Apostles."—*Comp. Syst. Divin., B. V., ch. 22, sec. 2.*

FIELD says:

" The baptism of infants is, therefore, named a *tradition*, because it is not expressly delivered in Scripture that the Apostles did baptize infants; nor any express precept found there that they should do so."—*On the Church, p. 375.*

NEANDER says:

" Baptism was administered at first only to *adults*, as men were accustomed to conceive of *baptism* and *faith* as strictly connected. We have all reason for not deriving infant baptism from apostolic institution."—*Ch. Hist. Vol. I., p. 311; Torrey's Trans. Plant. and Train., Vol. I., p. 222.*

OLSHAUSEN says:

" We cannot, in truth, find anywhere a reliable proof-text in favor of infant baptism."—*Comment, Acts 15 : 14, 15.*

HAHN says:

"Neither in the Scriptures, nor during the first *hundred and fifty years*, is a sure example of infant baptism to be found."—*Theology, p. 556.*

ROBERT BARCLAY says:

"As to the baptism of infants, it is a mere human tradition, for which neither precept nor practice is to be found in all the Scriptures."—*Apology, Propo. 12.*

WILLIAM PENN says:

There is "not one text of Scripture to prove that sprinkling in the face was the water baptism, or that children were the subjects of water baptism in the first times."—*Defence of Gospel Truths, p. 82.*

PROF. L. LANGE, of Jena, says:

"All attempts to make out infant baptism from the New Testament fail. It is totally opposed to the spirit of the apostolic age, and to the fundamental principles of the New Testament."—*Inf. Bap., p. 101; Duncan's Hist. Bap., p. 224.*

DR. HAGENBACH says:

"The passages from Scripture cited in favor of infant baptism as a usage of the primitive Church, are doubtful, and prove nothing."—*Hist. Doct., Vol. II., p. 200.*

DR. JACOBS says:

"Notwithstanding all that has been written by learned men upon this subject, it remains indisputable that infant baptism is not mentioned in the New Testament." "There is no trace of it until the last part of the second century."—*Eccl. Polity of the N. T., pp. 270–71.*

PROF. JACOBI says:

Infant baptism was established neither by Christ not by the Apostles."—*Art. Baptism, Kitto's Bib. Cyclop.*

DR. HANNA says:

" Scriptures know nothing of the baptism of infants."— *North Brit. Review, Aug., 1852.*

Observe that none of these authorities cited were Baptists. Many more witnesses from the ranks of Pedobaptist scholars and divines could be adduced to the same effect; but let these suffice.

II. HOUSEHOLD BAPTISMS

Some, however, have supposed that the " household baptisms " mentioned in the New Testament must have included children, and thus constitute a warrant for the baptism of such.

This argument, like the others in its support, is founded on the faintest and most illogical inference. It is inferred that these households certainly had infant children in them, and that such children certainly were baptized ; both of which are wholly gratuitous. There probably are but few Baptist churches in the world, of any considerable standing and numbers, that do not have one or more entire households in their communion, each member of which was baptized on a profession of faith.

1. *Lydia and her Household*

The case of Lydia, baptized at Philippi, mentioned

in Acts, 16th chapter, is especially relied on as a strong case. Now observe, Lydia was a merchant woman, "a seller of purple," from "the city of Thyatira," and was at Philippi, some three hundred miles from home, on business, when she heard Paul preach, was converted, and then "she was baptized, and her household." There is not the least evidence that she had either husband or children. If she had a husband why was *she* so far from home on mercantile business? If she had infant children, they would not likely have been with her on such a journey, so far away, and for such a purpose. Her "household," doubtless, were adults, and employed by her in her business—her company. The most reckless sophism alone could build infant baptism on such a case. A poor cause it must be that relies for support on such evidence as this.

DR. NEANDER says:

"We cannot prove that the Apostles ordained infant baptism: from those places where the baptism of a whole family is mentioned, we can draw no such conclusion."—*Planting and Training, p. 162. Ed. 1865.*

PROF. JACOBI, with reference to these household baptisms, says:

"In none of these instances has it been proved that there were little children among them."—*Kitto's Bib. Cyclo., Art. Bap.*

DR. MEYER says:

"That the baptism of children was not in use at that time appears evident from 1 Cor. 7 : 14."—*Com. on Acts 16 : 15.*

DR. DE WETTE says:

" This passage has been adduced in proof of the apostolical authority of infant baptism; but there is no proof here that any except adults were baptized."—*Com. N. T., Acts 16: 15.*

DR. OLSHAUSEN says:

" Baptism ensued in this case, without doubt, merely upon a profession of faith in Jesus as the Messiah. But for that very reason it is highly improbable that her house should be understood as including infant children." And he adds: " There is altogether wanting any conclusive proof-text for the baptism of children in the age of the Apostles."—*Com. Acts 16: 14, 15, Kend's Trans.*

Most manifestly, all of her household, whether old or young, *believed*, as she herself did, before they were baptized. Of this opinion, also, were *Whitby, Lawson,* the *Assembly of Divines,* and other Pedobaptist authorities.

2. *The Philippian Jailer and his Household*

The case of the Philippian jailer and his household, mentioned, also Acts, 16th chapter, is often referred to as of force by the advocates of this practice.

Now observe that Paul and Silas, being released from their confinement, spoke the word of the Lord to the jailer, " and to all that were in his house." Whether adults or infants, any one can judge; the Gospel was preached to them. And the jailer " was baptized, he and all his, straightway." Then " he rejoiced, *believing* in God, with all his house." Observe, the jailer's family was baptized; but first, they listened to the preaching of the Word, then they believed in God; and then they rejoiced in their new-found hope. Who believes that such a record as this could ever have been made of unconscious infants? There is not the remotest allusion to children, and the narrative does not fit them at all. Those who were baptized were those who believed and who rejoiced. It was therefore " believers' baptism," beyond which fact the particular age of the subjects is of no consequence whatever.

BLOOMFIELD says:

" It is taken for granted that his family became Christians, as well as himself."—*Com. on Acts 16:31. Greek N. Test.*

Such is the faith of Baptists, and such the command of Christ : " Believe and be baptized." Calvin, Doddridge, Henry, and other Pedobaptist scholars, declare that in this case they all *believed*, and therefore were baptized.

3. *The Household of Stephanas*

Paul speaks, in 1 Corinthians, 1st chapter, of having baptized " the household of Stephanas." This is also quoted as giving some support to the infant baptismal theory. The course of argument, or inference, is the same. It is supposed that the household contained children, and that these children were baptized. How entirely gratuitous! Households are constantly being baptized and admitted to the fellowship of our churches, but without infants in them. Doddridge, Guise, Hammond, Macknight, and others, consider this case as giving no countenance to the custom of baptizing infants.

This same family of Stephanas, Paul, in 1 Cor., 16th chapter, says were "the first fruits of Achaia;" and he adds, "they have addicted themselves to the ministry of the saints." This could not have been spoken of baptized infants, but well describes the Christian activities of adult believers. No infants can be found in the household of Stephanas.

III. RISE OF INFANT BAPTISM

But, it will be asked, if the baptism of unconscious infants and unconverted children was not appointed by Christ, nor practised by his Apostles, nor known in the primitive age, from whence was it, how did it arise, and when did it come into use ?

These questions are readily answered by the testimony of its friends.

TERTULLIAN is the first writer who mentions it in history, and he opposes it.* This was at the close of the second century, or about A.D. 200. His opposition proves two things. *First*, that it was in occasional use, at least. *Second*, that it was of recent origin, and not generally prevalent. For it must

---

* Neander supposes that the much-disputed passage of Irenæus has reference to this custom—a little earlier than *Tertullian's* mention of it. See *Neander's* Ch. Hist. Vol. I., p. 311.

have been in use to be discussed and opposed, and had it been long prevalent, it would have been earlier mentioned.

BINGHAM, with all his scholarship and industry, could find no earlier allusion to it than that of Tertullian, though he believed it to have previously existed. Had there been any earlier historic record he would surely have found it. It must therefore, as is generally admitted, have arisen about the beginning of the third century after Christ.

VENEMA says :

" Nothing can be affirmed with certainty concerning the custom of the Church before Tertullian; seeing there is not anywhere, in more ancient writers, that I know of, undoubted mention of infant baptism."—*Eccl. Hist., Vol. III., ch. 2, secs. 108, 109.*

CURCELLÆUS says:

" The baptism of infants in the *two first* centuries after Christ was altogether unknown, but in the *third* and *fourth* was allowed by some few. In the *fifth* and following ages it was generally received."—*Inst. Christ. Religion, B. I., ch. 12.*

HIPPOLYTUS, bishop of Pontus, writing in the first half of the third century, bears this testimony :

" We, in our days, never defended the baptism of children, which had only begun to be practiced in some regions." —*Hippol. and his Age, Vol. I., p. 184. See Duncan's Hist. Bap., p. 115; Curtis Prog. Bap. Princs., p. 101.*

BUNSEN, the learned translator of *Hippolytus,* declares that infant baptism, in the modern sense,

" was utterly unknown to the early Church, not only down to the end of the second century, but, indeed, to the middle of the third century."—*Hippol. and his Age, Vol. III., p. 180.*

SALMASIUS says:

"In the *first two* centuries no one was baptized except, being instructed in the faith and acquainted with the doctrines of Christ, he was able to profess himself a believer."— *Hist. Bapt. Luicer. Thesaur., Vol. II., p. 1136.*

Such testimony, and from such sources, is quite conclusive. Infant baptism was unknown until the *first* part of the *third* century after Christ. Had it existed earlier, some trace of, or allusion to, it would have been discovered. But the most labored and learned research has failed to make any such discovery.

It should be added that when the baptism of children did begin to be practised, it was not the baptism of unconscious infants at all, but, as Bunsen says, of " little growing children, from six to ten years old." He declares that Tertullian in his opposition to infant baptism does not say a word of new-born infants. Cyprian, an African bishop, at the close of the third century urged the baptism of infants proper, because of the regenerating efficacy which the ordinance was supposed to exert. He and his associates were the first to take this ground. —*Hippol. and his Age, Vol. III., pp. 192-5; Curtis Prog. Bap. Prin., p. 125.*

IV.   FROM WHAT CAUSE DID IT SPRING?

If it be asked from what cause did infant baptism arise, the question is not difficult to answer.

It is well known that at a very early period in Christian history the notion began to prevail that the ordinances possessed some magical virtue. It was believed that baptism conveyed saving grace to the soul; that by it sins were washed away, and the spirit fitted for heaven. Thus the sick were thought to be prepared for death, and salvation secured, or made more certain by its efficacy. Anxious parents therefore desired their dying children to receive baptism, and thus, "washed in the laver of regeneration," be secured against the perils of perdition. Such was one of the errors of a superstitious age. Hence arose infant baptism, as one of the many perversions which early corrupted the doctrines and ordinances of Christianity.

VITRINGA says:

"The ancient Church, from the highest antiquity after the apostolic times, appears generally to have thought that baptism is absolutely necessary for all that would be saved by the grace of Jesus Christ. It was therefore customary in the ancient Church, if infants were greatly afflicted and in danger of death, or if parents were affected with a singular concern about the salvation of their children, to present their infants or children in their minority to the bishop to be baptized."—*Observ. ad Sacra.*, *Vol. I.*, *B. II.*, *ch. 4, sec. 9.*

SALMASIUS says:

"An opinion prevailed that no one could be saved without

being baptized; and for that reason the custom arose of bap tizing infants."—*Epist. Jus. Pac. See Booth's Pedobap. Ex., ch. 3, sec. 3.*

VENEMA says :

"The ancients connected a regenerating power and a communication of the Spirit with baptism." He further asserts that the early fathers believed baptism to possess a saving efficacy, and cites Justin Martyr, Irenæus, Clemens, Tertullian and Cyprian as of that opinion, the last-named of whom has been called "the *inventor* of infant baptism."— *Eccl. Hist., Vol. IV., p. 3, secs. 2, 3, 4.*

CHRYSOSTOM, writing about A.D. 398, as cited by Luicerus, says :

"It is impossible without baptism to obtain the kingdom. It is impossible to be saved without it." And, as cited by Wall, he says : "If sudden death seize us before we are baptized, though we have a thousand good qualities there is nothing to be expected but hell."—*Luicer. Thesaur., Eccl. Vol. I., p. 3.*

WADDINGTON, in his Church History, declares, touching the opinions of the third century :

"The original simplicity of the office of baptism had already undergone some corruption. The symbol had been gradually exalted at the expense of the thing signified, and the spirit of the ceremony was beginning to be lost in the form. Hence a belief was gaining ground among the converts, and was inculcated among the heathen, that the act of baptism gave remission of all sins committed previously." —*Hist. of the Church, ch. 2, p. 53.*

Thus we see plainly *why*, as well as *when*, infant baptism arose. An invention of men, based on a perversion of Scripture doctrine, it is now boldly claimed to be an ordinance of God. How can honest and pious men make such a claim ? We are reminded of the words of the pious Charnock : " The wisdom of God is affronted and invaded by introducing rules and modes of worship different from divine institution." And we venture to ask, with the devout Baxter, though both had reference to other subjects, " What man dare go in a way which hath neither precept nor example to warrant it, from a way that hath full current of both ?"

V.   BAPTISMAL REGENERATION

We have seen that the baptism of infants, with that of the sick and dying, originated in a belief in the saving efficacy of the ordinance. Thus, the unscriptural device of *infant baptism* grew out of the unscriptural dogma of *baptismal regeneration* — a dogma as pernicious as presumptuous, and as repugnant to common sense as it is to the Bible; but one to which the advocates of pedobaptism have ever clung.

EPISCOPIUS asserts that the Milevitan Council, A. D. 418, declared pedobaptism to be a necessary rite.— *Theol. Inst., B. IV., ch. 14.*

DR. WALL says :

" If we except Tertullian, Vincentius, A. D. 419, is the first man on record that ever said that children might be saved without baptism."—*Hist. Inf. Bap., part I., chap. 20, p. 232.*

HAGENBACH says :

" The Church of England taught the doctrine of baptismal

regeneration, yet with cautions." He cites Jewell, Jackson, Hooker, Taylor, Pearson, and Waterland, to justify the assertion, which the baptismal service of that Church plainly proves.—*Hist. of Doct., Vol. II., p. 366.*

The words of our Saviour, " Verily, verily, I say unto you, except a man be born of water and of the Spirit he cannot enter into the kingdom of God," were almost universally applied to baptism, and supposed to teach that there was no salvation without it.

WALL declares that,

" From Justin Martyr down to St. Austin," this text was so understood. " Neither did I ever see it otherwise applied in any ancient author." And he adds, " I believe Calvin was the first man who ever denied this place to mean baptism."—*Hist. Inf. Bap., Part II., ch. 6, p. 354.*

THE CATHOLIC CHURCH held to baptismal regeneration, and in the Council of Trent thus declared it :

" If any one shall say that baptism is not necessary to salvation, let him be accursed."—*Catechism Coun. Trent, pp, 165, 175.*

THE GREEK CHURCH holds the same dogma, Cyril, Patriarch of Constantinople, declares,

" That both original and actual sins are forgiven to those who are baptized in the manner which our Lord requires in the Gospel."—*Confes. of Faith, ch. 16, 1631.*

STAPFERUS says :

They hold the absolute necessity of baptism, and that " without it no one can become a real Christian ; and that it cannot be omitted, in respect to infants, without endangering their salvation."—*Theology, Vol. V., p. 82.*

THE PROTESTANT CHURCHES generally have held, and to a degree do still hold, the same pernicious doctrine.

BOOTH cites the following Confessions which embrace it :

"That of Helvetia, of Bohemia, of Augsburg, of Saxony, of Wittenberg, of Sueveland, of the Church of England, and of the Westminster Assembly."—*Pedobap. Examined, chap. 3, ref. 3.*

A large number of Pedobaptist scholars and divines are cited by the same author as holding this doctrine, including Luther, Gerhardus, Vossius, Deylingius, Fiddes, Whitby, Wilson, Scott, John Wesley, and Matthew Henry.

Do its advocates and defenders now maintain the same ground ? Do they make the same claim for its saving efficacy ? If not, on what ground, and for what reason do they hold to the baptism of infants ? Have they any reason for it, except that they have been accustomed to it ?

VI. REASONS FOR INFANT BAPTISM

Now, since this rite was not instituted by Christ, nor practised by the Apostles, nor known among Christians until about A. D. 200, how is it justified as a Christian ordinance by those who practice it ? And by what reasons is it sustained and defended ?

1. Some good and honest people really believe,

after all, that infant baptism is taught in the Bible, and are greatly astonished, if they examine the subject, not to find it there. A very little effort will show how utterly without foundation is such a supposition. Read the sacred records through, from beginning to end, and no allusion to such a practice appears.

2. Its antiquity commends it to some. It has been a long time in vogue, and very generally practised by various Christian communions. But does that make it right? Is a usage necessarily good and true because it is old? Heathenism is older than the institutes of Christianity. Shall we adopt and practise all the absurd superstitions of the early corrupted churches—the worship of images, invocation of saints, prayer to the Virgin, oblations for the dead, baptism of bells, and many others; not a few of which came into use about the same time as this, and some of which are still older; any one of which has as much scriptural authority as infant baptism? Why do Protestants preserve this relic of popery alone, and reject the others?

Not what is *old*, but what is *true* should be our rule. Not what antiquity, but what the Bible commends should we obey. Not tradition, but, as Chillingworth declared, "the Bible only is the religion of Protestants." As Basil said, so should we say, "It is a manifest mistake in regard to faith, and a clear evidence of pride, either to reject any of those things which the Scripture contains, or to introduce anything that is not in the sacred pages."

3. Some there be, who confess that there is neither clear precept nor example in the New Testament to commend this practice, yet hold that the general spirit of the Gospel favors it; fundamental truths are there taught, from which the practice may be inferred. A strange mode of reasoning, surely. For if we may, by remote deduction and vague inference, originate ceremonies, call them gospel ordinances, and impose them on the consciences of men, then the whole Jewish ceremonial, and, indeed, the ritual of the Papal Church entire may be adopted, used, and taught as of divine authority, binding on believers.

But what a reflection is this on the wisdom and goodness of God; that He should have left positive institutions, designed for universal observance in His churches, to be vaguely inferred from supposed general principles, rather than to have been plainly and explicitly taught in His Word! Such reasoning will not serve in matters of religion. This maxim of Tertullian should have due weight, " The Scripture forbids what it does not mention." And with Ambrose we may ask, " Where the Scripture is silent, who shall speak ? "

4. Some have claimed that baptism came in the place of *circumcision*. Hence, it is inferred—only *inferred*—that as all the male Jewish children were to be circumcised, so all the children of Christians, both male and female, should be baptized. What connection there is between these two institutions would require a philosopher to discover. And yet

this has been the argument chiefly relied on by theologians, scholars, and divines in this country especially, for generations past, to prove the divine authority of infant baptism. More recently this stronghold of the tradition has been less confidently resorted to by learned men, and it may be said the tradition itself is being slowly abandoned. It cannot well endure the light of Christian intelligence.

Baptism did not come in the place of circumcision; nor in the place of any other previously existing institution. It has no connection with, and no reference to, circumcision whatever. The following considerations will make this plain :

a. If baptism, a Christian ordinance, was designed to take the place of circumcision, a Mosaic rite, would not Christ have so stated, or the Apostles have mentioned the fact ? But no allusion is to be found to any such design.

b. Circumcision applied to males alone. If baptism was its substitute, why are females baptized ?

c. Circumcision was an external sign of an external union with a national congregation, to secure the separation of the Jews from all other nations and races, and their unity as a people. Baptism is an external sign of an inward spiritual work of grace already wrought in the heart. It indicates not the separation of races, but the unity of the true people of God, of all races, as believers in Christ, without distinction of blood or tongue.

d. If baptism did take the place of circumcision, as is claimed, evidently the Apostles did not know it, else they would have made some mention of it, either in the conference at Jerusalem or in Epistles written for the guidance of the churches, or on other occasions, when both these subjects were under discussion, and directions given respecting them. But no allusion is anywhere made to such a substitution.

e. Jewish Christians for a time insisted on the practice of *both* circumcision and baptism; which proves they did not understand the one to have displaced the other. With their strong Jewish predilections they wished to retain circumcision as the sign and seal of their fellowship with the Church of Israel, and at the same time received baptism as a sign and seal of their adoption into the faith and fellowship of Christ and His kingdom.

The attempt to found a Christian ordinance on a Jewish ceremony is unreasonable, futile and absurd.

VII.   OBJECTIONS TO INFANT BAPTISM

1. It is founded on a falsehood. It claims to be a Gospel ordinance, when it is an invention of men. Christ did not appoint it; the Apostles did not practise it; the Scriptures do not sanction it. This is a sufficient reason why it should not be held as a Christian rite.

2. It impugns divine wisdom and insults the divine authority, because it claims to be needful, or useful, to religion; though Christ, by not appointing it when he instituted the Church, virtually decided it to be neither needful nor useful. Also, by bind-

ing the service on the consciences of Christian parents, as of religious obligation when God has not commanded it, there is an unwarrantable assumption of authority, and a grievous wrong is committed. Divine wisdom knew best what institutions to ordain, and what commands to lay upon His people.

3. It deprives Christian converts of the pleasure and privilege of believers' baptism. For having received this rite in their unconscious infancy without their consent or knowledge, if in after years they become regenerate and truly united to Christ, they cannot go forward in the discharge of this duty and be baptized on a profession of their faith without discrediting their earlier baptism—if baptism it may be called.

4. Because it appears like a solemn mockery for parents and sponsors to become sureties for the child about to be baptized, and declare for it that they believe in God's holy Word, and in the articles of the Christian faith as contained in the Apostles' creed; that they will renounce the vain pomp of the world, the devil and all his works, with all covetous and sinful desires of the flesh.

5. Because it requires the officiating minister to declare what is false, in the very performance of what should be a most sacred service. He declares what is false when he says, "I baptize thee," since he *rantizes*, or sprinkles, and does not baptize at all. Still more, and still worse, when he asserts that in this act the child "is *regenerated* and grafted into the body of Christ's Church;" and, also, when

in prayer he thanks God " that it hath pleased Thee to regenerate this infant with Thy Holy Spirit; to receive him for Thine own child by adoption, and to incorporate him into Thy holy Church." This is solemnly declared, when no such thing is done, and when the minister who says it knows that no such thing is done, unless, indeed, he believes in baptismal regeneration. The child is not regenerated, nor adopted of God, nor incorporated into the Church of Christ by this act. The service falsifies the facts most flagrantly.

6. But, perhaps, worst of all, infant baptism still teaches, to an extent, *baptismal regeneration*. It is more than a false statement, it is a pernicious and destructive error. What could be more reckless than to assert, even by inference, that a few drops of water on the face, with any form of words—no matter what—can make one regenerate, and a child of God ? If the child, when grown, believes all this —and why should he not believe it, when thus solemnly taught by parents and minister ?—he believes himself an heir of heaven, sealed and sanctified by the Spirit, while blind to the fact that he is still in the gall of bitterness, a child of sin, an heir of wrath, and in the broad road to death. What blind leadings of the blind ! too sad to be countenanced by Christian men and Christian churches.

7. Infant baptism, in some sense—though its advocates are not agreed in what sense—makes the child a Church-member, and thus introduces an unsanctified element into the nominal body of Christ,

making that body carnal instead of keeping it spiritual. It thus destroys the distinction which the Divine Founder of the Church designed should be maintained between it and the world. For even if the infant, as such, is not a member, yet, when grown to maturity, he is admitted to full membership, with no other evidence of, or demand for, regeneration. The purely spiritual character of the Church is thereby destroyed, and, like other associations, the spiritual and the carnal indifferently make up its communion. " A regenerated Church-membership " cannot be the motto or the watchword of the advocates of pedobaptism.

PROF. LANGE'S protest should be pondered by Protestant advocates of this papal emanation:

" Would the Protestant Church fulfill and attain to its final destiny, the baptism of new-born infants must of necessity be abolished. It has sunk down to a mere formality, without any meaning for the child."—*Hist. Protestantism*, *p. 34.*

Other objections than these mentioned may be urged against this unscriptural practice. But these would seem sufficient to deter any candid and conscientious Christian, who takes the Bible for his guide, from giving it any countenance or support.

CHAPTER 18

BAPTIST HISTORY

BAPTISTS have a history of which they need not be ashamed—a history of noble names and noble deeds, extending back through many ages, in which the present generation well may glory. From the days of John the Baptist until now, a great army of these witnesses for the truth, and martyrs for its sake, has illumined and honored the march of Christian history. The ages since Christ have known no purer, nobler lives, no braver, more faithful witnesses for the Gospel of Christ, no more glorious martyrs for its sake, than many of those who honor us by being called " our fathers in the faith." They were true to conscience and to principle, and loyal to Christ, at a cost to which we are strangers. They went gladly to prison and to death in defense of the Gospel which they loved. Social ostracism, bonds and imprisonments, confiscations and fines, whippings, drownings, and burnings at the stake, not only in solitary cases, but by hundreds and thousands, are certified to, even by their enemies. Christian martyrology has no bloodier and no brighter page than that which tells, however imperfectly, of the persecutions and sufferings for conscience' sake of

Baptist confessors, received during past ages, not from pagan barbarians so much as from professed fellow-Christians. It is an equal honor to their record that, while they endured persecution for the truth's sake, *they never persecuted others for conscience' sake—never!* How could they, when one of their cardinal principles was, and is, entire freedom of conscience and liberty of faith and worship, without interference by any? And the one priceless heritage they have given to the world, with which the world's religious life of to-day—and its secular life as well—has become imbued, is that of entire religious liberty of faith, speech and worship, and entire separation of Church and State.

The time was when *toleration* in religion was hailed as a peculiar boon, granted through a gracious Providence. Baptists have contended and suffered, not for *toleration*, but for *liberty* in religion.

The world is slow to acknowledge its indebtedness to them; nevertheless, it remains. With a great price they purchased it. But they did it, not for glory, nor for gain, but for God and humanity.

No Baptist history, of adequate value, has thus far been written. Not a few attempts have been made, and much valuable material has been collected and preserved. We do not, however, place so much value on written history, as on present conformity to the teachings of Christ, a maintenance of the doctrines, and an imitation of the lives of the Apostles and the first Christians. It matters little whether a Church can trace its lineage back one century or twenty. The great question is, Does it inherit the spirit of Him who founded the Church, and does it hold the doctrines and imitate the examples of Christ and His Apostles ? Still, whatever of history can be brought within the range of vision to be studied should be claimed and cherished.

If it be asked, When and where did Baptist history begin ? Who were the first of their honored line ? Without hesitation we reply, They commenced with John the Baptist, or Jesus Christ, the Head of the Church. And the first of their faith were His disciples, constituting the primitive churches. And though, in the dim, uncertain light of subsequent ages of error and corruption, we cannot at all times follow their trail, or identify their presence with absolute certainty, yet we feel positively assured that they have always existed. Like a stream which pursues its way from the mountains to the sea, and never ceases, though its course at times be through mountain gorges, trackless deserts, and hidden caverns, we know it is somewhere, though we cannot trace it, but we recognize it when again it comes to light, with a grander sweep, a deeper current, and a stronger tide.

Baptists make no pretence of establishing, by documentary evidence, an unbroken succession of churches in form and name, as now existing, extending back to apostolic times. Such a claim would only make them ridiculous, as similar High-Church pretensions have made some other communions. Such a claim would be as impossible to prove as it would be useless if proven. The old is not always true or useful, nor the new false or useless necessarily. Falsehood and error are hoary with age, from Eden until now. Nevertheless, there is a survival of truth often hidden under the accumulated rubbish of human tradition, itself ages old; and he is wise who searches for truth as for hid treasures. Baptists trace their lineage, not through corporate designations, or forms of organic life, but by principles avowed, maintained and defended. The doctrines they professed, and the lives they lived, give us title to the inheritance we claim in their history.

THE EARLY SECTS

It is on all hands conceded that from the days of the Apostles to the Reformation there existed congregations and communities of Christians separate from the prevailing and dominant churches, claiming to be of a more primitive, and therefore of a purer, faith. As these dominant churches fell into alliance with the State, sought its patronage, became subservient to its spirit, proud, corrupt and carnal, departing from the simplicity and spirituality of the Gospel, these separate communities maintained their distinct existence, worshiped by themselves, and served God according to their understanding of the Scriptures and the dictates of their consciences. They maintained the doctrines of the Gospel nearly in their purity, as they were at first delivered to the saints, and were the true and faithful followers of

Christ in the midst of prevailing spiritual darkness and decay. Even in the apostolic age not a few errors from prevailing philosophies had crept into the profession of the Christian faith, but after that faith had been adopted by princes and became nationalized, its corruptions became more numerous and its perversions more glaring. All the more did these dissenting communities need to maintain their distinctive existence, not only for conscience' sake, but as a protest against the outrages perpetrated on the cause of Christ by others.

During all the dark ages since the kingdom of Christ appeared, these companies and communities have confessedly existed. They have been known by many names, and have differed somewhat among themselves in different ages and in different countries. By the prevailing and dominant secularized churches they were stigmatized as *heretics*, and were defamed and persecuted perpetually, not by pagans and barbarians, but by their professed fellow-Christians. Those are usually the *heretics* who differ from the majority, and have conscience and courage enough to defend their position, and, if need be, suffer for their faith. Thousands on thousands of those dissenting disciples were put to death by the most painful tortures for no other crime than a purer faith than their persecutors possessed, and because they would hold, profess and defend that purer faith. Those who were permitted to live were doomed to endure unequaled cruelties. Emperors, kings and princes, popes, priests and people,

Senates, Synods and Councils, pursued them with every device of cruelty which malice could invent or power execute, to waste, blot out and exterminate them from the face of the earth. Language is too weak to portray the diabolical and fiendish cruelties perpetrated upon the innocent, helpless and, for the most part, unresisting people of God by those who were able to invoke the secular power to execute their fell designs.

They were the few among the many, the weak oppressed by the strong; with none to plead their cause, or to defend their rights, they could do nothing but suffer. Though calumniated by their enemies, who accused them of every crime, and charged them with every enormity, they were the purest and the best of the ages and the countries in which they lived. The doctrines and ordinances of the Gospel they maintained nearly, if not quite, in their primitive purity. The greater part had never been connected with the Roman hierarchy, while many who had, separated themselves from the false, that they might enjoy the true Church of Christ.

Like some rivulet which pursues its way parallel to, but never mingling with, the broad and turbid stream, these people have come down from the first ages of Christianity, preserving and transmitting to posterity the purest forms of doctrinal faith and practical godliness known to history during those long succeeding ages of darkness and corruption. The reproaches and persecutions they suffered were because they bore witness against prevailing errors and crimes, perpetrated in the name of religion by the papal Church. No doubt they had some faults, and; perhaps, held some errors. How could it well be otherwise, surrounded, as they were, by an atmosphere of ecclesiastical falsehood and corruption ?

During the *first* and *second* centuries, Messalians, Euchites, Montanists, were the names by which some of these sects were known.

In the *third*, *fourth* and *fifth* centuries, the Novatians arose and became exceedingly numerous, spreading throughout the Roman Empire, notwithstanding the destruction wrought among them by persecution.

In the *seventh* and *eighth* centuries arose the Paulicians, attracting much attention, becoming very numerous, and drawing upon themselves the hatred and hostility of the papal Church.*

JONES states that in the first part of the *ninth century*, Claude, bishop of Turin, a truly godly and evangelical man, who preached righteousness, and opposed prevailing corruptions, both as to doctrines and morals :

"By his preaching, and by his valuable writings, he disseminated the doctrines of the kingdom of heaven." "His doctrine grew exceedingly. The valleys of Piedmont were filled with his disciples, and while midnight darkness sat enthroned over almost every portion of the globe, the Wal-

* See Benedict's, Orchard's, Robinson's, Jones's, *et al.*, Histories, with all current Eccl. Hists. of the early ages of Christianity.

denses preserved the Gospel among them in its native purity, and rejoiced in its glorious light."—*Jones's Ch. Hist., Vol. 1., p. 396; Rob. Eccl. Research., p. 447; Allix. Rem., p. 52.*

If not technically Baptists, the principal points in which they differed from the dominant churches, and for which they were persecuted, were those which Baptists have always emphasized, and in respect to which they still chiefly differ from other Christian communions. They held that none but regenerate persons ought to be received to membership in the churches; they rejected infant baptism; they baptized by immersion, as did all Christians during those ages; they rebaptized converts received among them from the Romish Church, and hence were called Anabaptists. These are distinguishing marks of them all, more or less clearly defined, as noted by their enemies, from whom we receive the greater part of our knowledge concerning them, their own writings having largely perished in the sore and bloody persecutions to which they were subjected. Robinson, the historian, called them "Trinitarian Baptists."

The Paulicians became exceedingly numerous, and were so cruelly persecuted that the Empress Theodora is said to have caused not less than *one hundred thousand* of these peaceable subjects to be put to death, after having confiscated their property.* They confined the ordinances to the regenerate, rejected infant baptism, and rebaptized con-

---

* See Orchard, Milner, Gibbon. *et al.*

verts received to their fellowship. They were also called Bogomilians, a name which became famous in the annals of persecution. These communities continued through several succeeding centuries, and spread through both the East and the West.

Near the close of the *tenth* century, the Peterines come into notice. They were substantially the same people as had previously existed under other names. Indeed, these various sects were the progenitors and the inheritors of each other's religious faith and practice. It was the irrepressible energy of truth and the spirit of God, working in regenerate souls to develop and reproduce the true Christian life, in the simplicity of Christ, according to the primitive type. Not only the individual, but the Church life of the saints. Europe was well-nigh flooded with these dissentients. The truly devout welcomed them, since they yearned for something better than the prevailing heartless and secularized religion. And the prevailing and shameless corruptions of the Romish clergy gave those of purer lives great currency with the masses. For there were no vices, however gross and degrading, which the clergy, from the highest to the lowest, from pope to priest, did not practise with greediness and impunity. They were examples to the people in all kinds of sin and iniquity.

In the *eleventh* and following centuries, the Waldenses, Albigenses, Vaudois, Cathari, poor men of Lyons, and Anabaptists, attracted renewed attention through Europe, and for generations continued to increase and to suffer. They differed slightly among themselves, but were variously named according to their locations, or the circumstances in which they attracted the notice of the public. Their prevailing characteristics were the same as have been noticed above. They filled Italy even, the very seat and centre of papal power, corruption and crime, with their influence and the truths they held.

In the *twelfth* century, so great became their influence, especially under the leadership of Arnold of Brescia, a pupil of the renowned Abelard, that the papal throne itself trembled to its foundation. Arnold was as brave a reformer as was Luther four hundred years later, and perhaps as learned. But the times were not ripe for such a work as the German reformer was raised up to lead. Arnold, however, dared to visit Rome itself, and by his attacks on the vices and the unjust authority of the clergy raised a revolt in the very face of the Vatican, which finally compelled the pope to flee, and changed the government for a season. But he had no powerful nobles to espouse his cause, as had Luther, and the people were unorganized and unreliable; while the the influence of the clergy, with all their vices, was still most potent. Wise and powerful leaders were needed for a reformation. The people could endure better than contend. This lesson they had learned through generations of suffering. But the time had not come for truth to triumph. A reaction set in, and Arnold, like Savonarola three hundred years later, whose early history was also associated with Brescia, fell a victim to the hatred of his foes, and his immediate followers were scattered.*   But their principles survived, as did countless numbers of the various communities of dissentients from the dominant communions.

WADDINGTON, the historian, gives the following statement, made by Saccho, one of their adversaries and persecutors, as to the Vaudois, or Leonists, of the *twelfth century:*

" There is no sect so dangerous as the Leonists, for three reasons: First, it is the most ancient—some say as old as Sylvester, others as the Apostles themselves.   Secondly, it is very generally disseminated; there is no country where it has not gained some footing.   Thirdly, while other sects are profane and blasphemous, this retains the utmost show of piety. They live justly before men, and believe nothing respecting God which is not good.   Only they blaspheme against the Roman Church and the clergy, and thus gain many followers."—*Waddington, Ch. Hist., p. 290.   See Mosheim, 12th Cent.*

ORCHARD says of the Piedmontese :

" Though we have no documents proving the apostolical foundation for these churches, yet it becomes evident that some communities did exist here in the *second century*, since it is recorded they practiced believers' baptism by immersion.*"
—*Hist. Bap., p. 255.   See also Rollinson, Allix, et al., Hist. Pied.; Wall's Hist. Inf. Bap.*

From the time of the Apostles to the Reformation these various sectaries may be said to have consti-

* See Gibbon's Decl. and Fall, Mosheim, Allix, Jones, *et al.*

tuted the true Church of God. Their faith was the most scriptural, and their lives were the purest the world had. Of course they were not perfect. How could they be with such environments? And if at times they did not wholly agree among themselves, what marvel in age of doubt, corruption and unrest, when the truest were the most reviled, and the purest were the most persecuted? In the sixteenth century they came into public notice, largely under the leadership of Menno Simons, whom the historian calls, " a reformer whose apostolic spirit and labors have thus far failed to receive the recognition they deserve." From him they were called Mennonites, and flooded Europe with tens of thousands. "Mennonites, the Anabaptists of the Netherlands first called themselves in 1536." "They were certainly among the most pious Christians the world ever saw, and the worthiest citizens the State ever had." They crowded into Russia for shelter, where in our times they have been persecuted and exiled. At length they have fled to our own country for peace and freedom which they found nowhere else for the past four hundred years.

At the time of the Lutheran Reformation these various sects to a large extent fraternized with, and were lost in, the multitudes of the reformers. So glad were they to find something, if not wholly to their wish, yet so much better than had previously existed in the papal churches, and to find leaders of power, as also to find some shelter from civil and ecclesiastical persecution, that they welcomed the

Reformation, even with its imperfections, as a boon from heaven. The Waldenses of Piedmont, and some others, abandoned dipping for baptism, adopted infant sprinkling, in common with State churches, and the Calvinistic reformers generally identified themselves with, and were largely lost in, the mass of Protestant Pedobaptists. Not so however with the Baptists, or Anabaptists, as by their opponents they were more generally called. They maintained their faith and their position, not only against their papal adversaries, but against their Protestant friends as well, whose reformation they insisted needed still further reforming.

These various protesting peoples through the generations had at times been joined by enthusiasts and fanatics, or such had sprung up within their fellowship, like the " mad men of Münster," whose extravagances brought upon the entire brotherhood reproaches they did not merit—their adversaries being ever ready to find occasion against them, and to magnify every fault and indiscretion to the largest possible extent. But they were, on the whole, so much superior in faith and life to the dominant churches as to command the wonder and admiration of those, who in a spirit of fairness, now study the imperfect fragments of their history. They all more or less strongly pronounced the following statements of their religious beliefs: 1. The Bible as the only and sufficient standard of faith and appeal in matters of religion. 2. Entire liberty of conscience, confession and worship for all. 3. Complete separation of Church and State, the Church acknowledging but one Lord, even Christ. 4. The churches to be constituted of spiritual members only, such as were regenerate by the Holy Spirit. 5. Baptism to be administered by immersion. 6. Infant baptism to be rejected, as alien to the New Testament. 7. The churches to be self-governing, and free from the domination of both lords spiritual and lords temporal.

Such facts identify them with Baptists of later ages, what no other denomination can claim.

II. THE SWISS BAPTISTS

The secluded valleys and mountain fastnesses of Switzerland and Piedmont have from the earliest ages been the home and refuge of the persecuted people of God. Not only those native to the soil but such as had fled from other countries to find shelter and freedom in those Alpine retreats. Paulicians, Albigenses, Vaudois, Pickards, Anabaptists, with many others, are names bound up in history with these wild mountain resorts. " The Vaudois and Waldenses," says a historian, "have from time immemorial inhabited the vales at the foot of the Cottian Alps."

ZWINGLI, the Swiss reformer and co-laborer with Luther, says:

"The institution of Anabaptism is no novelty, but for *thirteen hundred years* has caused great disturbance in the Church." *

* See Intro. Orchard, p. 17; also Benedict *et al.*, Ch. Hists.

If it had existed thirteen hundred years before Zwingli, it must have extended back to within two centuries of Christ, to say the least. And it is confidently affirmed that it can be traced as far back as to the fourth century. They too, in common with their brethren of similar faith, suffered persecution unto death, against which the strongholds of nature, in the midst of which they dwelt, could not wholly protect them.* The horrid massacre of these innocent people by the Duke of Savoy, about the middle of the *seventeenth century*, equaled the dreadful scenes of St. Bartholomew's day, and was protested against by Cromwell, then in power.

III.   THE WELSH BAPTISTS

Few denominations have better claim to antiquity than have the Welsh Baptists. They trace their descent directly from the Apostles, and urge in favor of their claim arguments which never have been confuted.

When Austin, the Romish monk and missionary, visited Wales at the close of the *sixth* century, he found a community of more than 2,000 Christians quietly living in their mountain homes. They were independent of the Roman See, and wholly rejected its authority. Austin labored zealously to convert them—that is, to bring them under the papal yoke —but entirely failed in the effort. Yielding things

* See Robinson, Allix, Danvers; especially Burrage and Schaff.

in general, he reduced his demands upon them to three particulars: 1. That they should observe Easter in due form, as ordered by the Church. 2. That they should give Christening or baptism to their children. 3. That they should preach the Word of God to the English, as directed. This demand proves that they neither observed the popish ordinance of Easter, nor baptized infants. They, however, rejected all his overtures, whereupon he left them with many threats of war and wretchedness. Not long after Wales was invaded by the Saxons, and many of these inoffensive Christians cruelly put to death, as was believed, at the instigation of this bigoted zealot, the exacting and heartless Austin.*

IV. THE DUTCH BAPTISTS

The Baptists of Holland are acknowledged by historians to have had their origin at a very remote period.

MOSHEIM, the historian, says:

"The true origin of that sect which acquired the name of Anabaptists, *is hid in the remote depth of antiquity*, and consequently extremely difficult to be ascertained."—*Eccl. Hist., Vol. IV., p. 427, Murd. ed.; Introd. Orchard's Hist.*

DR. DERMONT, chaplain to the king of Holland, and Dr. Ypeij, professor of theology at Graningen, a few years since received a royal commission to

*See Neal's Hist. Puritans; Rob. Hist. Bap.; Benedict.

prepare a history of the Reformed Dutch Church. This history, prepared under royal sanction, and officially published, contains the following manly and generous testimony to the antiquity and orthodoxy of the Dutch Baptists:

"We have now seen that the Baptists, who were formerly called Anabaptists, and in later times Mennonites, were the original Waldenses, and have long in the history of the Church received the honor of that origin. On this account, *the Baptists may be considered the only Christian community which has stood since the Apostles, and as a Christian society which has preserved pure the doctrines of the Gospel through all ages."—Hist. Ref. Dutch Ch., Breda, 1819. See Hist. Mennonites.*

MOSHEIM says of the persecutions of this people in the sixteenth century:

"Vast numbers of these people, in nearly all the countries of Europe, would rather perish miserably by drowning, hanging, burning, or decapitation, than renounce the opinions they had embraced." And their innocency he vindicates thus: "It is indeed true that many Anabaptists were put to death, not as being bad citizens, or injurious members of civil society, but as being incurable *heretics*, who were condemned by the old canon laws. For the error of *adult baptism* was in that age looked upon as a horrible offense." That was their only crime.—*Eccl. Hist., Cent. 16, sec. 3, part II., ch. 3; Fuller's Ch. Hist., B. IV.*

This testimony is all the more welcome, because it comes from those who have no ecclesiastical sympathies with Baptists, but who, in fidelity to history, bear honest testimony to the truth which history teaches.   The circumstances under which their evidence was produced give it additional force.

CARDINAL HOSSIUS, chairman of the Council at Trent says :

> "If the truth of religion were to be judged of by the readiness and cheerfulness which a man of any sect shows in suffering, then the opinions and persuasions of no sect can be truer or surer than those of the *Anabaptists ;* since there have been none, for these *twelve hundred years past,* that have been more grievously punished."—*Orchard's Hist. Bap., sec. 12, part XXX., p. 364.*

Many thousands of the Dutch Baptists, called Anabaptists and Mennonites, miserably perished by the hands of their cruel persecutors for no crime but their refusal to conform to established churches."*

V.   THE ENGLISH BAPTISTS

At what time the Baptists appeared in England in definite denominational form, it is impossible to say.   But from the *twelfth* to the *seventeenth* century, many of them suffered cruel persecutions, and death by burning, drowning, and beheading, besides many other and sometimes most inhuman tortures. And this they suffered both from Papists and Protestants, condemned by both civil and ecclesiastical tribunals, only because they persisted in worshiping God according to the dictates of their consciences, and because they would not submit their religious

---

* Benedict's Hist. Baptists, ch. 4 ; Neal's Hist. Puritans, Vol. II., p. 355, Supplement; Fuller's Ch. Hist., B. IV.

faith and worship to the dictates of popes and princes.* In 1538 royal edicts were issued against them, and several were burnt at the stake in Smithfield.

BRANDE writes that:

"In the year 1538, thirty-one Baptists, that fled from England, were put to death at Delft, in Holland; the men were beheaded, and the women were drowned."—*Hist. Reformers. See Benedict's Hist. Bap., p. 303; Neal's Hist. Puritans, Vol. I., p. 138; Note Vol. II., p. 355, Sup.* What crime had they committed to merit such treatment as this?

BISHOP LATIMER declares that:

"The Baptists that were burnt in different parts of the kingdom went to death intrepidly, and without any fear, during the time of Henry VIII."—*Lent. Sermons; Neal's Hist. Purit., Vol. II., p. 356.*

Under the rule of the popish Mary, they suffered perhaps no more than under that of the Protestant Elizabeth. During the reign of the latter a congregation of Baptists was discovered in London, whereupon several were banished, twenty-seven imprisoned, and two burnt at Smithfield. †

DR. FEATLEY, one of their bitter enemies, wrote of them, in 1633:

"This sect, among others, hath so far presumed upon the patience of the State, that it hath held weekly conventicles,

* See Histories of Baptists, by Crosby, Ivimey, Danvers, and Benedict.

† Wall, cited by Neal, Hist. Puritans, Vol. I., p. 137; Vol. II., p. 358, Supplement.

rebaptizing hundreds of men and women together in the twilight. in rivulets, and in some arms of the Thames, and elsewhere, dipping them all over head and ears. It hath printed divers pamphlets in defense of their heresy; yea, and challenged some of our preachers to disputation."—*Eng. Bap. Jubilee Memor., Benedict's Hist. Bap., p. 304.*

BAILEY wrote, in 1639, that :

" Under the shadow of independency they have lifted up their heads, and increased their numbers above all sects in the land. They have *forty-six churches* in and about London. They are a people very fond of religious liberty, and very unwilling to be brought under bondage of the judgment of others."—*Benedict's Hist., p. 304.*

The first book published in the English language on the subject of baptism was translated from the Dutch, and bears date 1618. From this time they multiplied rapidly through all parts of the kingdom. The first regularly organized Church among them, known as such in England, dates from 1607, and was formed in London by a Mr. Smyth, previously a clergyman of the established Church.

In 1689 the Particular Baptists, so called, held a convention in London, in which more than one hundred congregations were represented, and which issued a Confession of Faith, still in use and highly esteemed.

The last Baptist martyr in England was Edward Wightman, of Burton upon Trent, condemned by the Bishop of Coventry, and burnt at Litchfield, April 11, 1612. *

* Eng. Bap. Jubilee Memor., Benedict's Hist. Bap.

VI. AMERICAN BAPTISTS

The history of American Baptists runs back a little more than two and a quarter centuries. In this country, as elsewhere, they were cradled amid persecution, and nurtured by the hatred of their foes. This has been their fortune in every age and in every land.

ROGER WILLIAMS, a distinguished and an honored name, was identified with the rise of the denomination in America. He has been called their founder, because he organized the first Church, and was intimately connected with their early history. Williams was born in Wales, 1598, educated at Oxford, England, came to America in 1630, and settled as minister of the Puritan Church in Salem, Massachusetts. Not long after he adopted Baptist views of doctrine and Church order, on account of which he was banished by his fellow Puritans, and driven out of Massachusetts, in the depth of a rigorous winter, in a new and inhospitable country. Having wandered far and suffered much, finding the savage Indians more generous and hospitable than his fellow Christians, he finally reached and fixed his future home at what is now Providence, R. I. Here, with a few associates of like faith, he founded a new colony, calling both the city and the colony *Providence*, in recognition of the divine guidance and protection, which he had in so remarkable a manner experienced.

In 1639 Mr. Williams received baptism from one

of his associates, there being no minister to perform that service. He in turn baptized his associates, and a Church was organized, of which he was chosen pastor. He was also appointed first governor of Rhode Island. Full liberty was granted in matters of religion. Thus Roger Williams became the first ruler, and Rhode Island the first State which ever gave entire freedom to all persons to worship God, according to their own choice, without dictation or interference from civil or ecclesiastical authorities.

On account of this unrestricted liberty many Baptists, as well as other persecuted religionists from other colonies, and from Europe, collected in considerable numbers at Providence, and spread through the colony.

It is a mistake to suppose that all the Baptist churches in America grew out of the one which Roger Williams founded. It is even doubtful whether any single Church arose as an outgrowth of that. As immigration increased, other churches grew up, having no connection with that; and with considerable rapidity the sentiments of Baptists spread into adjoining colonies, particularly west and south. For a long time, however, they were sorely persecuted, especially in Massachusetts and Connecticut. Persecuted even by those who had themselves fled from persecution in their native land, to find freedom and refuge in these distant wilds.

In 1644 the present First Church in Newport,

R. I., was organized. But whether the present
First Church in Providence was constituted before
this date is still a disputed point. Both claim priority. In 1656 the Second Church, Newport, was
formed. Then followed, in order of time, the Church
in Swansea, Massachusetts, 1663; First, Boston,
1665; North Kingstone, R. I., 1665; Seventh-Day
Church, Newport, 1671; South Kingstone, R. I.,
1680; Kittery, Me., 1682; Middletown, N. J., 1688;
Lower Dublin, Pa., 1689; Charleston, S. C., 1690;
Philadelphia, Pa., 1698; Welsh Tract, Del, 1701;
Groton, Conn., 1705. Others, not mentioned, arose
within this period in these and other colonies.
With the increase of population Baptists rapidly
multiplied, and spread widely abroad over the
country.

VII. BAPTIST FACTS AND FIGURES

For the first hundred years of Baptist history in
America their growth was slow. The population
was small and scattered. They were still dissentients from the majority of their fellow Christians,
by whom they were defamed, opposed, and persecuted. Though, in this country, none were burned,
hanged, or drowned, because of their faith, yet in
New England they were banished, fined, imprisoned,
and publicly whipped at the stake, because they insisted on religious liberty, and would not submit to
the magistrates in matters of faith and conscience.
In the then condition of the country they lacked in

organization, intercourse, and mutual help. The first Baptist Church known to American history was organized by Roger Williams in Providence, R. I., in 1639.

Edwards' Tables gives the number of churches in 1768, more than a hundred years afterward, as *one hundred and thirty-seven.*

Asplund's Register reported for 1790, 872 churches, 722 ordained ministers, and 64,975 Church members.

Benedict's History states that in 1812 there were 2,633 churches, 2,143 ordained ministers, and 204,-185 members.

Allens' Register, for 1836, enrolls 7,299 churches, 4,075 ministers, and 517,523 Church members.

The Baptist Almanack, for 1840, gives the following figures: 7,771 churches, 5,208 ministers, and 571,291 members.

The Baptist Year Book, for 1860, reports the following numbers, 12,279 churches, 7,773 ministers, and 1,016,134 members.

It must be borne in mind, however, that the figures given are always less than the facts would warrant, since complete returns can never be obtained from Churches and Associations.

From the various sources of information accessible, the following table of statistics is compiled, and is doubtless approximately correct; though, as to the earlier dates the figures differ somewhat, according to the sources from which they are derived.

Date	Churches	Ministers	Members
1768	137		
1784	472	424	35,101
1790	872	722	65,000
1792	891	1,156	65,345
1812	2,164	1,605	173,200
1825	3,743	2,577	237,895
1832	5,320	3,618	384,926
1840	7,771	5,208	571,291
1842	8,546	5,600	649,138
1851	9,552	7,393	770,839
1860	12,279	7,773	1,016,134
1871	18,397	12,013	1,489,191
1877	23,908	14,659	2,024,224
1880	26,060	16,569	2,296,327
1882	26,931	17,090	2,394,742
1884	28,596	18,677	2,507,703
1886	30,522	19,377	2,732,570
1888	31,891	20,477	2,917,315
1890	34,780	22,706	3,164,124
1892	35,890	23,800	3,269,806
1893	36,793	24,798	3,383,160
1894	38,122	25,354	3,496,988
1896	40,658	27,257	3,824,038
1898	43,397	27,355	4,055,806

The Baptist Family

The Baptist family of the United States is sometimes spoken of as included in three sectional divisions: *First,* Baptists of the North, of whom there are, according to reports of 1927, 1,385,709; *Second,* White Baptists in the South and Southwest, numbering (1927) 3,708,253; *Third,* Negro Baptists, of whom there are 3,253,369. It may be noted that the Northern Baptists reported, in 1927, something more than $6,323,985 expended the previous year in Home and Foreign Missions. The Southern white Baptists reported, in 1927, total receipts for Home and Foreign Missions of $8,228,281. The Negro Baptists have their mission and educational enterprises under their own management, for which they raise and expend amounts very creditable to them, considering their circumstances.

First Things

The following table of historical data, believed to be correct, presents facts which may prove of substantial value for reference. The first Baptist Church in each State was organized at the date here given.*

1	Rhode Island	1639	19	Ohio	1790
2	Massachusetts	1663	20	Illinois	1796
3	Maine	1682	21	Indiana	1798
4	South Carolina	1682	22	Arkansas	1799
5	Pennsylvania	1684	23	Dist. Columbia	1802
6	New Jersey	1688	24	Missouri	1805
7	Delaware	1701	25	Alabama	1808
8	Connecticut	1705	26	Louisiana	1812
9	Virginia	1714	27	Michigan	1822
10	New York	1724	28	Indian Ter.	1832
11	North Carolina	1727	29	Iowa	1835
12	Maryland	1742	30	Wisconsin	1836
13	New Hampshire	1755	31	Texas	1837
14	Georgia	1759	32	Oregon	1844
15	Vermont	1768	33	Minnesota	1849
16	West Virginia	1774	34	California	1849
17	Tennessee	1780	35	New Mexico	1849
18	Mississippi	1780	36	Kansas	1854

* This table was compiled after laborious care in ascertaining the facts, and published by Rev. David Spencer, D. D.

37 Nebraska	1855	43 Montana	1871
38 Washington	1863	44 Nevada	1873
39 Colorado	1864	45 North Dakota	1879
40 Idaho	1864	46 Arizona	1879
41 Wyoming	1870	47 Utah	1880
42 South Dakota	1870	48 Oklahoma	1889

During One Decade

During the decade from 1874 to 1884 there was reported the following increase: churches, 7,086; ministers, 3,313; members, 1,806,542. Full returns in many cases, not obtainable.

Numbers Baptized

Some years have been marked by peculiar revival power in the churches, when the numbers baptized were very large. In 1886 there were reported 163,300 baptisms; in 1887, 158,373; in 1888, 134,563; in 1889, 140,058; in 1890, 155,300; in 1891, 160,247; in 1892, 166,322; in 1927, 325,386. Of course, it is possible that some of these persons baptized may not have been truly regenerate. There is always a liability to hasty admission to church fellowship, especially in times of high revival fervor. But they all profess to be genuine converts, and the rule universally recognized for admission is, that none except such as give evidence of the new birth can be received to baptism and church-membership.

Of the 325,386 reported as baptized during the church year of 1927, there were 65,486 among the Northern Baptists, 195,858 among the Southern white Baptists, and 64,042 among the Negro Baptists.

Other Baptists

There are in the United States various other smaller sections of the great Baptist family practising immersion, but differing in many other respects from our own churches. It is a satisfaction to know that no longer is there any division between the Free-Will Baptists of the North and the other churches of the Northern Baptist Convention, the Free-Will churches having entered into unity of fellowship and work with the Baptists of the North. Concerning some of the smaller branches of the Baptist family the *Year-Book* of 1927 reports: Dunkards (Brethren), 156,768; United Brethren in Christ, 410,631; Adventists, 150,891; Church of God (Winebrenner), 29,011; Disciples of Christ, 1,754,512; Mennonites, 90,310.

Institutions of Learning *

American Baptists have 18 theological seminaries, with 224 teachers, and 2,688 pupils, with property valued at $8,441,600; endowments, $7,807,916; volumes in the libraries, 246,700. They have 70 universities and colleges, with 3,493 instructors, 111,555 pupils, $85,-955,000 value in property; $108,849,218 in endowments; 2,454,900 volumes in the libraries.

They have 32 institutions (including theological seminaries) for the education of women and girls, with 673 teachers and 9,872 pupils, with property worth $15,082,600 and $4,360,456 in endowments, with 205,-100 volumes in their libraries.

* The statistics given are quoted with reserve, because of difficulties encountered in obtaining full returns to requests for information.

They have 195 coeducational institutions (including theological seminaries), with 4,196 teachers, 69,114 pupils, $95,472,800 value of property, $104,887,239 in endowments, and 2,591,100 volumes in their libraries.

There are some 60 schools (including theological seminaries) for Negroes, 3 schools among the Indians, and 11 among the people in Mexico. There are also schools for Chinese and other foreign-speaking peoples in the United States.

Sunday Schools

The churches reported 29,137 Sunday schools for 1927, with an enrolment of 3,859,734; that is, there are about six-sevenths as many Sunday schools as churches, and the enrolment in the schools reaches nearly four-fifths of the number of church-members.

Benevolent Contributions

Within the last two decades vigorous efforts have been made to increase the contributions of the denomination to missionary objects. According to the latest and most reliable reports available, they are credited with giving for foreign missions in the fiscal year 1927, $3,636,325; for home missions, $4,503,270; for education, $1,089,870; for miscellaneous purposes, in the neighborhood of two million dollars, or more; for salaries of pastors and other home expenses of the churches, $61,490,538; an aggregate of over seventy-two million dollars. The value of church property as reported was $426,416,000. It seems difficult to reconcile these facts with a sense of duty to Christ and the world, that they should expend nearly sixty-two million dollars on the churches at home and less than four millions for the conversion of the heathen world; or, that they should lock up more than $426,000,000 in church properties when there is so much need of funds for disseminating the gospel. At the same time they have more than $240,000,000 in property and endowments of educational institutions; or a total of more than $666,000,000 in property and endowments of churches and schools. Highly creditable in one sense, but the active work of giving the gospel to the world should claim a larger share.

Foreign Baptists

In the Canadas, about	140,474
West India Islands	57,944
Central America	1,843
Mexico	5,560
South America	30,872
Great Britain	416,665
Europe, exclusive of Great Britain	1,220,295
Asia	334,251
Africa	67,727
Australasia	32,811

It may properly be added that in all parts of the world where Baptists exist they are steadily, and in many places rapidly, increasing, both as to numbers, culture, wealth, and influence. But their polity is most in harmony with free civil governments and liberal institutions. In Russia, in common with some other religionists, they still suffer oppression and persecution. No missions among the heathen have shown such large results, in proportion to the means employed, as theirs; a fact in which they duly recognize the most gracious favor of God, to whom be the praise.*

* For many other facts see *American Baptist Year-Book* for 1928.

APPENDIX

A. CREEDS AND CONFESSIONS

WHILE all Evangelical Christians hold that the Bible alone is the complete and sufficient guide in matters of religious faith and practice, yet all denominations have, each for itself, prepared forms of doctrinal statement, setting forth, more or less fully, the fundamental truths which they understand the Scriptures to teach. These are put forth and accepted by the various communions as standards of doctrine for the instruction and unity of the people, and for appeal in controversy, while they are not held as binding the conscience, or limiting the faith of believers, save in a few cases. This function is—certainly by all Protestant Christians—conceded to the Bible alone, that of binding the conscience.

This dealing in Creeds and Standards, as a department in theological science, is termed *symbolics*.

These documents are very numerous, and some of them very widely accepted, and held in great reverence. They have served an important purpose in the economy of grace by holding the faith of the people to the fundamental truths of Christianity. For, however much they may differ in minor details, they do largely agree in the more prominent teachings of the Scriptures. These Creeds (*credo*, I believe), Confessions (*confessus*, assent, declaration), Symbols (*sumbolon*, a token, a sign), Articles of Faith (*articulus fidei*, something believed), as they are variously termed, have, to a considerable extent, been sent forth with catechisms for the systematic instruction of the young in the doctrines they teach. By this means the minds of the people become deeply imbued with essential religious truth in early life, the convictions of which usually abide through subsequent years.

These different Creed-forms, based on and drawn from the Word of God, as understood by those who framed them, have been of immense service to evangelical religion, by teaching the fundamental truths of the Scriptures, and guarding against many pernicious and destructive errors. It must be conceded, however, that with all their excellencies, they are not perfect, and do not fully, and, in some cases, may not faithfully, represent the sacred fountain of truth from which they are drawn. It is even asserted by some that they are mischievous in their tendency, by affecting to be ultimate, whereas they are only tentative, and progressive toward more complete and final statements; that they fetter investigation, and retard the progress of thought; hence it comes to pass that orthodoxy is measured more by the Creeds than by the Bible, and that heresy consists rather in the rejection of the Confessions than in the perversion of the Scriptures. But such results as these transpire only in exceptional cases, and the Creeds, on the whole, have served most beneficent purposes. They are to be valued and used as helpful, bearing in mind that the Bible alone is a complete standard of faith and practice. Also, that the Creeds are subject to still further revision, since all of them have been more or less frequently and materially revised.

Later in Christian history creed-making became common, in the hope of fixing a universally accepted standard of faith.   Indeed, the sixteenth and seventeenth centuries, the period of the Reformation, became the era of doctrinal symbols.   The effort was to unify the faith of the churches by putting forth new statements of doctrine, hoping to gain general assent to some one, and thereby to secure uniformity of faith.   But, to a large extent, the asperities of theological discussion embittered and divided, more than the Creeds harmonized and united, the various sections of Protestant Christendom.

Many of these confessions have become historic.   Those of Augsburg, of Basle, Heidelberg, the Helvetic, Belgic, that of Saxony, the Synod of Dort, the Thirty-nine Articles of the Anglican Church, the Westminster Assembly Con· fession, based on, and similar to, the Thirty-nine Articles; the Savoy, a modification of the Westminster's, and many others of lesser note.   Each denomination of Christians has its own; and, save the Apostles' Creed, the oldest and briefest of them all, there is no one in which all professed Christians can agree as to its entire statements.

THE APOSTLES' CREED

The Apostles' Creed, so-called, the oldest summary of Christian doctrine now extant, and one which the Roman, Greek and Protestant Churches all accept, originated, as is agreed, as early as the fourth century.   It is not known by whom it was prepared—certainly not by the Apostles, whose name it bears, and to whom tradition long ascribed it.   Truly, in fact, it teaches apostolic truth.   Perhaps, however, instead of being made, it *grew*, as most enduring things have done.   Possibly, also, the brevity of its form, as well as the substance of its truth, has helped to preserve it from oblivion.   Augustine pronounced it *brevis et grandis*—brief as to the number of its words, grand as to the weight of its teachings.

It is as follows:

" I believe in God the FATHER Almighty, maker of heaven and earth:
	"And in JESUS CHRIST, His only SON, our Lord,
	" Who was conceived by the Holy Ghost,
	" Born of the Virgin Mary,
	" Suffered under Pontius Pilate,
	" Was crucified, dead and buried.
	" He descended into hades:
	"The third day He rose again from the dead.
	" He ascended into heaven, and sitteth on the right hand of God the Father Almighty;
	" From thence He shall come to judge the quick and the dead.
	" I believe in the HOLY GHOST; the holy catholic church; the communion of saints; the forgiveness of sins; the resurrection of the body; and the life everlasting. Amen."

II.   THE NICENE CREED

The Nicene Creed also belongs to the fourth century—which was a creed-making era—having been adopted by the Council of Nice A. D. 325, enlarged and approved by the second Council of Constantinople A. D. 381, in which form it is commonly used, and is given below. It is somewhat longer than the Apostles', and much briefer and more satisfactory than the Athanasian. It made emphatic the divinity of Christ, and was designed as a breakwater against the incoming heresy of the Arians.

It is as follows:

" I believe in one God, the Father Almighty, Maker of heaven and earth, and of all things visible and invisible, and in one Lord Jesus Christ, the only begotten Son of God, begotten of His Father before all worlds; God of God, Light of Light, very God of very God, begotten, not made, being of one substance with the Father, by whom all things were made; who for us men, and for our salvation, came down from heaven, and was incarnate by the Holy Ghost, of the Virgin Mary, and was made man; and was crucified also for us, under Pontius Pilate; He suffered, and was buried; and the third day He rose again, according to the Scriptures, and ascended into heaven, and sitteth on the right hand of the Father. And He shall come again with glory to judge both the quick and the dead; whose kingdom shall have no end. And I believe in the Holy Ghost, the Lord and Giver of life, who proceedeth from the Father and the Son, who with the Father and the Son together, is worshiped and glorified; who spake by the prophets. And I believe in one catholic and apostolic Church. I acknowledge one baptism for the remission of sins; and I look for the resurrection of the dead and the life of the world to come. Amen.''

III.   THE ATHANASIAN CREED

This also was the product of the fourth century, but is not thought to have been prepared by Athanasius himself, though he may have produced the original basis on which it was built, while the superstructure underwent various modifications by other hands before it crystallized into its final form, after several centuries of use and change.   It is longer than the other ancient symbols, and less satisfactory to the faith of the present age.   In its final shape it was designed to stem the current of Arian heresy by strongly teaching the absolute divinity of Christ, and his co-equality with the Father.   A large part of the text is devoted to this doctrine, the phraseology of which is as offensive to a good literary taste as the doctrinal teaching is perplexing to a simple Christian faith.   It will do to stand with the metaphysical subtleties of the schoolmen rather than with the teachings of Christian truth.   The greater part of it to common minds conveys no sense whatever. Of course it embodies much truth.

It is as follows:

" Whoever will be saved, before all things it is necessary that he hold the catholic faith. Which faith, except every one do keep whole and undefiled, without doubt he shall perish everlastingly. And the catholic faith is this: That we worship one God in Trinity, and Trinity in Unity; neither confounding the persons nor dividing the substance. For there is one person of the Father, another of the Son, and another of the Holy Ghost. But the Godhead of the Father and of the Son, and of the Holy Ghost is all one; the glory equal, the majesty co-eternal. Such as the Father is, such is the Son, and such is the Holy Ghost. The Father uncreate, the Son uncreate, and the Holy Ghost uncreate. The Father incomprehensible, the Son incomprehensible, and the Holy Ghost incomprehensible. The Father eternal, the Son eternal, and the Holy Ghost eternal. And yet they are not three eternals, but one eternal. As also there are not three incomprehensibles, nor three uncreated, but one uncreated and one incomprehensible, so likewise is the Father Almighty, the Son Almighty, and the Holy Ghost Almighty. And yet there are not three almighties, but one almighty. So the Father is God, the Son is God, and the Holy Ghost is God. And yet there are not three Gods, but one God. So also the Father is Lord, the Son is Lord, and the Holy Ghost is Lord. And yet not three Lords, but one Lord. For like as we are compelled by the Christian verity to acknowledge every person by himself to be God and Lord, so are we forbidden by the catholic religion to say there be three Gods and three Lords.

" The Father is made of none, neither created nor begotten. The Son is of the Father alone: not made nor created, but begotten. The Holy Ghost is of the Father and the Son, neither made, nor created, nor begotten, but proceeding. So there is one Father, not three Fathers; one Son, not three Sons; one Holy Ghost, not three Holy Ghosts. And in this Trinity none is afore or after the other; none is greater nor less than another. But the whole three persons are co-eternal together, and co-equal. So that in all things, as is aforesaid, the Unity in Trinity and the Trinity in Unity is to be worshiped. He, therefore, that will be saved, must thus think of the Trinity.

'' Furthermore, it is necessary to everlasting salvation that he also believe rightly the incarnation of our Lord Jesus Christ. For the right faith is that we believe and confess that our Lord Jesus Christ, the Son of God, is God and man. God the substance of the Father, begotten before the worlds; and man, the substance of His mother, born in the world, perfect God and perfect man, of a reasonable soul and human flesh subsisting. Equal to the Father as touching His Godhead, and inferior to the Father as touching His manhood. Who, although He be God and man, yet He is not two but one Christ. One, not by conversion of the Godhead into flesh, but by taking of the manhood into God. One altogether not by confusion of substance, but by unity of person. For, as the reasonable soul and flesh is one man, so God and man is one Christ.

'' Who suffered for our salvation, descended into hell, rose again the third day from the dead. He ascended into heaven, He sitteth at the right hand of the Father Almighty. From whence He shall come to judge the quick and the dead. At whose coming all men shall rise again with their bodies, and shall give account of their own works. And they that have done good shall go into life everlasting, and they who have done evil, into everlasting fire.

'' This ' is the catholic faith, which except a man believe faithfully, he cannot be saved. Glory be to the Father, and to the Son, and to the Holy Ghost. As it was in the beginning, is now, and ever shall be, world without end. Amen.' ''

IV. LATER CONFESSIONS

The Augsburg Confession is the principal standard of doctrine for the Lutheran churches, and constitutes what is considered " the first Protestant Confession," though Luther had previously prepared articles for the Convention of Schwalbach, which, however, had not yet been published. The Emperor Charles I. called a German Diet to meet at Augsburg, 1530, and directed the Protestants to present a statement of their faith. The Elector John of Saxony requested the doctors of Wittenberg to draw up such a summary. Among them were Luther and Melancthon, who were chiefly instrumental in the work. These articles were presented and accepted, 1530, having been completed by Melancthon.

The Schmalcald Confession, drawn chiefly by Luther, as a protest against the traditions and false teachings of the papacy, was presented to the Protestant league of princes, electors, and nobles, at Schmalcald, and by them approved in 1537, and published in German and Latin, at Wittenberg, the next year. These articles are regarded as authoritative by the Lutheran churches throughout the world.

The Thirty-nine Articles, so-called, constitute the Confession of the Church of England. Originally these were forty-two. They were prepared by a royal commission, appointed in 1551, under Edward VI., for this purpose. At the head of it was Archbishop Cranmer, who had previously prepared some articles, drawn largely from the Augsburg Confession. These became the basis of the thirty-nine. Calvin, Melancthon, Bullinger, Peter Martyr, and others, conferred as to their preparation. In 1553 they were presented to the Convocation. Various changes were made in them before they were confirmed by Parliament. Various further changes were made by Convocation in 1562, 1566, and 1571, but it was not till 1628 that they were issued by royal authority under Charles I. In 1801 they were adopted by the Episcopal Church in America, with some further alterations, and the omission of one article, and with still further changes they have become the accepted Confession of the Methodist Episcopal Church in America.

The Heidelberg Confession, called also the Palatinate Catechism, was prepared under the direction of Frederick III., prince of the Palatinate, who had espoused the cause of the Reformation. Its preparation was committed to Ursinus, a pupil of Melancthon (who is regarded as its principal author), aided by Olevianus, court preacher and professor at Heidelberg. Catechisms of Luther, Calvin, Melancthon, and Lasco, furnished materials, and the work was completed, presented to, and accepted by, a synod of the Palatinate, December, 1562, and published in 1563. It has been published by millions, and translated into nearly every known language. It has become the venerated symbol and the accepted doctrinal standard of the German and Dutch Reformed Churches everywhere. It is strongly Calvinistic in tone, and is, beyond question, one of the most admirable compends of Christian doctrine extant.

The Canons of Dort were prepared by a national synod, called to settle the disputes which had arisen between the Calvinists and the Arminians. In this bitter controversy the great Grotius and the equally noble Barneveldt were engaged ; the latter of whom lost his life through the hostile and heartless jealousy of Maurice, Stadtholder of Nassau. The synod opened its sessions, November, 1618, in the great church of Dort, Holland, and closed them in May, 1619. They approved as orthodox both the Heidelberg and Belgic Confessions, and issued their own Canons of Doctrine, which are accepted as authoritative by the Reformed Dutch Church, and some other communions.

The Westminster Confession is the leading docrinal standard of the Presbyterian churches throughout the world, and, with some exceptions, is one of the best compends of Christian faith of modern history. It was prepared by the Westminster synod, known as the " Assembly of Divines," appointed by Parliament, and composed of Presbyterians, Episcopalians, Independents, and Erastians :* one hundred and twenty-one divines and thirty laymen from England, and five from Scotland. The meetings were held in Westminster Abbey, London, having been convened in the presence of both houses of Parliament, July 1, 1643. The assembly continued its sessions until the dissolution of the Long Parliament by Cromwell in 1653. Their labors included the larger and smaller Catechism, and a Directory for public worship, in addition to the Confession. This was based on, and largely conformed to, the Thirty-nine Articles of the English Church ; indeed, it was little more than a revision of that document, prepared a hundred years before, adopting it, article by article, with few changes, to the close of the fifteenth article, where their revision terminated. The work was approved by the House of Commons, 1647, and adopted by the Presbyterian General Assembly of Scotland, 1648. The Episcopalian and Independent churches did not accept the Confession. Various changes have since been made in it, and the form now used in this country—about which so much has been said during recent years— as issued by the Presbyterian Board of Publication,

---

* Erastians were followers of Erastus, a German divine and physician of the sixteenth century, who taught that the Church ought to be wholly dependent upon the State for its support, government, and discipline.

consists of Thirty-three Articles, or Chapters, with numerous subdivisions, or sections, accompanied with scriptural proof-texts, making a considerable book of 166
pages.

The Savoy Confession, so-called from the Savoy palace,
the residence of the bishop of London, in which was held
the Conference, 1658, appointed by royal commission to
formulate a declaration of faith, which should, if possible,
harmonize the Nonconformists with the Anglican Church.
Both the Anglican and the Dissenting clergy were engaged
in the Conference, but the effort proved unavailing. The
Confession prepared is largely a reproduction of the
Westminster Assembly's, and to a considerable extent
verbally identical with it ; containing thirty-two articles,
one less than the Assembly's. It is an accepted standard
of the Independents and Congregationalists, though not
held as binding.*

V. BAPTIST CONFESSIONS

The Protestant doctrine that the Bible alone is an authoritative standard of religious truth, and the only sufficient guide in faith and doctrine, is emphasized by Baptists. All Protestant Confessions are professedly founded
on, and drawn directly from, the word of God, utterly rejecting the Romish claim that tradition is of equal authority
with the Scriptures. Baptists have their Confessions, or,
as they are more commonly called, " Articles of Faith."
Most churches have these summaries, and each Church
uses such form as it may prefer ; or no form at all, if such

* For a full discussion of this subject see Schaff's *Creeds of
Christendom.*

be its choice. None are binding on the conscience of any, and members are not required to subscribe to any. The New Testament alone is their authoritative and binding standard. But these confessional compends constitute convenient formularies for reference, and for the instruction of the young. They help also to hold the minds of the people to the radical forms of evangelical truth.

Among American Baptists are to be found great numbers of these formularies, in a great variety of expression. as the churches which use them, or the pastors who constructed them may be inclined, but with a remarkable— it may be said, with a marvelous—harmony of doctrinal statements. Some of these have attained local notoriety, and have been accepted by particular Associations. But *two* in particular have gained wide currency, and have been adopted over extensive fields. These are, the *New Hampshire Confession*, so-called, generally adopted by the churches of the North, East, and West ; and the *Philadelphia Confession*, extensively used by the churches of the South and Southwest. The former is much the briefer of the two, and for that reason partly, no doubt, is in more common demand. For that reason, also, largely, and because of its general excellency, it has been chosen for insertion in the Directory and in the author's other manuals. It now consists of twenty articles, with a covenant. A part of the proof-texts are omitted from this work, as being inapposite, and to save space.

The *Philadelphia Confession* is substantially that of the English Baptists, issued in London, 1689, by the ministers and messengers of more than one hundred "*baptized* congregations" in the United Kingdom, as an answer to the misrepresentations and slanders of their enemies. That was based on, and an enlargement of, the Confession published in London, in 1644, by seven churches for the same purpose, and for substance of doctrine does not differ from that. In 1742 the old Philadelphia Association, feeling the need of some standard for the use of its own members, and to which inquirers could be referred, adopted this, which has since borne the name of that body. But in its adoption some changes were made. Two articles were added, one on " singing in worship as a holy ordinance of Christ," and one on " the laying on of hands with prayer upon baptized believers, as an ordinance of Christ."* To these articles was added an essay on *Church Discipline*. But both the added articles and the essay were subsequently omitted. This Confession consists of *thirty-two* articles, or chapters, with numerous subdivisions, and an appendix on baptism. That of 1644 is much more brief, though it contains fifty-two articles, but without subsections.†

---

* The laying hands on the newly baptized before they left the water was practised in many, if not in most churches, and is still the custom of some ministers.

† On this subject see Neal's Hist. Puritans, Vol. II., p. 475, Append.; Cutting's Hist. Vindications, Append., p. 113; Cathcart's Bap. Ency., Art. Confessions.

The Philadelphia Confession is a most admirable statement of Christian doctrine, but is quite too long, and theologically too abstruse for general circulation. Its length alone precludes it from this work, as it would fill forty of these pages. Probably the best edition now accessible is the reprint of Mr. Spurgeon's, issued by Wharton & Baron of Baltimore, Md. It is somewhat more pronounced as a Calvinistic symbol than the majority of our present standards, though all claim to be Calvinistic—moderately.

THE NEW HAMPSHIRE CONFESSION

The New Hampshire Confession was of slow growth, as most enduring standard documents have been. Its origin dates back to 1830, when the New Hampshire Baptist State Convention, holding its session at Concord, June 24th, authorized the preparation of a "declaration of faith," which might secure the approval and serve the purpose of all the Baptist Churches in that State. The proposition met with general approval, and a committee of three was appointed to do the work, and report. As the Convention met only annually the matter was finally referred to the Board. The committee underwent various changes, and it was not until 1833, after many modifications from the first draft, that the "Declaration" was approved, article by article, and unanimously adopted as their standard of faith.

When, in 1889, the writer was contemplating the preparation of a new and much enlarged edition of the Baptist Church Directory—or, rather, a new and larger work on the same plan—he sought in vain for definite information as to the origin of the New Hampshire Confession. It has been generally supposed that the late Rev. J. Newton Brown, D.D., was the author, as it was known he held some connection with its preparation, and had in more recent years issued a copy under his own name. Finally, I wrote to my old friend, Rev. W. H. Eaton, D. D., so long the honored pastor at Keene, N. H., who was very familiar with denominational affairs in that State, to know if he could give me any light on the subject. After some delay, I received the following letter in reply, which it gives me pleasure to insert, and for which I am under special obligations.

" KEENE, April 9, 1889

"MY DEAR DR. HISCOX:

"When I received your first communication I was satchel in hand for the cars on a thirty-mile exchange. I came home sick, and staid in the house nine days. I am gaining now quite fast.

"I will inform you about our Declaration of Faith. The first edition was published in *1833;* the last, in *1882.* The history seems to be as follows: In the Convention at Concord in June, 1830, Rev. Noah Nichols of Rumney introduced the following: ' *Whereas,* The Baptist denomination of Christians are believed to be united in their views of the important and essential doctrines and practices of our holy religion (although their declarations of faith are not in precisely the same language as it is desirable they should be), therefore,

"'*Resolved,* That Brethren N. W. Williams, Wm. Taylor, and I. Person be a committee to prepare and present, at our next annual session, such a Declaration of Faith and Practice, together with a Covenant, as may be thought agreeable to, and consistent with, the views of all our churches in this state.' This was adopted. At Hopkinton in June, 1831, I find this record: ' The committee appointed last year to prepare and present a concise and scriptural Declaration of Faith and Practice, reported that they had made some progress in the work assigned them, but, owing to peculiar circumstances, had not been able to complete it.'

"At their request, the committee were discharged, and Rev. I. Person appointed to finish the work and report to the Board of this Convention as soon as convenient. By this vote the whole thing was transferred to the *Board.*

"At the Board Meeting June 26, 1832, ' Rev. I. Person presented his report in relation to the Articles of Faith and Practice, which he was some time since appointed to prepare.' And they were referred to a select committee, consisting of Stow, Brown and Going, with the author. Again, in Convention at Portsmouth in June, 1832, I find this record:

"' The committee, to whom the Board had referred the Articles of Faith and Practice prepared by Brother Person, reported in favor of adopting them with some slight alterations; but after some discussion it was resolved to refer them to the disposition of the Board.'

" At the Board Meeting June 29, 1832, they were presented and referred to Brethren Stow and Brown for revision.

" At the Board Meeting Oct. 10, 1832, they were presented and considered, article by article; then Bro. Brown was appointed to prepare a copy with such alterations as had been suggested by the Board.'

" At the Board Meeting in Jan., 1833, it was voted to erase the word 'article' or 'articles' wherever it was found, and substitute the word 'Declaration.' Then Bro. Brown presented the copy he had prepared, and they adjourned for one hour. Then, after a second adjournment, it was

" '*Resolved*, That the Declaration of Faith and Covenant prepared by Brethren Stow and Brown, and now read before the Board of this Convention, are entitled to their unanimous approbation, and are by them cordially recommended to the adoption of the churches.' Then arrangements were made for publishing them.

" You will see by the above that the proceedings about the Declaration were all in the Convention and Board.

" You understand that Stow was Baron Stow, D.D., and that Brown was J. Newton Brown, D.D. The *tradition* has always been that the Declaration was the work of J. N. Brown. I trust that the above will be satisfactory. If anything now is omitted, please let me know.

" Yours most truly,

" W. H. EATON "

At the meeting of the New Hampshire Historical Society at Concord, Oct. 21, 1891, Rev. Wm. Hurlin of Antrim, N. H., presented to that body a carefully prepared history of the " Declaration," to which service he had been previously appointed, which history was accepted, with the thanks of the body. I wish to acknowledge my indebtedness to Rev. Mr. Hurlin for a copy of this report, which he was kind enough to send me.   Omitting the details, the following is the summary of that report :

" The following is a summary of the Records on this matter : In 1830 the Convention appointed a committee of three to prepare a Declaration of Faith and a Covenant.   That committee made some progress, and then in 1831 they were, at their own request, discharged, and one of their number, Rev. I. Person (afterward spelt Pearson), was appointed to *finish* the work.   He presented what he had done to the Convention of 1832, and it was accepted and referred to a select committee of three persons in addition to the author.   This committee reported in favor of adopting the articles ' prepared by Bro. Person, . . . with slight altera-tions,' but after discussion, the Convention voted ' to refer them to the disposal of the Board.'

" The Board referred them to two members of the select com-mittee, Brethren Stow and Brown, to be revised and presented at a future meeting.   In October, 1832, Rev. J. N. Brown pre-sented the report of this committee, and after a long and pro-tracted consideration, article by article, it was accepted, and Rev. J. N. Brown was requested to prepare a copy of it, including such alterations as had been suggested by the Board.   At a subsequent meeting the Board voted still further amendments, and then Bro. Brown presented the amended copy, and it was unanimously ap-proved by the Board, and recommended to the churches of the State.

" Thus far the indications are that it is the work of Rev. I. Per-son, revised by Revs. B. Stow and J. N. Brown, and largely altered by the full Board, and then finally prepared for the press by Rev. J. N. Brown.   It is to be noted here that in the Resolution by which the Board approved and recommended it, they speak of it as " The Declaration of Faith and Covenant pre-pared by Brethren Stow and Brown,' thus speaking of these two as joint authors.

" But in 1853 Rev. J. N. Brown republished the Declaration and Covenant, under the title of *The Baptist Church Manual*, ' with such revision as on mature reflection he deems called for after the lapse of twenty years,' and also 'supplying two new articles, one on Repentance and Faith, and the other on Sanctification.' In the advertisement to this pamphlet Mr. Brown claims the authorship of the original publication, and this would seem to settle the question, which is otherwise obscure."

As first published, there were sixteen articles. Subsequently Dr. Brown added two : one on Repentance and Faith, and one on Sanctification. When this author prepared them for his Standard Manual in 1890, he divided the article on Baptism and the Lord's Supper, making two, and increasing the number to nineteen. Some verbal changes were also made, which seemed to be improvements, and a few of the proof-texts, which did not appear pertinent, were omitted. For this work a further change has been made by dividing the article on Repentance and Faith, giving one to each subject, and adding an article on Adoption, which seems to deserve a place in such a document. It is to be noted, however, that none of these changes have modified, or in any way altered, the doctrinal substance, or teaching of the Confession. It now consists of twenty articles, intelligible as to statement, simple as to form, and loyal to New Testament truth. No other creed form has attained to anything like its general circulation among American Baptists.* It is as follows:

* About 100,000 copies have been circulated with the author's manuals alone, besides its wide dissemination by other means. In the Directory, not far from 60,000 have been sent out. In the Star Book on Church Polity more than 30,000, and in the Standard Manual about 10,000. On the whole, for common use among Baptists, no other form of doctrinal statement has so much to commend it as this, though none can be claimed as perfect.

ARTICLES OF FAITH

I. THE SCRIPTURES

We believe that the Holy Bible was written by men divinely inspired, and is a perfect treasure of heavenly instruction; that it has God for its author, salvation for its end, and truth without any mixture of errror for its matter; that it reveals the principles by which God will judge us; and therefore is, and shall remain to the end of the world, the true centre of Christian union, and the supreme standard by which all human conduct, creeds, and opinions should be tried.

"All Scripture is given by inspiration of God, and is profitable for doctrine, for reproof, for correction, for instruction in righteousness; that the man of God may be perfect, thoroughly furnished unto all good works."— 2 Tim. 3 : 16, 17. Also, 2 Pet. 1 : 21; 2 Sam. 23 : 2; Acts 1 : 16; 3 : 21 ; John 10 : 35; Luke 16 : 29–31; Ps. 119 : 3; Rom. 3 : 1, 2.

"Every word of God is pure. Add thou not unto His words, lest he reprove thee, and thou be found a liar."—Prov. 30: 5, 6. Also, John 17 : 17; Rev. 22 : 18, 19; Rom. 3: 4.

"As many as have sinned in the law, shall be judged by the law."—Rom. 2 : 12. "If any man hear my words, the word that I have spoken, the same shall judge him in the last day."—John 12:47, 48. Also 1 Cor. 4 : 3, 4; Luke 10 : 10–16; 12 : 47, 48.

II. THE TRUE GOD

We believe the Scriptures teach that there is one, and only one, living and true God, an infinite, intelligent

Spirit, whose name is JEHOVAH, the Maker and Supreme Ruler of Heaven and Earth; inexpressibly glorious in holiness, and worthy of all possible honor, confidence and love; that in the unity of the Godhead there are three persons, the Father, the Son, and the Holy Ghost; equal in every divine perfection, and executing distinct but harmonious offices in the great work of redemption.

"God is a Spirit."—John 4 : 24.   " His understanding is infinite."—Ps. 147 : 5.   " Thou whose name alone is JEHOVAH, art the Most High over all the earth."—Ps. 83: 18; Heb. 3:4; Rom. 1:20; Jer. 10:10.

" Who is like unto Thee—glorious in holiness ? "—Ex. 15: 11: Isa. 6: 3; 1 Pet. 1: 15, 16; Rev. 4: 6–8.

" Thou shalt love the Lord thy God with all thy heart, and with all thy soul, and with all thy mind, and with all thy strength."—Mark 12: 30. "Thou art worthy, O Lord, to receive glory, and honor, and power."—Rev. 4: 11; Matt. 10 37; Jer. 2: 12, 13.

"Go ye therefore and teach all nations, baptizing them in the name of the Father, and of the Son, and of the Holy Ghost."—Matt. 28: 19; John 15 : 26; 1 Cor. 12 : 4 -6; 1 John 5 : 7.

III.   THE FALL OF MAN

We believe the Scriptures teach that Man was created in holiness, under the law of his Maker; but by voluntary transgression fell from that holy and happy state; in consequence of which all mankind are now sinners, not by constraint but choice; being by nature utterly void of that holiness required by the law of God, positively inclined to evil; and therefore under just condemnation to eternal ruin, without defense or excuse.

"God created man in His own image."—Gen. 1 : 27.
"And God saw everything that He had made, and behold,
it was very good."—Gen. 1 : 31; Eccles. 7 : 29; Acts 17 :
26; Gen. 2 : 16.

"And when the woman saw that the tree was good for
food, and that it was pleasant to the eyes, and a tree to
be desired to make one wise, she took of the fruit thereof,
and did eat; and gave also unto her husband with her, and
he did eat."—Gen. 3 : 6–24; Rom. 5 : 12.

"By one man's disobedience many were made sinners."—Rom. 5 : 19; John 3 : 6; Ps. 51 : 6; Rom. 5 : 15–
19; 8 : 7.

"We have turned, every one to his own way."—Isa. 53:
6; Gen. 6 : 12; Rom. 3 : 9–18.

"Among whom also we all had our conversation in
times past in the lusts of our flesh, fulfilling the desires of
the flesh and of the mind; and were by nature the children of wrath even as others."—Eph. 2 : 3; Rom. 1 : 18;
Rom. 1 : 32; 2 : 1–16; Gal. 3 : 10; Matt. 20 : 15.

"The soul that sinneth it shall die."—Ezek. 18 : 19, 20.
"So that they are without excuse."—Rom. 1 : 20.   "That
every mouth may be stopped and and all the world may
become guilty before God."—Rom. 3 : 19; Gal. 3 : 22.

IV.   GOD'S PURPOSE OF GRACE

We believe the Scriptures teach that *election* is the
eternal purpose of God, according to which He graciously
regenerates, sanctifies and saves sinners; that being perfectly consistent with the free agency of man, it compre-
hends all the means in connection with the end; that it is
a most glorious display of God's sovereign goodness, being
infinitely free, wise, holy and unchangeable; that it utterly

excludes boasting, and promotes humility, love, prayer, praise, trust in God, and active imitation of His free mercy; that it encourages the use of means in the highest degree; that it may be ascertained by its effects in all who truly believe the Gospel; that it is the foundation of Christian assurance; and that to ascertain it with regard to ourselves demands and deserves the utmost diligence.

" But be thou partaker of the afflictions of the Gospel, according to the power of God; who hath saved us and called us with a holy calling, not according to our works, but according to His own purpose and grace which was given us in Christ Jesus before the world began."—2 Tim. 1 : 8, 9.

" But we are bound to give thanks always to God for you, brethren beloved of the Lord, because God hath from the beginning chosen you to salvation, through sanctification of the Spirit and belief of the truth; whereunto He called you by our Gospel, to the obtaining of the glory of our Lord Jesus Christ."—2 Thess. 2 : 13, 14.

" Therefore I endure all things for the elects' sake, that they also may obtain the salvation which is in Christ Jesus with eternal glory."—2 Tim. 2 : 10; 1 Cor. 9 : 22; Rom. 8 : 28–30; John 6 : 37–40; 2 Pet. 1 : 10.

"Knowing, brethren beloved, your election of God."— 1 Thess. 4 : 10.

"Moreover, whom He did predestinate, them He also called, and whom He called, them He also justified, and whom He justified, them He also glorified."—Rom. 8 : 28– 30; Isa. 42 : 16; Rom. 11 : 29.

V.   THE WAY OF SALVATION

We believe the Scriptures teach that the salvation of sinners is wholly of grace; through the mediatorial offices of the Son of God; who according to the will of the Father, assumed our nature, yet without sin; honored the divine law by His personal obedience, and by His death made a full atonement for our sins; that having risen from the dead, He is now enthroned in heaven; and uniting in His wonderful person the tenderest sympathies with divine perfections, He is every way qualified to be a suitable, a compassionate and an all-sufficient Savior.

"By grace ye are saved."—Eph. 2 : 5; Matt. 18 : 11; 1 John 4 : 10; 1 Cor. 3 : 5–7; Acts 15 : 11.

"For God so loved the world that He gave His only begotten Son, that whosoever believeth in Him should not perish, but have everlasting life."—John 3 : 16; John 1 : 1–14; Heb. 4 : 14; 12 : 24.

"Who being in the form of God, thought it not robbery to be equal with God; but made himself of no reputation, and took upon Him the form of a servant, and was made in the likeness of men."—Phil. 2 : 6, 7; Heb. 2 : 9; 2 : 14; 2 Cor. 5 : 21.

"He was wounded for our transgressions, He was bruised for our iniquities; the chastisement of our peace was upon Him; and with His stripes we are healed."—Isa. 53: 4, 5.

"Wherefore He is able also to save them to the uttermost that come unto God by Him, seeing He ever liveth to make intercession for them."—Heb. 7 : 25. "For in Him dwelleth all the fulness of the Godhead bodily."—Col. 2 : 9; Heb. 2 : 18; Heb. 7 : 26.

VI. OF REGENERATION

We believe the Scriptures teach that *regeneration*, or the new birth, is that change wrought in the soul by the Holy Spirit, by which a new nature and a spiritual life, not before possessed, are imparted, and the person becomes a new creation in Christ Jesus; a holy disposition is given to the mind, the will subdued, the dominion of sin broken, and the affections changed from a love of sin and self, to a love of holiness and God; the change is instantaneous, effected solely by the power of God, in a manner incomprehensible to reason; the evidence of it is found in a changed disposition of mind, the fruits of righteousness, and a newness of life. And without it salvation is impossible.

" Verily, verily, I say unto you, except a man be born again, he cannot see the kingdom of God." —John 3 : 3.

" That which is born of the flesh is flesh; that which is born of the spirit is spirit."—John 3 : 6.

" Born again, not of corruptible seed, but of incorruptible, by the Word of God."—1 Pet. 1 : 23.

"Of His own will begat He us, with the word of truth."—James 1 : 18.

" If any man be in Christ, he is a new creature."—2 Cor. 5 : 17.

"Ye know that every one that doeth righteousness is born of Him."—1 John 2 : 29.

" And that ye put on the new man, which after God is created in righteousness and true holiness."—Eph. 4 : 24.

" And you being dead in your sins, and the uncircumcision of your flesh, hath He quickened together with Him."—Col. 2 : 13.

" But yield yourselves unto God, as those that are alive from the dead."—Rom. 6 : 13.

" Who hath delivered us from the power of darkness and hath translated us into the kingdom of His dear Son."— Col. 1 : 13.

" Which were born not of blood, nor of the will of the flesh, nor of the will of man, but of God."—John 1 : 13.

" And such were some of you, but ye are washed, but ye are sanctified, but ye are justified, in the name of the Lord Jesus, and by the Spirit of our God."—1 Cor. 6 : 11.

VII. OF REPENTANCE

We believe the Scriptures teach that *repentance* is a personal act, prompted by the Spirit; and consists in a godly sorrow for sin, as offensive to God and ruinous to the soul; that it is accompanied with great humiliation in view of one's sin and guilt, together with prayer for pardon; also by sincere hatred of sin, and a persistent turning away from, and abandonment of, all that is evil and unholy. Since none are sinless in this life, repentance needs to be often repeated.

" In those days came John the Baptist preaching in the wilderness of Judea, and saying, Repent: for the kingdom of heaven is at hand."—Matt. 3 : 1, 2.

" From that time Jesus began to preach, and to say, Repent: for the kingdom of heaven is at hand."—Matt. 4 : 17.

"Saying, The time is fulfilled, and the kingdom of God is at hand: repent ye and believe the Gospel."—Mark 1 : 15.

" Repent ye therefore and be converted, that your sins may be blotted out."—Acts 3 : 19.

" The times of this ignorance God overlooked, but now He commandeth all men everywhere to repent."—Acts 17 : 30.

" Testifying both to the Jews and also to the Greeks, repentance toward God, and faith toward our Lord Jesus Christ."—Acts 20 : 21.

"Godly sorrow worketh repentance to salvation, not to be repented of."—2 Cor. 7 : 2.

"And that repentance and remission of sins should be preached in His name, among all nations, beginning at Jerusalem."—Luke 24 : 47.

"Him hath God exalted with His right hand to be a Prince and a Savior, to give repentance to Israel, and remission of sins."—Acts 5 : 31.

"But thou, after thy hardness and impenitent heart, treasurest up unto thyself wrath against the day of wrath, and revelation of the righteous judgment of God."—Rom. 2 : 5.

"Let the wicked forsake his way, and the unrighteous man his thoughts; and let him return unto the Lord, and He will have mercy upon him; and to our God, for He will abundantly pardon."—Isa. 55 : 7

VIII.   OF FAITH

We believe the Scriptures teach that *faith*, as an evangelical grace wrought by the Spirit, is the medium through which Christ is received by the soul as its sacrifice and Savior.   It is an assent of the mind and a consent of the heart, consisting mainly of *belief* and *trust;* the testimony of God is implicitly accepted and believed as true, while Christ is unreservedly trusted for salvation; by it the believer is brought into vital relations with God, freely justified, and lives as seeing Him who is invisible.   Faith cannot save, but it reveals Christ to the soul as a willing and sufficient Savior, and commits the heart and life to Him.

"Believe on the Lord Jesus Christ, and thou shalt be saved."—Acts 16 : 31.

" For Christ is the end of the law for righteousness, to every one that believeth."—Rom. 10 : 3.

" Therefore, being justified by faith, we have peace with God, through our Lord Jesus Christ."—Rom. 5 : 1.

" Now, faith is the substance ot things hoped for, the evidence of things not seen."—Heb. 11 : 1.

" But without faith it is impossible to please God."—Heb. 11 : 6.

" For therein is the righteousness of God revealed from faith to faith; as it is written, The just shall live by faith."—Rom. 1 : 17.

" And the Scripture was fulfilled which saith, Abraham believed God, and and it was imputed to him for righteousness."—James 2 : 23.

" Blessed is the man who trusteth in the Lord, and whose hope the Lord is."—Jer. 17 : 7.

" They that trust in the Lord, shall be as Mount Zion which cannot be removed, but abideth forever."—Ps. 125 : 1.

" The Lord redeemeth the soul of his servants, and none of them that trust in Him shall be desolate."—Ps. 34 : 22.

" For we walk by faith, not by sight."—2 Cor. 5 : 7.

" Even the righteousness of God, which is by faith of Jesus Christ, unto all, and upon all them that believe."—Rom. 3 : 22.

" With the heart man believeth unto righteousness, and with the mouth confession is made unto salvation."—Rom. 10 : 10.

IX.   OF JUSTIFICATION

We believe the Scriptures teach that the great Gospel blessing which Christ secures to such as believe in Him is *justification;* that justification includes the pardon of sin, and the promise of eternal life on principles of right-eousness; that it is bestowed, not in consideration of any works of righteousness which we have done, but solely through faith in the Redeemer's blood; by virtue of which faith His perfect righteousness is freely imputed to us of God; that it brings us into a state of most blessed peace and favor with God, and secures every other blessing needful for time and eternity.

"Of His fulness have all we received."—John 1 : 16; Eph. 3 : 8.

" By Him all that believe are justified from all things."— Acts 13 : 39; Isa. 3 : 11, 12; Rom. 8 : 1.

" Being justified by His blood, we shall be saved from wrath through Him."—Rom. 5 : 9; Zech. 13 : 1; Matt. 9: 6; Acts 10 : 43.

"Being justified by faith, we have peace with God, through our Lord Jesus Christ: by whom also we have access by faith into this grace wherein we stand, and re-joice in hope of the glory of God."—Rom. 5 : 1, 2; Rom. 5 : 3; Rom. 5 : 11; 1 Cor. 1 : 30, 31; Matt. 6 : 33; 1 Tim. 4 : 8.

X.   OF ADOPTION

We believe the Scriptures teach that *adoption* is a gra-cious act, by which the Father, for the sake of Christ, ac-cepts believers to the estate and condition of children, by a new and spiritual birth; sending the Spirit of adoption into their hearts, whereby they become members of the family of God, and entitled to all the rights, privileges and promises of children; and if children, then heirs, heirs of God, and joint-heirs with Jesus Christ, to the heritage of the saints on earth, and an inheritance reserved in heaven for them.

" For as many as are led by the Spirit of God, they are the sons of God."—Rom. 8 : 14.

" But ye have received the spirit of adoption, whereby we cry, Abba, Father."—Rom. 8 : 15.

" The Spirit Himself beareth witness with our spirit, that we are the children of God."—Rom. 8 : 16.

" For ye are the children of God, by faith in Jesus Christ."—Gal. 3 : 26.

" And because ye are sons, God hath sent forth the Spirit of His Son into your hearts, crying, Abba, Father."—Gal. 4 : 6.

" Wherefore thou art no more a servant, but a son: and if a son, then an heir of God through Jesus Christ."—Gal. 4 : 7.

" Having foreordained us unto the adoption of children, through Jesus Christ."—Eph. 1 : 5.

" Behold what manner of love the Father hath bestowed upon us, that we should be called the sons of God."—1 John 3 : 1.

" To redeem them that are under the law that we might receive the adoption of sons."—Gal. 4 : 5.

" If ye endure chastening, God dealeth with you as with sons."—Heb. 12 : 7.

" But ye are a chosen generation, a royal priesthood, a peculiar people: that ye should show forth the praises of Him who hath called you out of darkness into His marvelous light."—1 Peter 2 : 9.

XI. OF SANCTIFICATION

We believe the Scriptures teach that *sanctification* is the process by which, according to the will of God, we are made partakers of His holiness; that it is a progressive work; that it is begun in regeneration; that it is carried on in the hearts of believers by the presence and power of the Holy Spirit, the Sealer and Comforter, in the continual use of the appointed means—especially the Word of God, self - examination, self - denial, watchfulness, and prayer; and in the practice of all godly exercises and duties.

"For this is the will of God, even your sanctification."—2 Thess. 4 : 3. "And the very God of peace sanctify you wholly."—1 Thess. 5 : 23; 2 Cor. 7 : 1; 13 : 9; Eph. 1 : 4.

"The path of the just is as the shining light, which shineth more and more, unto the perfect day."—Prov. 4: 18; 2 Cor. 3 : 18; Heb. 6 : 1; 2 Pet. 1 : 5–8; Phile. 12–16.

"Work out your own salvation with fear and trembling, for it is God which worketh in you both to will and to do, of His good pleasure."—Phil. 2 : 12, 13; Eph. 4 : 11, 12; 1 Pet. 2 : 2; 2 Pet. 3 : 18; 2 Cor. 13 : 5.

"Exercise thyself unto godliness."—1 Tim. 4 : 7.

XII.   THE PERSEVERANCE OF SAINTS

We believe the Scriptures teach that such as are truly regenerate, being born of the Spirit, will not utterly fall away and finally perish, but will endure unto the end; that their persevering attachment to Christ is the grand mark which distinguishes them from superficial professors; that a special Providence watches over their welfare; and they are kept by the power of God through faith unto salvation.

"And this is the Father's will that hath sent me, that of all which He hath given me, I should lose nothing, but should raise it up again at the last day."—John 6 : 39.

"Then said Jesus, If ye continue in my word, then are

ye my disciples indeed."—John 8 : 31; 1 John 2 : 27, 28:
3 : 9; 5 : 18.

" They went out from us, but they were not of us; for
if they had been of us, they would no doubt have continued with us; but they went out that it might be made
manifest that they were not all of us."—John 2 : 19; John
13 : 18; Matt. 13 : 20, 21; John 6 : 66–69.

" And we know all things work together for good unto
them that love God, to them who are the called according
to His purpose."—Rom. 8 : 28; Matt. 6 : 30–33.

" He who hath begun a good work in you will perform
it until the day of Jesus Christ."—Phil. 1 : 6; Phil. 2 : 12.
13; Jude 24 ,25; Heb. 1 : 14, 13 : 5; John 4 : 4.

XIII.   THE LAW AND THE GOSPEL

We believe the Scriptures teach that the Law of God is
the eternal and unchangeable rule of His moral government; that it is holy, just, and good; and that the inabil-
ity which the Scriptures ascribe to fallen men to fulfill its
precepts arises entirely from their sinful nature; to deliver
them from which, and to restore them through a Mediator to unfeigned obedience to the holy Law, is one great
end of the Gospel, and of the Means of Grace connected
with the establishment of the visible Church.

" Do we make void the law through faith ? God forbid.
Yea, we establish the law."—Rom. 3 : 31; Matt 5 : 17;
Luke 16 : 17; Rom. 3 : 20; 4 : 15.

" The law is holy, and the commandment holy, and
just, and good."—Rom. 7 : 12; Rom. 7 : 7, 14, 22; Gal.
3 : 21; Psalm 119.

" The carnal mind is enmity against God; for it is not
subject to the law of God, neither indeed can be.   So

then they that are in the flesh cannot please God."—Rom. 8 : 7, 8.

" For the law of the Spirit of Life in Christ Jesus hath made me free from the law of sin and death. For what the law could not do, in that it was weak through the flesh, God sending His own Son in the likeness of sinful flesh, and for sin, condemned sin in the flesh; that the righteousness of the law might be fulfilled in us, who walk not after the flesh, but after the Spirit."—Rom. 8 : 2, 4; Rom. 10 : 4; 1 Tim. 1 : 5; Heb. 8 : 10.

XIV.   A GOSPEL CHURCH

We believe the Scriptures teach that a visible Church of Christ is a congregation of baptized believers, associated by covenant in the faith and fellowship of the Gospel; observing the ordinances of Christ; governed by His laws; and exercising the gifts, rights, and privileges invested in them by His word; that its only scriptural officers are bishops or pastors, and deacons, whose qualifications, claims, and duties are defined in the Epistles to Timothy and Titus.

" Then they that gladly received His word were baptized; and the same day there were added to them about three thousand souls."—Acts 2 : 41, 42; Acts 5 : 11; 8 : 1; 11 : 31; 1 Cor. 4 : 17; 1 Tim. 3 : 5.

" They first gave their own selves to the Lord, and unto us by the will of God."—2 Cor. 8 : 5; Acts 2 : 47; 1 Cor. 5 : 11, 18.

" Now I praise you, brethren, that ye remember me in all things, and keep the ordinances as I delivered them to you."—1 Cor. 11 : 2; 2 Thess. 3 : 7; Rom. 16 : 17–20; 1 Cor. 11 : 23; Matt. 18 : 15–20; 1 Cor. 5 : 5.

" Teaching them to observe all things whatsoever I have commanded you."—Matt. 28 : 20; John 14 : 15; 15 : 10; 1 John 4 : 21; 1 Thess. 4 : 2; 2 John 6.

" With the bishops and deacons."—Phil. 1 : 1; Acts 14 : 23; 15 : 22; 1 Tim 3; Titus 1.

XV.   CHRISTIAN BAPTISM

We believe the Scriptures teach that Christian Baptism is the immersion in water of a believer in Christ, into the name of the Father, and Son, and Holy Ghost; to show forth, in a solemn and beautiful emblem, our faith in the crucified, buried, and risen Savior, with its effect, in our death to sin and resurrection to a new life; that it is prerequisite to the privileges of a Church relation, and to the Lord's Supper.

" And the eunuch said, See, here is water; what doth hinder me to be baptized ?   And Philip said, If thou believest with all thy heart thou mayest. . . . And they went down into the water, both Philip and the eunuch, and he baptized him."—Acts 8 : 36–39; Matt. 3 : 5, 6; John 3 : 22, 23; 4 : 1, 2; Matt. 28 : 19; Mark 16 : 16; Acts 2 : 38; 8 : 12; 16 : 32–34; 18 : 8.

" Baptizing them in the name of the Father, and of the Son, and of the Holy Ghost."—Matt. 18 : 19; Acts 10 : 47, 48; Gal. 3 : 27, 28.

" Therefore we are buried with Him by baptism into death; that like as Christ was raised from the dead by the glory of the Father, even so we also should walk in newness of life."—Rom. 6 : 4; Col. 2 : 12; 1 Peter 3 : 20, 21; Acts 22 : 16.

" Then they that gladly received His word were baptized, and there were added to them, the same day, about three thousand souls. And they continued steadfastly in the Apostles' doctrine and fellowship, and in breaking of bread, and in prayers."—Acts 2 : 41, 42 ; Matt. 28 : 19, 20.

XVI.   THE LORD'S SUPPER

We believe the Scriptures teach that the Lord's Supper is a provision of bread and wine, as symbols of Christ's body and blood, partaken of by the members of the Church, in commemoration of the suffering and death of their Lord; showing their faith and participation in the merits of His sacrifice, and their hope of eternal life through His resurrection from the dead; its observance to be preceded by faithful self-examination.

" And He took bread, and gave thanks, and brake, and gave unto them, saying, This is my body which is given for you; this do in remembrance of me. Likewise also the cup after supper, saying, This cup is the New Testament in my blood, which is shed for you."—Luke 22 : 19, 20; Mark 14 : 20–26; Matt. 26 : 27–30; 1 Cor. 11 : 27–30; 1 Cor. 10 : 16.

" For, as often as ye eat this bread, and drink this cup, ye do show the Lord's death until He come."—1 Cor. 11: 26; Matt. 28 : 20.

" But let a man examine himself, and so let him eat of that bread, and drink of that cup."—1 Cor. 11 : 28; Acts 2 : 42, 46; 20 : 7, 11.

" And they continued steadfastly in the apostles' doctrine and fellowship, and in breaking of bread and in prayers."—Acts 2 : 42.

XVII.   THE CHRISTIAN SABBATH

We believe the Scriptures teach that the first day of the

week is the Lord's Day; and is to be kept sacred to religious purposes, by abstaining from all secular labor, except works of mercy and necessity, by the devout observance of all the means of grace, both private and public;
and by preparation for that rest that remaineth for the
people of God.

" On the first day of the week, when the disciples came
together to break bread, Paul preached to them."—Acts
20 : 7; Gen. 2 : 3; Col. 2 : 16, 17; Mark 2 : 27; John 20 :
19; 1 Cor. 16 : 1, 2.

" Remember the Sabbath Day, to keep it holy."—Ex.
20 : 8.   " I was in the Spirit on the Lord's Day."—Rev. 1 :
10; Ps. 118 : 24.

" If thou turn away thy foot from the Sabbath, from
doing thy pleasure on my holy day; and call the Sabbath
a delight, the holy of the Lord, honorable; and shalt honor
Him, not doing thine own ways, nor finding thine own
pleasure, nor speaking thine own words; then shalt thou
delight thyself in the Lord, and I will cause thee to ride
upon the high places of the earth, and feed thee with the
heritage of Jacob."—Isa. 58 : 13, 14; Isa. 56 : 2–8.

"Not forsaking the assembling of yourselves together,
as the manner of some is."—Heb. 10 : 24, 25. " The next
Sabbath Day came almost the whole city together to hear
the Word of God "—Acts 13 : 44.

" Let us labor, therefore, to enter into that rest."—Heb.
4 : 3–11.

XVIII.   CIVIL GOVERNMENT

We believe the Scriptures teach that civil government
is of divine appointment, for the interest and good order
of human society; and that magistrates are to be prayed

for, conscientiously honored and obeyed, except only in things opposed to the will of our Lord Jesus Christ, who is the only Lord of the conscience, and the Prince of the kings of the earth. But that civil rulers have no rights of control over, or of interference with, religious matters.

"The powers that be are ordained of God. For rulers are not a terror to good works, but to the evil."—Rom. 13: 1–7.

"Be subject to every ordinance of man, for the Lord's sake."—1 Pet. 2 : 13.

"Render therefore unto Cæsar the things that are Cæsar's, and unto God the things that are God's."—Matt. 22 : 21; Titus 3 : 1; 1 Pet. 2 : 13; 1 Tim. 2 : 1–8.

"We ought to obey God rather than man."—Acts 5 : 29. "Fear not them which kill the body, but are not able to kill the soul."—Matt. 10 : 28; Dan. 3 : 15–18; 6 : 7, 10; Acts 4 : 18–20.

"Ye have one Master, even Christ."—Matt. 23 : 10. "Who art thou that judgest another man's servant?"—Rom. 14 : 4. "And He hath on His vesture and on His thigh a name written, KING OF KINGS AND LORD OF LORDS."—Rev. 19 : 14; Ps. 72 : 11; Ps. 2; Rom. 14 : 9–13.

XIX.   RIGHTEOUS AND WICKED

We believe the Scriptures teach that there is a radical and essential difference between the righteous and the wicked; that such only as through faith are justified in the name of the Lord Jesus, and sanctified by the Spirit of our God, are truly righteous in His esteem; while all such as continue in impenitence and unbelief are, in His sight, wicked and under the curse; and this distinction holds among men both in this life and after death.

" Ye shall discern between the righteous and the wicked; between him that serveth God and him that serveth Him not."—Mal. 3 : 18; Prov. 12 : 26; Isa. 5 : 20; Gen. 18 : 23; Jer. 15 : 19; Acts 10 : 34, 35; Rom. 6 : 16.

" The just shall live by faith."—Rom. 1 : 17. " If ye know that He is righteous, ye know that every one that doeth righteousness is born of Him."—Rom. 7 : 6; 1 John 3 : 7; Rom. 6 : 18, 22; 1 Cor. 11 : 32.

" And we know that we are of God, and the whole world lieth in wickedness."—1 John 5 : 19. " As many as are of the works of the law, are under the curse."—Gal. 3 : 10; John 3 : 36; Isa. 57 : 21; Ps. 10 : 4; Isa. 55 : 6, 7.

" The wicked is driven away in his wickedness, but the righteous hath hope in his death."—Prov. 14 : 32. " Thou in thy lifetime receivedst thy good things, and likewise Lazarus evil things; but now he is comforted, and thou art tormented."—Luke 16 : 25; John 8 : 21–24; Luke 12 : 4, 5; 11 : 23–26; John 12 : 25, 26; Matt. 7 : 13, 14.

XX. THE WORLD TO COME

We believe the Scriptures teach that the end of the world is approaching; that at the Last Day, Christ will descend from heaven, and raise the dead from the grave for final retribution; that a solemn separation will then take place; that the wicked will be adjudged to endless sorrow, and the righteous to endless joy; and this judgment will fix forever the final state of men in heaven or hell, on principles of righteousness

" But the end of all things is at hand; be ye therefore sober, and watch unto prayer."—1 Pet. 4 : 7; 1 Cor. 7 : 29–31; Heb. 1 : 10–12; Matt. 24 : 35; 1 John 2 : 17; Matt 28 : 20.

" This same Jesus, which is taken up from you into heaven, shall so come in like manner as ye have seen Him go into heaven."—Acts 1 : 11; Rev. 1 : 7; Heb. 9 : 28; Acts 3 : 21.

" There shall be a resurrection of the dead, both of the just and unjust."—Acts 24 : 15; 1 Cor. 15 : 12–58; Luke 14 : 14; Dan. 12 : 2; John 5 : 28, 29; 6 : 40; 11 : 25, 26; 2 Tim. 1 : 10; Acts 10 : 42.

" The angels shall come forth, and sever the wicked from among the just."—Matt. 13 : 49; Matt. 13 : 37–43; 24 : 30, 31.

" And these shall go away into everlasting punishment, but the righteous into life eternal."—Matt. 25 : 35–41. " He that is unjust let him be unjust still; and he which is filthy let him be filthy still; and he that is righteous let him be righteous still; and he that is holy let him be holy still."—Rev. 22 : 11: 1 Cor. 6: 9, 10; Mark 9 : 43–48; 2 Pet. 2 : 9.

" Seeing it is a righteous thing with God to recompense tribulation to them who trouble you, and to you who are troubled, rest with us when He shall come to be glorified in His saints, and to be admired in all them that believe."—2 Thess. 1 : 6–12; Heb. 6 : 1, 2; 1 Cor. 4 : 5.

" SEEING THEN THAT ALL THESE THINGS SHALL BE DIS- SOLVED, WHAT MANNER OF PERSONS OUGHT YE TO BE IN ALL HOLY CONVERSATION AND GODLINESS, LOOKING FOR AND HASTING UNTO THE COMING OF THE DAY OF GOD ?"—2 Pet. 3 : 11, 12.

COVENANT

Having been, as we trust, brought by divine grace to embrace the Lord Jesus Christ, and to give ourselves

wholly to Him, we do now solemnly and joyfully covenant with each other, TO WALK TOGETHER IN HIM, WITH
BROTHERLY LOVE, to His glory, as our common Lord. We
do, therefore, in His strength, engage—

That we will exercise a Christian care and watchfulness
over each other, and faithfully warn, exhort, and admonish each other as occasion may require:

That we will not forsake the assembling of ourselves
together, but will uphold the public worship of God, and
the ordinances of His house:

That we will not omit closet and family religion at
home, nor neglect the great duty of religiously training
our children, and those under our care, for the service of
Christ, and the enjoyment of heaven:

That, as we are the light of the world, and salt of the
earth, we will seek divine aid to enable us to deny ungodliness, and every worldly lust, and to walk circumspectly
in the world, that we may win the souls of men:

That we will cheerfully contribute of our property, according as God has prospered us, for the maintenance of
a faithful and evangelical ministry among us, for the support of the poor, and to spread the Gospel over the earth:

That we will in all conditions, even till death, strive to
to live to the glory of Him who hath called us out of
darkness into His marvelous light.

" AND MAY THE GOD OF PEACE, WHO BROUGHT AGAIN
FROM THE DEAD OUR LORD JESUS, THAT GREAT SHEPHERD
OF THE SHEEP, THROUGH THE BLOOD OF THE EVERLASTING
COVENANT, MAKE US PERFECT IN EVERY GOOD WORK, TO DO
HIS WILL, WORKING IN US THAT WHICH IS WELL PLEASING
IN HIS SIGHT THROUGH JESUS CHRIST; TO WHOM BE GLORY,
FOREVER AND EVER. AMEN."

B. OPTIONAL RESOLUTIONS

A Christian Church should be recognized, in the community where it is located, as professing and maintaining a higher standard of morality than that of worldly society about it. It should be the avowed friend, defender, and example of all the virtues, and the uncompromising opponent of all wrong and evil. So carefully should they bear themselves, not only as individuals, but as a corporate society, as to command the respect of the world, and have a good report of them that are without. Divinely set forth as a light to the world, and as the salt of the earth, they should recognize their commission, and be true to it. In all that is pure, irreproachable, and of good report, the pastor should be the wise and courageous teacher, leader, and example of the flock.

There are certain questions of moral reform and social good order, in respect to which there is often a wide difference of opinion, but in respect to which the churches should have settled convictions, and hold a well-defined attitude. It is not wise to put definitions and restrictions touching such questions into covenants or articles of faith. Nor does it seem wise to construct elaborate constitutions and by-laws for the guidance of a Church, to forestall possible violations of the code of Christian morals. A better way is, for it, after due consideration, to adopt a *standing resolution* on each such subject claiming attention, to be placed on its records as a guide for future action as to such subjects.

Something like the following, to be varied at the option of the body, would serve as a declaration of principles and guide for action:

1. *Resolved*, That this Church expects every member to contribute statedly to its financial support, according to his ability, as God has prospered him; and that a refusal to do this will be considered a breach of covenant.

2. *Resolved*, That this Church will entertain and contribute to Home and Foreign Missions, and to other leading objects of Christian benevolence, approved and supported by our denomination.

3. *Resolved*, That the religious education of the young, and Bible study, as represented in Sunday-school work, commend themselves to our confidence, and we will, to the extent of our ability, give them our aid, by both our personal coöperation and our contributions, as we are able.

4. *Resolved*, That in our opinion the use of intoxicating drinks as a beverage, and also the manufacture and sale of the same for that purpose, are contrary to Christian morals, injurious to personal piety, and a hindrance to the Gospel; therefore, persons so using, making or selling, are thereby disqualified for membership in this Church.

5. *Resolved*, That we emphatically discountenance and condemn the practice of Church members frequenting theatres, and other similar places of amusement, as inconsistent with a Christian profession, detrimental to personal piety, and pernicious in the influence of its example on others.

6. *Resolved*, That the members of this Church are earnestly requested not to provide for, take part in, or by any means encourage dancing or card playing, nor furnish intoxicating drinks to guests, on any occasion; but, in all consistent ways to discountenance the same, as a hindrance to personal godliness in their associations and tendencies, a stumbling-block in the way of the unconverted, and a grief to brethren whom we should not willingly offend.

7. *Resolved*, That we disapprove of Christians connecting themselves with secret, oath-bound societies, as being needless, profitless, and an offense and grief to many good people, and not conducive to piety or to Christian usefulness.

C. GLOSSARY OF AUTHORITIES

A list of the authorities cited in the foregoing pages is here appended for the satisfaction of readers. The figures which follow the names indicate the date of birth. The abbreviations show denominational connections : as, *Epis.*, Episcopalian ; *Presb.*, Presbyterian ; *Meth.*, Methodist ; *Cath.*, Catholic ; *Luth.*, Lutheran ; *Ref.*, Reformed; *Cong.*, Congregational; *Gr. Ch.*, Greek Church; *Diss.*, Dissenting; *Morav.*, Moravian.

ALSTIDIUS, John Henry, 1588. *Ref. Luth.* A learned German divine, professor of theology at Herbon. and author of many works.

AMBROSE. One of the early Christian Fathers, who flourished about A. D. 374.

ANTHON, Charles, LL.D. *Epis.* Professor of Greek and Latin in Columbia College, New York.

AUGUSTI, Christian, D.D. 1772. *Luth.* Professor of theology in the universities of Basle and Bonn, Germany.

BARCLAY, J. T., M.D. *Christ.* For several years missionary at Jerusalem, under the patronage of the American Christian Missionary Society.

BARNES, Albert. *Presb.* A distinguished clergyman, and author of the well-known *Notes* on the books of the Bible.

BARROW, Isaac, D.D. 1630. *Epis.* Eminent as a divine and mathematician. Vice-chancellor of, and professor of Greek in, Cambridge University, England.

BASIL. One of the Christian Fathers, who flourished about A. D. 360.

BAXTER, Richard. 1615. *Presb.* An eminent Nonconformist divine, author of the *Saint's Rest*, and other works.

BENGEL, John. 1687. *Luth.* Distinguished as a pious and learned German divine, biblical critic, and commentator.

BENSON, Joseph. 1748. *Meth.* One of the most eloquent preachers and able scholars of the early Methodists.

BEZA, Theodore. 1519. *Presb.* One of the most eminent of the reformers ; an associate of Calvin, and professor of theology at Geneva.

BINGHAM, Joseph. 1668. *Epis.* Rector of Havant, England ; author of the great work on Christian antiquities, the *Origines*.

BRENNER, Frederick, D.D. 1784. *Cath.* A distinguished writer, member of the cathedral chapter at Bamberg, Bavaria.

BUDDEUS, John Franz. 1667. *Luth.* One of the first scholars of his day ; professor at the universities of Halle, Coburg, and Jena.

BLOOMFIELD, S. T., D.D. *Epis.* Vicar of Bisbrook, England. Editor of the Greek New Testament, and author of various works.

BOSSUET, James. 1627. *Cath.* Bishop of Meaux, and state councilor of France. Distinguished as a preacher, author, and controversialist.

BROUGHTON, Thomas. 1704. *Epis.* Vicar of Bedminster, England ; author of various works.

CAVE, William, D.D. 1637. *Epis.* Vicar of Islington, England ; eminent as a scholar and author.

CALVIN, John. 1509. *Presb.* The great German reformer and theologian, whom Scaliger pronounced the most learned man in Europe.

CAMPBELL, George, D.D. 1719. *Presb.* President of, and professor of divinity in, Marischal College, Scotland.

CHRYSOSTOM, John. A. D. 347. *Gr. Ch.* Patriarch of Constantinople ; called the "golden-mouthed" preacher.

CLARK, Adam, LL.D. 1760. *Meth.* A distinguished antiquarian and Oriental scholar. The great Methodist commentator.

CLARKE, Samuel, D.D. 1675. *Epis.* An eminent English divine, scholar, and author.

CONYBEARE, W. J. *Epis.* A clergyman of the English Church ; joint author of the *Life and Epistles of St. Paul.*

COLEMAN, Lyman, D.D. *Cong.* Professor of biblical literature in Lafayette College, Pa. Author of several works.

CURCELLÆUS, Stephen. 1586. *Dutch Ref.* An eminent Greek scholar ; professor of divinity at Amsterdam.

CYRIL. One of the Christian Fathers, who flourished about A. D. 375.

DEYLINGIUS, Solomon. 1677. *Luth.* A German theologian ; professor in the University of Wittenberg.

DIODATI, John. 1576. *Ref.* An Italian divine, professor of Hebrew and theology at Geneva.

DWIGHT, Timothy, D.D. 1752. *Cong.* President of Yale College, and professor of theology.

DONNEGAN, James, M.D. Author of a Greek and English lexicon extensively used.

DODDRIDGE, Philip, D.D. 1702. *Diss.* A pious and popular English preacher ; author of the *Family Expositor*, and various other works.

DE WETTE, William. 1780. *Luth.* Theological professor at Basle ; eminent in biblical learning.

DICK, John, D.D. 1764. *Presb.* A learned Scotch divine ; professor of theology at Glasgow.

ESTIUS, Wm. von, D.D. 1542. *Cath.* Chancellor of, and professor of theology in, the University of Douay, France.

EUSEBIUS of Cæsarea. About A. D. 270. One of the early Christian Fathers, intimate friend of the Emperor Constantine. Called the father of church history.

FELL, John, D.D. 1625. *Epis* A learned English prelate ; Bishop of Oxford, and Vice-Chancellor of the university.

FLATT, Frederick, D.D. 1759. *Luth.* Professor of theology at Tübingen; associated with Störr in theological works.

FRANKIUS, Aug. Herman. 1663. *Luth.* Professor of Oriental and Greek languages in the University of Halle; author of various works.

FRITZSCHE, Karl Frie. Aug. 1801. *Luth.* One of the most learned of German philologists ; professor of theology in the University of Rostock.

GREENFIELD, William. 1799. *Epis.* Noted as a linguist and lexicographer. Editor of *Bagster's Comprehensive Bible.*

GREGORY. One of the early Christian Fathers, who flourished about A. D. 360.

HAGENBACH, Karl Rudolph, D.D. 1801. *Luth.* Professor of theology in the University of Basle, and author of various learned works.

HAMMOND, Henry, D.D. 1605. *Epis.* An eloquent English divine, rector of Penshurst ; nominated Bishop of Worcester.

HENRY, Matthew. 1662. *Presb.* Distinguished as a preacher and an expositor of the Scriptures.

HERMAS. About A. D. 95. One of the apostolical Fathers, and supposed author of a work called the *Shepherd*.

HIPPOLYTUS. One of the Christian Fathers. Supposed Bishop of Portus, near Rome. Flourished about A. D. 225.

JUSTIN MARTYR. One of the early Christian Fathers, who flourished about A. D. 140.

KING, John Glen, D.D. 1731. *Epis.* A distinguished English divine and antiquarian.

LEIGH, Edward. 1602. *Presb.* An English layman, distinguished in biblical lexicography and exegesis. A member of Parliament and of the Westminster Assembly.

LEIGHTON, Robert. 1611. *Epis.* A learned and pious Scotch prelate, Archbishop of Glasgow.

LIGHTFOOT, John, D.D. 1602. *Epis.* Distinguished for learning, especially as a Hebraist ; Vice-Chancellor of Cambridge University, and member of the Assembly of Divines.

LIMBORCH, Philip. 1633. *Dutch Ref.* Professor of theology at Amsterdam, and author of various works.

LIDDELL, Henry George. *Epis.* Dean of Christ Church, Oxford, England. Associated in lexicography with Robert Scott, D.D., *Epis.*, Master of Baliol College, Oxford.

LUTHER, Martin, D.D. 1483. *Ref.* The celebrated German reformer, preacher, and author.

MACKNIGHT, James, D.D. 1721. *Presb.* A learned Scotch divine and commentator on the Epistles.

MEDE, Joseph, B.D. 1586. *Epis.* A learned English divine, eminent for scholarship in Greek.

MELANCTHON, Philip. 1497. *Ref.* The most learned and eminent associate of Luther in the German Reformation.

MEYER, Frederick, D.D. *Luth.* A distinguished German theologian, jurist, and scholar.

MOLDINATUS, John. 1534. *Cath.* A brilliant and learned writer, and teacher in theology and philosophy.

MOSHEIM, John von, D.D. 1694. *Luth.* Chancellor of the University and professor of theology at Gottingen. Church historian.

MURDOCK, James, D.D. 1776. *Cong.* A profound scholar, professor in Theological Seminary, Andover, Mass. Translator of Mosheim.

NEANDER, John Aug. Wil. 1789. *Evang. Luth.* The great German scholar and ecclesiastical historian ; professor in the universities of Heidelberg and Berlin.

NEWTON, Thomas, D.D. 1704. *Epis.* Bishop of Bristol, England, and author of various works.

OLSHAUSEN, Herman, D.D. 1796. *Luth.* Professor of theology in the University of Erlangen, in Bavaria.

PARKHURST, John. 1728. *Epis.* A learned English divine and lexicographer.

PASSOW. 1786. *Luth.* A distinguished German philologist, professor in the University of Breslau.

PICTETUS, Benedict. 1655. *Presb.* A learned Protestant divine ; professor of theology at Geneva.

POOLE, Matthew. 1624. *Presb.* A learned English divine and commentator.

RICAUT, Sir Paul. 1628. *Epis.* An English traveler, author, and diplomatist, consul at Smyrna.

ROBINSON, Edward, D.D. *Cong.* Professor of biblical literature in Union Theological Seminary, New York. Author of N. T. Greek Lexicon.

ROSENMÜLLER, John George. 1736. *Luth.* A German scholar, and divinity professor at Erlangen and Leipsic.

SALMASIUS, Claude. 1596. *Ref.* A French Protestant, noted for scholarship ; professor of ecclesiastical history at Leyden.

SAURIN, James. 1677. *Ref.* A celebrated French Protestant pulpit orator and author.

SCAPULA, John. 1540. A native of Lausanne, chiefly known for his work in lexicography.

SCHAFF, Philip, D.D. *Presb.* Eminent as a scholar and historian ; professor in Union Theological Seminary, New York.

SCHLEUSNER, Frederic, D.D. *Luth.* Professor of theology at Wittenberg. Distinguished in New Testament lexicography.

SCHOLZ, John Mar. Aug. *Luth.* A distinguished biblical scholar, author, and professor of theology.

SOPHOCLES, E. A., LL.D. Born in Greece, professor of Greek in the University of Cambridge, Massachusetts.

SCHOETTGEN, Christian. 1687. *Luth.* Professor in various German institutions of learning.

SCHREVELIUS, Cornelius. 1615. *Dutch Ref.* An eminent critic and lexicographer of Leyden, Holland.

SHERLOCK, Thomas. 1678. *Epis.* An English prelate ; Bishop successively of Bangor, Salisbury, and London.

SCOTT, Thomas, D.D. 1747. *Epis.* An English divine, well known for his Bible commentary.

STACKHOUSE, Thomas. 1680. *Epis.* An English divine, well known as author of the *History of the Bible.*

STANLEY, Arthur Pen, D.D. *Epis.* Dean of Westminster, and professor of ecclesiastical history at Oxford, England.

STORR, Christian, D.D. 1746. *Luth.* A German divine and author, associated with Flatt in biblical learning.

STOURDZA, Alexander. 1738. *Gr. Ch.* A Russian scholar, traveler, and diplomatist.

TAYLOR, Jeremy, D.D. 1613. *Epis.* An eloquent English prelate and distinguished author. Bishop of Down and Connor.

TERTULLIAN, Septimus Florens. One of the early Christian Fathers ; author of several works. Flourished about A. D. 200.

THOMSON, W. M., D.D. *Presb.* Missionary of the American Board, for twenty-five years, in Syria and Palestine.

TILLOTSON, John, D.D. 1630. *Epis.* A noted English prelate, Archbishop of Canterbury.

TOWERSON, Gabriel, D.D. 1630. *Epis.* A divine of the English Church ; author of various works.

TURRETIN, John Alph. 1681. *Presb.* A celebrated scholar ; professor of theology at Geneva.

TYNDALE, William. *Epis.* The great English reformer of the sixteenth century ; suffered martyrdom in 1536. Translated the New Testament.

VALESIUS, Henry. 1603. *Cath.* A distinguished French critic and scholar ; appointed historiographer of France.

VENEMA, Herman. 1697. *Dutch Ref.* Distinguished as a scholar ; professor in the University of Franeker, Friesland.

VITRINGA, Campegius, D.D. 1659. *Luth.* A learned divine, professor of Oriental languages, history, and divinity at Franeker, Friesland.

Von Cölln, Daniel Geo. Con. 1788. *Morav.* Professor of theology at Breslau, and author of theological works.

Vossius, Gerhard. 1577. *Epis.* Professor at Leyden. Eminent as a critic and philologist.

Waddington, George. *Epis.* An English divine, Fellow of Trinity College, and prebendary in the Cathedral church of Chichester.

Wall, William, D.D. 1646. *Epis.* Vicar of Shoreham, England ; author of the learned *History of Infant Baptism.*

Wesley, John. 1703. *Meth.* Founder of Methodism in England. Most distinguished of the Wesley family. An able scholar and preacher.

Wetstein, John James. 1693. *Luth.* Distinguished as a biblical scholar ; professor at Amsterdam. Editor of the New Testament.

Whitby, Daniel, D.D. 1638. *Epis.* An English divine and commentator.

Whitefield, George. 1714. *Epis.* The celebrated preacher ; associate of Wesley and the Calvinistic Methodists.

Witsius, Herman. 1636. *Dutch Ref.* An eminent Dutch divine ; professor of divinity at Franeker, Utrecht, and Leyden.

Winer, George B. 1789. *Luth.* A German scholar and theologian, celebrated for his knowledge of New Testament literature.

Zanchius, Jerome. *Cath.* Professor of theology at Heidelberg. Embraced Protestantism with Peter Martyr.

Zwingli, Ulrich. 1484. *Ref.* The great Swiss reformer: coadjutor and friend of Luther; scholar and author.

D. RULES OF ORDER

The ordinary parliamentary rules of order commonly u ed in all deliberative bodies are those which govern churches and other religious societies in their meetings for business, in case no other rules are adopted at the commencement of their deliberations. Any body has the right to adopt any system of rules it may see fit to prefer. While in ordinary Church meetings it may not be wise to be over-punctilious as to order, it is wise to be very orderly, and to avoid confusion and disorder in the proceedings. The spirit of worship should pervade the business meetings of the Church. They should be opened with singing, reading the Scriptures and prayer. The pastor is, of right, moderator, and on him, more than on any one else, will depend the good order, and the efficiency of the proceedings.

Motions

1. All business shall be presented by a *motion*, made by one member, and seconded by another, and presented in writing by the mover, if so required.

2. No discussion can properly be had until the motion is made, seconded, and stated by the chairman.

3. A motion cannot be withdrawn after it has been discussed, except by the unanimous consent of the body.

4. A motion having been discussed, must be put to

576

vote, unless withdrawn, laid on the table, referred or postponed.

5. A motion lost should not be recorded, except so ordered by the body at the time.

6. A motion lost cannot be renewed at the same meeting, except by unanimous consent.

7. A motion should contain but one distinct proposition. If it contains more, it must be divided at the request of any member, and the propositions acted on separately.

8. Only one question can properly be before the meeting at the same time. No second motion can be allowed to interrupt one already under debate, except a motion to *amend*, to *substitute*, to *commit*, to *postpone*, to *lay on the table*, for *the previous question*, or to *adjourn*.

9. These subsidiary motions just named cannot be interrupted by any other motion; nor can any other motion be applied to them, except that to *amend*, which may be done by specifying some *time*, *place*, or *purpose*.

10. Nor can these motions interrupt or supersede each other; only that a motion to *adjourn* is always in order, except while a member has the floor, or a question is being taken, and, in some bodies, even then.

Amendments

1. Amendments may be made to resolutions in three ways : By *omitting*, by *adding*, or by *substituting* words or sentences.

2. An amendment to an amendment may be made, but is seldom necessary, and should be avoided.

3. No amendment should be made which essentially changes the meaning or design of the original resolution.

4. But a *substitute* may be offered, which may change entirely the meaning of the resolution under debate.

5. The amendment must first be discussed and acted on, and then the original resolution as amended.

Speaking

1. Any member desiring to speak on a question should rise in his place and address the moderator, confine his remarks to the question, and avoid all unkind and disrespectful language.

2. A speaker using improper language, introducing improper subjects, or otherwise out of order, should be called to order by the chairman, or any member, and must either conform to the regulations of the body, or take his seat.

3. A member while speaking can allow others to ask questions, or make explanations; but if he yields the floor to another, he cannot claim it again as his right.

4. If two members rise to speak at the same time, preference is usually given to the one farthest from the chair, or to the one opposing the motion under discussion.

5. The fact that a person has several times arisen and attempted to get the floor, gives him no claim or right to be heard. Nor does a call for the question deprive a member of his right to speak.

Voting

1. A question is put to vote by the chairman, having first distinctly restated it, that all may vote intelligently. First, the *affirmative*, then the *negative* is called, each so deliberately as to give all an opportunity of voting. He then distinctly announces whether the motion is *carried*, or *lost*.

2. Voting is usually done by "aye" and "no," or by raising the hand. In a doubtful case by standing and being counted. On certain questions by ballot.

3. If the vote, as announced by the chairman, is doubted, it is called again, usually by standing to be counted.

4. All members should vote, unless for reasons excused; or unless under discipline, in which case they should take no part in the business.

5. The moderator does not usually vote, except the question be taken by ballot; but when the meeting is equally divided, he is expected, but is not obliged, to give the casting vote.

6. When the vote is to be taken by ballot, the chairman appoints *tellers*, to distribute, collect, and count the ballots.

Committees

1. Committees are nominated by the chairman, if so directed by the body, or by any member, and the nomination is confirmed by a vote of the body. More commonly the body directs that all committees shall be *appointed* by the chairman, in which case no vote is needed to confirm.

2. Any matter of business, or subject under debate, may be *referred* to a committee, with or without instructions. The committee make their *report*, which is the result of their deliberations. The body then takes action on the report, and on any recommendations it may contain.

3. The report of a committee is *received*, when it is listened to, having been called for, or permitted by the moderator, with or without a vote of the body. The report is *accepted* by a vote, which acknowledges their services, and places the report before the body for its ac-

tion. Afterward, any distinct *recommendation* contained in the report is acted on, and may be *adopted* or *rejected*.

4. Frequently, however, when the recommendations of the committee are of a trifling moment or likely to be generally acceptable, the report, having been *received*, is *accepted* and *adopted* by the same vote.

5. A report may be *recommitted* to the committee, with or without instructions, or, that committee discharged and the matter referred to a new one for further consideration, so as to present it in a form more likely to meet the general concurrence of the body.

6. A committee may be appointed *with power* for a specific purpose. This gives them power to dispose conclusively of the matter, without further reference to the body.

7. The first named in the appointment of a committee is, by courtesy, considered the *chairman*. But the committee has the right to name its own chairman.

8. The member who moves the appointment of a committee is usually, though not necessarily, named its chairman.

9. Committees of arrangement, or for other protracted service, *report progress* from time to time, and are continued until their final report, or until their appointment expires by limitation.

10. A committee is *discharged* by a vote when its business is done and its report accepted. But usually, in routine business, a committee is considered discharged by the acceptance of its report.

Standing Committee

A committee appointed to act for a given period, or during the recess of the body, is called a *standing commit-*

tee. It has charge of a given department of business assigned by the body, and acts either with power, under instructions, or at discretion, as may be ordered. A standing committee is substantially a minor board, and has its own chairman, secretary, records, and times of meeting.

Appeal

The moderator announces all votes, and decides all questions as to rules of proceeding and order of debate. But any member who is dissatisfied with his decisions may *appeal* from them to the body. The moderator then puts the question, " *Shall the decision of the chair be sustained?* " The vote of the body, whether negative or affirmative, is final. The right of appeal is undeniable, but should not be resorted to on trivial occasions.

Previous Question

Debate may be cut short by a vote to take the *previous question.* This means that the original, or main question under discussion, be immediately voted on, regardless of amendments and secondary questions, and without further debate. Usually a *two-thirds* vote is necessary to order the previous question.

1. If the motion for the previous question be *carried*, then the main question must be immediately taken without further debate.

2. If the motion for the previous question be *lost*, the debate proceeds as though no such motion had been made.

3. If the motion for the previous question be *lost*, it cannot be renewed with reference to the same question during the same session.

To Lay on the Table

Immediate and decisive action on any question under discussion may be deferred by a vote to *lay on the table* the resolution pending. This disposes of the whole subject for the present, and ordinarily is, in effect, a final dismissal of it. But any member has the right subsequently to call it up, and the body will decide by vote whether or not it shall be taken from the table.

1. Sometimes, however, a resolution is laid on the table for the present, or until a specified time, to give place to other business.

2. A motion to lay on the table must apply to a resolution, or other papers. An abstract subject cannot be disposed of in this way.

Postponement

A simple *postponement* is for a specified time or purpose, the business to be resumed when the time or purpose is reached. But a question *indefinitely postponed* is considered as finally dismissed.

Not Debatable

Certain motions, by established usage, are *not debatable*, but when once before the body, must be taken without discussion.

These are : the *previous question*, for *indefinite postponement*, to *commit*, to *lay on the table*, to *adjourn*.

But when these motions are modified by some condition of *time*, *place*, or *purpose*, they become debatable, and subject to the rules of other motions, but debatable *only in respect to* the time, place, or purpose which brings them within the province of debate.

A body is, however, competent, by a vote, to allow debate on all motions.

To Reconsider

A motion to *reconsider* a motion previously passed must be made by one who voted *for* the motion when it passed.

If the body votes to reconsider, then the motion or resolution being reconsidered stands before them as previous to its passage, and may be discussed, adopted, or rejected.

A vote to reconsider should be taken at the same session at which the vote reconsidered was passed, and when there are as many members present. But this rule, though just, is frequently disregarded.

Not to be Discussed

If, when a question is introduced, any member objects to its discussion as foreign, profitless, or contentious, the moderator should at once put the question, *"Shall this motion be discussed?"* If this question be decided in the negative, the subject must be dismissed.

Order of the Day

The body may decide to take up some definite business at a specified time. That business therefore becomes the *order of the day* for that hour. When the time mentioned arrives the chairman calls the business, or any member may demand it, with or without a vote, and all pending questions are postponed in consequence.

Point of Order

Any member who believes that a speaker is out of order, or that discussion is proceeding improperly, may at any time *rise to a point of order*.　He must distinctly state his question or objection, which the moderator will decide.

Privileges

Questions relating to the *rights* and *privileges* of members are of primary importance, and, until disposed of, take precedence of all other business, and supersede all other motions, except that of adjournment.

Rule Suspended

A rule of order may be *suspended* by a vote of the body to allow the transaction of business necessary, but which could not otherwise be done without a violation of such rule.

Filling Blanks

Where different numbers are suggested for filling blanks, the *highest number*, *greatest distance* and *longest time* are usually voted on first.

Adjournment

1. A simple motion to *adjourn* is always in order, except while a member is speaking, or when taking a vote.　It takes precedence of all other motions, and is not debatable.

2. In some deliberative bodies a motion to adjourn is in order while a speaker has the floor, or a vote is being taken, the business to stand, on reassembling, precisely as when adjournment took place.

3. A body may adjourn to a specific time, but if no time be mentioned, the fixed or usual time of meeting is understood.　If there be no fixed or usual time of meeting, then an adjournment without date is equivalent to a dissolution

E. FORMS AND BLANKS

There are no fixed or necessary forms for Letters of Dismission, Calls for Councils, Minutes of Conventions, and the like. The customs of churches may differ, and the taste of those who prepare these forms will vary. They should be concise, intelligible and definite as to the purpose for which they are designed. The following constitute substantially the forms in common use:

1. *Letters of Dismission*

The   Baptist Church of
       To the Baptist Church of
Dear Brethren:
     This is to certify that   is a member in good and regular standing with us, and at   own request, is hereby dismissed, for the purpose of uniting with you. When   has so united,   connection with us will cease. May the divine blessing rest on   and on you.
     Done by order of the Church.

Ch. Clerk

New York, June   , 19
     This Letter is valid for *six* months.

NOTE I.—It is customary to limit letters to a specified time, after which they are not valid, but may be renewed at the discre-

585

tion of the Church, if satisfactory reasons are given for their non-use.

NOTE 2.—A letter may be granted to "any Church of the same faith and order," instead of to a specified Church, when the member is uncertain with what one he may unite.

NOTE 3.—But a letter granted to a particular Church is valid for some other Church, should that other see fit to accept it. Each Church is sole judge of the fitness of those whom it receives.

2. *Letter of Commendation*

This certifies that   is a member in good standing in the   Baptist Church in   , and is hereby commended to the confidence and Christian fellowship of sister churches wherever Providence may direct   course.

Pastor, or Clerk

New York, June   , 19

NOTE.—This form of letter is for members during a temporary absence from home, and may be given by the pastor personally, or by the Church's formal action.

3. *Letter of Notification*

New York, June   , 19

To the   Baptist Church.

Dear Brethren:

This certifies that   was received by Letter from you, to membership in the   Baptist Church, June   , 19

Ch. Clerk

NOTE 1.—This form is attached to, or enclosed in, every letter granted, and filled by the Church receiving the member, and returned to the one granting it.

NOTE 2.—When members are dismissed to constitute a new Church, that fact should be stated in the letters.

4. *Minutes of Church Meeting*

New York, June , 19

The Church held its regular meeting for business this evening at o'clock.

Pastor, moderator.

After singing, and reading the Scriptures, prayer was offered by

Minutes of the last meeting were read and approved.

[Then follows a faithful record of the business transacted.]

Meeting adjourned.

Ch. Clerk

NOTE.—The records of a Church should show not only bare minutes of its business, but a concise mention of important events and changes in its current history, for reference and information in after years.

5. *Call for an Ordaining Council*

New York, June 19

The Baptist Church of

To the Baptist Church of

Dear Brethren:

You are requested to send your pastor and two brethren to sit with us in Council, July , at o'clock P. M., to consider and advise as to the expediency of publicly setting apart to the work of the Gospel ministry our brother The Council will meet in

The following churches are invited:

By order of the Church,

Ch. Clerk

6. Call for a Recognizing Council

New York, June   , 19

To the   Baptist Church of

Dear Brethren:

In behalf of a company of brethren and sisters in Christ, you are requested to send your pastor and two brethren, to meet in Council at   , July   , at   o'clock P. M., to consider the propriety of recognizing said company as a regular and independent Church of Christ.

The following churches are invited:

Fraternally yours,

Com., or Clerk

7. Call for an Advisory Council

New York, June   , 19

The   Baptist Church of

To the   Baptist Church of

Dear Brethren:

You are requested to send your pastor and two brethren, to sit in Council July   , 19   , at   o'clock P. M., to consider and advise as to certain difficulties existing among us, which disturb our peace, and threaten serious injury to the welfare of our Church.

The Council will meet in

The following churches are invited:

By order of the Church,

Ch. Clerk

NOTE 1.—All Councils are *advisory*, in the sense that none are *authoritative*. But it is usual to call those advisory which are called to advise, especially as to the settlement of difficulties.

NOTE 2.—Advisory Councils may be called by either *churches* or *individuals,* and also as to other matters than pending difficulties. The call should state the object.

NOTE 3.—For directions as to calling and using Councils, see the chapter on that subject.

8. *Minutes of a Council*

New York, June , 19

An Ecclesiastical Council, called by the Church, convened at this day, at o'clock P. M.

Organized by choosing , moderator, and , clerk.

Prayer was offered by

The credentials of pastors and messengers were presented. The following churches were represented by the following brethren:

Churches	*Messengers*
....	....
....	....
....	....
....	....

The records of the Church relating to the call of the Council were read, also the *letter missive,* showing the object to be

[Then follows a faithful record of the proceedings as they transpired.]

Council dissolved, or adjourned *sine die.*

Moderator
Clerk

NOTE.—A true copy of the minutes, signed by the moderator and clerk, should be furnished to the parties calling the Council.

9. *Minutes of a Committee*

New York, June   , 19

The   committee met at   , at o'clock P. M.

Present:

Brother   in the chair.   Prayer was offered by

Minutes of the last meeting read and approved.

[Record of business.]

Adjourned.

Secretary

10. *Minutes of a Convention*

New York, June   , 19

A convention called to consider   met at at   o'clock P. M., this day.

was chosen chairman and   secretary.

After prayer by   , the chairman stated the object of the meeting to be

[Then follows a true record of proceedings.]

Adjourned, or dissolved.

Chairman
Secretary

NOTE.—The rules of order to be observed in all meetings, whether religious or secular, are substantially the same—the ordinary parliamentary rules.   But any organization or deliberative body has the right to make its own rules at the commencement of its sessions.   If none are then adopted, common rules prevail.

11. *Form of a License*

It is customary for young men who believe themselves called of God to the work of the Gospel ministry, to ask from their Church a *license*, granting the Church's approval of their exercise of ministerial gifts. Some theological seminaries require a license for every student admitted to divinity studies. A license confers no clerical authority, but simply approves the course of the licentiate in the matter.

There is no invariable form of license, but the following substantially serves the purpose:

License

This certifies that Bro.   is a member of the   Church, in good standing, and held by us in high esteem; and, after having opportunity for judging, we believe him to have been called of God to the work of the Gospel ministry, and hereby give him our entire consent and cordial approval in the improvement of his gifts in preaching the Gospel, as Providence may afford him an opportunity. And we pray the great Head of the Church to endow him with all needful grace, and crown his labors with abundant success.

Done by order of the Church, this day, June 19

                               Pastor
                               Clerk

New York.

NOTE I.—A license can be annulled or withdrawn at any time, should the Church have, in its judgment, sufficient reason for such action.

NOTE 2.—A license in no sense invests the licensee with ministerial functions, beyond approval in conducting religious services and expounding the Scriptures.

NOTE 3.—Quite commonly a license includes advice or approval of the candidate's pursuing appropriate studies, the better to prepare him for the work of the ministry, since a license by no means implies an immediate entrance upon full ministerial functions.

12. *Certificate of Ordination*

This certifies that our Brother   was publicly ordained and set apart to the work of the Gospel ministry with appropriate religious services, prayer, and the laying on of hands, according to the usages of Baptist churches, at   , Aug.   , 19

That he was called to ordination by the   Church, of which he was a member, and which, after full and sufficient opportunity for judging of his gifts, were agreed in the opinion that he was divinely called to the work of the ministry.

That   churches were represented in the Council by   ministers, and   laymen, and that, after a full, fair and deliberate examination, being satisfied on all points, the Council did unanimously recommend his ordination.

That our Bro.   did accordingly receive the full, entire and hearty approval of the Council in his official entrance upon the work of the ministry, administering the ordinances, and otherwise assuming all the functions of a Christian minister. And may the blessing of the great Head of the Church attend him, crown his labors with abundant success, and make him an honored instrument of good to Zion and the world.

Moderator

Clerk

New York, Sept.   , 19

NOTE.—As a rule, men are not ordained, except as pastors of churches, or to become missionaries and raise up churches. To ordain men to occupy semi-secular positions, because it may class them with clergymen, or enable them occasionally to serve the churches by administering the ordinances, when they neither do, nor expect to, enter fully into ministerial service, is not generally approved, or deemed orderly.

INDEX